Schoolchildren as Propaganda Tools in the War on Terror

Sonja C. Grover

Schoolchildren as Propaganda Tools in the War on Terror

Violating the Rights of Afghani Children under International Law

Springer

Dr. Sonja Grover
Lakehead University
Faculty of Education
955 Oliver Road
Thunder Bay, Ontario P7B 5E1
Canada
sonja.grover@lakeheadu.ca

ISBN 978-3-642-17899-3 e-ISBN 978-3-642-17900-6
DOI 10.1007/978-3-642-17900-6
Springer Heidelberg Dordrecht London New York

Library of Congress Control Number: 2011924348

Cover design: eStudio Calamar S. L.

Printed on acid-free paper

Springer is part of Springer Science+Business Media (www.springer.com)

In loving memory and in honour of my parents, Gina and David Gazan who first taught me that children and youth are worthy of respect, and of my brother Albert Gazan who struggled for the rights of the dispossessed as social worker, psychologist and educator

About the Author

Sonja C. Grover, PhD, is a Professor with Lakehead University and an Associate Editor of *The International Journal of Human Rights*. She has authored over 80 refereed articles primarily on the topic of human rights/children's human rights published in leading international human rights and law journals. She has also presented numerous papers at various international conferences on the topic of human rights including at UNESCO and contributed chapters to edited books such as a volume on children's human rights in Canada. She is the single author of several books such as: Children's Human Rights: Challenging Global Barriers to the Child Liberation Movement (Sandstone Academic Press); The Child's Right to Legal Standing (Lexis Nexis); Prosecuting International Crimes and Human Rights Abuses Committed Against Children: Leading International Court Cases (Springer); The European Court of Human Rights as a Pathway to Impunity for International Crimes (Springer); and Young People's Human Rights and the Politics of Voting Age (Springer).

Preface

This inquiry explores in what ways schoolchildren are being used as propaganda tools by terrorists in their global terror campaign (more specifically the Taliban insurgents in Afghanistan), but also by States waging the so-called 'war on terror' in their propaganda relating to claims about alleged progress in stabilization and development of the conflict-affected State in question. It is emphasized, however, that there is no argument here that there is validity in the view that education should be a part of an emergency aid response wherever feasible and where the security situation permits. This given the importance of education to children's sense of normalcy and to their future success in life (assuming, of course, that the quality of education delivered is such as to allow, at a minimum, for the development of functional literacy skills and, hopefully, a complete adequate basic education). This author is, in fact, in accord with the view that providing education services to children in fragile conflict-affected States *where the children's safety can be assured* is vital to meeting the population's humanitarian and development needs and entitlements. The reality is, however, that many millions of children live in States that are in a *perpetual* state of conflict with only periodic interruption (as is the case for Afghanistan). It is devastating to the children and to the country when this leads, as it inevitably does, to a shutting down of part or all of the education system. However, the suggestion by 'Save the Children' and other NGOs that education cannot wait *in any instance* for the State's 'post-conflict' development phase, but must be delivered also in the midst of intense conflict and despite high levels of organized terrorist activity, belies the fact that security cannot always be adequately provided to schoolchildren in that circumstance as will be discussed. It is specifically the latter situations with which this inquiry is concerned.

As to the scope of the book a few points need to be made. The book deals with targeted terrorist attacks on schools, schoolchildren, teachers of children at the elementary and secondary school level carried out by organized terrorist groups such as Al-Qaeda and the Taliban extremist element as part of a systematic campaign of terror. The issue of accidental damage to schools and injury or killing of schoolchildren, teachers or other school personnel while at school unintentional and collateral to military action is addressed only to the extent that such accidents were a foreseeable risk given the location of the schools. Note that the focus of this book concerns terror attacks on basic education and on schoolchildren; their teachers; allied school staff and on humanitarian aid workers rather than on terror attacks on universities, university students and academics. There is no doubt that terror attacks on higher education internationally have also increased in recent years. However, the present inquiry focuses on schoolchildren since the children generally have no say in whether they will attend school or not in contrast to university students. The fact that children are forced to attend school often in insecure conflict zones where there is a high risk of terror attack on the school, plus the fact that children are entitled to special protections under international humanitarian law, raises unique issues. Thus, the issue of schoolchildren attending school in 'hot terror zones' – that is zones where the terror activity level is high – is a topic that needs to be addressed separately from the issue of attacks upon university students, professors and higher education institutions. The latter topic, though also pressing, is then beyond the scope of the book.

Further, the book concentrates on organized, systematic and repeated targeted terror attacks on basic education in Afghanistan by the Taliban and other insurgents as opposed to isolated terror incidents carried out by individuals not associated with organized terror groups. The former pose a significant threat to the West, and to the stability of the States in which they occur. It is beyond the scope of this book to consider what strategy or strategies, military or non-military; or combinations, would in fact lead to greater security in Afghanistan. That weighty topic will be left to others with expertise regarding security in fragile conflict-affected States. Rather, the focus here will be on: (a) the responsibility of the international humanitarian community and the Afghan and coalition States in safeguarding schoolchildren by all means feasible and necessary including suspending school operation in hot conflict zones within the State (Afghanistan) until security for education at the sites in question can be reasonably guaranteed; (b) the potential civil liability of NGOs and States where school attendance is encouraged despite the known inadequate security situation for education and (c) potential criminal and/or civil liability under international law for individual officials most responsible for the education sector (and, at times, perhaps also for frontline workers), who encouraged school attendance at particular education sites which they knew would put the children at high risk of being victimized by a terror attack. The encouragement and facilitation of school attendance under these circumstances amounts then to the individual potentially violating international humanitarian norms (i.e., the prohibition against intentionally engaging in acts that potentially inflict or do result in avoidable and legally unjustifiable suffering – physical and/or psychological – for civilians or instigating or participating or contributing in any way to acts that place civilian lives in significant jeopardy).

As to the issue of any potential or actual civil and/or criminal liability under international law for encouraging and facilitating school attendance where security is quite inadequate, nothing in what follows, or implied therefrom, is intended to, or should be taken as being a statement attributing actual or potential culpability to any particular conflict-affected State or its allies, particular NGO organization or humanitarian or human rights entity or particular individual as a factual matter. As far as individual culpability for violations of international humanitarian law, those are matters potentially to be investigated by a Prosecutor if there is a reasonable basis for doing so (whether there is such a reasonable basis for an investigation in any particular instance is something only a Prosecutor can decide based on the available facts). Any attribution of culpability would be a finding made by a court, should the case be heard by a national court (where there are statutes concerning 'war crimes' and 'crimes against humanity' incorporated into the domestic statutes), or by the International Criminal Court in The Hague (where all jurisdictional criteria have been met), based on all the facts in the particular case, as well as consideration by the court of defences raised and of any mitigating and aggravating factors. As far as civil liability in respect of States, NGOs and human rights bodies, those are matters that would be heard in an international court of human rights or a national court depending in part on the jurisdictional criteria operative. Rather, the intent here is simply to critically examine the conduct of the Afghan government and its Western allies, as well as that of international and national NGOs, and UN bodies in regards to basic education initiatives (primary and secondary schooling) in Afghanistan. More specifically, a challenge is mounted regarding the alleged moral and legal legitimacy of encouraging and facilitating school attendance when security for education is grossly inadequate (as is occurring in Afghanistan in certain hot combat zones). Further, the author offers her views based on extensive research from diverse sources on the potential international law violations which derive from such conduct (with actual or potential liability of any particular individual or entity here acknowledged as being factually undetermined unless and until assessed by the proper judicial authority).

The objective of this book then is to raise awareness of the fact that various democratic States, certain high profile NGOs and the United Nations are inadvertently arguably complicit in the rapidly rising numbers of schoolchildren internationally who have been successfully targeted by terrorists in contemporary armed conflicts. Though this is certainly not the result that the West and its democratic allies or human rights/humanitarian aid organizations desire; it appears to be a result that the aforementioned are quite prepared to risk. We will explore why this is the case by looking beyond the 'right to education' rhetoric which has served as something of a smokescreen for the international community's prioritizing of education over the schoolchildren's personal security in certain conflict-affected States. The *inadvertent* complicity of the West and its allies, as well as the U.N. and its organs and certain national and international NGOs, in placing schoolchildren in harm's way arises in that these players in the 'war on terror' have too often: (a) contributed to or facilitated the building and maintenance of schools operating in hot combat zones notwithstanding the acknowledged woefully inadequate security situation both at the school as well as on the children's route to and from school, and (b) encouraged parents to send their children to school despite the grossly inadequate security situation (i.e., frequently by giving parents assurances about alleged 'improved' security when in fact the security was still substandard and would be ineffective in preventing harm to the children and to school personnel). There is no way to determine from the data available whether such assurances when given were or were not intentionally misleading or, instead, given in good faith.

There is no suggestion here that schools can only be built or operational in areas where there is an 'iron-clad guarantee' of safety for such a guarantee is not possible in any State whether conflicted or not. However, there ought to be a reasonably and factually-based almost certain guarantee of safety since schoolchildren and adults associated with the basic education effort are entitled to no less under international human rights and humanitarian law.

Thunder Bay, Ontario, Canada
November 11, 2010

Sonja Grover

Acknowledgements

I thank my husband Roshan Grover for his love and his infinite patience in listening to my ramblings about the book and for his constant support, and faith in my ability to complete this rather ambitious work. I also acknowledge the support of our daughter Angeline whose confidence in her mom is a source of great encouragement to me and whose own human rights advocacy work is to be admired. In addition, I especially thank Dr. Brigitte Reschke, Executive Editor for law with Springer for her invaluable advice regarding this monograph and extend my appreciation to those others also who reviewed and commented on the manuscript. My thanks also to the Springer production team and especially Umamaheswari Gnanamanni for their excellent work.

Contents

Part I
Re-Examining the Role of Education Aid as a Component of the 'Humanitarian' Agenda in Conflict-Affected States

Chapter 1
Introduction

There is no question that education is a basic human right and essential to a decent quality of life; though not a guarantee thereof. Yet, there are in the year 2010, 77 million children out of school and of these over half (53 million) live in conflict-affected fragile States[1] where CAFS is defined as "countries that are impacted by conflict, income-disparity, weak governance and/or inequality in resource allocation.[2] While the absolute numbers of children who are out of school is higher in conflict-affected countries; it is also the case that the rate of school enrollment is slower compared to that in countries that are not experiencing conflict-related fragility.[3] Furthermore, completion of primary school and regular school attendance are also substantially lower in CAFS compared to more stable States not currently affected by conflict.[4] There is no debate here that children in conflict-affected, developing countries deserve and are entitled to educational equity compared to children in developed, non-conflict affected States. That is a non-issue. The contention explored in this book is rather that simply getting children into school when they are at high risk of terror attack at that school or on the way to or from school does not genuinely amount to increased access to education in any meaningful and legitimate sense. In any case, another terror attack on their school will have many if not most of the students dropping out again; at least for a time. Yet, too often enrolling and retaining students in school no matter the cost in personal security to the children, their teachers and other school staff as well as to frontline education humanitarian workers is where the focus of the international community appears to be. Keeping the numbers of school attendees as high as possible despite the lack of school security or security for children and education personnel on their way to and from school creates the *illusion* of progress. That is, the illusion is crafted of movement toward stability and normalization not only in the education sector but also in the *perceived* overall security situation of the conflict-affected State itself. In fact, in CAFS such as Afghanistan, as will be discussed in detail in

[1]Dryden-Petersen (2010), p. 4.

[2]Dryden-Petersen (2010), p. 7.

[3]Dryden-Petersen (2010), p. 4.

[4]Dryden-Petersen (2010), p. 8.

S.C. Grover, *Schoolchildren as Propaganda Tools in the War on Terror*,
DOI 10.1007/978-3-642-17900-6_1, © Springer-Verlag Berlin Heidelberg 2011

what follows, level of school attendance is an *unreliable* indicator of the overall security situation in any particular region of the conflict-affected State. This is the case given the pressure from the international aid community and the national government and its allies that children attend school notwithstanding gross deficiencies in school security.

Persistence in school attendance, as mentioned is also of major concern to the international aid community as is not surprising. The concern is often communicated *as if* it were one that is purely based on the fact that children's educational interests are undermined by dropping out of school:

> . . .Five or six years of schooling . . .represent a threshold. With less than that amount of education, people remain functionally illiterate. From a human capital perspective, it is completion that matters more than enrollment. . .Primary Completion rates . . .are almost always substantially lower than net enrolment ratios in any given country.[5]

However, the national government and international aid community's concern with school attendance and completion rates in Afghanistan, as we shall see, has as much, if not more, to do with the bureaucratic and propaganda interests of the aforementioned as with the welfare of children.

There certainly has been tremendous change in the school attendance in Afghanistan since 9/11. According to a 2009 report by Human Rights Watch (HRW) "We have the Promises of the World", in 2002 less than one million children were enrolled in formal education in Afghanistan and by the school year 2008–2009, this number had risen to over six million "more than at any point in Afghanistan's history".[6] The greatest gains were in school enrollment in primary school and participation drops off substantially in secondary school for both boys and girls with the dropout rate being considerably higher for girls. The aforementioned HRW report states in fact that the number of girls enrolled in grade seven drops to half the number of girls enrolled in grade six. Only 11 percent of Afghani secondary-school aged girls are enrolled in grades 7–9 and this drops to 4% in grades 10–12.[7] In this regard, note that low school attendance and significant school dropout jeopardizes NGO funding and undermines the West's use of school attendance and completion rates as a propaganda tool for communicating to the international community progress in the global conflict designated as the 'war on terror':

> Since then [the 2007 UNESCO report on attacks on education globally] there have been thousands more reported cases of students, teachers, academics and other education staff being kidnapped, imprisoned, beaten, tortured, burned alive, shot, or blown up by rebels [including terrorists and by other forces] . . .The effects on education of such incidents will be felt long after the funerals have taken place, through loss of teachers and intellectuals, flight of students and staff, fear of turning up to class, grief and psychological trauma among students and personnel, damage to buildings, materials and resources, and degradation

[5]Dryden-Petersen (2010), p. 8.

[6]Human Rights Watch (2009), p. 76.

[7]Human Rights Watch (2009), p. 76.

> of the education system through staffing recruitment difficulties ***and halted investment*** (emphasis added).[8]

When significant numbers of basic education students fail to attend school for a considerable time or drop-out due to fear related to lax security around education, it is likely to stimulate others in the same school or alternate education site and schoolchildren in nearby locales to do the same. Poor school attendance and high drop-out rates in any region of a conflict-affected State such as Afghanistan would be perceived by the international community as reflective of the fact that: (a) security in the education sector is inadequate and (b) the students in a particular region(s) of the CAFS have directly or indirectly been exposed to terror attacks due to the victims' involvement with education. Thus, there is, it is suggested, a tremendous push from the international aid community and the national government and its military allies to increase enrollment and retain students despite inadequate security for school buildings and alternate education sites in certain regions of Afghanistan (the same pattern repeating itself also in other conflict-affected States). In this regard, note that:

> [Afghanistan is] [T]he only complex emergency where all *major donors [of international humanitarian aid to education and other sectors] are also belligerents* (the exceptions being Switzerland and India). *As a result the* ***militarization of aid*** *has reached unprecedented levels* (emphasis added).[9]

This author is agreed with the notion expressed in the quote immediately above regarding the 'militarization of aid' in several conflict-affected countries globally; Afghanistan included; for the reason that belligerents have also become aid donors. There has thus indeed been at least a perceived blurring of the lines between neutral humanitarian aid *versus* aid as part of a military strategy to "win hearts and minds" to the West's military cause (i.e., that cause being expressly stated by the West as that of defeating Taliban insurgent extremists, Al Qaeda and other terror groups). This author does *not* agree, however, with the position taken by some NGOs operating in Afghanistan (i.e., CARE and certain others) that agreeing to protection for schools and for various other humanitarian projects from the allied forces amounts to the militarization of aid. It is the obligation of NGOs and all humanitarian organizations under international humanitarian and human rights law to do what they can to protect civilians-accepting protection from allied forces against terror attacks is frequently the only viable option in that regard in the present circumstance. The current author is in disagreement then with the contention in a recent UNESCO report[10] and other NGO documents that negotiations with the Taliban insurgents in Afghanistan (or Pakistan for that matter) regarding school safety is a reasonable less incendiary approach. Consider in this regard the following admission by CARE:

---

[8]O'Malley (2010), p. 14.

[9]Donini (2010), p. 3.

[10]O'Malley (2010), p. 124 [citing Glad (2009), p. 57].

> The CARE study in Afghanistan recommends that where potential attackers are known, community leaders might consider engaging in *preventative negotiations* with them *to try to reach agreement on continuing education locally. But it warned that this option must not be taken lightly and only local leaders would know if it was appropriate,* ***might achieve the opposite effect*** *or would be beyond their reach* (emphasis added).[11]

In other words, attempting negotiations with Taliban extremists for schools as safe sanctuaries is a high risk proposition at best and, at times, may even increase the risk of school attacks and terror attacks directly on schoolchildren and education personnel. Children cannot give informed, voluntary consent to gambling with their security in this way. Further, under no scenario under international humanitarian law can such a gamble (sending children to unsecured schools on the basis of a promise by the Taliban not to launch a terror attack) be considered legally or morally supportable. One may rightfully raise the question 'how humanitarian is the humanitarian aid community when it takes such risks with children's lives and psychological and physical well-being?' It would seem that the international aid community in encouraging and facilitating school attendance even in various regions within Afghanistan where there is inadequate security for basic education is focused in that instance on self-interest. The motivation in such circumstances is, in large part, to meet the need of the NGOs, as bureaucratic entities, to maintain donor monies. It is relevant to note in this regard that "countries with the most children *already* accessing primary education receive the most aid".[12] There is a move, however, by UNESCO to shift the thinking such that the number of out-of-school children would be considered in determining need and more aid per child would be provided where large numbers of children are out of school as "these children may require more investment than a child already in school in terms of ensuring access to the education system".[13] Were the UNESCO proposal for assessing need in the education sector adopted, conflict-affected countries would then not be as disadvantaged in accessing donor monies as is currently the case (given the large numbers of children out-of-school in CAFS and the practice, at present, of donors giving more aid where more children are *already* in school).

Thus, currently, having large numbers of children out of school in conflict-affected countries (due to non-attendance, irregular attendance, or dropping out) does not translate into large amounts of donor monies for the work of NGOs as well as for other sectors of the international humanitarian aid community. Before they maintain their donor contributions at the same or higher levels, international donors want to perceive that there is progress in development and stabilization in the CAFS. Such progress, it is claimed by the international community, is *supposedly* accurately indexed, in part at least, by the numbers of children in school. Conflict-affected States, at present, thus wish to demonstrate to their allies/donors the *alleged* progress they are making in stabilizing the situation and moving toward

[11] Dryden-Petersen (2010), p. 13.

[12] Dryden-Petersen (2010), p. 13.

[13] Dryden-Petersen (2010), p. 38.

establishing the regular institutions of civil society in a democratic State. One vehicle for doing so is purportedly the education sector (building and operating schools and increasing the school attendance and completion rates). We will discover, however, that in conflict-affected States such as Afghanistan, school attendance rates are not unflawed as indicators of improvements in security. This is the case given the pressures that families are under from the national government and the national and international humanitarian education aid sector to send their children to school even where security is far below minimally acceptable standards for ensuring the children's safety. In this regard, note that Daniel Toole, UNICEF Regional Director for South Asia in 2009 had the following to say about the security situation in Afghanistan and the consequences for children: "Afghanistan today is without doubt the most dangerous place to be born".[14] The security situation has in fact deteriorated greatly since 2006 and is likely to get even worse with the planned withdrawal of most of the American troops in the very near future.

There is no challenge here to the view that education development work is particularly vital in all low-income States including especially those in a 'post-conflict' stage of development and those recovering from natural disasters. The prime issue addressed in this book is rather whether children who are living in the midst of ongoing armed conflict, in States impacted by organized terror campaigns that include the targeting of education, are unconscionably being used as pawns in a counter-terrorism propaganda campaign. That counter-insurgency strategy, *in practice*, involves, in part, children attending government or non-government community schools even where the schools are highly vulnerable to terror attack as are the routes to and from school (That strategy also potentially puts in harms way teachers, and frontline education aid workers affiliated with national and international NGOs working in insecure zones, and, on occasion, even educational policy-makers and administrators). Thus, there is no counter-argument being raised here disputing the notion that education is a useful and key element of an emergency humanitarian aid response in conflict-affected or disaster zones if and when reasonable security from armed attack becomes feasible. However, in conflict-affected States such as Afghanistan with intense armed conflict still ongoing; reasonable security for education often cannot be provided in every region of the country given the limited necessary military or other security resources available. One may question therefore the wisdom and legality of sending children to school in those unsecured regions where they are at high risk of being targeted for a terror attack given their status as schoolchildren. It would appear then that focusing on education provides the *appearance* at least of a neutral, purely humanitarian rallying point for international donors who wish to contribute to Afghanistan's development. As discussed, however, education in Afghanistan and other conflict-affected areas has become a tool used by both sides for propaganda purposes: (a) by the West to try and communicate the notion that progress is being made in stabilization and development, and (b) by the terrorists to send the opposing message;

[14] Donini (2010), p. 3.

namely that the country will remain unstable and no development progress of any kind made unless the government accedes to extremist Taliban demands.

In all of this, it is important to acknowledge the fact that in Afghanistan having the focus of the government and the international humanitarian aid community on education generally, and regardless whether or not minimal security has been established in the particular region in question, comes at a cost to the personal well-being of civilians. That cost, as discussed, comes, in part, in the form of increased risk to the safety of schoolchildren and education personnel from terror attack. It also, however, involves a 'cost' related to the comparative neglect of the vital survival needs of Afghanis. That is, those urgent needs for food, decent shelter and the like are being addressed relying on less financial support from the international humanitarian aid donor community. These additional potential funds have been diverted instead to education despite schools being unsecured in many regions where schools are being built and repaired after a terror attack using international donor monies. Consider in this context then the following sobering statistics relating to the urgent survival needs of civilians in Afghanistan:

> Nine million Afghans (36 percent of the population) live in absolute poverty, and five million 'non-poor' live on less than US$2 a day.[15]
>
> [Afghanistan has] some of the world's worst social indicators: highest infant mortality rate; second-highest maternal mortality rate; the only country in the world where women have lower life expectancy than men.[16]
>
> According to UNAMA, there has been a 40% increase of civilian casualties in 2008. The human security of ordinary Afghans is rapidly deteriorating because of the combination of conflict, appalling levels of poverty, food shortages, difficulties of access, and the accumulated consequences of three decades of war. Conflict-related displacement is a seriously under-addressed issue.[17]

Clearly, especially where security is still a grave concern in various parts of the country, the first priority ought to be the basic survival needs of all civilians. Under international law, those basic survival needs cannot legitimately take second place to education initiatives for school-aged children. Yet, this is in large part happening given a modus operandi of national and international humanitarian bodies in Afghanistan that would be more suitable for a *genuine* 'post-conflict' situation but not for an ongoing conflict such as is occurring in Afghanistan (i.e., a modus operandi of using donor dollars to build and repair schools as a top priority across the country *regardless the security situation* where those schools are located). Even though Afghanistan has been described as the "world's longest running major armed conflict";[18] in practice, NGOs often prioritize their activities as if the situation were a 'post-conflict' one. At the same time, international donors have responded to civilian needs in Afghanistan in recent years largely as centering allegedly around support for 'recovery' from conflict as opposed to needs relating

---

[15] Donini (2010), p. 3.

[16] Donini (2010), p. 3.

[17] Donini (2009), p. 2.

[18] Donini (2010), p. 3.

to a humanitarian crisis. In fact, donor money for purely humanitarian aid is quite low.[19] Donini attributes this to the fact that there is little hard data on the scope of the humanitarian crisis in Afghanistan as humanitarian agencies have not focused on collecting such data and there are not uncommonly issues of accessibility to the civilian population in need of humanitarian aid in those regions where the security concerns are significant.[20] International donors typically adopt the perspective that "unless you can prove that there is a humanitarian crisis, we see no need to shift our funds from recovery to humanitarian activities".[21] It is not surprising then that scholars of the situation have critiqued "the continued acceptance of [alleged] 'post-conflictness' by many NGOs"[22]:

> From a humanitarian perspective, the consequences of the early declaration of "post-conflict" and of the subsequent closing down of OCHA (U.N. Office for the Coordination of Humanitarian Affairs) and downgrading of the UN's humanitarian capacity in early 2002 are now in stark relief. While OCHA was re-established in early 2009, its capacity remains uncertain and its ability to negotiate humanitarian access and space untested. *This is compounded by the absence of reliable data on the depth and breadth of the crisis as well as donor reluctance to acknowledge that a robust humanitarian response is necessary* (emphasis added).[23]

It is noteworthy that donation of international aid monies for education to conflict-affected States such as Afghanistan is not in any way contingent on the State in question (with the assistance of allies and the international aid community) meeting any requirement for adequate monitoring of school attacks or threats of attacks and providing an effective means of prevention. Further, when it comes to the international humanitarian aid community, it, too, has only fairly recently come to discuss in earnest the issue of attacks on education. Suggested prevention measures from the humanitarian aid community regarding attacks on education by anti-government insurgents include things such as attempts at negotiation with extremist insurgent Taliban and other such groups. This despite the fact that many academics and field workers knowledgeable about the human rights situation in Afghanistan contend that:

> . . .there is little understanding of, and respect for, humanitarian principles by the Taliban and other insurgents who tar the UN and NGOs with the occupiers' brush [though of course there can be no justification for the violation of *jus cogen* humanitarian principles under any circumstance].[24]

The notion of NGOs operating in Afghanistan refraining from encouraging and facilitating school attendance where the safety of the schoolchildren and education personnel cannot be reasonably assured has, in practice, *not* been a preventive

[19]Donini (2009), p. 10.
[20]Donini (2009), p. 6.
[21]Donini (2009), p. 6.
[22]Donini (2010), p. 5.
[23]Donini (2010), p. 5.
[24]Donini (2010), p. 3.

strategy that has been widely discussed or promoted within the international humanitarian education aid community. Rather, the goal has generally been, for instance, to reopen schools as soon as possible after a school attack (after repairs to the school). This may in part be the case in that most NGOs in Afghanistan are not strictly dedicated to humanitarian aid; but rather have mandates focused largely on development and advocacy[25] and function "on the increasingly erroneous assumption that Afghanistan is a postconflict country".[26] The result of all this for schoolchildren is that more often than not:

> Students are afraid when they attend school. They are [rightfully] afraid of kidnappings and explosions [Principal Heart].[27]

With the increasing rate of school attacks in Afghanistan and the deteriorating overall security situation in the country,[28] it would seem that schoolchildren attending school in that troubled State have very good reason to be afraid; at least in certain regions of the country if not in most:

> Between January 2006 and December 2008, 1153 attacks or threats towards the education sector in Afghanistan were reported. The number of attacks started increasing in late 2005 and . . .almost tripled in 2008 . . .the phenomenon of attacks on schools is [furthermore] not confined to one region of the country in particular.[29]

One may, therefore, legitimately highlight the possibility that encouraging and facilitating school attendance knowing the children are under constant and high risk of being victimized by a terror attack, and that the children are consequently terrified of the same, amounts to a crime against humanity involving the intentional infliction of grave psychological harm on a highly vulnerable civilian population. The latter being in violation of Article 7(1)(k) of the Rome Statute dealing with: "Other inhumane acts of a similar character intentionally causing great suffering, or serious injury to body or to mental or physical health".[30] In regard to this latter issue of the potential commission of "crimes against humanity" (depending on the unique facts of the particular case) by individual government officials and humanitarian education aid workers in the field and their superiors (as a consequence of knowingly putting children at high risk in particular locales by encouraging school attendance in insecure zones in Afghanistan) consider the following:

> A second aspect [influencing fluctuations in the number of school attacks aside from the role of the number of armed insurgents in the area and the "resources and priorities" of the terrorists and other insurgents] that could influence the frequency of attacks is the prevalence of school closure. At the end of June, 2009, a total of 695 schools were reported

---

[25]Donini (2009), p. 2.

[26]Donini (2009), p. 2.

[27]Glad (2009), p. 42.

[28]Glad (2009), p. 15.

[29]Glad (2009), p. 22.

[30]Rome Statute entered into force 1 July 2002. http://untreaty.un.org/cod/icc/statute/romefra.htm. Accessed 7 Oct 2010.

> closed across the country . . .***The Ministry of Education is making a concerted effort to reopen schools and keep education alive even in those areas where school attacks are at its worst.*** ["School construction continues also in areas where security threatens construction companies".[31]] ***But many of these re-opened schools are subsequently attacked and shut down again.*** In Helmand province, for example, 180 schools, or 71% of the total, were inactive from March to July 2009, but 100 schools were re-opened over the same period. ***In many of these areas there appears to be an endless, and costly [costly also in terms of civilian deaths and serious injuries], process of attack, closure, rehabilitation, opening and attack*** (emphasis added).[32]

At what price then in terms of deaths and injuries for students, teachers and other education-related personnel, as well as for humanitarian education aid workers, are these schools in hot terror zones within the country re-opened again and again after repair subsequent to a terror attack? Insofar as delivering education as a humanitarian emergency aid response in conflict-affected Afghanistan (and many other conflict-affected States where the fighting is ongoing and there are hot terror zones) is concerned, this author is thus in accord, at least to a degree, with the view that: ". . .there is at best limited interest or support for principled humanitarian action. . ."[33] in these conflict-affected contexts by various parties including the international aid community. This less than full adherence to humanitarian principles is reflected in the willingness to put children at risk in the manner described in order to demonstrate to international donors that development progress is being made. As previously mentioned, most of these donors are also belligerents in the 'war on terror' in Afghanistan and, hence, anxious to use education (i.e., rates of school attendance etc.) as a supposed marker for alleged progress in suppressing insurgents. This is the case presumably, in large part, due to the need to garner support for the 'war effort' at home. The pressure to have children return to school after a terror attack is an ongoing challenge for the international humanitarian aid community and the national government in Afghanistan as:

> It is a natural reaction from a parent to be more hesitant to send their children to school after the school they go to has been attacked or threatened. But a direct incident on the school is not the only factor that keeps people away. 'Each incident affects the risk assessment that parents and students undertake nearly every day. Single episodes, even from far away districts, accumulate to establish a pattern: in a country as traumatized by violence as Afghanistan, teachers, parents, and students are keenly attuned to fluctuations in this pattern and decide to continue or stop their education based on how they view the general climate of insecurity and how it will manifest itself in their immediate environment'.[34]

The emphasis has been on drawing a rosy picture focusing on increased school enrollment in particular regions in Afghanistan, new schools built or schools repaired etc. with comparatively less attention paid by the humanitarian community,

---

[31]Glad (2009), p. 25.

[32]Glad (2009), p. 25.

[33]Donini (2010), p. 3.

[34]Glad (2009), p. 42 [Citing Human Rights Watch, Lessons in Terror (2006) http://www.hrw.org/en/node/11295/section/7].

or the international media, when schools and schoolchildren are victimized by a terror attack. A 2010 briefing paper issue by the Feinstein International Centre of Tufts University in fact states that Afghanistan hosts:

> An aid community that is ill-equipped ***(or unwilling?)*** to make the necessary effort to build up a composite picture of the extent of conflict-related human suffering and vulnerability, and to address it (emphasis added).[35]

This lack of willingness to address fully the suffering induced by terror in Afghanistan is especially the case in regard to attacks on education. This is reflected, for instance, in the fact that the international humanitarian community and UN bodies to date have collected mostly only unverified anecdotal evidence on school attacks and direct attacks on schoolchildren and teachers. The numbers of such incidents reported are in all probability underestimates due to the fear that likely adversely impacts on the likelihood of community members reporting such attacks to government officials or humanitarian education aid workers given their concerns regarding possible retaliation by insurgents for such contacts. The national government and the international aid community operating in Afghanistan appear then often to encourage and facilitate school attendance even in highly insecure areas within the country (according to NGO reports of this practice in Afghanistan); thus putting schoolchildren and teachers at considerable risk of death or grievous injury. Given this apparent phenomenon, one can well imagine that these parties would be unwilling to 'make the necessary effort to build up a composite picture of the extent of conflict-related human suffering and vulnerability and address it' *and their potential contribution to it*; at least insofar as the impact of the violence on education and the *necessary preventive is concerned- the latter being school closing until security can be reasonably assured*:

> ...some provinces reporting a decrease or only moderate increase in attacks...figure amongst those provinces with the highest number of closed schools. *This suggests that if a school is closed it may be less likely to be attacked. While important to bear this possibility in mind, statistically across the country* [*Afghanistan*] *the association between* ***the rate of attacks*** *vs. permanent school closure is in fact quite variable and thus such a conclusion should not be considered universally valid* (emphasis added).[36]

What is clear is that where schools are closed due to lack of security, children and education personnel are not killed or injured at the school or on their way to or from the school. That is, of course, the key point from a purely humanitarian perspective. There would appear to be sufficient data to conclude that insurgents are less interested in attacking closed schools where there is no possibility of inflicting grievous physical harms on civilians. There may, however, be some instances where insurgents have wrongly assumed that the school, though permanently or temporarily closed, is operational at that time and have attacked. There may be other instances where the attack on a temporarily closed school is intended

[35]Donini (2010), p. 5.

[36]Glad (2009), p. 25.

to send a message that the government's educational enterprise is futile as when a just repaired or newly built school is attacked. What can be the possible point of comparing the *rate of terror attacks on schools* to the number of permanent school closures (see quote above), and suggesting that there is not always a perfect inverse relationship between the two (as occurs in the CARE study conducted on behalf of the World Bank and the Afghan Ministry of Education)? The answer would, of course, be speculative. However, what can be said is that the foregoing statistic (the variability in the rate of school attacks *versus* number of permanent school closings in various areas across Afghanistan), included as it is in a high profile NGO report, is thus made available to those in government (the Afghan Ministry of Education) to use in the service of a sort of perverse and distorted logic. That distorted logic can be summarized as 'why not keep the schools open even after a terror attack, once they are repaired, since closing them permanently is not a guarantee that the schools will not be attacked'. That 'illogic' purports to support a justification for schools being kept open even where security is quite inadequate (and even where the schools in question may have suffered a terror attack) and where the civilians attending there are, therefore, at high risk of being grievously harmed by the insurgents:

> Despite the security situation some schools resume activities fairly quickly after attacks, remaining closed for just days or weeks. . .Across those provinces studied in the field assessment, schools normally remained closed for between 1 and 3 months [the times may be longer in the more insecure provinces].[37]

NGOs in Afghanistan have *not* taken a position on humanitarian grounds, or any other, vigorously opposing the government of Afghanistan's desire and practice of keeping government schools open even in unsecured terror zones. Indeed, keeping schools open despite the abysmal security situation in various regions in the country is consistent with the development mandate of most of the NGOs; operating as they are with the illusion of being in a 'post-conflict' environment and as partners with the Afghan government in development efforts. Nor, therefore, have NGOs in Afghanistan set an official policy for themselves of closing NGO-based schools wherever these schools are at any level of credible risk of terror attack *until and unless* such time arrives when security can be reasonably assured (though there have been temporary school closings in particular locales by some NGOs and a scale back of education projects by certain high profile NGOs[38]). That scale back and some school closings by select NGOs may in fact be due, in part, to the difficulty in recruiting Afghan nationals –teachers and humanitarian aid workers- to go into particular hot conflict areas to do education aid work soon after a terror attack on a school or when such an attack has been perpetrated directly against schoolchildren and teachers (as well as due to the reluctance of many parents to send their children to school soon after a terror attack). In this regard, note that international humanitarian NGOs operating in conflict-affected countries such as

[37]Glad (2009), p. 41.

[38]Glad (2009), p. 26.

Afghanistan have come in recent years to rely heavily on nationals of the conflict-affected State to carry out the agency aid operations especially in the highly insecure and most volatile areas within the State:

> International staff travel minimally or not at all outside these areas [protected green zones]. Risk has by and large been transferred to national staff of INGOs [international NGOs] and Afghan NGOs. . .[39]

While government schools appear to be at highest risk of terror attack in Afghanistan, NGO-based and private schools are also not immune.[40] Just how many attacks on NGO-supported schools are occurring in Afghanistan is not at all clear. This is the case in that these schools "are not necessarily linked up to an official monitoring system" regarding such attacks though they appear to be less targeted than are government schools. NGO-based schools are, to some extent, apparently less targeted for terror attack than are government schools as they are not as visible structurally (being placed most often in multi-purpose community buildings, and, most often in private homes as opposed to being located in separate identifiable school buildings) and perhaps also for other undetermined reasons.[41] Furthermore, there is evidence that communities (and thus likely also insurgents) in Afghanistan are generally aware of where funding for a school comes from: international donor *versus* Afghan government funded, and this, too, may impact on the likelihood of an attack on the school.[42]

What is further evident is that in conflict-affected fragile States (CAFS) such as Afghanistan where the conflict is ongoing and intense, government departments responsible for education have assumed no particular responsibility for the security of schools (i.e., in preventing or repelling terrorist attacks). Protecting schools against terror attacks may indeed be beyond the capabilities of the Ministries of Education in these conflict-affected countries. Yet, the issue arises as to the questionable legitimacy morally and legally of these same education government departments (i.e., Afghan Ministry of Education) of: (1) promoting school attendance knowing that the schools, in many instances, are not adequately secured, and (2) encouraging the practice of reopening schools as soon as possible after a terror attack on a school (i.e., as soon as repairs are complete) despite there being, in most if not all instances, no significant, if any, improvement in the security for the previously attacked schools. Often school attendance has become the objective in and of itself in conflict-affected states such as Afghanistan where the fighting is intense and ongoing. That is to say that NGOs and government encourage school attendance in Afghanistan often in large part ignoring whether a quality education is being offered as well as the frequent high security risk in attending school especially for girls. School attendance under these circumstances then serves

[39]Donini (2009), p. 7.

[40]Donini (2009), p. 25.

[41]Donini (2009), p. 26.

[42]Donini (2009), p. 55.

primarily NGO and government political objectives as opposed to meeting the children's best interests:

> The question of what children are learning in schools looms especially large in CAFS. . . . much of the humanitarian literature has been about the role of education in restoring normality. . . *"the implication is that it would almost be enough to get the children back into school and the routines of schooling are as important as the content"*. . .*situations of conflict and fragility often require urgent responses* that *focus more on inputs like constructing a school* [*or repairing or re-constructing a school after a terror attack*] *than on much harder to plan for and evaluate outputs such as learning* [*and improved school security*] (emphasis added).[43]

NGOs in Afghanistan, at present, then focus on 'inputs' (building and repairing schools) and encouraging children to attend school, putting it appears, much less emphasis on 'outputs' in providing education aid in this and other armed conflict situations (i.e., learning outcomes, indicia of improved school security outcomes). Those learning outcomes are adversely affected by poorly educated and trained teachers, large classes and poor learning resources. Human Rights Watch reported in 2006 the following in this regard:

> Classes are typically very large—with an average of seventy-one students per teacher at the primary level—and meet for only around three hours a day. Schools lack teaching materials and schools supplies; many teachers rely on poor teaching methods such as rote-learning, use corporal punishment, lack knowledge of basic subjects, and are frequently absent; the curriculum is poor (although steps have been taken to reform the curriculum); and teachers and students may discriminate against children from minority ethnic groups. . .. Many teachers have not finished grade twelve.[44]

The tragic 'output' so-called (as a result of this NGO and government 'recovery focus' in what is *not* in fact a post-conflict situation) is not only less than adequate learning outcomes in many instances, but also a significant increase in child deaths and injuries flowing from stepped up terror attacks on government schools and on alternate community education sites such as has occurred over the last number of years in Afghanistan.

In the rush to get children back into school despite the lack of security, various justifications are often proffered by international aid organizations. One prime example of such a justification is the notion that returning children back to their normal school routine quickly has psychological therapeutic benefit for children traumatized by conflict and a recent terror attack on education i.e., a terror attack on their school or on a school in a nearby locale etc. While that rationale for sending children back to school makes sense if children are returning to a school that is genuinely a 'safe zone' or where the country is in a 'post-conflict' stage, it is highly dubious when children are returning to schools or alternate education sites that are not secured as is most often the case in Afghanistan. There is no psychological benefit in children attending school with justifiable fear knowing that the next terror

---

[43]Dryden-Petersen (2010), p. 38.

[44]Human Rights Watch (2006) p. 92.

attack on their centre of learning may come at any time. Indeed, there appears in many ways to be more emphasis on getting children back into school at all costs after a terror attack to create *the appearance* of 'normality' rather than on any theoretical potential benefit to the children educationally and psychologically in school attendance in the midst of intense conflict. In fact, this focus on returning children back to school as soon as possible after a terror attack, even before security and educational curricula are well worked out, would seem to be one of the tell-tale signs that factors in addition to, or even instead of, the children's best interests are operative in those instances. Those factors include, but are not limited to, the need to show international aid donors for the conflict-affected State, as well as the parents of prospective schoolchildren, that: (a) NGO and national government activity is allegedly having a positive impact in terms of stabilization and development, and that (b) there is purported significant progress being made as a result in the education sector.

Human Rights Watch has reported on the lack of planning and implementation of strategies around monitoring and preventing attacks on education in Afghanistan:

> Human Rights Watch found nobody monitoring early warning signs for attacks, such as night letters [letters from the Taliban warning of violent attacks if children are sent to school], a school being located very near a district government office, or being the only representation of government in an area, or other factors. . .*in Afghanistan there is no nationwide policy for preventing attacks on schools, and there is no policy for ensuring individual schools receive assistance after an attack* (emphasis added).[45]
>
> *The Ministry of Education* [*in Afghanistan*] *takes the position that ensuring security for education is beyond its mandate and capabilities.* Mohammed Azim Karbalai, the head of the Ministry of Education's planning department, explained that: "The Ministry of Education cannot do anything about security. Maybe the Ministry of Defence, the Ministry of Interior or ISAF [International Security Assistance Force provided by the North Atlantic Treaty Organization under mandate of the United Nations] or other forces". Karbalai went on to explain that *when the ministry receives word that a school building or tent has been destroyed "we refer it to the Ministry of Interior, and we try to reconstruct the building if it is possible* . . . (emphasis added)[46]

UNESCO's 2010 report 'Education Under Attack'[47] and other recent reports by various international NGOs discussed here reveal that there is still a gross lack of adequate security for education in many conflict-affected States internationally including Afghanistan. Security is the foundational issue which must be addressed if 'access to education' is to be considered a meaningful concept in very fragile conflict-affected States. That is, attending school only to be victimized by a terror attack does not genuinely amount to 'accessing education'. One can readily concur that:

> *the macro-level barrier* [*to education*] *of conflict and fragility overlays all other barriers to accessing education.* Whether they are poor, rural, girls, disabled, ethnic or linguistic minorities, over-age [for school] or displaced, children in CAFS [conflict-affected fragile

[45] Human Rights Watch (2006), p. 105.

[46] Human Rights Watch (2006), p. 105.

[47] O'Malley (2010).

States] are vulnerable to exclusion from education [due to violence] *before* analysis on other barriers to access begins (emphasis added).[48]

The fact is, of course, that NGOs partnering most often with the national government in delivering education aid have no direct control over security matters in conflict-affected States such as Afghanistan. Nevertheless, the international aid community (along with the various State governments participating in the so-called 'war on terror' in foreign lands) shares in the legal and moral responsibility to encourage school enrollment at particular sites only when the security of school buildings and alternate education settings is adequate in that particular locale within the CAFS. It is *not e*nough that the international humanitarian community simply calls time and again for greater security for schools and for improved safety measures for students and school personnel in conflict-affected fragile States. The latter has certainly been done, and done repeatedly. For instance, the NGO 'Education International' in 2009 issued a 'Declaration on Violent Political and Military Attacks Against Education Institutions, Students, Teachers, Academics and All Other Education Personnel (including Support and Transport Staff, Education Officials, Education Trade Unionists, and Education Aid Workers)'. The Declaration, among other things, called upon the UN Security Council, government and the parties to the conflict to protect those involved with the education sector and to prosecute under international criminal law those responsible for perpetrating violent attacks on education:

Declaration on Violent Political and Military Attacks Against Education Institutions, Students, Teachers, Academics and All Other Education Personnel (including Support and Transport Staff, Education Officials, Education Trade Unionists, and Education Aid Workers) [Proclaimed by the NGO 'Education International']

Article 2: Take practical measures to ensure protection: Take all practical measures to protect students, teachers, academics, and all other education personnel from all deliberate violent political or military attacks on their way to or from, or at, their places of learning or work; and to take all possible measures to deter such attacks.

Article 3: End impunity for attacks on students, teachers, academics, all other education personnel and education facilities: The international community shall assist in ending impunity for attacks on education, and bring those culpable to justice. . .This explicit focus on attacks on students and staff in addition to buildings and facilities must also be included in the investigations of the International Criminal Court and the U.N. Secretary-General's monitoring of the grave violations against children in armed conflict.[49]

There is no question that for the countless children excluded from school in conflict-affected fragile States due to the security risks; States not yet in the 'post-conflict' stage; such exclusion represents an additional devastating barrier to a future decent quality of life. Thus:

Measured in terms of scale and impact on life chances, the out-of-school population represents a crucial human development challenge. More than that, it represents an indictment of national and international policy failures.[50]

---

[48]Dryden-Petersen (2010), p. 44.

[49]Education International (2009).

[50]Dryden-Petersen (2010), p. 45.

However, where national governments of conflict-affected fragile States (CAFS), and the international community, including the international aid community, encourage school attendance in locales within these CAFS despite the lack of security for education, this represents no less "an indictment of national and international policy failures". It is this violation of children's fundamental right to security masked by rhetoric concerning the indisputable right of all children to education, and the use of children in this way in the counter-terrorism propaganda wars, that is the subject of this book. Thus, on the one hand, there is recognition here that millions of children in CAFS are being excluded from education due to the conflict in violation of their fundamental right to an education. For instance, "Currently [in 2010], 5 million children in Afghanistan do not have access to education, approximately 43% of the total school-age population".[51] At the same time, there must be recognition that sending children to school where there is inadequate security and where their very lives and physical safety are in jeopardy does *not* in fact constitute access to education (i.e., the implementation of the 'right to education'), nor serve children's interests. Rather, sending children to school regardless of the security situation for education in the CAFS serves adult agendas at the cost of children's fundamental protection rights as guaranteed under international humanitarian and human rights law.

This book was stimulated by the images broadcast on worldwide media of young Afghan schoolgirls with their faces burned leaving them horribly disfigured; victims of an attack on education. The questions which arose for this author in viewing these images included not just: 'How do we stop this from happening?' – that is, 'How do we stop the terrorists?'; but also: 'How do we stop those responsible for sending the children to school despite their knowing that there was inadequate security for the school facilities and for the children as they made their way to and from school?' In all the background research for this book and the innumerable research reports read on the issue of attacks on education specifically, this author has only once come across even a mention of the fact that sending children to school in zones where there is a high risk of attack raises serious moral issues [aside from the implications under international law]. The passage in question appears in a paper by Alexander, Boothby and Wessells included in the 2010 UNESCO report 'Protecting education from attack: A state-of-the-art review' and reads as follows:

> Attacks on schools. . .weaken access to education, undermine the quality of education, and exact a heavy toll of suffering on learners, teachers, other educational staff, and of course, parents and communities. *Such attacks raise a host of disturbing questions about protection: Is it appropriate to place large numbers of children in a single space that may become a target and where attacks and abductions can have mass effects? Do not only governments but also civil societies and the international community have a responsibility to protect against attacks on schools? How can they fulfill that responsibility?* If schools are subject to

[51] Office of the Special Representative of the Secretary-General for Children and Armed Conflict (2010). Mission Report on the Visit of the Special Representative of the Secretary-General for Children and Armed Conflict to Afghanistan (20–26 February 2010), p. 68. http://www.unhcr.org/refworld/docid/4c0e143b2.html. Accessed 11 June 2010.

> attack with impunity, what are the implications for other public sites that house vulnerable people? Are attacks on education institutions like any other attacks or do they cause special harm...? Have adequate steps been taken internationally and with warring parties to advocate for strong prohibitions against attacks on education?
>
> *Too often, these and related questions are either not asked or are considered in a cursory manner that is wholly disproportionate to the magnitude of the problem* (emphasis added).[52]

This book addresses some of these disturbing questions that have to date received less than the required attention, if they have been addressed at all; particularly: (i) whether sending children to school in zones within CAFS where their security is at high risk (due to armed conflict involving terror campaigns specifically targeting education) is immoral and moreover an illegal practice under international law; and (ii) what is the nature of the culpability and who is culpable when children are sent off to school only to be victimized by a terror attack that was in fact reasonably foreseeable. Alexander, Boothby and Wessells respond to the aforementioned questions they raise in their paper thus:

> What is needed is nothing less than a concerted international campaign to criminalize attacks on schools and other education institutions, hold perpetrators accountable for attacks, and *to organize education in ways that prevent or minimize the risk of attacks on learning environments* (emphasis added).[53]

It is here contended that Alexander, Boothby and Wessells' suggestion that we must "organize education in ways that prevent or minimize the risk of attacks on learning environments" implies an overly optimistic picture of what is possible in terms of outcome regarding security when children are attending a school situated in the midst of an active terrorist operating zone. Negotiations with terror groups to regard schools as "safe zones" is a risky and unreliable proposition at best; even in those infrequent circumstances where it occurs (i.e., as, for instance, where the NGO allows the terror group to dictate constraints on curriculum). Reliance on community leaders to provide security is also a "double-edged sword" since "they [local elites] have the power [also] to provide or withdraw security".[54] In any case, the ability of local community leaders to provide security in the face of terrorist attacks is highly dubious and generally amounts to nothing more than their warning NGOs that insurgents are in the area and that the humanitarian workers should cease their activity at least for a time.[55] Furthermore, a key element missing in the commonly suggested necessary responses of the international community to prevent or mitigate attacks on education (including attacks on school buildings) is the need for a re-evaluation of the morality, wisdom and legality of NGOs, UN organizations, national governments in CAFS and Western States encouraging school attendance where security is at high risk and cannot be reasonably guaranteed. It is that issue,

[52] UNESCO (2010), p. 1.

[53] UNESCO (2010), p. 1.

[54] Azarbaijani-Moghaddam et al. (2008), p. 42.

[55] Azarbaijani-Moghaddam et al. (2008), p. 42.

and the matter of accountability and impunity; both in regards to the terrorists, and in respect of those responsible for facilitating school enrollment and attendance when schoolchildren are attending education sites known to be situated in the midst of the hot conflict zone, that is the focus of this inquiry and analysis.

References

Azarbaijani-Moghaddam S, Wardak M, Zaman I, Taylor A (2008) Afghan hearts, Afghan minds: exploring Afghan perceptions of civil-military relations. Research conducted for the European Network of NGOs in Afghanistan (ENNA) and the British and Irish Agencies Afghanistan Group (BAAG). http://www.humansecuritygateway.info/documents/ENNA_BAAG_Afghanistan_afghanheartsafghanminds.pdf. Accessed 29 May 2010

Donini A (2009) Afghanistan: humanitarianism under threat. Feinstein International Centre Briefing Paper. http://www.reliefweb.int/rw/rwb.nsf/db900sid/EGUA-7Q9QX4?OpenDocument. Accessed 11 Oct 2010

Donini A (2010) Afghanistan: humanitarianism unravelled? Feinstein International Centre Briefing Paper, Tufts University. http://www.alnap.org/pool/files/feinstein-afghan.pdf. Accessed 3 Oct 2010

Dryden-Petersen S (2010) Barriers to accessing primary education in conflict-affected fragile states: literature review. A report written on behalf of International Save the Children Alliance. http://www.savethechildren.org.uk/en/docs/Barriers_to_access_Literature_Review_Final.pdf. Accessed 3 June 2010

Education International (2009) Education international declaration on schools as safe sanctuaries (22 September 2009). http://www.ei-ie.org/library/en/pdf.php?id=151. Accessed 10 June 2010

Glad (2009) Knowledge on fire: attacks on education in Afghanistan; risks and measures for successful mitigation (CARE). http://care.ca/ckfinder/userfiles/files/Knowledge_on_fire-attacks_%20schools.pdf. Accessed 3 June 2010

Human Rights Watch (2006) Lessons in terror: attacks on education in Afghanistan, vol 18, no. 6 (C). www.hrw.org/reports/2006/afghanistan0706/index.htm. Accessed 18 May 2010

Human Rights Watch (2009) We have the promises of the world: women's rights in Afghanistan. http://www.hrw.org/en/node/86805/section/9. Accessed 6 June 2010

O'Malley (2010) Education under attack. A report commissioned by Mark Richmond, Director, Division for the Coordination of United Nations Priorities in Education, Education Sector, UNESCO, p 14. http://unesdoc.unesco.org/images/0018/001868/186809e.pdf. Accessed 26 Apr 2010

UNESCO (2010) Protecting education from attack: a state-of-the-art review. http://unesdoc.unesco.org/images/0018/001867/186732e.pdf. Accessed 18 June 2010

Chapter 2
Paradoxes Resulting from the Militarization of Education Aid

Save the Children declared in its 2006 report 'Rewrite the future: Education for children in conflict-affected areas' that it was "calling upon the international community and national governments to ensure that the 43 million children in conflict-affected countries get the quality education to which they are entitled".[1] At present, not only are these children facing daunting barriers in accessing basic education, but they often drop out once enrolled; not in small part due to terror attacks on their schools, teachers and other school personnel and on the students themselves.[2] What has transpired since the aforementioned report was released is a dramatic increase in terror attacks on education in many conflict-affected countries, including Afghanistan, and the victimization of schoolchildren and school personnel as a result. Security for schools, schoolchildren, teachers, education officials and humanitarian education aid workers has been woefully inadequate in conflict-affected States such as Afghanistan, Iraq and certain other States dealing with organized terror groups. International and national NGOs lament in their reports the lack of security in places such as Afghanistan where there is a continuing high rate of terror attacks on education. Yet, these same NGOs and organs of the UN, such as UNICEF, continue, in these highly insecure zones within the conflict-affected States, to build new schools and reopen schools that have previously suffered a terror attack and which are at considerable risk of subsequent attack. Thus, the international humanitarian community has, *in effect*, assigned the education of schoolchildren a higher priority in conflict-affected zones than the security of the person rights of the schoolchildren (right to be safe from harm). This means that the 'right to education' has, *in practice*, been distorted and implemented *as if* it did not automatically incorporate also the right to security which, of course, is not the case:

> *The fundamental human right to education includes the right to a safe education.* Children have the right to safety in school establishments that are conducive to a positive learning environment [Statement of the Special Rapporteur Vernor Munoz Villalobos on right to

[1] Save the Children (2006), p. 2.

[2] Human Rights Watch (2006), p. 101.

S.C. Grover, *Schoolchildren as Propaganda Tools in the War on Terror*,
DOI 10.1007/978-3-642-17900-6_2, © Springer-Verlag Berlin Heidelberg 2011

> education 19 April 2006 on the occasion of the terror rocket attack on Salabagh School in Afghanistan] (emphasis added).[3]

Further, the international and national NGOs have, *in practice*, downplayed the lack of security in those areas where they are running education classes for schoolchildren or wish to operate schools. This they have done, in part, by erroneously generalizing a model for delivery of education services in the context of emergency aid response in *post-conflict* societies, and in situations of natural disaster, to situations where the model is inapplicable. A 'post-conflict' recovery-oriented aid response is inapplicable to situations involving conflict-affected areas where there is: (1) still intense fighting ongoing; (2) a systemic campaign of terror that in significant part specifically targets education, (3) inadequate security for the education enterprise and (4) an urgent need for humanitarian aid regarding basic survival (i.e., need for delivery of food etc.). Yet, international and national NGOs seek to build and re-open schools even in the midst of terror zones within the CAFS *as if* school could provide a safe place in those regions. For example, Save the Children in its 2006 aforementioned report expresses the following view reflective of this assumption of school as an alleged safe place even in the midst of conflict thus over-generalizing the post-conflict delivery model to situations of ongoing armed conflict where school is most often *not* a safe place:

> Education can and should be part of all humanitarian responses-**including those to conflict situations**... *In countries affected by conflict, the risk to children increase*, and *education can play a vital role in protecting them*. ...***Well managed school spaces can help protect children from physical harm, psychological and emotional distress, recruitment into armed groups, family separation and other abuses*** (emphasis added)[4]

Save the Children's view is no doubt correct that education spaces can offer protection for children in certain circumstances; such as in situations that are genuinely 'post-conflict', and in natural disaster situations (i.e., children at school in a post-conflict situation are less subject to being harmed by landmines, being abducted etc. as they are supervised in a protected area). However, the view that "well managed school spaces" can protect children from physical and psychological harm is fallacious as applied to situations in which organized terror groups such as the Taliban target schools and schoolchildren for elimination or physical injury and school security, and the general security situation in the country, or in certain regions of the country where the education classes are conducted, is grossly inadequate. The latter situation is generally the case in Afghanistan, Iraq and many other States where organized terror groups operate and have a predilection for attacking civilian targets; in particular, schools, schoolchildren, teachers and education-related personnel including education aid workers. The steady increase since at least 2005 in attacks on schools, teachers and education officials in conflict-affected regions such as Afghanistan and Iraq, and in many other States, attests to the folly of presuming that education sites (be they school buildings, education

[3] United Nations (2006).

[4] Save the Children (2006), p. 19.

classes in tents or open air spaces) are, or can always be made, 'safe zones' for the schoolchildren attending (i.e., in Afghanistan most schools are sites that are not buildings but rather unsecured outdoor sites that are particularly vulnerable to total destruction should there be a terror attack).

Save the Children states in its 2006 'Rewrite the Future' report that: "*Unless children affected by conflict are protected and educated*, their futures, and the future of their nation, are seriously imperilled (emphasis added)".[5] This author has no dispute with the latter contention. However, integral in the immediately foregoing quote is the notion of "protection" as associated with the enterprise of educating children in conflict-affected areas: "Unless children affected by conflict are *protected* and educated". What is evident in the data discussed and analyzed in the pages that here follow is that the international humanitarian community, along with local and national governments in conflict-affected areas have, for reasons we will explore, ploughed ahead with education in conflict-affected areas such as Afghanistan without the necessary associated protections for children's physical security. In that circumstance, education is not at all a humanitarian response since it does not further the security or well-being of the children, but rather puts them at high risk of physical and psychological harm. Do not misunderstand; there is no suggestion here that NGOs do not wish to see an improved situation in conflict-affected States in regards to security generally, and for education security in particular; quite the contrary. For example, consider the statement of CARE which follows:

> Recognizing this need for security, CARE has been one of the NGOs calling for expansion of international military forces outside of Kabul. The aim of CARE's advocacy in repeated policy briefs and more than three hundred interviews with the international press in 2002 and 2003 is to promote the security rights and reconstruction needs of ordinary Afghans.[6]

Yet, at the same time, where that adequate security does not exist, it appears that many national and international NGOs are still prepared to continue with the project of building new schools and repairing and re-opening schools and encouraging children to attend. In addition, some NGOs such as CARE even go so far as to refuse protection from coalition forces for their specific projects (i.e., building and repairing schools, etc.):

> CARE's advocacy repeatedly urged international military forces to avoid blurring the lines between military and civilian, activities and, *to date has refused to work alongside them or to accept any form of armed protection for their activities* (emphasis added).[7]

NGOs in Afghanistan that refuse to work alongside the coalition forces to receive protection for their (NGO) education aid efforts (such as building, maintaining and operating schools) take this stance for fear of blurring the line between the military and civilian. NGOs in these instances believe that working as part of

[5]Save the Children (2006), p. 2.
[6]O'Brien (2004), p. 35.
[7]O'Brien (2004), p. 35.

a team with the military providing them protection will endanger the lives of the humanitarian aid workers and put their education projects at risk of terror attack. Declining protection from coalition forces, however, has not stemmed the ever-increasing and high rate of terror attacks on schools, schoolchildren, teachers or on humanitarian education aid workers. The aforementioned are, afterall, ideal targets for spreading terror and, as a bonus, relatively 'soft targets' (not particularly well protected unlawful military objectives).

Attacks on schools in Afghanistan since the fall of the Taliban continue to rise at an alarming and unabated rate. When schools are protected by local villagers and by the parents using licensed guns, the fear is that direct attacks on the schoolchildren *outside* of the building where they are more vulnerable are even more likely:

> It is not difficult to destroy schools in Afghanistan - only 40% of the 8,500 schools in the country are run out of buildings. The rest operate out of tents or are simply run under trees. *Officials worry that the Taleban* [sic] *may have begun targeting school children because of the "relative success" of a programme* to *protect schools.* Over the past eight months, the government has spent $500,000 launching what it calls a "special school protection programme" - which works by *groups of parents and local villagers keeping a watch on the schools, sometimes keeping licensed guns.* Some 1,000 schools have been covered under the programme , and officials say the protection scheme is yielding results - 35 of the 381 schools shut down by the Taleban [sic] have been reopened (emphasis added).[8]

The fact remains that most international and national NGOs in Afghanistan receive funding from the U.S. and/or certain of its allies that are also belligerents in the conflict. There is no way then for the international and national NGOs in doing their education aid work to avoid having their work portrayed by both sides in the 'war on terror' as something other than purely independent humanitarian activity. This is clearly perceived as a problem by increasing numbers of these NGOs:

> CARE works in Afghanistan to promote the human rights (including political, economic, and security rights) and [the] aspirations of the poor and marginalized. Claims by the United States that we [CARE] are here as part of the "war on terror" not only undermine CARE's security, but also CARE's pro-poor political philosophy.[9]

It is important to understand that the international norms safeguarding civilians are binding *directly* on individuals (as relates to individual conduct under Common Article 3 of the Geneva Conventions and additional Protocol II to the Geneva Conventions; the latter pertaining to non-international conflicts), and do not apply just to the conduct of States that are a party to the relevant treaty:

> Today there is no longer any doubt as to the existence of treaty-based and customary rules applicable in internal conflicts. *Moreover with regard to the question of whether the rules of humanitarian law are binding only on States –which would thus be held solely responsible in the event of non-observance-or whether they also apply to individuals, who could violate them directly by their conduct, it would seem that the second option clearly outweighs the first, regardless whether the conflict is internal or international in nature* . . .the substance

[8]Biswas (2007).

[9]O'Brien (2004), p. 35.

> of the rules contained in Article 3 common to the four Geneva Conventions of 1949 and in Protocol II additional to the Conventions ... makes frequent reference to the acts of individuals ... point[ing] to the fact that *the law applicable in such [non-international] conflicts also governs the conduct of individuals* (emphasis added).
>
> In this connection, it would be remiss not to mention the following assertion made by the International Military Tribunal at Nuremberg:' Crimes against International Law are committed by men, not by abstract entities, and only by punishing individuals who commit such crimes can the provisions of International Law be enforced". (emphasis added)[10]

Note that it is accepted that 'crimes against humanity' and genocide can occur in the context also of non-international conflicts and that individuals by their personal conduct can be held individually culpable for the same.[11] According to the International Law Commission, the same is true for 'war crimes' committed in the context of an internal conflict. As was mentioned previously, the conflict in Afghanistan is typically characterized as non-international (as opposed to a conflict between States); though it clearly has internationalized elements (international allies assisting the national government; an international web of terror organizations supporting the Taliban and other insurgents etc.).[12] Note that the Rome Statute under Article 8 (2)(c)incorporates a category of 'war crimes' regarding *individual culpability* for the violation of one or more of the provisions of Common Article 3 occurring in the context of a non-international conflict. Further, the Rome Statute under Article 8(2)(e) addresses war crimes involving "serious violations of the laws and customs applicable in armed conflicts not of an international character, within the established framework of international law".[13] Thus, individuals can be held directly accountable criminally for violations of international humanitarian law stemming from their personal conduct in the context of either an international or non-international armed conflict as will be discussed in some detail here in a later section.

The discussion in the chapters that follow, it should be recognized, is not intended in any way to undermine the importance of providing education to children in conflict-affected areas *if and when security is adequately ensured for all involved in the basic education enterprise*. Consider on the point of the feasibility of providing education services in the midst of conflict; the example of Save the Children's accomplishments in West Darfur. Save the Children established more than 20 children's centres in 11 refugee camps for displaced persons in West Darfur, Sudan that provided education services to 55,000 children.[14] However, the fact is that even UN refugee camps are rarely fully secure as evident from an interview with a 'Save the Children' child protection specialist regarding the security issues in the refugee camps in Sudan:

---

[10]Graditzky (1998), p. 2.

[11]Graditzky (1998), p. 7.

[12]Graditzky (1998), p. 7.

[13]International Committee of the Red Cross (2005).

[14]Save the Children (2006), p. 19.

> . . . armed militia continue to roam the inside [of] the camps and prey outside of them. When family members leave the camps in search of basics such as water, firewood and grass to feed their animals, they are targets for brutal attacks. Men do not leave the camps at this point because they are routinely killed. That leaves women and children, who are more vulnerable, to do the work. Hoping to reduce the chances of being beaten or raped, they go out at night or early in the morning, when the army is sleeping, but many do not make it back safely. [Children have also been abducted from UN refugee camps for forced participation in armed conflict as 'child soldiers' and for other purposes].[15]

The question arises as to the legality and morality of concentrating a multitude of civilians in facilities that are inadequately protected and highly vulnerable to armed attack (as with the UN IDP refugee camps in West Darfur). Bringing refugees together in camps where their needs can be better met in certain respects as to required essential services (food, shelter, medical care etc.), and where education for the children is provided to the extent possible, is unquestionably a useful humanitarian intervention; at least in principle. At the same time, the grossly inadequate security at a significant number of U.N. refugee camps in Sudan and elsewhere is something that needs addressing urgently. Suffice it to say that if security reaches an unacceptable extremely low standard; there comes a point at which the UN refugee camps for internally displaced persons or other refugees potentially may pose more risk then benefit to the civilians housed there. The humanitarian character of the camps at that point would be undermined, or even largely negated. In the same way, facilitating school attendance in particular hot terror zones within Afghanistan ceases to be a humanitarian enterprise where there are known high risks of terror attack on schools, schoolchildren and education personnel and grossly inadequate protection for the education sector in the particular region at issue.

The focus here is on the misguided; and in no small measure (though certainly not completely) self-interested practice of having children attend school buildings, open air education classes, classes in tents, community schools or any other education site in hot combat zones with high levels of terror activity. The problem is that encouraging children to attend school in the latter circumstance puts them at a *foreseeable* grave risk of terror attack since the organized terror group specifically targets schools and school sites and children on the way to and from those known school sites where security is most often inadequate. There have been urgent calls from international NGOs, UNICEF and UNESCO at least since 2006 for increased security in Afghanistan and other conflict-affected States. However, to date, that increased security has not materialized for many if not most schools in numerous provinces in Afghanistan or for schools in other conflict-affected regions of the world. Yet, national governments (including the Afghan government) and the international humanitarian aid community continue to push for school attendance even in unsafe regions within conflict-affected States where terror activity is high.

[15]Interview with Save the Children child protection specialist Christine Knudsen: Children in Sudan still not safe. http://www.savethechildren.org/emergencies/africa/interview-with-child-protection-specialist.html. Accessed 25 May 2010.

This risking of the lives of their schoolchildren is marketed to the parents and the community not only as a sign of courage and good parenting (i.e., wanting to obtain a better future for the children via providing them access to education), but also as a show of loyalty to the State government, to anti-terrorist international coalitions, devotion to democratic ideals, to the objective of building a democratic State and to the anti-terrorist military objectives of the conflict-affected State's national government and its allies. Despite the foregoing, the complicity here in contributing to children being harmed in school attacks, or on the way to or from school, is categorized as 'inadvertent' insofar as there is no intention by these actors (NGOs, donor countries to humanitarian aid initiatives, organs of the U.N etc.) that the children be harmed. Yet, at the same time, the acts which put the schoolchildren at a foreseeable high risk of terror attack (encouraging and facilitating school attendance without regard to the security situation for education, or the general security situation in the region) *are* intentional thus leading to potential criminal culpability for the individuals involved.

The increase in numbers of schools built or repaired, and in teachers trained is widely publicized by the conflict-affected State and its Western allies as well as by NGOs and certain organs of the U.N. through innumerable government and NGO and UN reports and through the online and print press and diverse other media. The target audience for the information thus disseminated is not only the national public in the conflict-affected State, but, importantly, also the international community. The objective of such propaganda is to suggest to the international community that monies provided by donor countries for the work of NGOs and UN organs working in conflict-affected countries where the fighting and terror is ongoing, is yet money well spent. That is, the message is that the donor money is making a significant difference in development and steady progress toward stabilizing the country in question.

Even if progress overall were being made in stabilization of Afghanistan i.e., an overall improved security situation (which is arguably far from the case at present), this book argues that education must *not* be used as a benchmark for security. To do so, as will be explained, leads unconscionably to children too often being used as pawns in the counter-terrorism effort and their placement in harm's way due to lack of security for basic educational activities (i.e., lack of protection for the operation of basic education classes for schoolchildren at the primary and secondary school level, and on school routes). The propaganda imperative in the context of the war on terror (i.e., that of the national government and its allies as well as of NGOs and other members of the international aid community) has resulted in children in conflict- affected States (i.e., Afghanistan) being encouraged to attend schools not simply in secure areas, but also in specific locales within the conflict-affected State where there is a gross lack of security. Hence, ever- increasing numbers of children and education personnel, as well as humanitarian education aid workers, are being killed or grievously injured as a result of targeted terror attacks on their schools while classes are in session, or on the routes to and from school.

Given the right to life and to security of the person under international human rights and humanitarian law, no new schools ought to be built, or any school operational in zones where there is ongoing systemic violence and a foreseeable terrorist threat combined with inadequate security with the only question being precisely where and when in that zone the next attack on schools and on schoolchildren and education personnel will occur. Yet, there is a tremendous impetus to have children in conflict-affected States attend school even in circumstances where there is an extreme lack of security for at least two reasons: (a) the pressure experienced by the conflict-affected State and its allies to demonstrate to the international community that the counter-terrorism effort is proving successful, combined with: (b) the international aid community's desire to demonstrate progress in meeting key millennium goals, (such as in the area of education i.e., gender equity internationally in the numbers of children completing primary schooling by the year 2015 and the elimination of gender disparity in access to primary and secondary schooling by 2005) in no small part in order to ensure that international aid funding from the World Bank and other sources for work in conflict-affected States not be cut. The new schools built, the schools repaired and again ready for operation soon after a terror attack, and the new teachers trained are all for naught if, due to a significant lack of security, schoolchildren do not attend. Further, a dramatic drop in school attendance undermines confidence in the stabilization and development initiatives and threatens to reduce international donations for the so-called 'recovery' effort. Hence, in practice, there are aggressive campaigns carried out by the conflict- affected States at the national and local level, and by the international aid community to keep the children coming to school notwithstanding the alarming, and most often foreseeable safety risks to the schoolchildren and teachers posed by organized terror groups in the region that target education as part of *their* propaganda effort.

Diverse organized terror groups internationally have a long history of targeting education as do the terrorist elements of the Taliban. In targeting education, these groups seek to communicate the message to the conflict-affected State's public and to the international community that: (1) stabilization has not, and allegedly will not be achieved until the terror group in question operating in a particular State is in charge politically and militarily and that (2) both the civilian population and government armed forces and their allies are allegedly helpless in the face of terror.

The gender issue as it relates to education and terror attacks is also addressed in what follows. Note that UNICEF reports that of the almost 60 million children out of school in countries and territories plagued by conflict; over half are girls.[16] It has been noted that "Despite the progress made [in enrolling girls in school in developing fragile countries]. . .violence against girls continue[s] to jeopardize the achievement of the education-and gender-related Education for All and Millennium Development Goals by 2015".[17] Gender-based disparity in educational opportunity is a stark reality also in Afghanistan where "in some rural regions 92% of girls do

[16]UNICEF (2009).

[17]United Nations Girl's Education Initiative (UNGEI) (2010).

not attend schools".[18] Globally in various States affected by conflict (such as Afghanistan now embroiled in an ongoing struggle with the Taliban), girl children are also at a disproportionately higher risk of being the victims of a terror attack compared to their male counterparts simply because they are attending school. Yet, Western parties to the armed conflict and their allies, international NGOs as well as human rights organizations, in particular those advocating for women's rights, have not infrequently pushed for girls' schools to be built or re-opened *even in insecure combat zones with high terror activity*. Having girls attend school is a laudable goal, but sadly a dubious one in those particular local areas within the conflict-affected State where there is extremely inadequate security for schools and schoolchildren. In fact, girl children attending school are at an especially high and increasing risk of loss of life or grievous injury in certain unsecured locales in Afghanistan and other countries where terror groups oppose the education of females. Building or operating schools in these unsecured locales for boys or girls is an extremely high risk enterprise; while operating a girl's school at these sites is like marking the site for terrorists with a visible 'bull's-eye' target. Such sites (unsecured education sites) are the terrorists' ideal target; maximal carnage and terror created with minimal expenditure of the terror group's resources. Further, it is highly questionable whether education classes in conflict-affected States such as Afghanistan can be successfully held in clandestine locations (i.e., in private homes) indefinitely given the level of infiltration by the terrorists of the local population.

The 2010 UNESCO report titled "Education under Attack" by Brendan O'Malley notes that systematic attacks on schools, teachers and students have "intensified dramatically in Afghanistan, Pakistan, India and Thailand" as well as being reported in a greater number of countries than was the case from 2004-2007.[19] The number of terror attacks on schools, students and school-related staff in Afghanistan, for instance, from 2007 to 2008 tripled from 242 to 670[20] according to the aforementioned 2010 UNESCO report. The situation is such in Afghanistan that:

> It is impossible to consider the education performance of Afghanistan outside of the context of the ongoing conflict. *Children have just one in four chances of surviving until their fifth birthday-and if they do, the outlook in terms of education remains bleak* (emphasis added).[21]

Certainly attending school in unsecured zones where education is at high risk of terror attack does nothing to increase the already abysmal survival odds for Afghani children. What is clear is that aid to education in Afghanistan has increased dramatically since military intervention by the West in that State post 9/11 (i.e., from 2 million US dollars of aid in 1999 amounting to one dollar a day per child of

[18] Shaharazad et al. (2010).

[19] O'Malley (2010), p. 21.

[20] O'Malley (2010), p. 21.

[21] Shaharazad et al. (2010), Interview with Save the Children child protection specialist Christine Knudsen under section titled 'Children of Afghanistan: In conflict and out of school'.

primary school age to 168 million in 2007 which translates to 37 dollars per child of primary school age[22]) but with little or no improvement regarding the security for education.

Adding to the risk to schoolchildren is the fact that unoccupied schools are *not* specifically mentioned in international humanitarian law as completely off-limits in terms of their use for military purposes in contradistinction to hospitals for instance.[23] Thus, if school buildings, even those damaged and non-operational for education purposes, are used by any party to a conflict for any military operation, this places *all* schools (occupied or unoccupied) at an even greater risk of terror attack. Should terrorists occupy a school, Afghan forces or their allies could consider the school a legitimate military target under international law (the rules of war) under conditions of pressing military necessity thus placing any children still inside who the terrorists may be using as human shields at incredibly high risk. The blame for any injury or deaths inflicted on the children by the government or its allies would, under international law, be attributed to the terrorists for their use in the first instance of human shields and use of a civilian building for a military purpose.

Schoolchildren have become a vital piece of the propaganda war on terror for both sides to the conflict in Afghanistan (the government and its allies as well as the anti-government insurgents). As a consequence, significant numbers of schoolchildren have been killed or injured by terrorists who have a pattern of targeting schools and schoolchildren, especially girls, wherever they are easily located. (In a later chapter, we will examine in what specific respects the use of schoolchildren as propaganda tools by both the terrorists in Afghanistan, and the national government and its allies, constitutes serious violations of international human rights, humanitarian and criminal law). In short, child civilians are being involuntarily utilized by both sides in the conflict–terrorists and their opponents- in the attempt to further their respective military objectives i.e., to gain a psychological advantage over the enemy, and to mark certain territory as allegedly under the full control of that particular party to the conflict.

We will consider in later section issues related to ending the impunity for the loss of life and injuries suffered by schoolchildren, education personnel and humanitarian education aid workers as the result of terror activity directed against education. Addressed will be both: (a) the terrorists' targeting of schoolchildren and of adult civilians (those supporting or involved in the education of schoolchildren) for violence of various forms, *and* (b) the actions of human rights leaders, NGO's and UN personnel and State officials working on the ground to encourage parents to place schoolchildren in harm's way while knowing full well that in many, if not most instances, proper security cannot be guaranteed for the children and teachers at their schools or on the way to and from those schools located in hot combat zones.

[22]Shaharazad et al. (2010), Interview with Save the Children child protection specialist Christine Knudsen under section titled 'Children of Afghanistan: In conflict and out of school'.

[23]O'Malley (2010), p. 145.

The decision of a significant proportion of the parents in conflict-affected States such as Afghanistan to jeopardize their children's security by sending them to school, even if that school is located in a high risk armed conflict area, is technically most often made 'voluntarily' by the parents or other legal guardians, but often *without* true informed consent. That is, the parents may have been intentionally or unintentionally misled to believe that adequate security would be provided to allow for safe school attendance. Parents who have kept their children home from school for any period after a terror attack (especially where the attack was on the very school their children previously attended, or on one in a nearby region) are not uncommonly pressured by local government representatives, government propaganda and/or NGO frontline workers to return the children to school though the security, in actuality, is still not adequate.[24]

It should also be kept in mind that the children, particularly the younger children, cannot generally be regarded as having given voluntary *and* informed consent to attending school despite inadequate security to assure their safety as schoolchildren. In any case, no individual assessment is being done, or even practicable, to ascertain whether: (1) every child who attends school in a conflict-affected area without adequate security is cognizant of the risks inherent in school attendance under these conditions and (2) whether he or she wishes, nevertheless, of his or her own free and informed will, to attend despite the security risk. The children's fundamental liberty rights, as well as potentially their right to life and security of the person, are violated when they are forced to attend school in high risk combat zones. The latter is especially the case where there is significant terrorist activity targeting education such as is in fact occurring with ever increasing frequency in contemporary armed conflicts internationally. Forced school attendance is involved in that the children are attending first and foremost at their parents' behest; and as a result of the direct and/or indirect pressures that not infrequently have been applied to the parents from outside the family. There are generally great pressures brought to bear on parents to return their children to school both by NGO workers who tout the benefits of education, and by national and local government that, in addition, view parents permitting their children to attend school despite the instability in the country as a show of loyalty to the State. In the process, the security concerns regarding education are being ignored or minimized in these persuasive attempts to convince parents to once again have their children attend school. Further, the fact that attendance at school in many conflict-affected States is compulsory by law – as it has been in Afghanistan since 2004 – may also play a role in the parents' decision regarding their children's school attendance (i.e., the parents may be expected to send their children back to school when the local government education representatives deem it safe to do so-regardless how accurate that assessment may be- and the school has reopened after a terror attack on the school or on schoolchildren in the area). This expectation of local government that the children, after a time, return

[24] Filkins (2009).

to school following a terror attack may exist even when no substantive changes have been made to better ensure the schoolchildren's safety in attending school.

Various NGOs such as CARE have endorsed the notion that the security responsibility for schools in Afghanistan and other conflict-affected States should be largely or completely assigned to the local communities themselves (i.e., in Afghanistan security attended to through local village councils or *shura* charged with the protection of the schools).[25] The theory is that this may help reduce the perception of insurgents that schools are merely an extension of the government and the West's combined military/development plan. This may, on its face, appear to be an attractive public relations move in terms of suggesting a handover of a key education matter-security of schools and schoolchildren, teachers and other school personnel- to local control. However, this approach generally cannot be relied upon to effectively meet the ongoing complex and pressing security requirements for education in conflict- ridden States such as Afghanistan. This is evidenced by the high number and significantly increasing number of school attacks and their severity since 2004 in Afghanistan and elsewhere. Such data regarding attacks on education contradict the claims by the Afghan Ministry of Education made in 2008, for instance, that shura were reducing the incidence of terror attacks on schools in 2006 and 2007 in Afghanistan.[26] The Ministry of Education in Afghanistan had instituted school security shuras involving local communities in 2006, hoping unrealistically, it now appears, that this would help dampen the number of school attacks and ultimately at least 8000 such shuras were established.[27]

A 2010 report commissioned by the Afghan Analysts Network (AAN) states that weapons are used rarely by shuras in their attempts to protect schools. There are no records of armed engagement between any shura security charged with protecting schools and insurgents. Rather, shuras rely on recruiting mullahs, elders and police into their ranks in the hopes that this will mobilize support for the school and reduce or eliminate attacks. Clearly, from the data on the trends in numbers of attacks over time in a variety of geographically dispersed provinces within Afghanistan, this is a strategy that overall is not working:

> UNICEF reports 236 violent incidents in schools in 2007, including armed attacks, arson and explosions. In 2008, 290 such incidents resulting in 92 deaths and 170 injuries. In the first half of 2009, UNICEF recorded 171 incidents in which 60 students and teachers were killed and 204 wounded.[28]

Further, it has been noted as far back as 2006 that local warlords or their proxies have often infiltrated these local 'shura' and provincial councils such that the local peoples, as a result, are in many instances being ruled by intimidation when it comes to those schools that are operating under the watchful eye of the shura in

[25] O'Malley (2010), p. 29.

[26] Giustozzi (2010), p. 18, citing Samadi (2009).

[27] Giustozzi (2010), p. 18, citing Samadi (2009).

[28] Giustozzi (2010), p. 18, citing Samadi (2009).

various locales.[29] In fact, even local notables (i.e., village elders) are not uncommonly dubious about *their* having any actual control in running local schools or making security decisions in respect of schools:

> Already in 2006 administrative and security officials in the south were pointing [out] how 're-opening of schools without local cooperation was impossible', although *village elders were sometimes sceptical* [sic] *of the willingness of either government or Taliban to allow them to play a role* (emphasis added).[30]

NGOs operating in Afghanistan continue to press for negotiation with insurgents for the reopening of particular schools when clearly all schools in Afghanistan remain at considerable risk of terror attack (even if reopened through such negotiation) given that the Taliban "clearly were [are] not ready to entirely renounce their stand on the [alleged] corruption of schools by foreign influence and their [alleged] use as centres for the spread of Christianity".[31] Further, the Afghan government continues to rely largely on local shuras for school protection despite shura vulnerability to infiltration by insurgent sympathizers, and the high risk and tenuous security situation for operating schools in these circumstances. Given both of these factors, it seems that, in practice, many, if not all, NGOs operating in Afghanistan as well as Afghan government officials working for the Ministry of Education are prioritizing school openings above children's security.

So desperate is the situation in Afghanistan regarding school attacks that some communities have tried to negotiate with potential attackers (insurgents of various descriptions) not to attack schools and to provide "permission" for continued teaching of the children.[32] However, the high number of school attacks in Afghanistan and the dramatically increasing numbers of such attacks suggest that any alleged 'successful' negotiations with insurgents regarding keeping schools an 'attack-free zone' in a particular locale, should they have occurred, have most often been short-lived. Further, anything short of complete compliance with Taliban dictates will likely result in a school attack in any limited instance where schools may have been kept open for a time based on 'negotiation' so-called. According to the AAN, "whatever success the shuras achieved in defending the schools, it seems to have been due to negotiation and compromise with the opposition more than to improved defense".[33] Local communities are generally helpless and unable, therefore, to protect schools should any compromise solution with local insurgents break down. Thus, the safety of schoolchildren and that of their teachers and of humanitarian education aid workers is essentially being left to the discretionary whims of insurgents in these instances with the government, for all intents and purposes, acting for the most part as but a bystander to the carnage if and when a school attack occurs.

---

[29]Human Rights Watch (2006), p. 19.

[30]Giustozzi (2010), p. 18, citing Samadi (2009).

[31]Giustozzi (2010), p. 18, citing Samadi (2009).

[32]O'Malley (2010), p. 10.

[33]Giustozzi (2010), p. 18, citing Samadi (2009).

Attempted compromise with organized terror groups to keep schools open in conflict-affected States appears then to be an approach supported enthusiastically by many high profile NGOs such as CARE, and also by certain organs of the U.N., for instance UNESCO (if NGO and UN reports are any indicator of the likely position of these organizations on this matter). This is the case despite: (1) the constraints placed on the education rights of the schoolchildren by insurgents (which restrictions in curriculum and/or gender equity in education are the precondition for such school re-openings as may have occurred through 'negotiation'); and (2) the uncertainty of whether insurgents will in actuality respect the schoolchildren's entitlement to security. That is, the children's freedom of expression, freedom of thought, right to access accurate and diverse sources of information and the global media, right to non-discrimination in education and enjoyment of other rights that are incorporated into the notion of the 'right to education' as understood under international human rights law; namely the Convention on the Rights of the Child[34] are generally all compromised by acquiescence to insurgent dictates. For instance,

> With Farouq Wardak as minister and under pressure because of the wave of violence unleashed against schools, The MoE (Ministry of Education in Afghanistan) started allowing greater flexibility with the curricula at the local level, avoiding to raise issues if certain parts of textbooks were ignored or pages were even torn off the books [as per the demands of the insurgents].[35]

This is *not* to make a statement on the value of private religious education or even State-funded schools that have a religious instruction component and how that intersects with the children's human rights entitlements (i.e., where the schools the children attend are chosen by parents and offer curricula freely endorsed by parents). It should be noted in this regard that the Convention on the Rights of the Child acknowledges the importance of parental guidance and community values in general, and the significant role of parents in respect of religious education; while also recognizing that children have an inherent autonomous right to religious freedom:

> Article 14
>
> 1. States Parties shall respect the right of the child to freedom of thought, conscience and religion.
> 2. *States Parties shall respect the rights and duties of the parents and, when applicable, legal guardians, to provide direction to the child in the exercise of his or her right in a manner consistent with the evolving capacities of the child.*
> 3. Freedom to manifest one's religion or beliefs may be subject only to such limitations as are prescribed by law and are necessary to protect public safety, order, health or morals, or the fundamental rights and freedoms of others (emphasis added).[36]

---

[34]UN Convention on the Rights of the Child. Adopted (entry into force 2 September 1990). http://www2.ohchr.org/english/law/crc.htm. Accessed 18 May 2010.

[35]Giustozzi (2010), p. 18, citing Samadi (2009).

[36]UN Convention on the Rights of the Child. Adopted (entry into force 2 September 1990). http://www2.ohchr.org/english/law/crc.htm. Accessed 18 May 2010 (Article 14).

In the case of Afghanistan, in those limited instances where there have been negotiated school openings; the reality is that an organized terror group (the Taliban extremists), as well as other insurgents, are dictating curriculum guidelines though *not* having been elected to do so (i.e., as members of the local body overseeing school functioning having been elected by the majority of the community in free and fair elections). The community is in such instances, in all probability, intimidated by the threat of violence against its children and acquiesces to the insurgents' demands in exchange for the *promise* of security. The community thus succumbs to pressure to have a curriculum that has the insurgents' stamp of approval but does little, if anything, to promote tolerance and peace.

We will in what follows explore further the incentives for, and broader ramifications of NGOs, government officials and community leaders negotiating with organized terror groups to keep schools open. Such negotiations are essentially a trade of the tenuous *promise* of security at the sacrifice of fundamental rights i.e., education rights; aspects of one's liberty etc.:

> *A . . . calculus of security-versus-rights is re-emerging now . . .* There has been a tectonic shift in Afghanistan's public mood . . . It is prompted by a host of factors: growing disappointment with western governments and the ineffectiveness of billions of dollars in aid that seems to go nowhere except into the bank accounts of foreign consultants or local politicians; a sense that there can be no military solution to the new civil war and that outsiders are deliberately prolonging it; grief and despair over the mounting toll of civilian casualties. . .rising nationalist anger and a feeling of humiliation; and a desire to return to an Afghan consensus in which Afghans create their own space and find their own solutions (emphasis added).[37]
>
> In practice, agreements to reopen schools involved purging teachers who were not acceptable to the Taliban and local conservative elements and *hiring conservative mullahs with some leaning towards the Taliban to exercise some kind of supervision on behalf of the Taliban, affecting in particular the curricula* (emphasis added).[38]

The reader should make no mistake; the current author is making *no* attempt whatsoever to suggest that children are not entitled to an education- in fact a high quality education- if they happen to find themselves by accident of birth in an armed conflict situation; one where there is a high level of terror activity. Rather, the suggestion is that international humanitarian and human rights law requires that these children be educated only where their security can be reasonably assured. This in that international humanitarian and human rights law stipulates that children are not to be placed in a situation that puts them at foreseeable significant risk of loss of life or other grievous harm. Yet, just such high risk is present when children are schooled at education sites in conflict-affected States that are insecure and located in areas where terrorists have systematically targeted schools (government schools, community schools, schools in private homes etc.), schoolchildren and teachers. Terrorists cannot be relied upon to cease violent attacks on education short or long-term even when agreements are ostensibly reached that embody that

[37]Steele (2010).

[38]Giustozzi (2010), pp. 18–19, citing Samadi (2009).

promise. To intentionally and knowingly place children in such a precarious and potentially deadly situation under the banner of fulfilling their education entitlement would appear to amount, in effect, to 'aiding and abetting' the potential commission of international crimes against children by the terrorist group. We will explore that possibility in some considerable detail in later sections.

The current author takes the view that relying on the terrorists' promise not to attack schools in a particular locale within the conflict-affected State, notwithstanding the terror group's international and ongoing systemic attacks on civilians and civilian objects of every description, constitutes a cavalier disregard for the safety of schoolchildren, teachers and humanitarian education aid workers. The sad fact is that accessing the entitlement to education which is a fundamental human right is not feasible in a conflict circumstance where terror activity is high and security cannot be reasonably guaranteed for the children attending school. *Furthermore, the right to life and freedom from physical harm must take precedence over access to education which, without security, in fact does not lead to realization of the 'right to education' in its fullest sense in any case.* It is time that the international community (including the national governments of conflict-affected States) finally acknowledge that children are being victimized by *both* sides in the terror wars when encouraged and supported by NGOs and government to attend school where there is a known high risk of a targeted terror attack combined with evident inadequate protection for education. The extent of victimization of schoolchildren due to terror attacks on education in the context of the 'war on terror' thus is importantly impacted by the fact that both parties to the conflict have played their respective roles in exposing the schoolchildren to grave potential harm. This they have both done as a result of organizational self-interest and propaganda objectives.

It is important for the reader to note that the critical importance of education to 'development' and're-construction' or 'recovery' in *post-conflict* zones is not at all under attack in this book. Alternate safe education secret in-home sites or other clandestine sites and /or the use of the internet where possible and the like could theoretically provide a safe education alternative in some conflict settings. However, these strategies realistically may be feasible in only limited instances, if at all, in conflict-affected States where the conflict is ongoing and intense; there is no set frontline per se and acts of terror can occur virtually anytime and anywhere within the region such as in Afghanistan. Such alternative safe education sites seem an unlikelihood then where there is no *general* minimal state of adequate security in the region. Consider also that separate school buildings or community schools housed in multi-purpose buildings are visible symbols of government and/or Western presence or influence and are, therefore, high value targets for organized terror groups operating in conflict-affected States such as Afghanistan.

Given the lack of a significant financial and moral commitment from the international community to ensure adequate security for schools in Afghanistan (and in other conflict-affected States); and the general lack of security in the country, the fact that international NGO's, and the local and national government in Afghanistan are encouraging school attendance also in unsecured regions within the country is legally and ethically insupportable. In the final analysis, the children's right to life and freedom from physical harm and violence must take precedence over the right to access education where these rights are pitted against each other as is so often the case in areas where intense terror activity is occurring. Yet, for propaganda reasons this seemingly self-evident axiomatic prioritizing of the 'right to life' over the 'right to education' (where the latter is understood to refer here to a limited right without the necessary prerequisite security for the education enterprise) has often as not been intentionally forsaken when it comes to schoolchildren.

Schoolchildren must *not* be used as pawns in the propaganda war with terrorists by being encouraged to attend school despite inadequate security with their risk of harm dramatically increased as a result. It is beyond naïve, in this author's respectful view, to suggest, as is done in the 2010 UNESCO report 'Education Under Attack' that sending children to school as soon as possible after a terror attack is a feasible and legitimate element of a counter-insurgency strategy:

> The international community, UN agencies and NGOs should work with governments of conflict – affected states and governments assisting in preventing or limiting conflict to develop .... ways to *rapidly reconstruct, repair, and resupply attacked educational institutions* [i.e., schools etc.] *in order to guarantee a zero tolerance policy towards violations of the right to education* (emphasis added)[39]

UNESCO and other UN bodies and various NGOs appear to be communicating the following arguably misguided and potentially destructive message to the general populace in conflict-affected fragile States such as Afghanistan that are still in the midst of conflict: 'as an act of resistance to the terrorists, just keep sending your children back to school (whether classes are held in free-standing buildings known by the insurgents to be schools or in tents or open air spaces etc.) *despite the high risk of repeated terrorist attacks* on those school buildings or alternate education sites and on the schoolchildren who attend them'. There is in fact (contrary to the suggestion in the quote from the aforementioned UNESCO report 'Education Under Attack'[40]), no correlation whatsoever between moves to "rapidly reconstruct, repair, and resupply attacked educational institutions" and "zero tolerance ...towards violations of the right to an education" where schoolchildren remain at grave risk of harm from a terror attack in the repaired, reconstructed and refurbished school as they most often do. That is, repairing schools and re-opening them as soon as possible after a terror attack; or building new schools soon after a terror attack and encouraging school attendance, does nothing whatsoever to reduce the number of such terror attacks on schools or on the routes to and from school or the child casualties that result contrary to the objectives of a 'zero tolerance' policy or practice. Encouraging and facilitating children attending school in as yet unsecured zones subject to a continued high risk of terror attack thus is not, contrary to the implicit suggestion in the aforementioned 2010 UNESCO report,

[39]O'Malley (2010), p. 39.

[40]O'Malley (2010), p. 39.

consistent with implementing the right to education which presupposes a safe learning environment.

Education then has become a propaganda tool for the West with the number of schools built or reopened, and the number of students attending in places such as Afghanistan and Iraq, used as one of several prime measures of alleged achievement of ultimate combined military-development objectives i.e., reclaiming of territory from terrorists and re-stabilization of the country. Such propaganda becomes all the more important where there is a deteriorating or at least an extremely tenuous security situation. This is reflected, for instance, in the U.S. pointing to the number of schools repaired and reopened in Iraq as evidence of Iraq purportedly being firmly in a 'reconstruction/post-conflict' phase:

> Although [reconstruction] efforts in Iraq have progressed, the U.S. government has faced criticism about the pace of reconstruction. In response, *U.S. officials have argued that thirty years of neglect under Saddam Hussein's regime is to blame for the poor state of the country and that* ***insufficient credit has been given to important reconstruction achievements, such as repair and reopening of schools*** (emphasis added).[41]

The figures as to new schools built, schools repaired and reopened after a terror attack, and number of school attendees are touted in national and international media campaigns for consumption by the public in the conflict-affected State and by the international community as indicators of the West's alleged progress and success in the 'war on terror'. This is an instance then of the melding by governments of military and political interests with the humanitarian domain. While it is the case that international humanitarian organizations have in recent years made an urgent call for better security for schools (i.e., as stated in various key NGO reports to be discussed here); to the extent that they continue to build, repair and re-open school buildings or set up education sites in tents and open air spaces without adequate security, they, too, are mixing political agendas (those of their own bureaucratic organizations) with the humanitarian domain. Thus, while one can concur with De Torrente that: "humanitarian action is not itself a political project";[42] it has become apparent that national and international NGO operations in the education domain in conflict-affected States where terrorists specifically target schools, schoolchildren and education personnel have often times become less about humanitarianism, and more about politics and NGO funding.

It is essential in consideration of NGO education aid initiatives in Afghanistan (and in other conflict-affected States not yet in the post-conflict stage) to keep in mind the obvious point that while adult civilians may choose to risk their lives in an anti-terrorist act (i.e., such as voting in a free election despite the risks posed by terrorists intent on disrupting the elections), schoolchildren must *not* be purposely placed in harm's way as a show of anti-terrorist resistance. When a State exposes schoolchildren to an increased risk of terror attack by encouraging or coercing school attendance despite: (a) inadequate security for schools and (b) organized

[41]De Torrente (2004), p. 20.

[42]De Torrente (2004), p. 5.

terror groups targeting schools, schoolchildren, education personnel and humanitarian education aid workers, it violates international humanitarian law and the rights of the child. Note that the Convention on the Rights of the Child at Article 38 (1) and 38(4) makes reference to the obligation of States to adhere to international humanitarian law as it affects children:

> 1. States Parties undertake to respect and to ensure respect for rules of international humanitarian law applicable to them in armed conflicts which are relevant to the child.
> 4. In accordance with their obligations under international humanitarian law to protect the civilian population in armed conflicts, States Parties shall take all feasible measures to ensure protection and care of children who are affected by an armed conflict.[43]

Clearly, the Afghan State and its Western allies are not meeting their obligations under the Convention on the Rights of the Child (CRC)[44] to adequately protect schoolchildren from terror attack (i.e., which requires encouraging school attendance only in zones and at schools that are adequately protected). In fact, in too many instances the Afghan State (often partnered with national and Western NGOs and UN agencies) is exposing schoolchildren to a known increased risk of terror attack. This situation arises in Afghanistan as a consequence of the State and NGO intense campaign to increase enrollment in primary and secondary school even in unsecured zones and at poorly protected education sites that are known to be highly vulnerable to targeted terror attack. Such State activity contributing to the endangerment of the safety of a specific especially vulnerable civilian population (schoolchildren) in order to advance a combined military-development objective (gaining some psychological advantage over the enemy, marking reclaimed territory with civilian buildings such as schools etc.) is in direct contravention of the Geneva Conventions, customary international humanitarian law and various international human rights conventions such as the CRC which call for every effort to be made to protect civilians; especially children.

International human rights and humanitarian law clearly sets out State obligations to protect children in times of armed conflict and thus, by implication, prohibits the use of schoolchildren (without regard to their personal safety or ability to provide informed, voluntary consent) as instruments of any State 'counterinsurgency' or 'counter-terrorist' propaganda. To the extent then that the Afghan State, frequently partnered with national and international NGOs, as part of its national education strategy is encouraging and facilitating school attendance even where security is known to be inadequate, the State and its partners are, it is suggested, potentially violating international law. The government officials (of the conflict-affected State) most responsible in this regard then are potentially culpable for international crimes prosecutable under the Rome Statute *depending on the unique and total facts of the case*, crimes including but not limited to; for

---

[43] UN Convention on the Rights of the Child. Adopted (entry into force 2 September 1990). http://www2.ohchr.org/english/law/crc.htm. Accessed 18 May 2010 (Article 38).

[44] UN Convention on the Rights of the Child. Adopted (entry into force 2 September 1990). http://www2.ohchr.org/english/law/crc.htm. Accessed 18 May 2010 (Article 38).

instance: (1) complicity in various 'war crimes' as a result of facilitating schoolchildren becoming the victims of terror attacks directed against education and of systemic persecution by organized terror groups (i.e., the Taliban) despite knowing the risks of this eventuality and (2) perpetrating 'degrading treatment' of schoolchildren by knowingly exposing them to a heightened risk of, or actual terror attacks by the Taliban or other insurgents (by sending them to schools that are known to be unsecured and, therefore, highly vulnerable to terror attacks). Likewise, the NGO personnel who participate in encouraging and facilitating school attendance at schools that are known not to be secure and to be instead vulnerable to terror attacks are also potentially prosecutable under the Rome Statute depending on the specific facts and circumstances (as nationals of a State party to that statute and/or persons operating in a State that is a party to the Rome Statute i.e., Afghanistan is a party to the Rome Statute by accession since 10 February 2003). To date, the International Criminal Court (ICC), to this author's knowledge, has not investigated or prosecuted (under the Rome Statute) the act of intentionally placing children in potential harms way in conflict-affected States with ongoing fighting and terror attacks by encouraging and facilitating school attendance even in unsecured locales within a CAFS (knowing that doing so will place the children at grave risk of physical and/or psychological injury). However, the ICC Office of the Prosecutor (OTP) has been conducting investigations and prosecutions of crimes that include armed attacks on education (i.e., violent attacks on teachers and students) and/or abduction of schoolchildren for child soldiering in the context of conflict in the DRC, Uganda, the Central African Republic and Darfur.[45] An OTP spokesperson has described the work thus:

> Our mission is to end impunity for the most serious crimes of concern to the international community as a whole-war crimes, crimes against humanity and genocide-and to *contribute to the prevention of such crimes in the future which might include 'attacks on education'*(emphasis added).[46]

Typically those most responsible for encouraging and facilitating school attendance in conflict zones *despite grossly inadequate security* have not been viewed as potentially having committed a 'war crime'; or 'crime against humanity'; or any other serious international crime. In part, this may be due to the fact that the actions of those responsible in this way are clouded by: (1) characterizations of their activities in terms of 'rights' and 'development' work rhetoric, and (2) the obvious lack of malice of government officials and NGO workers toward the children victimized in this manner. That is, the social reality of children being grievously injured or dying as a result of being encouraged and supported to attend school without adequate protection against terror attack has not to date been translated in the public consciousness or the application of the Rome Statute into a recognized international crime. However, it is still the case that the acts of these government education officials, NGO personnel and other education aid workers and their

[45] O'Malley (2010), p. 150.

[46] O'Malley (2010), p. 153.

superiors in intentionally jeopardizing children's safety in the way described potentially meet the criteria for international crimes (such as war crimes as defined in the Rome Statute, and according to the ICC rules set out as to the elements of the crime). It is time then (as will be argued in some detail in a later chapter) that acts of encouraging and facilitating school attendance in an ongoing conflict zone without providing adequate security, and intentionally using children for propaganda purposes in this way, be evaluated on a case-by-case basis for potential prosecution as an international crime.

The Afghan government and its State allies, to the extent that these States actively support and have supported this aspect of the Afghan education strategy (namely the enrollment of children in schools or alternate education sites where their safety was known to be grossly inadequately protected and they were at high risk of terror attacks), have also potentially violated various international human rights conventions and humanitarian law treaties/conventions to which they are State Parties. This they have done by undermining a number of the children's fundamental human rights. For instance, encouraging school attendance at insecure education sites where there is a high risk of terror attack constitutes inhuman and degrading treatment causing fear and mental suffering due to the fear of attack (where the attack occurs there may be, furthermore, physical injury for some, death for others thus resulting in the State having been complicit in causing these injuries and deaths in violation of the child's right to be protected from violence and his or her right to survival). Thus, facilitating school attendance without adequate security for the education sites in a CAFS leads to violations of various fundamental rights of the child including, but not limited to, the following rights stipulated in various international conventions ratified or signed by various State parties involved in the non-international conflict in Afghanistan as allies of the Afghan State in fighting organized terror:

1. **Convention on the Rights of the Child**[47] (i.e., ratified by Afghanistan 28 March 1994, ratified by the United Kingdom 16 December 1991 ratified by Canada 13 December 1991, and signed by the U.S. 16 February 1995): the right to such State protection and care as required including adequate protection at government institutions providing services to the child such as schools (Article 3); the right to survival and development (Article 6); the right to protection from mental and physical violence (Article 19); the right to education in the interests of developing his or her individual potential (the child's education when occurring at a site known to be vulnerable to terror attack is fulfilling first and foremost a propaganda military objective not in the best interests of the child's immediate survival, development, or security needs) (Article 29); the right to be protected from exploitation prejudicial to the child's welfare (here Afghani schoolchildren are arguably being exploited for a State and international community of States' military propaganda purpose despite the risk to the children's physical and

[47]UN Convention on the Rights of the Child. Adopted (entry into force 2 September 1990). http://www2.ohchr.org/english/law/crc.htm. Accessed 18 May 2010.

psychological safety)(Article 36); the right to be protected from cruel and inhuman treatment (exposing schoolchildren to the high risk of a terror attack at school or on the way to or from school by encouraging attendance when schools and schoolchildren are being targeted for terror attack and security is inadequate amounts to inhuman and degrading treatment (Article 37); the right to be afforded the protections of international humanitarian law (Article 38).

2. **International Covenant on Civil and Political Rights**[48] (i.e., accession by Afghanistan 24 January 1983, accession by Canada 19 May 1976, ratification by the United Kingdom 20 May 1976, ratification by the U.S. 8 June 1992): the right to life (Article 6); protection from inhuman and degrading treatment (Article 7); protection from servitude (arguably when children are being sent to school where there is compulsory schooling and the children must also obey the parents whilst, in addition, the government is encouraging school attendance despite the high risk to safety of the attendees; this amounts to servitude i.e., where increased school enrollment despite the lack of security meets adult needs regarding counter-insurgency propaganda); the right to security of the person (Article 9); the right of every child to that State protection required due to the individual having the status of minor (Article 24).
3. **International Covenant on Economic, Social and Cultural Rights**[49] (accession by Afghanistan 24 January 1983; Accession by Canada 19 May 1976, ratification by the United Kingdom 20 May 1976 and signed by the United States 5 October 1977): The right to "special measures of protection and assistance" as a child or young person (Article 10(3)); the right to education "directed to the full development of the human personality and the sense of its dignity" and strengthening "the respect for human rights and fundamental freedoms" (Article 13) (where encouraging and facilitating schoolchildren attending schools is a State policy and practice *even in zones within the CAFS where there is a high risk of targeting of those particular schools by organized terror groups given the inadequate protection*; this is not consistent with education directed first and foremost to developing the child's full human potential, or with educational practice that respects the child's human dignity, or education that fosters respect for human rights by demonstrating, in the first instance, respect for the child's fundamental human rights).

The truth is that encouraging children to attend schools that are inadequately protected from terror attack creates a propaganda stalemate for both sides in the terror war. If schoolchildren are killed or maimed as a result, the terrorists lose favour among the populace. On the other hand, the terrorists gain the fact that the public's confidence in the government to protect them has been severely shaken. If , in contrast, schoolchildren in the conflict-affected State are able in some locales to

[48]International Covenant on Civil and Political Rights entry into force 23 March 1976. http://www2.ohchr.org/english/law/ccpr.htm. Accessed 16 Oct 2010.

[49]International Covenant on Economic, Social and Cultural Rights, entry into force 3 January 1976. http://www2.ohchr.org/english/law/cescr.htm. Accessed 16 Oct 2010.

attend school with few if any casualties due to terror attacks, *at least for a time*, this provides a tremendous psychological and propaganda advantage for the West. This being the case in that the populace regains faith, often illusory to some extent, that the country is indeed returning to normal and the terrorists are losing substantial ground. The latter misperception also tends to stimulate more funding for international humanitarian efforts directed to the education sector in these conflict-affected States. In the war on terror, perception is almost as important as reality. Thus, when it comes to the education domain, the belligerent parties, as well as international humanitarian organizations, are too often, in practice, more concerned with shaping positive public perceptions in a way that serves their own respective political interests rather than with the reality of the security situation. Thus, amidst NGO urgent calls for better security and notwithstanding the abysmal lack of security and the risk to the schoolchildren and their teachers, international NGOs and local and national governments nevertheless move forward with their educational agenda even in hot conflict zones within the CAFS. The end result then is that the schoolchildren have become mere props in a propaganda campaign fuelled in no small part by decidedly non-humanitarian interests.

De Torrente and many others who are influential in the international human rights and humanitarian community contend that national and international NGOs must ensure that their humanitarian work not become part of the overall military strategy. This "politicization of humanitarian aid"[50] they contend creates disfavor and mistrust among the populace that the NGOs are working with and undermines humanitarian efforts. The irony is that when it comes to education as part of a so-called NGO emergency humanitarian response, NGOs who disengage from the U.S. military and its allies in places such as Afghanistan and Iraq are nevertheless deeply embroiled in politics. They have, in effect, potentially sacrificed the safety of schoolchildren (who are attending education classes at insecure sites unprotected by Western military forces) in order to keep school enrollment numbers as high as possible ostensibly for their own organizational financial and political bureaucratic interests. This then inadvertently furthers the chances for a successful insurgent terror strike against the school or on the routes to and from the school. In some limited cases, NGO's have come to rely, as previously discussed, on the tenuous discretionary decision of the organized terror group (i.e., the Taliban) to refrain from school attacks; something bartered for by the local village council with the enthusiastic support of the NGOs in many instances. Any respite from school attacks for some indeterminate period, where forthcoming, comes typically at the price of acquiescence to Taliban dictates regarding educational practice.

There is often confusion among the populace as to where NGO loyalties lie. On the one hand, reconstruction is part of the U.S and allied coalition overall military strategy for Afghanistan (trying to 'win the hearts and minds' of the people is part of the approach to undermining the power of the Taliban). NGOs are often perceived as part of that military effort. In addition, NGOs working in Afghanistan

---

[50]De Torrente (2004), p. 6.

are largely funded by the US. and for this reason also, segments of the population have mixed feelings about their work (i.e., do not view the work as purely humanitarian in its objectives or implementation). Afghan NGOs more often work with coalition PRTs (Provincial Reconstruction Teams), while international NGOs, in many instances, are attempting to distance themselves from PRTs so as to have a better relationship with the local civilians in areas where they hope to do their so-called development work.[51] The PRTs, however, are not a substitute for effective government and the rule of law. Hence, it is not surprising that the sentiment often is expressed by Afghan civilians, amongst others, that an adequate security situation must be pre-existing; otherwise "projects and development work [i.e., building new schools and repairing damaged schools etc.], although welcome, [are] pointless and would remain so until the [adequate] security situation is previously [first] established". [i.e., otherwise the schools are subject to ongoing terror attacks].[52]

In sum then, a co-operative effort regarding education initiatives between NGO's and the coalition reconstruction teams in Afghanistan which include small contingents of armed forces to provide protection has deeply political ramifications. However, by the same token, reliance on the Taliban, or supposedly more moderate so-called 'neo-Taliban' elements (who some contend are less opposed to girls' education[53]), and reliance on the local village elite, is also a political maneuver that may breed suspicion among segments of the general population in Afghanistan. Hence, it is apparent that: (1) the delivery of education as an NGO emergency response in the midst of a conflict situation where schools are being targeted for terrorist attack and security is grossly inadequate is not practicable if international human rights standards are to be observed in regards to both the protection of children and their education rights in any meaningful sense and (2) the need for protection of schools and schoolchildren and the education enterprise generally in a conflict-affected State does *not* allow for the complete independence and neutrality that is the traditional hallmark of humanitarian aid work. The latter reality is reflected, for instance, in both situations where the NGOs are negotiating with the terror groups, such as the Taliban, for school security, or, in contrast, where they are relying on coalition reconstruction forces for protection as they undertake small education development projects.

It should be noted that attacks on humanitarian aid workers have sharply increased in Afghanistan further underlining the fact that the so-called 'post-development' phase is not yet firmly in place in most areas of the country if any:

> **Growing Insecurity for Aid Organizations**
> According to UN figures there were [in Afghanistan] at least 120 attacks against aid workers in 2008 resulting in 30 deaths and 92 abductions. . .NGO staff report an increase in

[51] Azarbaijani-Moghaddam et al. (2008), p. 20.

[52] Azarbaijani-Moghaddam et al. (2008), p. 51.

[53] Steele (2010).

> raids [of NGO offices] by anti-government elements looking for proof of links to international military forces.[54]

It appears that Afghans doing aid work, especially young people working for international NGOs, have significantly higher fatality rates due to attacks by the Taliban, warlords and other anti-government elements than do non-Afghans doing aid work in Afghanistan. According to a report by Afghan Analysts Network (AAN), it is not clear why this is the case. The higher fatality rate for Afghan humanitarian aid workers may be due to the fact that: (1) they are Afghans working in fragile conflict zones in their own country, and as such, are especially mistrusted by the anti-government forces, or (2) they may tend to underestimate the security risks, or (3) they are simply more willing to take extra risks by going into the less secure areas where the donor monies are available to be directed, or, alternatively, the disproportionate fatality rate may instead be linked to some other factor or combination of factors. It also appears to be the case that Afghan NGOs personnel are less likely to withdraw from a conflict zone when security is especially poor compared to international NGO aid workers who more readily do so.[55]

All of this demonstrates the futility of maintaining the illusion that education as part of an emergency humanitarian response is feasible and advisable in areas of the country that are as yet highly insecure. While one can but admire humanitarian aid workers that deliver life-sustaining services and supplies under these circumstances, they must not be put at this risk simply for the purpose of building and re-opening and operating schools that in short order must be closed due to a systemic pattern of terror attacks targeting education. This exercise of opening and then closing schools due to terror attacks that in fact materialize, in reality, does nothing to further development or lift the people's spirits or hope for the future:

> According to UNICEF, there were 256 attacks against schools resulting in 58 deaths and 46 injuries in 2008. *Afghan Ministry of Education officials are reported as estimating more than 600 schools in the south to be closed due to insecurity and threats with up to 300,000 unable to attend school* [*as a result of the terror attacks and threats*]... These attacks and threats reveal significant setbacks in development progress (emphasis added).[56]

Research from the field in Afghanistan by NGOs reveals that negotiations with anti-government forces regarding security for humanitarian work is becoming increasingly more difficult as the insurgent forces are more heavily comprised of foreign Taliban and other foreign insurgents without ties to the local Afghan communities or even any particular experience with Western aid organizations.[57] Local village leaders cannot also always be relied upon, and they too can divert humanitarian resources from the target group and/or withdraw assistance on security issues (i.e., decline to warn NGO workers of a Taliban imminent threat).[58]

[54]Canada's Coalition to End Global Poverty (2009), p. 3.

[55]Azarbaijani-Moghaddam et al. (2008), p. 41.

[56]Canada's Coalition to End Global Poverty (2009), p. 3.

[57]Azarbaijani-Moghaddam et al. (2008), p. 36.

[58]Azarbaijani-Moghaddam et al. (2008), p. 42.

Thus the security situation for humanitarian work in Afghanistan continues to deteriorate while donor countries (those providing billions in aid) continue to demand more progress with respect to development.

Etzioni points out that:

> Human rights are not self-implementing; they need to be promoted through educational means, moral suasion, incentives, and the coercive powers of the state, all of which command resources. Given that the resources needed to promote human rights are limited and substantially short of that which full implementation requires, various rights must be ranked so that we may effectively allocate these resources.[59]

What is little recognized, however, is that when education is regarded as a vital component of a humanitarian aid 'emergency response' in high conflict zones infected with terrorist activity, and where adequate security cannot be provided, schooling is too often promoted at all costs; even at the cost of the schoolchildren's physical security. In those cases, there is no cessation of education initiatives in the high conflict areas unless: (1) the parents decide to keep the children home such that schools close due to extremely poor attendance subsequent to an attack or threat of imminent attack (i.e., the threat delivered by night letter from the Taliban that the school/schoolchildren/teachers will be attacked unless the education activities are terminated) or (2) the school has been destroyed by armed insurgents or is so damaged after an attack that it must be closed for repairs or complete rebuilding.

Increasingly, Afghanis are becoming disillusioned with humanitarian aid efforts in the highly insecure zones within the country including with the building of schools and re-opening of schools that flounder in the face of insecurity (as when these same schools must subsequently close after a terror attack). The entire education initiative in those particular circumstances amounts to what is not infrequently perceived by the Afghan people as but a fruitless Western-driven 'show exercise' that does not really serve the interests of the Afghan people. The Afghan people not illogically desire first and foremost "effective government and the rule of law".[60] Both of the latter are the necessary prerequisites for truly effective delivery and distribution of humanitarian aid in whatever form (be that food, schools, health clinics etc. that can reach even the most remotely located and neediest of peoples within a conflict-affected State). Security and the rule of law, furthermore, are the necessary preconditions for sustained and meaningful progress in development including full implementation of the right to education (as that right is described in the Convention on the Rights of the Child).

Katy Webley, Head of Education, Save the Children, reflects the view of many international NGOs when she states: "Education must become part of emergency responses, alongside food, nutrition, health and shelter".[61] However, while it is the case that the delivery of humanitarian aid to meet medical needs, sustenance and shelter needs saves lives in conflict zones where there is still intense fighting, the

---

[59] Etzioni (2010), p. 101.

[60] Care International UK (Media release) (2008).

[61] Webley (2010).

same cannot generally be said with regard to the delivery of services directed toward basic education (i.e., literacy training, primary education etc.) in no small part since the latter is, in contrast, very often putting children's lives at high risk in various conflict contexts. Yet, basic education (directed mostly at the primary school level) as a component in an emergency aid response is marketed by the international aid community as part of a 'life-sustaining' strategy even in high conflict areas when too often this is clearly *not* the case (i.e., as evidenced by the attacks on schools and schoolchildren in conflict zones globally; attacks that keep increasing with the result that more and more children are injured or lose their lives as victims of terror attacks on education). This is the situation in conflict-affected States internationally where terrorism is prevalent. To date the impassioned pleas from the national and international NGOs and the UN for adequate security in the education sector in conflict-affected States has, for the most part, not had the desired result and this is the situation also sadly in Afghanistan.

At present, there are many international and national groups that have an interest in donor monies for education continuing to flow into insecure areas (i.e., NGOs that have a bureaucratic interest in self-preservation and retention of personnel, numerous private international and national contractors engaged by NGOs and other entities to build and repair schools in CAFS such as Afghanistan etc.). 'Development Initiatives' has commented on the "big business" aspect of international humanitarian aid[62] which is, in many ways, self-perpetuating regardless of any negative effects it may have on the victims of man-made or natural disasters it is actually supposed to serve. The children too often benefit little if at all, or are short-changed in important ways as, for example, when: (1) these donor monies are used to build or repair schools that are then closed in short order due to the imminent threat of a terror attack or actual terror attack,[63] or (2) after a terror attack against the schools, the private contractors engaged charge exorbitant prices and do not always do quality work in building and repairing the damaged schools.[64]

The strategy then, as discussed, has been to elevate a very limited notion of the right to education to such a point that it takes precedence over the right to life and the right to be protected from violence. The underlying reason for this appears to be to gain the propaganda value of schoolchildren actually attending school in the context of the war on terror (i.e., the numbers of children of both genders attending school as an alleged concrete measure of progress toward peace, democratization, modernization, respect for human rights, gender equality etc). However, schoolchildren being intentionally exposed to the high risk of death or grievous injury by terrorists carrying out systematic and repeated targeted attacks against education; with the casualties to be replaced by the next batch of schoolchildren serving, in effect, as sacrificial lambs is not in any sense an expression of the democratic spirit or respect for fundamental human rights. As mentioned, these children are largely

[62]Overseas Development Institute (2009), p. 144.

[63]O'Malley (2010), pp. 43–49.

[64]Azarbaijani-Moghaddam et al. (2008), p. 49.

unsuspecting of the risks they are undertaking and do so without knowing and voluntary consent. This state of affairs hardly seems consistent with Western democratic ideals and values such as those in the American constitution which affirms the *right to life*, liberty and the pursuit of happiness.

Etzioni points out that:

> One cannot rely on the primacy of life as the leading normative principle to guide and legitimate the foreign policy of a nation—or the policies of a group of nations or international institutions—if the life to be protected is only of the citizens of a given nation. *Even a modicum of consistency, a major foundation of robust ethnical* [sic] [ethical] *judgments, requires that all lives be respected* (emphasis added).[65]

When it comes to schoolchildren in conflict-affected developing States internationally where the conflict is still ongoing, intense and involves terror activity, it appears that the lives of these children are, in practice, not always being equally respected compared to the lives of Western children. In this regard, consider that it would be unthinkable to expose Western children to such security risks as Afghani children are expected by the international community to endure for the sake of State and NGO education 'development'/'recovery' initiatives. The stark and tragic reality of attacks on education by terrorist groups appears to underscore Etzioni's observation that ". . . the primacy of the right to life implies that *basic* security must be provided before democratization and a general promotion of human rights can take off . . . ."(emphasis added).[66] By encouraging school attendance despite high insecurity at school sites and on the routes to and from school in various zones within the CAFS, the international humanitarian community is, in fact, very much engaged in the course and conduct of the conflict by unwittingly having entered into the counter-terrorism propaganda strategy of the West and its allies (i.e., encouraging school attendance at all costs as a purported measure of an improved general security situation and progress in the war on terror).

It should be noted that the current author adopts the position of the UNESCO 2010 report 'Education Under Attack' in viewing the abduction of children from school or on their way to or from school for use as child soldiers and other roles with the armed group as also being an instance of an attack on education since it deprives these children of an education. So, too, the use of school facilities for child soldier recruitment and other military purposes constitutes an attack on education by co-opting learning facilities for non-humanitarian objectives.[67] The author concurs with the aforementioned UNESCO report that there may be 'grey area' cases such as when suicide bombers attack in a place where students gather even if outside of a school where the injured and killed are not exclusively students. If the attack was carried out on a known usual student gathering place; or place where students were expected to be for some special occasion, then this too is considered a targeted attack on education. So, too, attacks on schoolchildren and teachers in their homes or in

---

[65]Etzioni (2010), p. 107.

[66]Etzioni (2010), p. 107.

[67]O'Malley (2010), p. 19.

informal learning settings where terrorists are suspected, or have claimed responsibility and where there have been threats by terror groups to do violence to those involved with education are also considered as an attack on education. With regard to the latter, the UNESCO 2010 report, for instance, notes that many such threats are placed on the doors of the homes of teachers in Afghanistan.[68]

Education is a huge sector for the international aid community bringing in very substantial donor dollars and hence helping to rationalize the existence of particular NGOs and their own bureaucratic personnel and financial requirements:

> *... since the fall of the Taliban, education has been almost completely dependent on international support, provided directly to the government or to private contractors and NGOs*. The largest international donors for education in Afghanistan are the United States (via USAID) and the World Bank.... Other donors include... UNESCO and UNICEF. Donor money has gone to school construction and rehabilitation, textbook printing and distribution, teacher training and school equipment such as tents, blackboards and carpets *[with] the focus of donors and the Ministry of Education ... on primary education largely to the exclusion of secondary* (emphasis added).[69]

International donor dollars supporting the humanitarian education response in conflict-affected States (and more generally in less developed poor States also) are disproportionately directed to primary school education. This may be because the international community, in practice at least, adopts the view that access to a free, compulsory primary level education is a basic human right which States must take urgent steps to meet as opposed to the right to access secondary education which purportedly can be legitimately relegated to being realized progressively as State resources permit.[70] This *relative* lack of support from the international aid community for secondary education in conflict-affected fragile States (CAFS) then results in inequity for students attending secondary school or those who could attend were there sufficient secondary schools, qualified secondary school teachers, adequate security etc. (i.e., a resultant discrimination based on age, if you will; though it is the case that there are instances of secondary school-aged children in CAFS, such as Afghanistan, still attending primary school having been shut out of the opportunity for schooling previously for a variety of reasons).

The significance of the size of the potential pool of school-aged children not currently enrolled in school in places such as Afghanistan then is not simply that it represents the tremendous need of the populace for educational/development intervention. Rather, the large number of school-aged children not yet in school in Afghanistan also represents a potential way for NGOs and the national government to garner tremendous international donor support that automatically legitimizes international NGOs, their resources in terms of personnel and in other areas, and the work that NGOs and government do in the education domain:

---

[68]O'Malley (2010), p. 19.

[69]Human Rights Watch (2006), p. 29.

[70]Johnson (2010), pp. 191–192.

> Afghanistan has one of the youngest populations on the planet-although exact numbers do not exist, an estimated 57 percent of the population is under the age of eighteen. . .The [Afghan] Ministry of Education estimates that [since the fall of Taliban rule] 40 percent of children aged six to eighteen, including the majority of primary school-aged girls, were still out of school in 2005. Older girls have particularly low rates of enrollment: at secondary level, just 24 percent of students were girls in 2005, and the gross enrollment rate for girls in secondary education was only 5 percent in 2004 compared with 20 percent for boys . . . Enrollment has also varied tremendously by province and between rural and urban areas. Many children in rural areas have no access to schools at all. *Seventy-one percent of the population over age fifteen –including 86 percent of women-cannot read or write, one of the highest rates of illiteracy in the world* (emphasis added).[71]

It bears repeating this last time that nothing in this book should be understood as intended to devalue the need to educate children in every region globally; including children in conflict-affected areas where this can be done without posing a security risk to the children. Rather, the issue focused on here is the failure of the international community to adequately prioritize the life and security of schoolchildren in Afghanistan, Iraq and other hot zones of terror activity in the drive to educate at all costs. It is the case that in places such as Afghanistan and other conflict-affected States with high levels of ongoing terror activity that: ". . . the lack of effective rule of law has rendered this landscape of conflicts. . .complex-in some cases creating a security minefield for NGOs".[72] The personal security of humanitarian education aid workers, schoolchildren, their teachers and other education-related personnel and administrators is in many regions of the conflict-affected State severely endangered as a result. The time is well overdue then that the international community stop over-generalizing a 'post-conflict' model of education emergency aid and development intervention to situations where it is inapplicable (i.e., situations where the high intensity conflict is ongoing and which involve a systematic terror campaign waged by organized terror groups directed at civilians including also the targeting of schoolchildren and educators as is the case in the unsecured regions of Afghanistan). The continued overgeneralization of a 'post-conflict model' for educational intervention in Afghanistan at this time will only mean that more schoolchildren and their teachers, as well as humanitarian education aid workers, will lose their lives or be injured as pawns in what ironically is, to date at least, a 'politically correct' counter-terrorism propaganda effort ('politically correct" given that the education of poor and suffering children is a 'motherhood' issue; one that when de-contextualized is not generally conceptually associated with placing the children at high risk of loss of life or grave physical harm though the latter is in fact the tragic reality).

Note also a key point that emerged from 2008 research interviews with a sample of key stakeholders in the Afghan situation (i.e., interviews were conducted with aid organization staff, government employees, religious and local Afghan leaders, policy makers, military personnel, donor agency staff and academics). The perception of most of the *Afghan interviewees* was that:

---

[71]Human Rights Watch (2006), pp. 25–26.

[72]Azarbaijani-Moghaddam et al. (2008), p. 48.

> ... *the idea that development leads to stability and security is contrived.* In fact more interviewees linked security to improved governance and the removal of unsavory [corrupt] characters from positions of power rather than the roll-out of small infrastructure projects (emphasis added).[73]

While education can, when reformed system-wide (i.e., to promote significant improvements in literacy rates, gender and class equity in access to high quality education, and the promotion of peace and tolerance education etc.) facilitate stability, the facts in Afghanistan appear to bear out what the aforementioned interviewees surmised. Small scale infrastructure projects such as the building of new schools and re-opening of schools here and there across a huge territory where the conflict is ongoing and the risk of terror attacks still very high has *not* lead to more stability or security. Nor has this been the case for large-scale projects where terror threats or acts of terror have interfered with the completion of projects and/or actual attacks have damaged or destroyed completed education projects. Rather, this education development exercise in the context of ongoing armed conflict, marked as it is by terror attacks, has led frequently to placing schoolchildren in harms way and in seriously undermining the confidence of the people in the possibility of peace as a result. It is apparent that development can strengthen security and stability once a minimum adequate level of security has been achieved as the starting point. However, the evidence is that development cannot automatically create security; at least not in the context of the war on terror.

This book then in what follows attempts, in part, to highlight the many paradoxes that are embedded in the use of development in the education domain as a propaganda tool in a counter-terrorism strategy in States such as Afghanistan (i.e., States experiencing organized terror attacks on civilians which include the targeting of students, teachers; other education related personnel as well as education aid workers). The summary below highlights some of the key paradoxes which are separated here for convenience and ease of communication into categories; but which in fact have a considerable degree of overlap:

2.1 Education and Politics (Paradox One)

2.1.1 Education as Apolitical and Tolerant

- Humanitarian education aid workers hold that schools are politically neutral and therefore should be 'safe zones' even in the midst of armed conflict.
- The Right to Education as defined under the *UN Convention on the Rights of the Child* requires the teaching of tolerance and respect for the inherent human dignity of all persons and communities.

[73]Azarbaijani-Moghaddam et al. (2008), p. 51.

2.1.2 The Politicization of Education

- In return for tenuous promises of security, some NGOs have acceded to the demands of terror groups such as the Taliban regarding school curriculum thus limiting freedom of expression and access to information for students and risking the teaching of intolerance and gender inequity.
- Schools are not uncommonly built with international aid monies in areas where they are viewed by terrorists as the major symbol of the contested State government and of Western influence and therefore are considered by these insurgent groups as a high value target for violent attack.

2.2 Education and Security (Paradox Two)

2.2.1 Education as a Benchmark for Security

- Many NGO's, such as Human Rights Watch for instance, hold that education should be used as one of the key benchmarks for overall level of security in the conflict-affected fragile State.
- The West and its allies use education; that is, the increase in absolute number of children enrolled in school, number of new schools opened, schools buildings repaired and functioning soon after a terror attack, the numbers of tent schools opened after terror attacks that destroy schools etc. as indicia of State development, resilience and/or stability.

2.2.2 Education as a Benchmark for Lack *of Security*

- As the international aid community, the national governments of conflict-affected States as well as their allies wish to show the public and the powers that be in donor countries progress in stabilization and the war on terror ; more children are being enrolled in school or sent back to schools where there is inadequate security.
- As the West (and its allies) and NGOs use the education of schoolchildren (mostly at the primary school level) to tout alleged progress in stabilization in conflict-affected States still being subjected to organized terror campaigns, there is globally a steady, dramatic and ongoing increase in violent attacks on schoolchildren, educators and related school staff and on schools and other education-related facilities and on humanitarian education aid workers.
- The increase in attacks on education undermines stabilization and development and spreads terror in a most effective manner.

- The numbers of school children, teachers, education-related personnel and education aid workers injured or killed in targeted terror attacks on education has increased dramatically in Afghanistan in recent years as it has elsewhere where educational intervention (i.e., the number of new schools built, increases in student enrollment etc.) is used to create the *illusion* of progress in establishing security (i.e. ..."between March and October 2010; 20 schools were attacked [in Afghanistan] using explosives or arson, and insurgents killed 126 students".[74]

2.3 Education and Basic Human Rights for Women and Girls (Paradox Three)

2.3.1 Education as a Route to Gender Equity

- Progress in achieving gender equity in schooling is used in PR campaigns by the international aid community and the West as an indicator of progress in development, democraticization and respect for education as a basic human right. Further, gender equity in schooling is viewed as a pathway for gender equity in society generally.

2.3.2 Education in the Context of Insecurity as a Facilitator of Gender Inequity

- As the international aid community and the West push for gender equity in societies where there is strong opposition from anti-government insurgents to the education of females (i.e., where national and international NGOs, perhaps partnered with the national government, open girls schools also in specific locales within conflict-affected States such as Afghanistan where there is inadequate security); female schoolchildren and teachers become the victims of terror attacks at a disproportionately high rate (either at school or on their way to or from school or other education related facility).

2.4 Education and Development (Paradox Four)

2.4.1 Education Aid Interventions as the Pathway to Development

- National and international NGOs and the West market their education humanitarian interventions as the pathway to development and modernization for conflict-affected States.

---

[74]Coursen-Neff, Z. and Sheppard, B. (2011).

2.4.2 Aspects of Education Aid Interventions Blocking Development

- NGO work and donor monies in respect of education focus on primary school education with a very weak concentration on secondary school. Yet, it is those who complete secondary school who might then go on to obtain higher education and become leaders in the new more developed State suggesting the need for a much greater emphasis also on secondary education. The over emphasis on primary education in international aid funding to the almost exclusion of secondary school education may arguably mean somewhat higher functional literacy rates (i.e., though the evidence demonstrates serious inadequacies in the quality of education being delivered at the basic education level in Afghanistan), but a greater delay in creating an available pool of adequately educated individuals who can help build civil society and change the status quo sooner in the direction of full stabilization and development.
- Educators teaching at the basic education level in conflict-affected States such as Afghanistan are not uncommonly unqualified such that learning outcomes are far from ideal for their students. This fact has led many in the international aid community to market basic education initiatives in States still plagued by conflict and terror campaigns with reference to the alleged therapeutic benefits of education rather than to the education benefits per se (increased literacy, numeracy etc). Those therapeutic benefits of education allegedly being the creation of a sense of normality in the midst of conflict and despite the risk of terror attacks on education sites, students, teachers and other school personnel.

2.5 Education and Militarization (Paradox Five)

2.5.1 Education Aid Intervention as Allegedly Non-Partisan

- Some NGOs hold they can negotiate with organized terror groups to respect schools as 'safe zones' that are not to be considered aligned with the government or with any foreign political or military interests and hence are to be spared from attack.

2.5.2 The Militarization of Education Aid

- Implementing education aid (so as to increase school enrollment numbers, numbers of children completing primary school, number of new schools opened or reopened after a terror attack, number of girl children attending school etc.) *even in unsecured locales within the CAFS* is part of 'counter-terrorism' propaganda. That propaganda is intended to convince the international community of progress in the war on terror. The latter is a military objective that if achieved is expected to inspire the support of the people of Afghanistan and the international public for the war on terror, to boost the morale of the Western allies and Afghan forces, to demoralize the terrorists etc.

- Sending children to schools notwithstanding grave security concerns to achieve these military propaganda objectives is, furthermore, to use the schools for a combined military-development purpose. This militarization of development intervention (i.e., education aid work serving propaganda purposes) serves to put schoolchildren in harm's way as it involves children attending also at unsecured education sites at high risk of terror attack.
- Negotiating with organized terror groups that have not officially renounced violence as a legitimate tool tacitly serves to embroil NGOs in legitimizing the terror group and hence involving themselves in reinforcing the insurgents' (military) propaganda objectives.

Now that we have in Part I considered the objectives of this inquiry, and what this book is and is not about; please note the following regarding the organization of the material yet to be discussed and analyzed: Part II examines: (a) the nature and scope of the problem of terror attacks on education in conflict-affected States that are as yet not in the post-conflict development stage and (b) focuses on the *unwitting* complicity of the West and the international aid community in the problem. We will then turn our attention in Part III to what can be done to: (a) end the use by the West and its allies of schoolchildren as propaganda tools in the 'war on terror' and (b) to hold to account both those who perpetrate the terror attacks on education (i.e., the Taliban) or in any way substantively contribute to the problem. In regard to the latter, we will consider the applicability of international law to the issue of accountability for both sides in the war on terror (the Afghan government and its allies, and the Taliban and other terror groups) and their respective roles in putting schoolchildren, education personnel and education aid workers in harm's way. Part IV offers some final reflections.

References

Azarbaijani-Moghaddam S, Wardak M, Zaman I, Taylor, A (2008) Afghan hearts, Afghan minds: exploring Afghan perceptions of civil-military relations. Research conducted for the European Network of NGOs in Afghanistan (ENNA) and the British and Irish Agencies Afghanistan Group (BAAG). http://www.humansecuritygateway.info/documents/ENNA_BAAG_Afghanistan_afghanheartsafghanminds.pdf. Accessed 29 May 2010

Biswas S (2007) Afghan schools try to make a new start (20 June 2007) (BBC News, Kabul). http://news.bbc.co.uk/2/hi/south_asia/6768801.stm. Accessed 28 May 2010

Canada's Coalition to End Global Poverty (2009) Aid in the cross-hairs: civil-military relations in Afghanistan. Briefing note to the Canadian government. http://www.ccic.ca/_files/en/working_groups/003_apwg_2009-04_brief_note_civil_military_afghanistan.pdf. Accessed 29 May 2010

Care International UK (Media release) (2008) Independent study published on Afghan perceptions of security and development in Uruzgan and Paktia. http://www.careinternational.org.uk/11406/media-releases/independent-study-published-on-afghan-perceptions-of-security-and-development-in-uruzgan-and-paktia.html. Accessed 29 May 2010

Coursen-Neff Z, Sheppard B (2011) Schools as battlegrounds:Protecting students, teachers and schools from attack. http://www.hrw.org/en/world-report-2011/schools-battlegrounds. Accessed 24 February 2011

De Torrente N (2004) Humanitarian action under attack: reflections on the Iraq war. Harv Hum Rights J 17:1–29

Etzioni A (2010) Life: the most basic right. J Hum Rights 9:100–101

Filkins D (2009) Afghan girls, scarred by acid, defy terror, embracing school. New York Times, 14 January 2009. http://www.nytimes.com/2009/01/14/world/asia/14kandahar.html. Accessed 29 May 2010

Giustozzi A (2010). Nation-building is not for all: the politics of education in Afghanistan. A report prepared for the Afghan Analysts Network. http://www.aan-afghanistan.org/uploads/AAN-Politics-of-Education.pdf. Accessed 30 May 2010

Graditzky T (1998) Individual criminal responsibility for violations of international humanitarian law committed in non-international armed conflicts. Int Rev Red Cross 322:29–56

Human Rights Watch (2006) Lessons in terror: attacks on education in Afghanistan, vol 18, no 6 (C). www.hrw.org/reports/2006/afghanistan0706/index.htm. Accessed 18 May 2010

International Committee of the Red Cross (2005) International humanitarian law: treaties and documents. http://www.icrc.org/ihl.nsf/WebART/585-08?OpenDocument. Accessed 11 Oct 2010

Johnson R (2010) The child's right to an education: 'consensus-minus-one'? Int J Children's Rights 18:185–216

O'Brien P (2004) Politicized humanitarianism: a response to Nicholas de Torrente Harvard. Hum Rights J 17:31–39

O'Malley B (2010). Education under attack. A report commissioned by Mark Richmond, Director, Division for the Coordination of United Nations Priorities in Education, Education Sector, UNESCO. http://unesdoc.unesco.org/images/0018/001868/186809e.pdf. Accessed 13 Oct 2010

Overseas Development Institute (2009). Aid and war: a response to Linda Polman's critique of humanitarianism (written by the Humanitarian Policy Group of the Overseas Development Institute)

Samadi A (2009) Education policy today will determine what Afghanistan is in 2020. Radio Free Europe, 31 August 2009

Save the Children (2006) Rewrite the future: education for children in conflict-affected areas. http://www.reliefweb.int/rw/rwb.nsf/db900SID/KHII-6TL3RG?OpenDocument. Accessed 2 May 2010

Shaharazad A, Barratt S, Coventry J, Fry L, Harris G, Hollow D, Longhurst S, Narayan S (2010) Back to school? The worst places in the world to be a schoolchild. A report for the 'Global Campaign for Education' sponsored by Actionaid, Education International, Oxfam, Plan International, Save the Children and VSO. http://www.reliefweb.int/rw/rwb.nsf/db900SID/MYAI-89N7R2?OpenDocument. Accessed 5 May 2010

Steele J (2010) Afghanistan: is it time to talk to the Taliban? 4 May 2010. http://www.guardian.co.uk/world/2010/may/04/afghanistan-taliban. Accessed 28 May 2010

UNICEF (2009) Beyond school books: education in emergencies (UN General Assembly thematic debate). http://www.unicef.org/emerg/index_49323.html. Accessed 12 Nov 2010

United Nations (2006) Special Rapporteur on right to education condemns attack on Salabagh School in Afghanistan (19 April 2006). Relief Web http://www.reliefweb.int. Accessed 12 Nov 2010

United Nations Girl's Education Initiative (UNGEI) (2010). Dakar declaration on accelerating girls' education and gender equity, Dakar, Senegal, 20 May 2010. www.ungei.org. Accessed 12 Nov 2010

Webley K (2010) Out of conflict and into school (youtube presentation by Katy Webley, Head of Education, Save the Children, 27 May 2010). http://efareport.wordpress.com/category/conflict/. Accessed 5 May 2010

Part II
Attacks on Education: The Scope of the Problem and the Unwitting Complicity of CAFS, their Coalition Allies and the International Aid Community

Chapter 3
Schooling as Counter-Terrorist Strategy

> Protecting children and teachers is a moral imperative as well as a matter of international law.[1]

The above quote from Asha-Rose Migro, then U.N. Deputy Secretary-General (made during the debate on education in emergencies at the U.N. General Assembly 18 March 2009) belies the fact that both the West and the international humanitarian and human rights community have too frequently not only failed to provide protection to schoolchildren and teachers; but in fact knowingly placed schoolchildren and their teachers in harm's way. The question is then what is going wrong? Why are there ever increasing numbers of terror attacks on schools? Why is there a strong focus by Western powers, through their affiliations with national and international humanitarian organizations, NGOs etc. in building and maintaining more and more schools even in insecure locales within Afghanistan and Iraq and other unstable regions such that these schools and those who attend there are at high risk of terror attack. That is the central question this author seeks to begin to address in this book. Consider first that within the elite and powerful circle of the professional international human rights/humanitarian aid community (amongst many high profile international NGOs, human rights lawyers and advocates, UN experts on post-conflict reconstruction, international Red Cross administrators involved in setting emergency relief policy and practice in conflict-plagued regions for the organization, academic and other international experts on education in fragile States and in conflict zones etc.), there can be no more *non*-contentious issue than the child's 'right to education'. Indeed, some might contend 'tongue- in cheek' that the paper spent on UN, UNESCO, UNICEF and other human rights organizational and NGO reports on the child's right to education, and on renewal of education in conflict and post-conflict regions of the world has significantly depleted the world's rainforests. Be that as it may, nothing in this book should be, or is intended to undermine the importance of, or claim to the inherent fundamental human right to basic education for every individual.[2] The current author is an unwavering advocate for every child's right to basic education at

[1]Asha-Rose Migro, U.N. Deputy Secretary-General cited in O'Brien (2004), p. 16.

[2]Grover (2004).

S.C. Grover, *Schoolchildren as Propaganda Tools in the War on Terror*,
DOI 10.1007/978-3-642-17900-6_3, © Springer-Verlag Berlin Heidelberg 2011

a minimum as an essential component in the prerequisites for realization of the child's entitlement to acceptable levels of physical and psychological well-being. The issue at hand for this inquiry is, however, that in various internal armed conflict situations, the focus on the child's right to education has too often become part of the propaganda effort in the war on terror. So much so in fact that the 'right to life'-construed as inclusive of the right to be protected from all forms and degrees of physical and psychological violence- has been *subordinated* to the 'right to education'. That is, schoolchildren have been intentionally placed in harm's way in pursuit of their education despite the fact that it is well-known that Taliban and/or Al-Qaeda are actively and specifically targeting elementary and secondary schools in the region also during school hours as well as attacking the schoolchildren and their teachers and other school staff on their way to and from school or in any other location where they might be especially vulnerable. The evidence to this effect will here be presented in detail shortly. This seems to be an example of what Neil Stammers refers to as the "paradox of the institutionalization of human rights" where human rights institutions and high-profile human rights groups and actors actually, at times, may end up, in part at least, doing a significant disservice to human rights rather than safeguarding them.[3,4] Consider the following:

> On October 27, 2003, suicide bombers slammed an ambulance packed with explosives into the compound of the International Committee of the Red Cross (ICRC) in Baghdad, killing eighteen civilian bystanders and wounding dozens more. Coming just two months after the bombing of the U.N. headquarters in Baghdad that claimed the lives of twenty-three people, including Special Representative of the Secretary-General Sergio Vieira de Mello, the attack on the ICRC sent shockwaves through the aid community. There was no mistaking the intentions of the bombers; the attack was a deliberate and targeted assault on civilians and aid workers, a blatant war crime. For many aid organizations, the attack on the ICRC jeopardized the possibility of keeping international staff in Iraq, particularly in the central part of the country where hostilities between the U.S. occupation force and insurgents were the most intense. *Many organizations withdrew entirely from the country while others, like Médecins Sans Frontières/Doctors Without Borders (MSF), scaled back their programs and temporarily withdrew international staff* (emphasis added).[5]

What is striking here is that while most often international humanitarian aid groups withdraw permanently or at least temporarily or scale back operations when under terror attack[6]; no such luxury is generally afforded schoolchildren under attack by terrorists. That is, these children (i.e., schoolchildren in Afghanistan) are still expected to attend what is left of their school and 'soldier on' in the period following a terror attack or attend soon after the school is repaired, or if the school is beyond repair, perhaps attend school in the open air or in tents or in a private home

[3]Stammers (2009).

[4]Pruce (2010).

[5]De Torrente (2004), pp. 1–2 [Dr. de Torrente is Executive Director, Médecins Sans Frontières/ Doctors Without Borders (MSF-USA)].

[6]De Torrente (2004), p. 12 and pp. 21–22 [Dr. de Torrente is Executive Director, Médecins Sans Frontières/Doctors Without Borders (MSF-USA)].

(sometimes while waiting for a new school to be built if the latter option is available). This expectation of school attendance by the national government and NGOs despite the lack of security exists in Afghanistan and in other conflict-affected States. This is the situation despite the unreasonableness under any international humanitarian law standard of the children being exposed to such a continuing tangible and high risk to their personal safety and very lives should they continue to attend school (i.e., the virtual certainty of another terror attack on the school or on the routes to and from school). This brings us then to the topic of the potential or actual politicization of humanitarian intervention in various conflict situations. Torrente asks the question:

> In contexts like Iraq and Afghanistan, where the United States and other Western powers assertively project their military power in support of ambitious political goals, is there still a space to provide humanitarian aid directly to the population? *Are aid organizations irrevocably intertwined with the U.S. and Western agenda in the minds of violent opponents and, even more alarmingly, of the local population? Are the fundamental principles that have typically characterized and guided humanitarian action, in particular impartiality, neutrality, and independence, still valid in such crises*? Do aid organizations have choices left other than to seek armed protection and to work in full cooperation with Western military and political forces or to simply retreat? (emphasis added).[7]

The contention here is that insofar as schoolchildren are being encouraged by aid organizations including NGOs and organs of the UN to attend school even in unsecured areas subject to a very high probability of terror attack, these organizations are, in fact, fulfilling not simply a Western political agenda, but also a political agenda *set by the organizations themselves*. That political agenda is to establish the global perception that progress is being made toward democratization, stability and normalization of the State's affairs. Children attending at school and schools being repaired or built are normally conspicuous indicators that peace is returning to a region and that the strategies of aid organizations, as well as Western military efforts, are proving successful. However, in contemporary times, in areas which are heavily infiltrated by terrorists and subject to relentless terror activity, this is no longer the case. In some regions of the world suffering intense armed conflict, such as Afghanistan for instance, school attendance and progress in restoring the rule of law, democracy and peace are *not* necessarily positively correlated and, in fact, may in some cases (i.e., particular hot combat zones within the country) oddly be negatively (inversely) correlated. That is, school attendance may actually show sharp increases overall as peace, and stability are undermined and the forces of democraticization undercut by extremist opponents though particular schools may close for a time in various regions due to the threat of attack. Schooling in such an instance then becomes part of the psychological propaganda used against the enemy to increase the enemy's perception that it is being defeated in its terror objective of de-stabilizing the society.

The picture being drawn here then is different in some key respects from that constructed by Torrente. Torrente suggests that humanitarian organizations are normally

[7]De Torrente (2004), p. 2 [Dr. de Torrente is Executive Director, Médecins Sans Frontières/ Doctors Without Borders (MSF-USA)].

separate from political ideology and that the U.S. is to blame for the linking of aid to its military and political objectives in Iraq such that these humanitarian organizations have had difficulty distinguishing themselves for the populace generally and for the insurgents as entities with independent non-military apolitical objectives and motives. The suggestion here instead is that the numbers of schools operational and the numbers of children attending in intense conflict situations or as yet unstable post-conflict zones are erroneously taken to be concrete measures of success in implementing the humanitarian aid mandate. This then reflects a lack of consideration of the numbers of children killed or seriously injured by being forced to attend school in what are in fact often unsecured areas. Thus, insofar as education of schoolchildren is concerned in these terror-ridden regions, the political agendas of humanitarian aid organizations and of Western powers in concert with the national government, are indistinguishable. Both use school construction and school attendance as a public relations tool; an indicator of their doing something supposedly indubitably good for the society no matter the cost to children in terms of injury and loss of life.

The end result of using schoolchildren as propaganda tools in this way is the potential violation of international human rights, humanitarian and criminal law depending on all the specifics of the individual case. That is to say that school children, civilian 'non-combatants', are being intentionally encouraged and supported to attend school sites (by NGOs and the national government), whether secured or unsecured, as part of the effort to psychologically defeat the terrorists. Those responsible then are placing the children at high and considerably increased risk of being victimized in a terror attack. For the first time in an armed conflict, and in the context of the 'war on terror' then, it is not just one or both direct parties to the conflict (the national government and as well as the terrorists) that are placing child and other civilians in harm's way; it is also the humanitarian aid agencies that are doing so insofar as they facilitate school attendance where security is less than adequate. It appears then that both the national government and Western allies involved in the conflict in Afghanistan, *in effect*, view school attendance- even where the risks to life and limb would normally preclude such attendance- as conducive to their military and propaganda objectives. Thus, education aid interventions in the context of the realities of conflict zones that are undergoing sustained terror attacks such as are occurring in Afghanistan *cannot* be simply be characterized in rosy terms as an enterprise beyond reproach.

It is important to stress that there is no dispute here that *where security can be adequately guaranteed* for schoolchildren, teachers, allied school staff and humanitarian aid workers in a crisis situation it is the case that:

> Quality and relevant education in times of crisis can be life-saving and life-sustaining, providing protection, psychosocial support, and a basis for social and economic development and peacebuilding. Access to quality education ensures communities and individuals have the support required to support their psychological well-being, [and] to rebuild their communities...[8]

---

[8]INEE (2010), p. 4.

Yet, school attendance at the elementary and secondary levels at the urging of Western powers, their allies and national and international humanitarian groups operative in the region, *despite the schools being located in zones with high frequency terrorist activity* raises serious and fundamental human rights and humanitarian concerns and it is that particular circumstance and those questions which this book explores.

Clearly, humanitarian groups view education as a prime vehicle for peace and conflict-resolution in "fragmented societies". This author herself has held that learning tolerance is an educational right and that curricula and teaching strategies conducive to the teaching of tolerance ought to be a mainstay of educational institutions. Yet, it is naïve at best and cynical at worst to suggest that tolerance is the likely outcome when the reality is that children are being sent to elementary and secondary school in unsecured regions such that they are at high risk of being killed or seriously injured. Consider in this regard the following statement from a 2010 Inter-agency Network for Education in Emergencies (INEE) report which would seem more applicable to post-conflict situations rather than situations where the fighting is ongoing:

> Crises may provide an opportunity for governments, communities and partners, such as NGOs and UN agencies, to rebuild the foundations of human security, including through teaching all members of a community new skills and values, such as the importance of inclusive education and participation in the social and political processes. Beyond reading, writing, and arithmetic, schools in these fractured societies lay the groundwork for peace, tolerance, conflict resolution, human rights, environmental conservation, and disaster prevention— helping prevent, mitigate, and respond to future crises. Simply put, *quality* education works. *Studies show that increased levels of high-quality primary and secondary education reduce wars ... Every additional year of formal schooling for males reduces their risk of becoming involved in conflict by 20 percent...*[9]

Thus while one can see the value in the INEE's agenda of reducing the likelihood of future conflict by educating children for tolerance, this laudable objective must not obscure the realities of the conflict situation on the ground *at present* in many regions such as Afghanistan. There is nothing conducive to teaching tolerance in having children forced to attend school by parents at the urging of humanitarian groups and Western military community liaisons as well as local government officials despite the risk to the children's lives. Any hope of the children's complete psychological rehabilitation from the traumatisation arising from exposure to armed conflict is seriously compromised by having being attacked at school or on the way to or from school. Yet, humanitarian groups themselves are being sullied by their participation in further exposing children to the high risk of terror attack by encouraging their attendance at school despite the lack of security in particular zones making those specific schools prime terror targets.

Let us turn then to some of those realities on the ground in this era of global terrorist campaigns:

---

[9] INEE (2010), p. iii

> On 12 November 2008 in southern Afghanistan, two motorcyclists rode up to a group of 15 girls and female teachers walking and chatting on their way to Mirwais Nika Girls High School, Kandahar. Some of the girls were wearing full burkhas, others just their school uniform of black coat and headscarf, with their faces exposed. When the motorcyclists threw a liquid over them, Atifa Biba, 14, screamed as she felt and smelled her skin burning. The liquid was battery acid. One of her friends quickly tried to wipe the liquid from her face. But she, too, was sprayed and as she called for help, the attackers struck again. Another girl, Latefa, 16, rushed to help her older sister, Shamsia. "One of them threw acid on my sister's face. I tried to help her and then they threw acid on me, too", she said. The attack left at least one girl blinded, two permanently disfigured and two others seriously hurt. *As news of the attack spread, countless more became afraid to walk to school. Atifa's aunt, Bib Meryam, said the family was now considering keeping her at home. The incident was covered prominently in the pages of the international press and stirred world opinion.* It showed that the issue of attacks on education has lost none of its ability to provoke shock at the lengths to which armed groups, armed forces and political elements are prepared to go to further their political aims (emphasis added).[10]

It is certainly the case that terror attacks on schools and school children as a means of deterring the education of the masses in particular regions globally- particularly in respect of girls- is indeed shocking. However, also extremely disturbing is the virtual absence of self-reflection and questioning among high profile international human rights institutions and national and international NGOs as to the wisdom of and rationale for putting schoolchildren at risk in terror zones by encouraging and facilitating school attendance despite the lack of security. Note that in the example above, the Guardian newspaper reports that only after the acid attack on their young daughter-an attack of this sort in some regions in Afghanistan being highly foreseeable- is the family reconsidering whether in fact the child should be attending at school given the security situation. Clearly, enormous pressures have been brought to bear on these families to act as if the situation has been normalized when in fact this is not the case.

It is the case that tens or even hundreds of schools may be closed temporarily or permanently in a region within the conflict-affected State due to damage to or complete destruction of school buildings, destruction of school materials and equipment subsequent to a terror attack, the difficulty of NGOs such as UNICEF in getting into the area to set up open air tent schools, the fears of the parents and students as well as teachers in returning to school after a terror attack etc. Yet, at the same time, there is considerable pressure coming from the national government and its Western allies as well as the international aid community to continue with education of the children in new schools or repaired schools even where the inadequate security in the areas where the school is located should be a barrier. One cannot imagine North American and European governments pressuring parents to comply with government urgings to send their children to school where these children would face the *ongoing risks* to personal safety from terror attacks that children face in many regions of Afghanistan.

[10]Clancy Chassay, *Acid Attacks and Rape: Growing Threat to Women Who Oppose Traditional Order*, The Guardian, 22 November 2008; Suzy Austin, *Schoolgirls Hurt in Afghan Acid Attack*, The Metro, 13 November 2008; and Aljazeera.net, *Afghan Girls Scarred in Acid Attack*, 12 November 2008. Cited in O'Malley (2010), p. 13.

Indeed, in North America schools are closed for such things as snow storms and evacuated at the hint of any threat to the children's safety with no school operational in the relevant area until the threat is completely eliminated.

3.1 The Scope of the Problem of Terror Attacks on Basic Education

What then is the scope of the problem of terror attacks on education at the elementary, middle and post-secondary level globally? There are no official statistics on the problem which in itself raises serious questions about whether there are efforts to downplay the frequency of attacks on schoolchildren, on teachers and allied staff and on the schools themselves. It becomes highly difficult thus to determine trends and much of the data comes from the field through anecdotal reports. The lack of efficacy of the West and its allies in mitigating the threat does not come easily into sharp focus given this absence of data revealing official numbers of such attacks on basic education. Neither do 'humanitarian' interventions that encourage school attendance in insecure conflict zones come under adequate scrutiny where the nature, frequency, and pattern of terror attacks on education are not adequately monitored. Perhaps the most accurate data available currently on the issue of terror attacks on education comes from two reports; one completed in 2007 and the other a 2010 report both commissioned by UNESCO. The 2007 report which covered a ten year period stated that the "reported number of targeted attacks on students, educational staff and institutions seemed to have risen dramatically [globally] in the three years from 2004 to 2006".[11] The 2010 UNESCO report concerning attacks on education covers the period from January 2007 to July 2009 and, according to the report, also addresses: "the measures that have been taken to increase protection for students and education personnel and to reduce impunity for perpetrators".[12] Clearly, as we shall see in what follows, discouraging school attendance in zones with active and ongoing terror activity is *not* one of the protective measures generally taken by international humanitarian groups and their Western military liaisons despite its being an obvious first order priority in any rational approach to enhancing the children's security. Note also that at the time of writing of the introduction to this book in May 2010, there were several gas poisoning attacks against girls' schools in Afghanistan sending the girl victims as well as affected teachers to hospital with the attacks suspected by authorities to be the cruel 'handiwork' of an organized terror group likely the Taliban.[13] The Taliban are suspect in these attacks on girl schoolchildren and girls' schools despite their disclaimers in regards to the recent incidents given that the group banned education for girls from

[11] O'Malley (2010), p. 14.

[12] O'Malley (2010), p. 15.

[13] Reuters. *Afghan girls hit again by suspected gas attack* (May 11, 2010 news report).

1996 to 2001 when they ruled Afghanistan and it has a history of terror activity in the contemporary conflict with the West.

Attacks on education by terror groups continue with a ferocious viciousness and the intensity of these attacks in terms of frequency appears unabated in many regions of the world including Afghanistan. The 2010 UNESCO report on attacks on education refers to terror attacks on education in 31 countries in Africa, Asia, Europe and Latin America in the three years preceding the report's release. The report refers, in addition, to: "sinister new tactics. . .from abducting children from schools for training and use as suicide bombers to mass poisoning of classes".[14] The UNESCO 2010 report speculates that these new odious terror incidents may be the result of "*new trends such as the blurring of the line between military and aid operations*" while "others [result] from the age-old strategies of wearing down the enemy by destroying their infrastructure (emphasis added)".[15]

3.2 On the Issue of Negotiating with the Taliban Regarding Schools as 'Safe Zones'

The claim is made in the 2010 UNESCO report that the findings from the field were that:

> . . .it is possible to negotiate with rebels, even rebels who seem ideologically opposed to education, to end attacks and reopen schools closed by threats; and second, that giving local communities a sense of ownership of the education process, and of the defense of schools in particular, may reduce the risk of attack.[16]

However, one may legitimately ask: 'Does playing Russian roulette with children's lives- as in effect NGOs are doing when relying for the safety of Afghan schoolchildren on a promise from a self-acknowledged terror group (the Taliban) known to specifically target this vulnerable civilian group (schoolchildren)- not also 'blur the line between military and aid operation'? That is, by encouraging children to attend school despite the lack of security; the illusion of stability is created (stability being a combined military-development objective in the context of the conflict situation in Afghanistan). NGOs then in: (1) encouraging and facilitating school attendance also in unsecured zones within Afghanistan and by (2) attempting at times to negotiate the reopening of schools with the Taliban (a group that relishes its identity as a terror group) can be said to be participating in furthering the combined military-development objective of creating the impression that development and security progress is being made when in fact this does not appear to be the

[14] O'Malley (2010), p. 15.
[15] O'Malley (2010), p. 15.
[16] O'Malley (2010), p. 15.

case in many parts of the country (where the security situation in fact may be deteriorating by all indications).

Perhaps the Taliban would like to take credit for the opening or re-opening of certain schools and the safety of schoolchildren in such instances where negotiations for school (re) openings are successful for a time, but it is unlikely to do so without conditions. The question thus arises as to just what are those conditions? Is the Taliban's occasional negotiating with factions of the local community, and national and/or international aid organizations regarding school openings directed toward the goal of thereby implicitly obtaining an affirmation of legitimacy from aid organizations in the hopes that the populace will also come to perceive the Taliban as their saviour? This is likely part of the explanation for such negotiations where they do occur. The message being communicated by the Taliban in such instances is that 'If you want your children to stay safe; you must cooperate with the Taliban and accept its dictates (one of those dictates commonly being the ban on education for females)'. It appears that: (1) schoolchildren remain central to the propaganda agenda of both sides to the armed conflict in Afghanistan (government and anti-government insurgents), and that (2) national and international aid groups working in Afghanistan in the education sector are not adequately protecting the children from terror attack, the prospect of terror attack, or exploitation as propaganda tools in the 'war on terror'. Given that there is no general cessation of terror attacks on schools in hot conflict zones within Afghanistan (in fact the trend is markedly in the opposite direction), one can justifiably be led to infer that the occasional 'negotiation' for a school (re) opening or temporary immunity from attack is but part of the terror group's overall cynical strategy of gaining control and the successful negotiation is likely to be short-lived.

3.3 Protocol II Additional to the 1949 Geneva Conventions and Its Implications for Protecting Schoolchildren Living in Hot Conflict Zones Within Afghanistan

One must ask: 'Since when is it acceptable to the international humanitarian aid community to strive to 'negotiate' children's right to access education despite the security situation when doing so involves having these vulnerable civilians attend school in dangerous high conflict areas in school buildings that in the near foreseeable future have every likelihood of becoming prime targets for a terror attack for the first or additional time?' In fact, the Protocol Additional to the Geneva Conventions of 12 August 1949, and relating to the Protection of Victims of Non-International Armed Conflicts (Protocol II), 8 June 1977 specifically refers to the need to *remove* child civilians from conflict areas (as opposed to, for instance, making them prime and easy targets for a terror attack at school or on the way to or from particular schools located within hot conflict zones within the conflict-affected State):

> 3(e) measures shall be taken, if necessary, and whenever possible with the consent of their parents or persons who by law or custom are primarily responsible for their care, to remove children temporarily from the area in which hostilities are taking place to a safer area within the country and ensure that they are accompanied by persons responsible for their safety and well-being.[17]

There is no assertion here that there is any indication, at present at least, that protected zones under IHL can currently be negotiated with the Taliban in Afghanistan (i.e., agreed upon 'no conflict' zones established pursuant to signatures on a formal agreement between the parties that includes also agreed upon arrangements for the care of civilians in the mutually respected 'safe' or 'protected' zones). The suggestion here rather is that the above quote from Protocol II sets out the basic humanitarian principle that what can be done to improve the safety of child civilians caught in a conflict situation must be done. While it may or may not be possible to remove the children to a safer part of the country where the fighting is less intense and/or the zone is better secured (which zone may yet not be an officially recognized no conflict zone), it appears reasonable to deduce that the aforementioned principle articulated in Protocol II precludes increasing the risk to children by facilitating their attendance at schools that are operating despite the high probability of terror attack.

3.3.1 The Applicability of Protocol II Additional to the 1949 Geneva Conventions to the Conflict in Afghanistan Since 2004

Protocol II pertaining to non-international armed conflict arguably has been applicable to the Afghan situation since the 'Afghan Interim Authority' (supported by the U.S.) assumed governmental control of the country in January 2004. At that point, the U.S. was on Afghan soil with the permission of the Afghan government (not as an occupying force) and as an ally in the government's fight against Afghan terrorists and other insurgents. At the same time, the Taliban and other insurgents were continuing with sustained and systematic attacks (against the Afghan government forces and the allied armed forces backing the government) as opposed to sporadic, isolated insurgent activities. Indeed, to date the Taliban still exert significant control over various regions in the county though not complete control. Hence, the conflict since 2004 can be characterized as an internal 'armed conflict' under international humanitarian law and, hence, Protocol II additional to the 1949 Geneva Conventions is applicable. Furthermore, Afghanistan acceded to Protocol II additional to the Geneva Conventions 10 November 2009. The conflict in Afghanistan

[17]Protocol II Additional to the Geneva Conventions of 12 August 1949, and relating to the Protection of Victims of Non-International Armed Conflicts, 8 June 1977. http://www.icrc.org/web/eng/siteeng0.nsf/html/genevaconventions. Accessed 11 May 2010.

then since 2004 has been between the Afghan government (backed by an international coalition) and the Taliban terrorists and other insurgents, some foreign. The anti-government insurgents are civilians as opposed to 'lawful combatants' since: (1) these terrorists, unlike lawful combatants, do *not*, for instance, wear insignia and do not carry arms openly to distinguish themselves as combatants thus undermining international humanitarian law (IHL) protections pertaining to civilians, (2) do engage in terrorist acts and other systemic war crimes and other international crimes in violation of Common Article 3 of the Geneva Conventions which prohibits attacks on civilians, and (3) may or may not report to a central command depending on the particular terror cell. (In any case, even if there is such a central command over various terror cells, it is not one that enforces or attempts to enforce adherence to international humanitarian law (IHL) and hence does not contribute to recognition of the Taliban terror organization as a combatant force under IHL).

Note that international humanitarian law does *not* recognize any such category as 'unlawful combatant' or "unlawful enemy combatant' (one belongs either to the category of 'combatant' which by definition is lawful or to the category of 'civilian'). Under Common Article 3 of the Geneva Conventions which also applies to non-international conflicts such as that currently ongoing in Afghanistan, there is no category of 'combatant' in any case (lawful or unlawful). That is, the captured enemy are *not* considered POWs though Common Article 3 stipulates minimum requirements for humane treatment of both civilians not engaged in the fighting and those deprived of their liberty in connection with their role in the armed conflict. Under Protocol II additional to the Geneva Conventions, civilians when hors du combat, that is, Taliban and other insurgent captives have the protection of the Geneva Convention Common Article 3 provisions incorporated into Protocol II.

Both sides in the current and ongoing conflict in Afghanistan are backed by international players. In regards to the government, the backers are other nation States; while the insurgents (i.e., the Taliban and other insurgents) are backed by other international terror groups such as Al-Qaeda. Since the fall of the Taliban government in Afghanistan, the international humanitarian aid community has worked in earnest to rebuild the Afghan education system and it is those efforts, backed by the West and the international community of States that provide the context for the legal and ethical questions addressed in this inquiry.

3.4 Ethical and Legal Obligations Relating to Humanitarian Educational Aid Interventions in the Midst of Ongoing Armed Conflict

National and international NGOs and UN organs implementing educational interventions in the midst of ongoing armed conflict do so in accord with international humanitarian law only if the safety of the schoolchildren and education related adult personnel can be reasonably assured. This may mean relocation to a safer area of the country or some clandestine educational enterprise (i.e., distance education delivered via internet if feasible, in-home schooling etc.). These options often appear to be less feasible in practice than in theory. In places such as Afghanistan, terror attacks are not confined to one region and in-home schools may be found out due to an informer since the Taliban and Al-Qaeda have infiltrated the regular civilian population. The failure of national and international humanitarian aid agencies to safeguard schoolchildren in this way can be considered a violation of the responsibility to do what can be done to protect them from terror attacks; such protection being a humanitarian rights entitlement implied under Article 4 (2)(d) of Protocol II Additional to the Geneva Conventions of 12 August 1949 which bans terrorism.[18] To the extent that government and NGO officials adopt policies and practices that expose schoolchildren to a heightened risk of, or actual terror attacks, they are on the analysis here potentially prosecutable under the Rome Statute.

In the final analysis, attacking schools is not first and foremost about "the age-old strategies of wearing down the enemy by destroying their infrastructure"; it is very much about manipulating a population in a systematic and calculated way; committing crimes against humanity and/or war crimes by a pattern of murder and maiming designed to instil terror and remove hope for the future by attacking the children. Unfortunately, international humanitarian organizations in 'negotiating' with terrorists about the safety of schoolchildren, teachers and school staff have become the ideal pawns in a deadly game of chess that can take a turn for the worse at any point in terms of the ultimate fate of both the humanitarian negotiators and the civilians who are the subject of the negotiations. This is the case as these negotiations are taking place in a context where the terror group i.e., the Taliban has not, as a group, renounced violence as a means to a political end. Rather, any such negotiations would be occurring in the context of high levels of terror activity. It is dangerous to the lives and well-being of schoolchildren and their teachers that some international humanitarian organizations have begun to conduct themselves as if the situation i.e., in Iraq and Afghanistan was a stable post-conflict situation when clearly we are a long way from that state of affairs in either country.

It was noted in the 2010 UNESCO report "Education Under Attack" that very little attention has been paid by the international community of human rights experts and academics to the issue of school attacks by terrorist organizations/groups:

> *Research into attacks on schools...is still at an early stage. Many aspects of this multi-faceted phenomenon have attracted little attention*, and there is much scope for more extensive investigation and deeper analysis. *So far, for instance, very little research has been carried out into why particular armed groups regard schools or even schoolchildren as legitimate targets...*Almost no research has been carried out on the impact of repeated attacks on education systems, as opposed to individuals and buildings. And *research into*

[18]Protocol II Additional to the Geneva Conventions of 12 August 1949, and relating to the Protection of Victims of Non-International Armed Conflicts, 8 June 1977. http://www.icrc.org/web/eng/siteeng0.nsf/html/genevaconventions. Accessed 11 May 2010.

the effectiveness of protective measures and negotiations with armed groups is very limited (emphasis added).[19]

One must ask why it is the case that despite systematic terror attacks on schools, schoolchildren, teachers and others involved in education having increased dramatically in number and ferocity every year for at least the last decade globally in conflict-affected States; so little attention has been paid to this issue by the international community. As O'Malley notes, despite Human Rights Watch and other groups recording repeated instances of attacks on education in various countries, it was "the launch of [UNESCO's report] "Education Under Attack"(2007) [that] put the issue on the international agenda as a distinct subject".[20]

It is here contended that the issue of why attacks on schools, schoolchildren, education personnel and education aid workers has been to date so neglected by the international community as a topic for study (with a view to amelioration of the situation) may not be completely unrelated to the fact that such studies would automatically raise the question of accountability. Thorough investigation and monitoring of this issue would raise the matter of accountability not just in respect of the perpetrators of the terror attacks on schools, schoolchildren, teachers and allied staff but also properly in regards to the local and national government education officials; humanitarian aid organizations and Western representatives who knowingly encourage school attendance even in locales without adequate security in place to reasonably assure the safety of the children, teachers and other staff. Some more in-depth study and discourse within international human rights and aid circles on this issue is beginning (as evidenced, for instance, by the 2007 and 2010 UNESCO reports regarding attacks on education). This has likely occurred, in part, due to the marked increase in attacks on education internationally which it is difficult to successfully downplay. It is critical, however, that the issue of accountability not be shaped as pertaining only to the perpetrators of attacks on education. Rather, the problem must be viewed as one that also potentially implicates parts of the international aid community; and various national government education officials and others who have inadvertently facilitated the schoolchildren being exposed to terror attacks by intentionally and knowingly encouraging and supporting school attendance regardless of the security situation. The inquiry in this book then examines, along with other matters, the issue of accountability of: (1) both the international human rights/ humanitarian aid community on an organizational level and CAFS government for their role in exposing schoolchildren to the risk of terror attack while assuming no responsibility for the same in any respect; and (2) the individual culpability in this regard of government officials as well as officials of national and international humanitarian education aid NGOs and international human rights organizations in this regard. To the extent that the matter is left unaddressed of the accountability of international humanitarian and human rights organizations, UN bodies as well as national government in encouraging

[19] O'Malley (2010), p. 16.

[20] O'Malley (2010), p. 16.

school attendance where the terror risk is unacceptably high within the conflict-affected State, the issue of attacks on education cannot be said to be fully and seriously on the international agenda.

The question has been raised by international humanitarian workers particularly in reference to Iraq and Afghanistan:

> How do humanitarian agencies [including UN agencies such as UNICEF and UNHCR] avoid being too closely identified with resisted political and military interventions [i.e., avoid being perceived as an arm of the U.S. in Iraq and Afghanistan] and 'How do we [international humanitarian organizations/personnel] balance the need for a secure political and military environment –essential for our [humanitarian] operations - without being seen as humanitarian cover for strenuously contested political action?'[21]

Building and maintaining operational schools in insecure areas at high risk of terror attack should *not* be considered a legitimate vehicle for attempting to draw the sought after distinction between (a) the Western combined military and political/development agenda and (b) the objectives and mandate of national and international humanitarian aid organizations. There is nothing politically neutral or humanitarian about such a strategy adopted too often by aid organizations working in the education sector. This approach may in part be an attempt to curry favour with the local populace by demonstrating an illusory lack of reliance and connection to Western military forces i.e., relying for the schoolchildren and teacher's safety on negotiations with terrorist organizations such as the Taliban and community resources as a supposed substitute for military protection from the West. Such a strategy as mentioned is wholly inconsistent with the raison d'être of national and international humanitarian organizations-to ensure to the maximum extent possible the safety and well-being of civilians. When national and international humanitarian organizations encourage and facilitate school attendance despite the high risk of terror attack at the sites concerned, this simply adds to the horrendous number of unwarranted civilian casualties that have been accumulating in the conflicts in Iraq and Afghanistan as elsewhere where civilians are, due to no fault of their own, caught up as victims in the midst of it all.

3.5 "Hearts and Minds" Campaigns in Their Various Forms in Conflict-Affected States: The Role of Humanitarian Aid/Human Rights Organizations

Torrente suggests that the U.S. must:

> . . .fulfill its obligations under IHL [International Humanitarian Law] in a straightforward and systematic manner instead of viewing the conduct of warfare and the provision of assistance primarily through the prism of a 'hearts and minds agenda'.[22]

[21]De Torrente (2004), pp. 22–23.

[22]De Torrente (2004), p. 25.

What has been suggested here is that many of the national and international humanitarian aid agencies and human rights organizations are no less guilty of failing to meet their international humanitarian law obligations when they encourage school attendance in every region of Afghanistan and other conflict-affected States without adequate regard to the security situation. That is, they too have replaced actions designed to meet positive duties under international humanitarian law (i.e., removing children from high conflict areas or otherwise working to ensure their safety) with actions intended to win over the local populace and international donors –the "hearts and minds' agenda implemented through means that put children at risk (i.e., building and operating schools in impoverished communities with continuing high levels of terror activity). Not surprisingly, the propaganda regarding the promise of schools even when built in highly insecure conflict areas does not fit the reality as parents soon come to know in burying their son or daughter or dealing with their children's grievous injuries after a terror attack on the school or on a group of schoolchildren while on their way to or from school.

It is to be understood that this author does not object to the notion that humanitarian agencies, institutions and frontline workers be involved in promoting peace and respect for universal human rights in the context of their relief work. This objective is often referred to as the 'integrated' or 'coherence approach':

> A number of NGOs have embraced the idea of enhancing the relevance of their relief work by placing it within a broader framework of resolving conflict and promoting human rights. *The availability of donor -funding for 'coherence- based' activities has also played a key role in bringing about this change [from a focus only on relief efforts]*(emphasis added).[23]

The building, repairing, reopening and operating of schools and the particular content of the school curricula is one of the key vehicles for creating the perception of working toward peace and respect for human rights in a move to win the "hearts and minds' of the people on the ground in conflict areas such as Afghanistan and Iraq. That enterprise is perceived as being non-contentious in the view of international donor countries that fund national and international aid organizations. The objection here is simply, but importantly, that these operations are too often occurring without any modicum of due and realistic regard for the safety of the schoolchildren, school personnel and frontline education aid workers involved. Further, there is frequently a failure of national and international humanitarian aid and human right organizations that are operating in conflict theatres rife with terror activity to own up to the fact that their trying to promote human rights using schoolchildren; especially girl schoolchildren as symbols; and placing the children's lives and safety at high risk in the process, is absolutely contrary to the tenets of international humanitarian law regardless the cloak of rights rhetoric and UN 'bureaucratic speak' draped over these activities.

Also of concern is that encouraging and facilitating school attendance in areas within the conflict-affected State where safety problems should preclude sending children to school (especially where attendance is at high visibility; easily identifiable

[23]De Torrente (2004), p. 26.

school buildings) may be importantly linked to the availability of funding for such 'humanitarian' interventions. This being one way to overcome 'donor fatigue'[24] in regards to straight emergency relief efforts and interventions focused first and foremost on saving civilian lives in conflict areas or other crisis situations. It is incumbent thus on international humanitarian aid organizations to re-evaluate their school/ education strategy in areas experiencing intense armed conflict and terror attacks. This to ensure that their aid organizations are not in fact contributing to the politicization of humanitarian aid intervention spurred on by donor countries interested in the propaganda value (in the context of the 'war on terror') of reopening schools damaged in terror attacks and building new schools across the country regardless of the security situation creating the *perception* that development progress and improved security is occurring. The international donors, hence, provide considerable (and increasing) financial and moral support for education aid interventions notwithstanding the pressing security concerns in the areas where the schools are attempting to operate.

Local bands of various insurgent terror groups in Afghanistan, on occasion, have demonstrated politically motivated, *discretionary* mercy in their halting of terror attacks on particular schools for a time as the outcome of negotiations with humanitarian organizations. That cessation of school attacks may last for an indeterminate period and too often may result in schoolchildren losing their lives or being gravely injured whenever the terrorists decide that the respite time is up (expired) in their estimation.

This author thus concurs with Torrente's concerns over the 'politicization' of humanitarian intervention and suggests that the issue arises also for those NGOs that have larger mandates aside from saving lives (NGOs thus moving away from the so-called 'classic approach to humanitarianism') and especially in regards to these organizations' involvement with the education of schoolchildren in high conflict zones. Consider then the statement below from a leading figure for the NGO CARE in Afghanistan:

> Many . . .international aid agencies have multiple mandates focused not just on saving lives through health interventions, but also on helping the living to rebuild after they are saved, by fighting extreme poverty, *educating children*, providing food and nutrition, and helping people to feed themselves. . . .*These larger mandates are born not out of a lack of humility, but out of a strong sense that ensuring human survival is simply not enough.*[25]

The point here then is that "these larger [NGO and Western] mandates" may *in principle* be born "out of a strong sense that ensuring human survival is simply not enough", but, *in practice*, operating schools *subject to a significant and foreseeable risk of terror attack* in areas with high levels of organized and systemic ongoing terror activity, is *not* consistent with claims of a mandate that prioritizes human survival; let alone a good quality of life. There is, in reality, no 'post-conflict' reconstruction context in Afghanistan for the general populace where turning to

[24]De Torrente (2004), p. 26.

[25]O'Brien (2004), p. 32.

recovery efforts *in every locale* across the country at the expense of basic humanitarian relief is feasible. The schoolchildren who have died or been seriously injured in terror attacks during this alleged designated 'post-conflict' period are a tragic testament to that fact. That is, the situation is very much, from the perspective of the surviving victims of the terror attack on the schoolchildren and teachers, and the families of the murdered and injured schoolchildren and educators, one of active conflict. The sooner this is acknowledged by the international community; the fewer schoolchildren's and teacher/education aid worker lives will be lost due to what, in many respects, amounts to a reckless education strategy that has more to do with propaganda objectives than the children's short or long-term best interests.

This is not at all to suggest, however, that such reconstruction efforts, including the operating and opening of new and of old repaired schools *en masse* is not of invaluable benefit to the people who have suffered as a result of armed conflict and terror activity once a true 'post-conflict' stage has been reached (i.e., where at least basic minimum adequate security is established; the latter being gauged in important part by the ability of national and coalition forces to adequately suppress the frequency of terror attacks or abort them before they wreak havoc). Thus, this author respectfully suggests that it is misleading for NGO leaders to characterize the operating of schools also in terror-rife zones as essentially non-problematic from an ethical and international humanitarian law standpoint and unquestionably consistent with humanitarian objectives. Yet, this suggestion is typical and is implicit also in the comment below which seeks to characterize the nature of humanitarian work in Afghanistan as legitimately focused on recovery or 'reconstruction' rather than relief-including education aid intervention- occurring in an alleged 'post-conflict' situation.

> What if all humanitarian NGOs in Afghanistan had adopted a limited and classical humanitarian mandate [focused on emergency basic survival relief efforts]? The vast majority would have left Afghanistan following the last humanitarian crisis of 2002 *because saving lives was no longer the main concern. As a result, many children would have gone without education. The reconstruction effort, already compromised by insecurity,* would have ground to a halt... Although humanitarian work in Afghanistan has moved beyond the' life and death' political choices of emergency response work and towards the far more explicitly political work of ***post-conflict*** reconstruction, it remains crucial to the people of Afghanistan. *NGOs that participate in such work cannot claim to be apolitical. Rather, they need to understand and articulate how their political solidarity with the people they serve trumps any political obligations they may have to their donors or to the sovereign governments where they work* (emphasis added) **[Quote from P. O'Brien; Advocacy Director for CARE in Afghanistan]**.[26]

The above comment disassociates the matter of 'saving lives' from the NGO efforts in regards to education; while yet acknowledging the insecure state of affairs in the ongoing alleged 'reconstruction' period in Afghanistan. In actuality, whether and how NGO's engage with education, and the building and operating of schools, and where specifically these efforts take place in conflict- ridden countries such as

[26]O'Brien (2004), p. 33.

Afghanistan, is very much still about 'saving lives'. This is the case given that the child casualties of terror attacks on schools and on school routes are the inevitable result of encouraging and facilitating school attendance despite inadequate security; an activity in which the humanitarian aid community is also heavily involved. Further, give the destitution of large segments of the populace in Afghanistan and issues such as critical food shortages which are still occurring in parts of the country, it seems quite premature to say that the need for basic emergency relief has passed.

Note that in the quote directly above, the first 'reconstruction task' listed which is said to justify the international NGO presence in the country at this time is that of children's education (despite the admitted insecurity existing in this *alleged* 'post-conflict' situation in Afghanistan). Clearly, the intense insurgent activity over the last years and the increasing number of school terror attacks in Afghanistan and in several other conflict-affected countries calls out for: (1) a revised set of criteria in the humanitarian aid community regarding what constitutes a genuinely 'post-conflict' situation, and (2) a new analysis regarding what is feasible and in the actual best interest of children under these conditions (i.e., in regards to the manner and timing of humanitarian interventions to provide basic education to school-children). We have *not* then in fact moved beyond "life and death political choices" associated with humanitarian intervention in Afghanistan and many other regions where NGOs choosing to operate a school in certain locales within the country may foreseeably cost some of the children and certain of their teachers their lives. It is time to come to grips with that political reality and the fundamental human rights and humanitarian issues it raises.

O'Brien's statement quoted directly above suggests that NGO's opening and operating schools and doing other so-called reconstruction work in allegedly 'post-conflict' societies must convey to the people in those countries: (1) their [NGO] "political solidarity with the people" and (2) the priority of the people's interests for the NGO over NGO obligations to donors or to the government of the host country. However the current author would contend, in contrast, that the reality is that the priority of the people's interests is too often lost in consideration instead of: (a) NGO interests as bureaucratic entities reliant on donors and host governments and (b) the demands of donors and host governments for highly visible donor-funded NGO activities that are palatable and marketable to the international community as *supposedly* apolitical and purely humanitarian efforts; such as the building and operating of schools regardless the security situation where the school is located. This author then challenges the notion espoused by O'Brien for instance that: (a) "humanitarians do not control or significantly influence humanitarian space" (that apolitical neutral space in conflict and post-conflict societies defined by humanitarians acting independently with only the best interests of civilians and those hors du combat in mind) and that (b) NGOs are but, in all instances, "one small voice in a complex political matrix".[27] When it comes to the prospect of operating schools in

[27]O'Brien (2004), pp. 33–34.

areas where there is an unacceptably high risk of terror attack, it is absolutely critical that NGOs oppose this precisely on humanitarian grounds; that opposition being very much consistent with their obligations under international humanitarian law. The voice of NGOs on this issue is not small at all, and would serve to expose the political propaganda agenda that fuels such reckless activities under the guise of apolitical reconstruction efforts in supposed post-conflict periods. While NGOs are largely reliant on international donors for funding and on host countries for cooperation, there is nothing inevitable about NGOs being complicit in encouraging and facilitating schoolchildren attending school even in areas within conflict-plagued States such as Afghanistan where doing so puts the children at extraordinarily high risk of injury or death.

O'Brien (Advocacy Director for CARE in Afghanistan) notes that terrorists are especially effective in creating terror when they carry out attacks on the "more innocent and apolitical".[28] Certainly, schoolchildren then fit the aforementioned criteria as preferred terrorist targets. There is simply no legally or morally supportable rationale for the West or cooperating international humanitarian agencies being complicit in knowingly putting schoolchildren in harm's way in the manner here described. Yet such NGO 'reconstruction' efforts pertaining to schools continue in highly insecure regions within Afghanistan and elsewhere. Contrary to paying sufficient regard to security needs in the construction of new schools and in the reopening of schools previously hit by terror attacks in Afghanistan, and to the safety needs of humanitarian workers themselves; CARE for instance "...has refused to work alongside them [military security forces] *or to accept any form of armed protection for their activities*".[29] as have certain other NGOs in Afghanistan. While the motivation for this may be to attempt to remain apolitical, the end result is that prime terrorist human targets are 'set up for the kill'; including schoolchildren.

3.5.1 Counter-Terrorism as Theatre and the Symbolic Function of Children Attending School Despite the Risk of Targeted Terror Attacks on Education

The support of the West, the U.N. and its organs and the national and international humanitarian aid community in repairing, constructing, reopening and operating schools in Afghanistan *even in areas with high terror activity* has both cultural and military significance. Operating schools even in highly unstable regions within Afghanistan is symbolic of the West's involvement and support for the government's combined military-development initiatives (i.e., its promotion of gender equality, attempt to develop democratic institutions, enhance literacy levels for the

[28]O'Brien (2004), p. 35.

[29]O'Brien (2004), p. 35.

general populace, promote free thought and access to information at the basic education level in schools and in independent institutions of higher learning etc.), and is symbolic also of alleged progress toward stabilization of the society and the purported regaining of government control over the life of the country.

One of the key points being made in this book is that the motives of terrorists such as Al-Qaida and the Taliban in attacking schools cannot be effectively de-legitimized in a context in which the national government and its Western allies *in effect* prioritize combined military-development objectives over and above the objective of preserving children's lives and their physical safety. This is especially the case when the national and international humanitarian aid community feeds into this tact as well by encouraging school attendance despite significant security concerns in particular regions within the conflict-affected country. The aforementioned approach sends the unwitting message to the general populace in the region (particularly if terror attacks on schools and schoolchildren materialize in a particular region) that it is Western ideology and security interests; as well as the bureaucratic interests of the U.N. and various national and international humanitarian organizations; which drives the push to operate schools where these schools are highly likely to be the target of terror attacks. That is, it becomes apparent sooner or later to most of the parents that there is, in practice at least, less than genuine concern for the lives and well-being of their children when measured in terms of the risks with their safety they as parents are being encouraged by government officials and NGOs to take in sending them to school where the security for education is so poor. Sending children to school in Afghanistan in regions of the country where security is highly inadequate is likely to invigorate terror attacks on education. This is the case in that the killing and maiming of children serves to demonstrate the terror group's resolve and the 'show no mercy' bravado that is their trademark and currency. In a sense, the slaughter of children serves not only to re-legitimize the perpetrators as full-fledged terrorists capable and prepared to carry out systemic campaigns of terror; but each 'success' in this regard sickeningly is claimed as an indicator that destiny and the divine is on their side.

This author is in accord with the view of Chowdhury and Krebs that the battle for legitimacy is a critical one in any counter-terrorism enterprise "One might have assumed that the battle for legitimacy would be tossed aside in the hail of bullets. One would have been mistaken".[30] What is remarkable is, however, that in many ways terrorists are winning the propaganda war despite their committing heinous international crimes. In killing schoolchildren, terrorists stay true to their objectives of instilling terror via the most horrendous of acts so as to attract a maximal audience:

> . . .legitimation requirements are perhaps particularly pressing in the arenas of terrorism and counter-terrorism, which are fundamentally communicative and symbolic enterprises

[30] Chowdhury and Krebs (2010), p. 127.

> ...Terrorism is open-air theatre, seeking to attract large audiences through spectacular displays ...[31]

However, in too often facilitating schoolchildren in Afghanistan attending school where security is grossly inadequate such that these children become easy and valued targets for the terrorists, the national government and its western allies as well as the national and international humanitarian aid community operating in the country are not staying true to the values embodied in international humanitarian law (i.e., values relating to the protection of civilians in times of armed conflict and the obligation to seek the preservation of civilian life by all feasible means in the circumstance). Chowdhury and Krebs state: "that which cannot be legitimated cannot be pursued" and point out that the legitimating process is a public one.[32] Clearly the West and international humanitarian organizations as well as the U.N. have, with inspirational rhetoric concerning rights, equity, development, peace and democracy, attempted to legitimate the repairing of schools, building of new schools and operating of schools even in hot terror zones in Afghanistan and in other conflict-affected regions where these schools will inevitably be attacked at some point. Further, this legitimization process has occurred via the public dissemination of literally several hundreds of public documents and speeches over the years on the topic of the importance of basic education to development and stabilization in areas such as Afghanistan and Iraq regardless of the risk of violence to schoolchildren and their teachers.

The education of children in regions subject to high levels of terror attack is considered by the national government and its allies as being a vital component in the counter-terrorism effort. In this regard, the current author is agreed that: "Counterterrorism is [in part at least] also theatre";[33] and holds that the operating of schools in regions plagued by insecurity and terrorism is just such theatre; here designed to symbolize alleged progress in defeating the terrorists. This theatre insofar as children's schooling is concerned, however, requires, in the first instance, the successful marketing to the international community of the legitimacy of prioritizing children's access to basic education *over* their security needs. Success in that regard is reflected in the garnering of increasing and significant financial support from international donors for the operation of schools even in regions where these schools cannot be secured adequately against the high and imminent risk of terror attacks. Operating schools in circumstances so extremely dangerous to the schoolchildren, teachers and other school personnel involved becomes a symbolic measure of the resolve of the government and the West to overcome terrorism and promote democratic regimes:

[31]Chowdhury and Krebs (2010), p. 133.

[32]Chowdhury and Krebs (2010), p. 133.

[33]Chowdhury and Krebs (2010), p. 133.

> If terrorists avidly seek publicity for their causes and adopt methods designed to signal their resolve, so too must the terror-fighting State be centrally concerned with what message it sends to what audiences.[34]

Of course, at some point, the number of deaths and severely injured amongst schoolchildren; their teachers and education aid workers due to targeted terror attacks may stimulate a re-assessment of the education strategy being encouraged by the national government and its allies This reconsideration of the value of a strategy of 'education at all costs' occurs, at least for the locals, due to their first-hand knowledge of the actual broad and intense scope of the violence against schoolchildren and educators in their region. For instance, in Afghanistan, parents are frequently led to reconsider whether education can continue to be the priority in the counter-terrorism strategy given: (a) the lax security in the region and (b) the fact that schools are a high value target for terrorists due to the shock and fear that attacks on schools engender in the local populace and the international community generally. A September 2009 CARE International in Afghanistan report titled: 'Knowledge on fire: Attacks on education in Afghanistan; Risks and measures for successful mitigation' states the following on this point:

> At the beginning of 2009, 670 schools were closed across the country [Afghanistan]. In southern provinces, between 65-81% of schools are currently closed due to insecurity. But closure of schools is not the only negative impact. *Insecurity also causes more parents to keep their children home from school in fear of their safety.* According to respondents in the field study, girls' attendance suffers slightly more than boys after a security incident at their school. Thirty six percent of the respondents in the field study indicated that fewer girls have frequented the school after the threat; while 27% said that it had led to a reduction in boys' attendance. *Fortunately, attacks do not appear to have that serious of an impact on teachers' attendance.* Male teachers were reported to have decreased their attendance by 3% of respondents after the incident and female teachers by 7% of respondents (emphasis added).[35]

Hence, while the national government and its allies and international aid organizations push for the operation of schools in insecure and secure zones in Afghanistan, schools are, at times, closed in various unstable regions in the country after terror attacks; at least for a time. It is noteworthy that the CARE 2009 report 'Knowledge on Fire' concerning the situation regarding targeted terror attacks on education in Afghanistan states 'Fortunately, attacks do not appear to have that serious of an impact on teachers' attendance'. Why is this fortunate if not for the reason that the perspective expressed in the CARE report is implicitly that education should, in practice, be prioritized above the security interests of the schoolchildren? That is, having most of the teachers still attending at the school means that the school will continue to operate immediately after or soon after a terror attack even if some parents choose to keep their children home from school for some indeterminate period after the attack. The terror attack then would not be successful in closing the school long-term and that would be scored as a victory by the West,

[34]Chowdhury and Krebs (2010), p. 133.

[35]Glad (2009), p. 3.

the Afghan government and the international community no matter the ongoing risk to the physical safety of the children still attending there.

3.6 Monitoring Targeted Terror Attacks on Education

The 2009 CARE Afghan study 'Knowledge on Fire' involved, in part, the collection of data on education attacks through interviews in eight provinces in Afghanistan (Logar, Khost, Kunar, Wardak, Ghazni, Herat, Balkh and Kapisa):

> A total of 1,037 individual and group interviews were conducted among Ministry of Education officers, Ministry of Education provincial department heads, representatives from the NGO community, parents, police officers, school principals, members of local shuras (community councils), teachers at different levels, and students. A total of 4,819 people were involved in the field exercise. Due to security concerns for the people that participated in this exercise, the exact villages and schools visited will not be revealed publicly... *Under-reporting, wrong information and partial information on attacks do not give the complete picture of all attacks. There are also certain inconsistencies within the figures generated by the databases themselves* (emphasis added)[36]

The international aid community- perhaps in part being concerned about the risk of undermining the prioritizing of the education of schoolchildren in conflict-affected highly unstable regions within countries such as Afghanistan-has to date not placed an emphasis on providing the international community or the local populace with official figures regarding the nature and number of terror attacks on schools, schoolchildren and teachers and other school personnel as well as on education aid workers. Rather, NGOs have relied on sparse anecdotal evidence in reporting such attacks which likely underestimates the actual scope of the problem. (This is not to deny, however, the obvious constraints posed by the circumstances that exist on the ground in gathering such information). There is, for instance, in the aforementioned 2009 CARE report, an acknowledgement of the underreporting of terror attacks on education (i.e., attacks on schools and school-related structures, on schoolchildren, teachers and other school personnel as well as on education aid workers). In addition, there are inconsistencies in UNICEF and NGO databases on the issue when compared with data collected through interviews in the field and the like not only in Afghanistan but likely also in other areas such as Iraq experiencing high levels of terror activity in some regions.

Note that the 2009 CARE study of terror attacks on education in Afghanistan mentions that:

> Due to security concerns for the people who participated in the exercise [that is, the people who participated in interviews regarding the targeted terror attacks on schools, school-related facilities, on students and on school personnel] the exact villages and schools visited will not be revealed publicly.[37]

[36]Glad (2009), p. 1.

[37]Glad (2009), p. 1.

It is apparent then that security is inadequate for the operation of schools in certain regions within the country heavily affected by terror activity and that all those involved in the education enterprise are at ongoing risk of being victimized by the terrorists. Concealing the identity of the CARE study participants (Afghan Ministry of Education personnel, NGOs, parents and students) in the interests of the participants' security; while at the same time expecting the children of these villages to attend school in the context of an abysmal security situation, is both ironic and tragic. This is not at all to say that UNICEF, CARE International, other NGOs and the West do not hope for a better security situation; it is rather to acknowledge the reality of the current situation in Afghanistan and in many other countries in respect of terror attacks on education:

> Throughout 2008 alone, 670 attacks on the Afghan education system were carried out including arson and the murder of teachers and students. Between January 2006 and December 2008, 1153 attacks of different natures were reported: grenades, night letters or verbal threats to teachers, killings of students and education personnel. According to the Ministry of Education . . .230 people died as a result of attacks on schools, students and personnel between 2006 and 2007. *The most frequent type of attack according to the UNICEF school security database is arson, where school buildings, tents or inventory was burned. Explosions in or near schools buildings (including throwing of grenades, mines and rocket attacks) and direct attacks against students or education personnel are also common.* Twenty percent of education personnel interviewed in the field assessment stated that they have been threatened. *Attacks on schools cannot be confined to a certain area of the country*. . .While in 2006, the provinces that reported most attacks were Helmand, Khost, Kandahar and Ghazni; in 2007 these were Khost, Kunar, Herat and Wardak; and in 2008 Kunar, Kabul, Nangarhar and Khost. Very few provinces have seen a decrease or even a light increase in attacks throughout the period.
>
> The nature of attacks varies from province to province. In some areas, arson is the most frequent form of attack, while in other areas, the attackers chose explosives. Grenades have been thrown in school windows and rockets fired at schools. Tents used for classes have been burnt down and children have been killed on their way home from school. Schools are more at risk at night and in the early months of the school year, although the latter trend has extended further into the school term with each passing year (emphasis added).[38]

The most common types of terror attacks on basic education in Afghanistan reported in the CARE 2009 study and which were not confined to any particular region of the country involved : (a) arson attacks on schools, tents or other structures where learning was taking place or education supplies were housed; (b) explosions in or near school buildings, and (c) direct attacks on schoolchildren and school personnel at school or on the way to or from school or in other locales where these persons were known to be and were targeted. The forgoing attacks resulted in large numbers of deaths and grave injury. Clearly, operating schools easily recognized as schools is a magnet for terror attacks. Marking the schools with some internationally recognized symbol that would signify that the facility was protected under international humanitarian law is unlikely to deter their being targeted for attacks. This seems evident as terrorists such as the Taliban insurgents have not

[38]Glad (2009), p. 2.

been at all reluctant to attack other installations or vehicles bearing such internationally recognized insignia such as the symbol of the International Red Cross. Anything that makes schools more visible is likely in fact to increase considerably the risk of their being attacked. The contention here is, furthermore, that steps such as marking schools with international symbols cannot legitimate operating schools in areas where terror attacks are foreseeable and highly likely (especially where the educational facility is easily identified as a school or school-related structure or place). The current author is in favor of recognizing armed attacks on schools as a specific and distinct international crime (a topic to be discussed in detail in a later section).

3.7 More on Counter-Terrorism Strategies That Include the Basic Education of Schoolchildren as a Component

What is especially unusual about the counter-terrorism strategy incorporating as a component the basic education of schoolchildren, *even in zones with high levels of terror activity*, is that, in many ways, this is a very counter-productive tact in terms of, for instance, its:

(a) Failure to reduce casualties and deaths of civilians and likely contribution to further civilians victims of terror attacks.
(b) Failure to reduce the terrorist resolve to engage in violence.
(c) Failure to show that the West and the international community will not concede to terror demands based on the threat of violence (i.e., as when NGOs not uncommonly are willing if possible to 'negotiate' with terrorists the terms and conditions of the school's operation in return for the *promise* of security for at least some period).

It is difficult to imagine a scenario under which prioritizing the right to education of schoolchildren *over* their right to physical security in conflict-ridden places such as Afghanistan would serve to de-legitimize terror attacks on education by insurgents. In fact, by placing schoolchildren and school staff potentially in harm's way as a consequence of encouraging school attendance despite the high risk of terror attacks; the opponents of terrorism, in effect, though not in intent, become potential contributors to it.

This author is agreed with the notion that: "States and insurgents [including national and international global terrorist organizations] are ... engaged in an intertwined struggle for legitimacy".[39] The West's and international aid community's involvement with basic education in terror afflicted regions (i.e., in Afghanistan and Iraq) is intended to be symbolic of their investment in the community, their alliance with the general populace including the ordinary folk in the villages, and their commitment to the future stability and prosperity of the particular country in

[39]Chowdhury and Krebs (2010), p. 135.

question. While schooling is presented then as a neutral 'rights issue', it is intricately related to the political objectives of re-stabilization and democratization of the States in which these largely Western endorsed and sponsored education initiatives are occurring. This sets up the education enterprise supported by international aid agencies for labeling as an alleged colonialist, imperialist effort with the children caught in the cross-fire. It should be pointed out, however, in regards to the disingenuous claim of basic education as a colonialist tool imposed by the West, that the States themselves which are experiencing high levels of terror attacks on education, and which are often allied with the West in fighting terrorism, have also in fact overwhelmingly ratified the U.N. Convention on the Rights of the Child (UNCRC) (entered into force 2 September 1990). The CRC includes in its provisions the right of every child to basic education[40] and emphasizes the 'best interests of the child principle' in State policy and practice. Clearly then the West is not imposing these education initiatives on the States concerned, but rather the States themselves endorse, in principle at least if not fully in practice, the move to improve education and literacy levels for the general populace, increase gender equity in education, and the role of education in teaching about the inherent right of every individual to basic human rights and fundamental freedoms. Conflict-affected States where international education aid interventions are a feature, and where the State endorses the U.N. Convention on the Rights of the Child (UNCRC) (and hence every child's right to a basic education) include, amongst others, Afghanistan, Iraq, Pakistan and Thailand as shown below:

State's Party to the UNCRC	Signature	Ratification
Afghanistan	27 September 1990	28 March 1994
Iraq		15 June 1994
Pakistan	20 September 1990	12 November 1990
Thailand		27 March 1992

Note that the right to education set out in the U.N. Convention on the Rights of the Child which States such as Iraq and Afghanistan have ratified sets out a guarantee of the right to be educated for tolerance and peace, the right to educational inclusion including for the disabled child and females and children of minority groups, the right to learn to respect fundamental human rights and democratic values, and to learn respect for diverse cultural groups:

UNCRC Article 28

1. *States Parties recognize the right of the child to education*, and with a view to achieving this right progressively and on the basis of equal opportunity, they shall, in particular:
   (a). *Make primary education compulsory and available free to all;*
   (b). *Encourage the development of different forms of secondary education, including general and vocational education, make them available and accessible to every child*, and take appropriate measures such as the introduction of free education and offering financial assistance in case of need;

[40]Convention on the Rights of the Child ratification status. http://treaties.un.org/Pages/ViewDetails.aspx?src=TREATY&mtdsg_no=IV-11&chapter=4&lang=en. Accessed 18 May 2010.

(c). Make *higher education accessible to all* on the basis of capacity by every appropriate means;
(d). Make educational and vocational information and guidance available and accessible to all children;
(e). *Take measures to encourage regular attendance at schools and the reduction of drop-out rates.*

2. States Parties shall take all appropriate measures to ensure that school discipline is administered in a manner consistent with the child's human dignity and in conformity with the present Convention.
3. States Parties shall promote and encourage international cooperation in matters relating to education, in particular with a view to contributing to the elimination of ignorance and illiteracy throughout the world and facilitating access to scientific and technical knowledge and modern teaching methods. In this regard, particular account shall be taken of the needs of developing countries (emphasis added).

UNCRC Article 29

1. States Parties agree that the education of the child shall be directed to:
   (a). The development of the child's personality, talents and mental and physical abilities to their fullest potential;
   (b). *The development of respect for human rights and fundamental freedoms, and for the principles enshrined in the Charter of the United Nations*;
   (c). *The development of respect for the child's parents, his or her own cultural identity, language and values, for the national values of the country in which the child is living, the country from which he or she may originate, and for civilizations different from his or her own;*
   (d). *The preparation of the child for responsible life in a free society, in the spirit of understanding, peace, tolerance, equality of sexes, and friendship among all peoples, ethnic, national and religious groups and persons of indigenous origin*;
   (e). The development of respect for the natural environment.
2. No part of the present article or article 28 shall be construed so as to interfere with the liberty of individuals and bodies to establish and direct educational institutions, *subject always to the observance of the principle set forth in paragraph 1 of the present article* and to the requirements that the education given in such institutions shall conform to such minimum standards as may be laid down by the State (emphasis added).[41]

The UNCRC right to education endorsed by Islamic and other States plagued by terror activity and targeted terror attacks on education thus incorporates values and principles that directly contradict the terrorist philosophy and agenda.

The aforementioned CARE International 2009 report 'Knowledge on fire: Attacks on education in Afghanistan' provides some considerable insight into how the rhetoric in the international humanitarian aid community is shaped to tacitly support the prioritizing of education over the life and physical security of schoolchildren, teachers and school personnel. This 2009 CARE report is but one example of the many reports by the U.N. and various international human rights and humanitarian organizations which do the same with respect to various conflict regions globally that have high levels of terror activity. In the next chapter we will delve

---

[41]UN Convention on the Rights of the Child Adopted (entry into force 2 September 1990). http://www2.ohchr.org/english/law/crc.htm. Accessed 18 May 2010.

into the CARE report in more detail as well as reports by UNICEF, UNESCO and various NGOs such as Human Rights Watch for examples of inconsistencies and propaganda relating to education in conflict-affected States experiencing high levels of terror activity and targeted attacks on education. That propaganda, on the analysis here, is held to undermine the current and likely also the future security interests of schoolchildren and school personnel.

It will become evident in considering the data from the field in conflict regions that the West, the international aid community and national governments in places such as Afghanistan and Iraq will inevitably fail to effectively de-legitimize organized terrorism and win the 'hearts and minds' of the people when they, too, are potentially contributing to the loss of life and injury of schoolchildren and of school personnel. This being the case due to national governments, international aid organizations and Western high representatives strongly encouraging; some would even say pressuring parents to send their children to schools notwithstanding the woefully inadequate security provided for schools and their attendees. Remedies are required as will be discussed for improving the security of schools, and holding those responsible for attacks on education accountable. In addition, the national governments of conflict-affected States and their Western allies must not tout the number of schools built, re-opened and number of children attending school *despite the lack of security and the risk to children's lives and physical safety* as a measure of *alleged* progress in the 'war on terror'. Rather, insofar as education and counter-terrorism is concerned; progress is to be claimed when terrorist propaganda attempting to justify attacks on schools, schoolchildren and educators is less and less accepted by the mass of the local population, the international community and academics; even those who profess to be opposed to Western combined military-development objectives in Afghanistan and elsewhere in conflict-affected regions.

Since we have been considering education initiatives in conflict-affected States implemented in circumstances and in ways that jeopardize children's security interests, let us digress briefly to consider what implementation of the right to education as envisioned by the U.N. Convention on the Rights of the Child embodies.

3.8 Performance Indicators for the Implementation of the Right to Education Grounded on Respect for Fundamental Human Rights: Relevance to Education in a Conflict-Affected State

Dr. Katrien Beeckman draws a very important distinction between 'education indicators' *versus* 'human rights indicators' pertaining to the implementation of the right to education.[42] She maintains that the performance indicators generally relied upon in the education domain are not necessarily "rights-based" indicators while:

[42]Beeckman (2004).

> Measuring the human right to education calls for the development of *rights-based indicators*, capable of reflecting the norms, principles, and values underpinning human rights in general, and the right to education particularly.[43]

The current author suggests that in the context of the international humanitarian aid community's efforts in implementing the right to education in States not yet genuinely in a post-conflict stage (i.e., Afghanistan); too often *non-rights* based educational performance indicators are utilized. For example, the number of schoolchildren enrolled at the beginning of the year is a 'performance indicator' that is *not* rights-based in a context where the reality is that a high number of those children are likely to be at considerable risk of a terror attack given the poor security situation. Increasing enrollment of girls at the basic education level may, on its face, appear to be a 'rights- based' indicator (indictor intended to reflect progress in rights attainment) since it pertains to increased gender equity in school attendance. However, the value of that performance indicator (the number of girls enrolled in basic education) *as a rights-based indicator* is offset in many conflict-affected States such as Afghanistan by the fact that the girls are at considerably higher risk of terror attack than are the boys; especially if attending an all girls' school.

Time and again in the reports of UN bodies such as UNESCO and NGOs reporting on basic education in conflict-affected fragile States (CAFS) such as Afghanistan (and despite the passing anecdotal references and rough estimates of numbers of attacks on education based on inadequate monitoring cited in the reports), 'the bottom line' for these agencies is most often framed in terms of allegedly neutral educational 'performance indicators'. One of the key performance indicators is often taken to be improvements in school enrollment interpreted as alleged evidence of the successful implementation of the 'right to education'. Those indicators, however, as discussed, mask fundamental rights issues. The implementation of the right to education requires *in the first instance* a safe environment such that anything less does *not* in any meaningful sense meet the criteria for fulfillment of the children's education entitlement. Yet, the focus of the national and international aid community working in the education sector and operating in Afghanistan and other conflict-affected regions is on how to increase enrollment and reduce drop-out and grade repetition *despite inadequate security* (the latter two problems -drop-out and grade repetition- often not being adequately addressed in NGO reports thus leading to artificially inflated figures regarding progress in school attendance as based on enrollment at the *beginning* of the school year).

Lack of security for basic education in Afghanistan and other conflict-affected States becomes an issue for the national and international aid community and the national government then *not* necessarily first and foremost because it threatens the lives and well-being of children and others involved in the education enterprise including humanitarian education aid workers. Rather, security becomes an issue, it appears, in large part because it interferes with school enrollment and thus threatens the international donor monies that are provided in support of humanitarian

---

[43]Beeckman (2004), p. 71.

education aid. Those donor monies help significantly in the financing of many humanitarian aid groups intervening in the education sector in CAFS. Thus, even before security problems in relation to schooling at the basic education level in Afghanistan can be adequately addressed (assuming such is possible which in the current situation is highly dubious), the children are encouraged to attend school and *to return to school as soon as possible after a terror attack despite the continuing lack of security*. In this regard, UNESCO speaks, for instance, of 'rapid response' after a terror attack on education (The so-called 'rapid response' is directed to returning the children to school as soon as possible and, in practice, even absent any change in terms of improved and adequate security at the school and on the routes to and from school). Any improvement in security soon after an attack is highly unlikely in CAFS such as Afghanistan in any case given that security forces are stretched thin. Afghan police do not have the numbers of sufficiently trained personnel available to protect every school and negotiations with terror groups, if they take place at all, are a risky basis for moving forward in re-opening schools after a terror attack. Further, as mentioned previously, many NGOs reject co-coordinating with coalition forces to provide for the protection of schools even should such an option be available in certain cases since they fear the perception that theirs is not purely humanitarian work but rather 'militarized aid' motivated by an alleged hidden Western political agenda.

A 2010 UNESCO report titled 'Protecting Education from Attack: A State-of-the-Art Review' reflects the inappropriate generalization of the 'rapid response' model from genuine 'post-conflict' and disaster situations where schools can potentially become safe zones to conflict-affected States (CAFS) where terror campaigns are still raging:

> Rapid response helps mitigate the effects of the attack. Authorities need to know about attacks so as to be able to respond e.g. with school materials and temporary shelter or building repairs. *They need to determine which students are not returning to school /classes and why, so that these disruptions can be responded to and addressed* (emphasis added).[44]

One may question what is meant by the above phrase: "Rapid response helps mitigate the effects of the attack". Certainly returning to school soon after a terror attack does not lessen the children's fears after their school has been burned or bombed and perhaps some of their schoolmates and/or teachers injured or killed. Nor does rapidly re-opening the school mitigate the chances for the occurrence of another terror attack. Rather, in this instance, the NGOs are likely considering 'mitigation' ('Rapid response helps *mitigate* the effects of the attack') to mean that there is less impact on school enrollment/attendance if the damaged school can be repaired and functioning again quickly soon after a terror attack, or if some alternative education site can be up and running soon after an attack and children encouraged once more to attend school This so-called 'rapid response', to the extent that it results in rendering the school or an alternate site for classes operational,

[44]UNESCO (2010), p. 15.

creates the *illusion* of a return to a semblance of normality while still placing children at risk of harm from future terror attacks.

Particularly disconcerting in the quote immediately above from the 2010 UNESCO report on preventing attacks on education (for this author at least) is the phrase "They need to determine which students are not returning to school/ classes [after the terror attack on the school, schoolchildren and/or teachers] and why, so that these disruptions can be responded to and addressed".[45] They (certain segments of the attacked school's population) are not returning to school because they have just experienced a terror attack directed at them due to their attendance at school, and they and their parents would prefer that they (the schoolchildren) enjoy some reasonable longevity. The meta-message in the phrase in question appears to be that efforts should be made to entice (pressure?) students to return to school and/ or recruit even more new students to replace any students who do not return to school after a terror attack directed at the school, the students or the staff.

NGOs such as Human Rights Watch contribute to aid organizations adopting such a high risk 'rapid response' approach to dealing with terror attacks on education which approach generally does not adequately address the security issue if at all. This by suggesting that "access to education be made one key benchmark" of security:

> On a practical level, because this benchmark lends itself to diagnostic, nationally comparable data analysis (for instance the number of operational schools, the number of students, the enrollment of girls) focused on outcomes instead of the number of troops or vague references to providing security.[46]

As we have seen, increases in school enrollment, numbers of schools operational and girls attending in Afghanistan in comparison to the situation when the Taliban were officially in power have been accompanied by increasing numbers of schoolchildren, teachers and education aid workers killed or maimed. Hence, such educational performance indicators as school enrollment and number of schools overall operational are not in any perfect or even rough positive correlative relationship with increases in security or genuine improvements in the human rights situation of children in Afghanistan (or in other conflict-affected States not yet in the post-conflict stage) or even with improvements in the quality of education offered (quality of education in Afghanistan has been an issue due to a variety of factors including; but not limited to: (1) a paucity of well-trained teachers, (2) a lack of emphasis on a quality curriculum and, at times, (3) modifications in curriculum made simply to appease the Taliban and other insurgent groups such that the curriculum may be a great deal less than inclusive in terms of the values espoused and deficient in a number of other respects as well according to UN standards for the right to education as set out in the Convention on the Rights of the Child).[47]

---

[45] UNESCO (2010), p. 15.

[46] Human Rights Watch (2006), p. 6.

[47] Dryden-Petersen (2010), pp. 34–42.

In discussing "prevention and early warning" the same 2010 UNESCO report 'Protecting Education from Attack: A State-of-the-Art Review' states:

> Monitoring should ideally be involved with providing early warning to prevent attacks, knowing why schools and education facilities are targeted, and what puts them at risk; discerning patterns of attack, such as seasons and times of day; and to inform prevention and protection e.g. protection of travel to and from school.[48]

One cannot easily imagine such advice as that in the quote immediately above being proffered for those working in the education sector in a developed State should tragically schools be under terror attack in that context. That is, one cannot easily imagine children in a developed state being expected to gamble with their lives based on probability calculations that bureaucrats and frontline workers in the education community have made regarding, in their estimation, for instance: (1) what time of day or season terror attacks on schools and schoolchildren are more versus less likely to occur, (2) how they (local community members, teachers, humanitarian education aid workers etc.) might appease potential attackers, at least for a time, (3) how many guards are needed on a school bus to ward off a terror attack (assuming of course that the bus with its load of students and teachers and the bus guards are not doomed at the outset given the insurgents' use of roadside IEDs); and (4) what type of school structure and school location might be more versus less susceptible to terror attack (Note that NGO- run schools in Afghanistan are often 'home-based' or run in community- based facilities as opposed to in government schools. Where this is the case, the NGO-run classes may therefore be somewhat less visible than would otherwise be the case-that is, if no one; such as a conservative pro-insurgent village leader for instance, betrays the location of the education classes rendering them highly vulnerable to attack).[49] Nor can one easily contemplate children in the West being encouraged to return to school after a terror attack as soon as a new school is opened (either a government or community-based school) ; or the old school is repaired; or a temporary educational site becomes operational (perhaps in tents or the open air as so often is the case in Afghanistan) with humanitarian education aid organizations, in consultation with the community, supposedly selecting for the re-established education classes "*discrete locations*" or "*where possible; ...discrete school structures*".[50] In sum, the children in CAFS where the fighting is intense and ongoing are being expected by the national government and its allies, and the international humanitarian education aid community to return to school soon after a terror attack on education. This, despite essentially often having to be in hiding while going to, for instance, an NGO sponsored community school, given the high risk to their personal safety of being found out by the insurgent groups that are waging a terror campaign and specifically targeting education (i.e., targeting for terror attack schools, schoolchildren, teachers

---

[48]UNESCO (2010), p. 15.

[49]Glad (2009), p. 25.

[50]Glad (2009), p. 4.

and other education staff, humanitarian education aid workers and others involved in the education domain).

The reality is that in most States where the conflict is ongoing such as in Afghanistan, monitoring of the alleged reasons for attacks, and attempts at deciphering and predicting the patterns of attacks are likely to be ineffective, in most instances, in providing the basis for preventing or escaping school terror attacks. To date, neither the security forces in Afghanistan (i.e., the Afghan national police), coalition forces nor neighborhood school protection committees have succeeded in providing a generally secure environment for the functioning of all schools in that conflict-affected State (whether due to lack of sufficient deployment of these forces to school protection, ineffective protection strategies employed in the enterprise of protecting schools or for some other reason). The problem of attacks on education is particularly acute in provinces classified by the UN as "high risk".

Knowingly exposing children through intentional acts (i.e., encouraging and facilitating school attendance despite significant security concerns) to the considerable risk of harm due to a potential terror attack at school or on the way to or from school, as mentioned previously, is here contended to constitute a violation of international humanitarian law, criminal and human rights law (as will be discussed in detail in a later section). No number of attempted mitigative measures can undo that fact.

In 2006, Human Rights Watch noted in its report 'Lessons in Terror: Attacks on Education in Afghanistan'; the "emergence of schools as a frontline in Afghanistan's internal military conflict".[51] That is, it is here suggested, the situation today in Afghanistan even more so than it was in 2006 and likewise schools are increasingly on the frontlines of armed conflict also in many other CAFS globally. Yet, it continues to this date to be the case that schoolchildren are being expected to attend at those 'frontlines' of armed conflict without adequate protection. This, ostensibly to attain an education and a brighter future; that is, assuming that: (1) the children escape the occurrence of a terror attack during their years of basic schooling, *or* (2) survive one should it occur; and, (3) should they experience an attack on their school, or on the way to or from school; that their parents can be convinced to send them to school once again notwithstanding the risks. This author is in full accord with Beeckman (a leading consultant in the international humanitarian education aid community) when she states:

> . . . ***the successful implementation of the right to education depends on the simultaneous co-realisation of other human rights*****, such as the right to food, the right to health** ***or the right to physical integrity***. Assessing the realisation of one right can thus not be uncoupled from progress achieved in the others (emphasis added).[52]

However, it is the case, it is here argued, that the international humanitarian education aid community has, in its work in CAFS such as Afghanistan that are still caught up in the fighting, in practice, uncoupled the *right to physical security* from

[51]Human Rights Watch (2006), p. 11.

[52]Beeckman (2004), pp. 75–76.

the right to education. This is not at all to say that the international humanitarian education aid community fails to recognize that adequate security will in fact promote better school attendance and school achievement. Rather, it is to highlight that the international humanitarian aid community working on education as a reconstruction aid intervention in CAFS that are *not* genuinely in a post-conflict phase (as well as national governments of CAFS and their international State allies) have prioritized the schoolchildren's right to education in these conflict-affected States over their right to physical security. While the right to education may well be "a key right in unlocking other human rights" for schoolchildren, it will *not* unlock/ provide access to better security in the face of the ever increasing incidence of terror attacks on education in many CAFS.

Beeckman goes on to make the point that:

> *Implementing human rights goes beyond realising rights*- stipulated *results* in the treaties, such as providing free primary public education [one of the UN prime millennium goals to which is attached a timeframe of 2015 for attainment]. *It also requires the implementation process to observe human rights standards, principles and values.* If free primary education does not respect the child's dignity, it is not congruent with human rights law (emphasis added).[53]

This book presents evidence and argument that in fact the attempted implementation of the right to basic education in at least several CAFS not yet in the post-conflict stage (such as Afghanistan) does indeed, in many instances, fail to respect the children's dignity or observe human rights standards, principles and values. This by employing a process that significantly endangers the children's physical security; namely sending children to school in various locales within UN- defined insecure 'high risk' provinces despite the poor; at times even extremely poor security for education and more generally. In order to maintain donor dollars from the World Bank and various other sources, the CAFS must show progress in development and one indicia of this is alleged progress toward universal primary education; a key UN millennium development goal.[54] There is then in CAFS, it would appear, a push to increase primary school enrollment in every part of the State notwithstanding the security risks; an approach apparently not challenged and, in practice, even supported by the international humanitarian aid community. This is not to suggest that international human rights/humanitarian aid organizations such as UNICEF and NGOs do not advocate for better school security. Rather, it is to suggest that these national and international bodies are prepared to open schools (and re-open them after a terror attack) in locales where school security is poor and the risk of attack high.

Western donor countries, national and international NGOs and various UN organs (such as UNICEF and UNESCO), the World Bank etc. most often advocate or adopt an approach to humanitarian education aid in CAFS where, in effect, the child's education rights are treated as if they supersede the child's security rights. This may not, however, be evident given the 'rights-talk' of these diverse donors or

[53]Beeckman (2004), p. 76.

[54]Johnson (2010), p. 195.

interveners (to be explored in the next chapter). NGOs encouraging and facilitating school attendance notwithstanding any security concerns are *not* then employing a 'rights-based' education strategy contrary to any protestations to the contrary. They are arguably functioning as if a "run-away train" where, in practice, reaching for the United Nation's MDG relating to achieving universal primary education for all States, including CAFS, has, in practice, become the goal in and of itself no matter the numbers of child casualties along the way due to terror attacks on education. In places such as Afghanistan there is a huge untapped reservoir of out-of-school primary school-aged children who, if they can be enticed to school (despite the considerable security risks that exist in various high-risk provinces and especially certain locales within those provinces) can take the place of those who will not be returning to class subsequent to a terror attack on their school or on the children as they made their way to or from school. Thus, terror attacks on education become a problem from this distorted perspective in that they interfere with the State and NGO bureaucratic interest in achievement of the MDG relating to education (to which many millions of donor dollars are linked) and ***not*** due to their devastating impact on the children's physical and psychological well-being per se. This subtle message is tacit, for instance, in the following UNESCO statement:

> *The international community has made a commitment to achieving Education for All (EFA) goals by 2015; wherever they occur, attacks on education threaten the realization of those goals.* UNESCO, tasked with the global coordination of EFA, has a mandate to promote full and equal opportunities for education for all, and this includes those whose access to education is threatened or prevented by targeted violence (emphasis added).[55]

The problem is then that there has been and is an ongoing concerted effort of the international humanitarian education aid interveners in States such as Afghanistan that are still undergoing conflict to increase enrollment in basic education despite inadequate security for all types of schools (government sponsored, NGO sponsored community-based schools, and private schools); and for the schoolchildren, teachers and other school staff associated with the schools as well as for humanitarian education aid workers.

References

Beeckman K (2004) Measuring the implementation of the right to education: educational *versus* human rights indicators. Int J Children's Rights 12:71–84

Chowdhury A, Krebs RR (2010) Talking about terror: counter-terrorist campaigns and the logic of representation. Eur J Int Relat 16:125–150

De Torrente N (2004) Humanitarian action under attack: reflections on the Iraq war. Harv Hum Rights J 17:1–29

Dryden-Petersen S (2010) Barriers to accessing primary education in conflict-affected fragile states: literature review. A report written on behalf of International Save the Children Alliance http://www.savethechildren.org.uk/en/docs/Barriers_to_access_Literature_Review_Final.pdf. Accessed 18 May 2010

[55]UNESCO (2010), p. vii.

Glad M (2009) Knowledge on fire: attacks on education in Afghanistan; risks and measures for successful mitigation. A study initiated and funded by the World Bank and carried out by CARE International in Afghanistan on behalf of the World Bank and the Afghan Ministry of Education. http://care.ca/ckfinder/userfiles/files/Knowledge_on_fire-attacks_%20schools.pdf. Accessed 18 May 2010

Grover SC (2004) Secondary education as a universal human right. Educ Law 16:21–30

Human Rights Watch (2006) Lessons in terror: attacks on education in Afghanistan, vol 18, no 6 (C). www.hrw.org/reports/2006/afghanistan0706/index.htm. Accessed 18 May 2010

INEE (Inter-agency Network for Education in Emergencies) (2010) Draft guidance notes on teaching and learning for emergencies, early recovery and preparedness (updated as of 10 May 2010) (New York City: INNE)

Johnson R (2010) The child's rights to an education: consensus-minus-one? Int J Hum Rights 18:185–216

O'Brien P (2004) Politicized humanitarianism: a response to Nicholas de Torrente. Harv Hum Rights J 17:31–39

O'Malley B (2010) Education under attack. A report commissioned by Mark Richmond, Director, Division for the Coordination of United Nations Priorities in Education, Education Sector, UNESCO. http://unesdoc.unesco.org/images/0018/001868/186809e.pdf. Accessed 26 Apr 2010

Pruce JR (2010) Book review of Neil Stammer's human rights and social movements. J Hum Rights 9:16–120

Stammers N (2009) Human rights and social movements. Pluto, London

UNESCO (2010) Protecting education from attack: a state-of-the-art review. UNESCO report in partnership with the Office of Her Highness Sheikha Mozah Bint Nasser Al-Missned of Qatar, UNESCO Special Envoy for Basic and Higher Educationat. http://unesdoc.unesco.org/images/0018/001867/186732e.pdf. Accessed 2 Oct 2010

Chapter 4
Analysis of UN and NGO Rights Rhetoric in Addressing Terror Attacks on Education: The Implications for Schoolchildren's Security Interests

Let us turn now to a closer look at key reports by UNESCO, UNICEF, CARE and Human Rights Watch concerning attacks on schools, schoolchildren, education personnel and education aid workers in Afghanistan. The problem of terror directed at education in Afghanistan in many ways reflects what is happening in this respect in other conflict-affected States. The reports provide some insight into the scope of the organized systemic terror threat to schools globally and the inadequacies of the international community's response to the same. We will consider the valuable data provided in these reports, but also importantly some of the inadequacies of the discourse of the reports that mirrors in large part that adopted by the international community as a whole. Our meta-purpose then is to: (a) consider the propaganda value of the particular way in which the issue of terror attacks on education is framed by international humanitarian groups and certain organs of the U.N. in these reports and (b) to contemplate the implications for children's security interests of the use of children's schooling as a counter-terrorist propaganda tool.

4.1 Schoolchildren Exploited for Propaganda Purposes: Education Initiatives Framed as a Component in Counterinsurgency Strategy

Statement of President Karzai on the occasion of International Women's Day, 2006:

> If you stop sending your children to school because one school is set ablaze or a child is threatened, or if a teacher is martyred, then you make your enemy succeed and make yourself fail. . .*if a million times they [the children] are threatened, send your children back to school a million times. If a million times schools are torched, build them a million times so that this nation can be freed from fear and horror* (emphasis added).[1]

[1]Human Rights Watch (2006).

DOI 10.1007/978-3-642-17900-6_4, © Springer-Verlag Berlin Heidelberg 2011

The problem is, of course, that Afghanistan has not been "freed from fear and horror" and the children of Afghanistan and their teachers and other school personnel continue too often to pay in blood for attending at schools. They are, as has been previously here stated, serving first and foremost as propaganda tools in the counter-terrorist efforts against the Taliban and Al-Qaeda. The aforementioned high casualty rate for Afghan schoolchildren and teachers due to terrorist attack is a very direct measure of the lack of adequate security provided for schooling in Afghanistan. One wonders whether those high officials of the Afghan government, Western leaders and personnel from national and international aid organizations and international women's groups promoting gender equality in education and access to education generally would be willing to risk the lives of their own children by sending them to school in areas with high terror activity. The latter seems a reasonable question given that they urge this upon the poor and largely dispossessed of Afghanistan. It is more likely that the stirring words of President Karzai cited above and similar rhetoric would ring rather hollow were it their own children (namely the children of Afghan government officials, Western leaders and of personnel from national and international aid organizations and international women's groups) whose physical and psychological security were at stake in attending school in an ongoing armed conflict zone.

Human Rights Watch (hereafter HRW) in its 2006 report 'Lessons in Terror: Attacks on Education in Afghanistan'[2] cites President Karzai's March 2006 statement that 100, 000 children in Afghanistan who had gone to school in 2003 and 2004 no longer attended school in 2006 in part "because some two hundred schools that we built were torched or destroyed".[3] HRW reported that in fact President Karzai had underestimated the number of schools at that time no longer operational due to terror attacks; HRW pegging the number at closer to three hundred such schools.[4]

The frequency of terror attacks on schools in Afghanistan has only increased since President Karzai gave his speech in 2006. Already in 2006, HRW maintained that:

> The Afghan government and its international supporters have largely failed to provide adequate assistance to promote and protect the development of Afghanistan's education system. *Neither the Afghan government nor the international community have developed a strategy to end attacks on girls, teachers, and schools*; to keep schools open [i.e., without temporary or permanent closings of particular schools due to repeated terror attack]; or to make education accessible to insecure and rural areas. Such a strategy must include preventing attacks, monitoring attacks and their effects, and responding to attacks once they occur (emphasis added).[5]

[2]Human Rights Watch (2006).

[3]Agence France-Presse (2006), p. 31.

[4]Esfandiari (2006).

[5]Human Rights Watch (2006), p. 101.

The 2006 HRW report 'Lessons in Terror: Attacks on Education in Afghanistan'[6] makes reference to the propaganda value for the Afghan government of increased rates of schooling of Afghan children as an indicator of alleged progress in development and level of State stability. There is then an impetus, according to the HRW report, to downplay and underreport attacks on schools, schoolchildren and educators. This being the case lest the government be perceived at home and abroad as ineffectual in managing security and development and perhaps also based on a well-founded fear that donor monies for education and other development initiatives may be reduced or cut off:

> The resuscitation of the educational system after the fall of the Taliban [as a ruling entity] is one of the major successes of the present government and its international backers, and. . .is often touted as such. *But the lack of monitoring and the pressure to present a positive image about advances in education in Afghanistan have impeded accurate reporting on the impact of insecurity on education* (emphasis added).[7]
>
> *Human Rights Watch encountered a shared impression by the Afghan government, UNICEF, and some NGO education providers that reporting attacks and school closures could cause donors to cut-off much -needed funding.* This concern may well be valid but is not a justification for covering up the problem (emphasis added).[8]

The fact that the handling (by the Afghan government, national and international aid organizations and the U.N.) of the issue of attacks on education by terror groups in Afghanistan could in any way be impacted by considerations regarding donor funding of the Afghan education system is very troubling. Such a likelihood as appears to be suggested in the HRW 2006 report suggests strongly that the issue of terror attacks on schools, teachers and students as well as on education aid workers in Afghanistan is very much tied up with propaganda considerations. That propaganda objective then likely importantly contributes to the tendency to downplay, to some degree at least, the scope of the problem of attacks on education across the country (i.e., the frequency of such terror attacks on education, and the number of victims etc.):

> . . .there is currently no domestic or international institution in Afghanistan that has a full picture of the attacks on education that are taking place and their impact. Collecting and analyzing this information is necessary to understand the causes and extent of the problem. *Yet, even in areas where the government is present, it is reluctant to share or even gather, information that may indicate that schools are not operating properly. . .The [Afghan] Ministry of Education told Human Rights Watch that it does not monitor attacks on schools or their effects. . .* (emphasis added).[9]

HRW acknowledged some of the logistical problems in NGOs and the Afghan government gathering information regarding terror attacks on education i.e., the fact that the government is lacking in basic information on education to begin with (such as the exact numbers of teachers, students and schools in the country) and the

[6]Human Rights Watch (2006), p. 101.
[7]Human Rights Watch (2006), p. 102.
[8]Human Rights Watch (2006), p. 102.
[9]Human Rights Watch (2006), p. 103.

fact that local educational officials who could gather information on school attacks are often times themselves driven out of the area by the violence. However, the 2006 HRW report on attacks on education in Afghanistan maintains that the information is also deliberately being ignored or perhaps even suppressed to a degree where such data exists in even limited form:

> . . .the failure to officially monitor [terror attacks on education in Afghanistan] also reflects a conscious attempt to avoid bad news. . . Deputy Ministry [sic] Mohammad Sediq Patman told us. "We don't bring information [on security incidents] to the center because it will have a negative effect on our morale".[10]

The lack of reasonably accurate statistics and other particulars regarding attacks on education in Afghanistan as elsewhere is still a problem in 2010:

> There remain serious challenges to collecting accurate data and information nationally and providing accurate global data and analysis of attacks on education. *Currently, no global database of attacks on education exists, nor are there reliable baselines in most contexts. This makes it impossible to provide a comprehensive assessment of the growth or reduction in the number of incidents or the actual numbers of victims or incidents* (emphasis added).[11]

Attacks on schools, it seems, are just beginning to be regarded as a distinct category of terror attack carried out with specific underlying objectives and devastating short and long term impacts for the direct and indirect victims as well as for the population as a whole. This emergent understanding of attacks on education as a key issue in its own right deserving of in-depth study and attention is reflected, for instance, in the commentary on an April 24, 2010 gas poisoning attack on a girl's school in Konduz Afghanistan by the spokesman for the President. That spokesman alluded to the deliberate nature of the attack and its terroristic nature:

> Poisoning schoolgirls is a horrific act; *in some ways it is a terror attack. . .*Whoever is trying to prevent kids from going to school is an enemy of Afghanistan, *and it is not different from any other terrorist act* (emphasis added).[12]

At the same time, it is the case that the phenomenon of terror attacks on education as a separate and distinct issue continues to receive relatively little attention in the public media both nationally and internationally, and spotty coverage rarely if ever with any in-depth analysis by independent investigative journalists. The topic of attacks on education in fact is only recently garnering some focused attention by the international aid community with the major outcome to date essentially being some of the key NGO and UN reports here discussed. The 2010 UNESCO report regarding terror attacks on education makes the claim that there has been "a mushrooming of the number of newspapers and particularly news websites reporting on the subject".[13] What constitutes "mushrooming" in the number of media outlets covering these stories is unclear given the lack of reference

---

[10]Human Rights Watch (2006), p. 103.

[11]O'Malley (2010), p. 54.

[12]Sahim (2010).

[13]O'Malley (2010), p. 54.

to any previous baseline figure in that regard in the UNESCO report or information on how frequently such news is reported by any particular outlet or how consistently the media covers any or all significant terror attacks on education in any particular country. It is this author's impression that print, online and radio news reports on the issue of terror attacks on education are exceedingly brief. These generally contain only bare facts as to estimated numbers of casualties and information on which group is suspected of being the perpetrator or has claimed responsibility with the inclusion also, at times, of some inspiring words from government officials promising to persist in their education initiatives and sometimes also from survivors of the attack vowing to return to school.

The print, and online news media, it seems, rarely if ever delve deeply, if at all, into the issue of the lack of adequate security for many schools in Afghanistan and other conflict zones with high levels of terror activity. A couple of fairly recent typical examples the author picked at random from 2009 and 2010 online news reports (Reuters) on terror attacks on education in Afghanistan are excerpted below. These news reports fail, for instance, to question why the international community has not made increased security for schools in Afghanistan and for Afghan schoolchildren and teachers on their way to and from school a priority. Neither do the news reports question the wisdom of school attendance in school buildings or alternate education sites (i.e., open air sites) that are at high risk of terror attack. Further, the news media reporting on attacks on education in Afghanistan and in other conflict-affected States generally avoid the issue of the violation of children's right to life and security that is potentially implicated in the government and international community's failure to provide adequate security to schoolchildren while simultaneously encouraging and facilitating the children's attendance at schools which are known to be highly vulnerable to a likely terror attack. Consider in this regard the typical news report cited below regarding recent terror attacks on education in Afghanistan specifically targeting girls' schools:

4.1.1 Excerpts of Typical News Reports Regarding Attacks on Girls' Education in Afghanistan

Reuters: Afghan girls hit again by suspected gas attack
May 11 2010
KABUL (Reuters) - Dozens of schoolgirls in Afghanistan were admitted to hospital on Tuesday after two suspected poisonous gas attacks on schools... the latest in a spate of similar incidents. Thirty schoolgirls in the northern city of Kunduz and six in Kabul were admitted to hospital,...The attacks are the latest in a string of incidents at girls' schools involving an airborne substance which officials say could be poisonous gas... One schoolgirl, a 15-year old called Samira, was on gate duty shortly before her classmates were taken ill. "I smelled something very sweet and when I went and told my teachers about it they said it was not a big incident but later on I saw girls falling down and collapsing and vomiting so we called the police", she said. Samira said she saw three men standing outside the school shortly before smelling the gas... It is not clear who is responsible for the attacks. In the

past officials have blamed the Taliban but the Islamist group has denied involvement and condemned the possible attacks. The Taliban banned education for girls when they ruled Afghanistan from 1996 to 2001, and in many rural areas where the Taliban hold sway, girls' schools remain closed, teachers have been threatened and some girls have been attacked with acid.[14]

It is interesting to note that Reuters reports in the above online news story that the Taliban denied responsibility for the May 2010 suspected gas poisoning attacks on girls' schools in various Afghan locales. It may be that the Taliban are becoming ever more sophisticated in using terror against education (attacks on schools, school-related facilities as well as direct attacks on schoolchildren, teachers and other school related personnel such as security guards) as a propaganda tool and in manipulating and managing the media on this issue. That is, rather than the Taliban claiming direct responsibility for the attacks, or suggesting that the attacks are inspired by the Taliban mission to rid Afghanistan of all vestiges of the so-called Western "infidel" imprint (the latter including then education for females even young girls); the Taliban denied direct or indirect responsibility for the gas poisonings of girl schoolchildren. The organized terror group-the Taliban- even went so far, according to the Reuter's news report cited above, to condemn the attack on the girl schoolchildren. This, of course, is an adept propaganda move in that the focus is shifted by the Taliban via this media savvy strategy to the government's inability to secure the schools. At the same time, the source of the terror threat is rendered in the reporting as being *allegedly* less than clear, more amorphous and, hence, perceived as even more difficult to counter and, therefore, more terrifying. The populace and the government all the while most often suspect, and rightfully so, that the Taliban have *not* in fact suddenly developed a new found favourable attitude toward gender equity in schooling nor a distaste for victimizing children and other civilians via targeted terror attacks on education; but are instead directly responsible for the recent attacks on the girl schoolchildren:

Afghan Girls Ill in Third School Poisoning
12 May, 2010

Afta Bachi, Afghanistan (Reuters) - Five young girls slipped briefly into comas and nearly 100 were taken to hospital after a gas attack on their school on Tuesday, the third in a series of such incidents north of Kabul, Afghan officials said. *The early morning mass-poisoning at Qazaaq school was likely the work of Taliban sympathizers hostile to girls' education, the head of security for Kapisa province told Reuters...*

"There was a very bad smell in my classroom this morning and the teacher immediately told us to evacuate. . .When I opened my eyes we were in hospital", said 12 year-old Leda. "I am so sad, what went wrong with our school? I want to study", the sixth-grader said from her hospital bed in a ward of around 20 pale girls, most with drips in their arms. "We knew about the incident in Charikar, but we didn't think such incidents would happen in our school. Right now we are very scared to continue with our education, to learn", said Aara Gul, 15, waiting for medication.

[14]Shalizi and Hamed (2010).

> EDUCATION UNDER ATTACK
>
> ..."Whoever has done this is against peace and security and improvement for women in the country. Surely it will have a negative impact on education, but we will never close the doors of schools for girls", said health chief Rahim...
>
> Attacks on girls' schools have increased in the past year, particularly in the Taliban's eastern and southern heartlands, as an insurgency has gathered strength (emphasis added).[15]

Note in the above report that the girl child victim expresses the opinion that all of the girls at her school fear continuing with their education and communicates her astonishment that *their* school was successfully targeted for a terror attack. At the same time, the official interviewed for the same news piece makes it clear that the girls' schools will remain open notwithstanding the high risk of terror attacks saying: "Surely it [the terror attack] will have a negative impact on education, but we will never close the doors of schools for girls". This common reaffirmation in international news reports of the stated intention of Afghan education and other government officials to continue with school operation and of parents to continue to send their children to school despite systemic terror attacks on schools is reflected also in the following online news report from 2009 below regarding acid attacks on girl schoolchildren Afghanistan. The 2009 report cited below thus provides a typical example of the inclusion in such news reports of the message that Afghan parents, the government and the international community all fully endorse the plan of children continuing to go to school despite the high risk of death or grievous injury resulting from a high probability of repeated terror attacks on schools in various regions of Afghanistan and the lack of adequate security for the schools. That message, Afghan children and parents defying terror, it would seem, is perceived to have particular value as counterterrorist propaganda whether or not it fully accords with reality (i.e., most if not all children attending school after a terror attack do so with much fear and trepidation and many parents choose not to send their children back to school after such an attack though some are coaxed to reconsider and do eventually have them return to school after a time). The 2009 online news story (here excerpted) reads as follows:

New York Times: Afghan Girls, Scarred by Acid, Defy Terror, Embracing School (14 January, 2009)

> KANDAHAR, Afghanistan —...if the acid attack against Shamsia and 14 others — students and teachers — was meant to terrorize the girls into staying home, it appears to have completely failed. Today, nearly all of the wounded girls are back at the Mirwais School for Girls... Perhaps even more remarkable, nearly every other female student in this deeply conservative community has returned as well — about 1,300 in all.
>
> *"My parents told me to keep coming to school even if I am killed*", said Shamsia, 17, in a moment after class. ... *Building new schools and ensuring that children — and especially girls — attend has been one of the main objectives of the government and the nations that have contributed to Afghanistan's reconstruction. ...Yet at the same time... the Taliban have made schools one of their special targets...* But exactly who was behind the acid attack is a mystery. The Taliban denied any part in it. ...One thing is certain: in the months before the attack, the Taliban had moved into the Mirwais area and the rest of Kandahar's outskirts. As they did, posters began appearing in local mosques. "Don't Let Your

[15] Salahuddin and Shalizi (2010).

> Daughters Go to School", one of them said. In the days after the attack, the Mirwais School for Girls stood empty; none of the parents would let their daughters venture outside. . . .*The governor promised more police officers, a footbridge across a busy nearby road and, most important, a bus. Mr. Qadari [the school's headmaster] . . . told the parents that there was no longer any reason to hold their daughters back. "I told them, if you don't send your daughters to school, then the enemy wins", Mr. Qadari said. "I told them not to give in to darkness. Education is the way to improve our society"*. The adults of Mirwais did not need much persuading. *Neither the bus nor the police nor the bridge has materialized, but the girls started showing up anyway.* Only a couple of dozen girls regularly miss school now; three of them are girls who had been injured in the attack (emphasis added).[16]

The 2009 news report immediately above thus is typical in offering no challenge whatsoever (i.e., from any mental health service provider to Afghan families in the terror zone, NGO, education official or other relevant source) to the questionable presumption that the vast majority of Afghan families in fact endorse their children risking their lives to attend school. The story claims that the parents "did not need much persuading" to send their daughters back to school after the terror attack. However, at the same time, the story reveals that the issue of sending the girls to school despite the repeated terror attacks on schools and schoolchildren in the region was framed as one of patriotism by the school headmaster in speaking to parents at a meeting he had called where hundreds of parents were said to have attended. Further, the governor of the region also spoke to the parents promising better security in the form of police patrols and a bus to transport the girls to and from school to afford them better protection; none of which actually materialized according to the same news report. The question thus arises whether these parents were in fact intimidated as a result of: (a) the suggestion by officials that not sending the girls to school was a way of assisting the enemy, and (b) the call by high local and regional government officials to have their daughters return to school. Chilling is the comment of one of the girls who had been most seriously injured by the acid attack that: "My parents told me to keep coming to school even if I am killed".[17] It seems highly unlikely that these parents went from the dread of sending their daughters to school based on the very real fear of another vicious terror attack on their children to doing so based on simple invocations to what essentially amounts to the message of "get with the program". Even if this were the case, the fact that the parents continued to send the girls to school even though no added security had been provided, makes it is more likely that the parents felt pressured to do so lest they be viewed by those in authority as disloyal to the State. The fact that basic schooling to the intermediate level is compulsory in Afghanistan (as per the Afghan constitution adopted in 2004) may also have played some indeterminate role in the parents sending the girls back to school despite the parents' and children's fears of another terror attack targeting the school and the children.

The actual numbers of school closings in any particular area of Afghanistan following terror attacks on or near the schools in that particular region of the

[16]Filkins (2009).

[17]Filkins (2009).

country suggest that fear among parents is rampant, as is to be expected, following a terror attack. Those attacks have been directed against unoccupied school buildings (i.e., arson, bombing etc.), on schools with the schoolchildren or teachers in the building and/or on the children or teachers on their way to or from school and/or on education aid workers. The majority of school closings after terror attacks on education are in fact related to the parents keeping the children home for fear regarding their children's security. That fact is not consistently mentioned in the news reporting on such incidents as more often the stress is placed on those children who return to school (as in the news stories cited above) to once again face the risk of a targeted terror attack at school:

> More than three hundred schools have been burned or, for the major part, have been shut down. . .*Most of the schools have been closed because of the fear of attacks by Taliban and Al-Qaeda forces,* ***and, due to the insecurity that the people in the region [feel], parents are refusing to send their kids to school*** (emphasis added)[18]

It would appear that Afghan parents are often pressured to send their children to school by school and government officials as a supposed act of patriotism despite the apparent lack of adequate school security in many; perhaps even most instances. This pressure tactic is referred to in uncritical terms in the aforementioned 2009 news report on the acid attack against female schoolchildren as is typical. The news item frames the parents' sending their daughters back to school after the acid attack as defiance in the face of terrorism. The news item thus implicitly frames sending the children back to school, despite the lack of security, as something admirable no matter the price in blood that the children may have to pay for their parent's decision (under what appears to be psychological pressure) to return them to school despite terrorists specifically targeting schools for attack:

> In the days after the attack, the Mirwais School for Girls stood empty; none of the parents would let their daughters venture outside. That is when the headmaster, Mahmood Qadari, got to work. After four days of staring at empty classrooms, Mr. Qadari called a meeting of the parents. *Hundreds came to the school — fathers and mothers — and Mr. Qadari* ***implored them*** *to let their daughters return* (emphasis added).[19]

It is most ironic and even sad that it is only now; in the midst of a terror campaign by Al-Qaeda and the Taliban that especially favours targeting symbolic and emotive targets such as schools, that there is such a great impetus by the West, by the national and local government in the conflict regions and by national and international NGOs to educate the populace including girls. There were most certainly education initiatives in Afghanistan by the UN and international NGOs, and a certain level of funding for the same provided by the international community after the end of Taliban rule in Afghanistan in 2001. However, there was not such a high level of urgency regarding the need to educate the populace in Afghanistan as after 9/11 and as in the so-called 'war on terror' period still ongoing. In this regard,

---

[18]Statement of Mr. Nader Nadery of the Afghan Independent Human Rights Commission, February 2006 cited in Human Rights Watch (2006), p. 31.

[19]Filkins (2009).

note that the 2009 aforementioned NY Times story regarding the acid attack on the Afghan school girls states that many of the students at the elementary school are in their late teens and early twenties. This reflects the new emphasis on education as part of the counter-terrorism effort for previously excluded individuals.

There are then, this author contends, significant biases embedded in the print and online news coverage of terror attacks on education in Afghanistan (and in the reporting of such attacks in other conflict-affected States). These biases lead to the framing of the parent sending the child back to school despite the security risk as hero. Such a slant feeds well into counterterrorism propaganda by focusing on the alleged resilience of the populace in the face of terror. At the same time, there appears to be rather sparse coverage generally on the major national and international television networks and in the print and online news outlets pertaining to terror attacks on schools and schoolchildren in conflict-affected fragile States (CAFS) such as Afghanistan. The scarcity of information on the topic of attacks on education by organized terror groups in comparison to the frequency and depth of coverage (i.e., televised coverage) regarding terror attacks on humanitarian installations or vehicles or on non-education related civilian buildings and personnel is noteworthy. It has major implications for the public's "take" on the issue nationally and internationally i.e., the public's perception of: (a) whether terror attacks on schools, students and educators is a significant and pressing issue in their State and/or internationally; (b) whether schooling in conflict zones with high terror activity is being handled appropriately by the national government and the international community as to the security of school buildings, and of students and teachers ; (c) whether the purported significant progress in basic education of schoolchildren in regions with high levels of terror activity is or is not an important vehicle for government propaganda that too often takes priority over the actual security interests of the schoolchildren. The news media, as well as reports by international NGOs and the UN, thus importantly shape the national and the international community's perception as to whether or not schoolchildren's security interests are being significantly compromised in the interest of counter-terrorism propaganda. While there is a de-emphasis on reporting terror attacks on education in Afghanistan and in other CAFS, there is a focus instead on reporting any progress in the education of schoolchildren, especially girls (that progress most often not being weighed against the price in terms of child casualties of terror attacks on education). That progress is, furthermore, held out to be a prime marker of purported success in re-stabilizing the conflict-affected country in question, in moving the State toward democraticization and in countering terrorism.

It seems most telling that according to the 2006 Human Rights Watch (HRW) report "Lessons in Terror" regarding attacks on education in Afghanistan; the World Bank and USAID (the two largest international donors in Afghanistan) do *not* monitor attacks on schools; and USAID only tracks attacks on its own education projects. The essential point here is that aside from any logistical issues (which certainly exist in respect of trying to monitor school attacks and attacks on education in all its forms in Afghanistan), there is an indisputable continuing lack of prioritizing of the need to provide adequate security to students and teachers. There is unlikely to be an improvement in the monitoring of terror attacks on schools and on education generally in Afghanistan, it is suggested, as long as there continues to be a lack of resources devoted by the national government (with assistance from the international community) to enhanced security for education.

It appears that schoolchildren in Afghanistan and other terror-plagued regions are too often learning that adults cannot be trusted to ensure their (the children's) safety even when promised. Theirs then is not uncommonly an education on the subject of fear and suffering as they become the victims of terror attacks at school or on the way to or from school. It would seem that the international community is, in practice, complicit with national and local governments in downplaying or sometimes even suppressing information regarding the full scope and nature of terror attacks on education in conflict-affected fragile States. To date, there has been largely a reliance on scattered, non-systematic, unofficial reports from the field and anecdotal case reports regarding such attacks, and no concerted cooperative effort involving local, national and international partners directed toward school protection and security for education generally. The aforementioned 2006 HRW report in fact stated that Human Rights Watch had received numerous complaints about the alleged unwillingness of the Afghan National Police to investigate or at times even respond to terror attacks on schools.[20] The U.N. High Commissioner for Human Rights Watch reported in March 2006 that the National Afghan police maintained that they had little access to insecure areas and a lack of resources to respond adequately to school attacks and that this had led to "reinforcing an environment of impunity and a climate of fear..."[21]

To date, no effective organized strategy has been implemented for the protection of schools in Afghanistan (a situation that is duplicated in various other regions that have also been subjected to systemic terror activity including attacks on education; some of which we will examine). Hence, the security situation for Afghan schools has improved little since the 2006 HRW report as is evident from the fact, for instance, that the UNESCO 2010 report on the topic of attacks on education: (a) noted a "dramatic intensification" of attacks on education in Afghanistan (and a number of other countries) since 2004 and (b) referred to the as yet unfulfilled need for co-ordinated school protection efforts spearheaded by various levels of the State government together with the international community and NGOs and the need for international funding for these protection of education efforts (i.e., protecting schools from attack, relocating threatened students, and teachers etc.):

> The international community, UN Agencies and NGOs should work with governments of conflict-affected states ... to develop...
>
> -mechanisms to protect threatened students, teachers ... education support staff... education officials and education aid workers ...and *assist them in relocating internally or externally where appropriate*

[20]Human Rights Watch (2006).

[21]Statement of the U.N. High Commissioner for Human Rights Watch, cited in Human Rights Watch (2006), p. 105.

-ways to rapidly *reconstruct, repair and resupply attacked educational institutions* in order to guarantee a zero tolerance towards violations of the right to education

-ways to *support the continuation of education in alterative places or via alterative methods and media in areas under attack*

The international community should consider providing funding to help capacity-building for local protection of education[22]

What is especially disturbing is that it appears that children in Afghanistan and certain other regions plagued by systemic terrorism are in fact often not being educated in safe alternative venues when their schools have been targeted for attack and have become non-operational. Indeed, children in Afghanistan have been, for example, moved to open air tents for their schooling when their school building has been destroyed or badly damaged by arson or bombing only then to have been attacked in the tents. ("...UNICEF ...policy is to provide tents and to replace damaged textbooks and furniture within five days" though UNICEF may not always be aware of each and every attack).[23]

The above quote from the UNESCO 2010 report on attacks on education reveals the inconsistency in the thinking on the issue of protection of schoolchildren and teachers in conflict-affected regions: On the one hand, the UNESCO 2010 report suggests the possibility of relocating students and teachers who have been threatened (i.e., as when the Taliban write 'night letters' to specific teachers or to the community with a warning to cease and desist the education of children, especially girls, in schools they view as an extension of the Western political-military agenda). The UNESCO report further suggests relocating to alternative sites if the school is located "in areas under attack".[24] At the same time, the UNESCO 2010 report essentially implicitly urges that schoolchildren continue attending at schools despite those schools being at a continued high risk of repeated terror attack. This the report does by suggesting that *after* a terrorist attack, the schools simply be reconstructed, repaired and resupplied and that things carry on as before the attack. This, as if doing so would somehow constitute a display of "zero tolerance towards violations of the right to education".[25]

The UNESCO report also suggests that "...where there is *a pattern* of attacks on or abduction of schoolboys or schoolgirls on the way to or from school... governments should find ways to provide safe transport of students to and from school".[26] The latter suggestion seems to disregard the reality that even U.S. and allied military convoys are subject to terror attacks and roadside explosives in Afghanistan. The same would be true for any mode of transportation provided to transport the schoolchildren to and from school where there have been repeated direct terror attacks on the children in the past directed to preventing them from attending

[22]O'Malley (2010).

[23]Human Rights Watch (2006), p. 106.

[24]Human Rights Watch (2006), p. 170.

[25]Human Rights Watch (2006), p. 170.

[26]Human Rights Watch (2006), p. 170.

school. It is unlikely, in any case, given the present level of inadequate financial commitment to school protection by the international community in Afghanistan and many other conflict zones, that most schoolchildren would have adequate armed protection on the way to and from school. One is reminded of the bus for school transport that was promised after the acid attacks against girls being schooled in the outskirts of Kandahar region (see the New York Times news item above: "Afghan Girls, Scarred by Acid, Defy Terror, Embracing School" (14 January, 2009)) and the fact that even that modicum of protection did not materialize after such a spate of vicious terror attacks against girl schoolchildren in the area while walking to school.[27]

It is quite unclear under what international humanitarian or human rights law or moral theory it is that schoolchildren should be expected to risk their lives in order to attend school (as is the expectation in Afghanistan and other conflict-affected States plagued by terror targeting education as well as other civilian objectives). In taking these risks, the children essentially become 'foot soldiers' in the 'war on terror' for the national government and the West. This by contributing to the counter-terrorist propaganda regarding the significant progress allegedly being made in re-stabilizing the country (this is not at all to deny that some progress has been made). These unwitting 'foot soldiers' in this propaganda war are thus being exploited by both sides in the war on terror for this propaganda purpose.

The 'right to education' does not contemplate children having to sacrifice their lives or sustain mental and physical injury to send a counter-terrorist so-called "zero-tolerance" propaganda message to the Taliban or to any other terrorist group. On the contrary, 'the right to education' as envisioned under the UN Convention on the Child,[28] for instance, is one of education in the context of a peaceful and supportive environment. The problem is, of course, that terror attacks on schools in Afghanistan are widespread in many regions throughout the country and though the attacks are foreseeable; their precise timing is unpredictable. Further, there is at present still a lack of funding (as the UNESCO report acknowledges) and perhaps even political will to support adequate protection for schools in regions being subjected to systemic terror attack. Hence, 'safe' zones for schools in Afghanistan may often as not at present be more fiction than reality as there is commonly no possibility of relocation of students and teachers to a truly safe alternate education venue. Further complicating the issue is the fact that schools in previously relatively secure regions can quickly become insecure and subject to attack (i.e., the 2006 HRW report cited terror attacks on previously secure schools in Kandahar city and Northern Afghan provinces such as Balkh).[29]

---

[27]Filkins (2009).

[28]Convention on the Rights of the Child (entered into force 2 September 1990) http://www2.ohchr.org/english/law/crc.htm (accessed 22 May 2010).

[29]Human Rights Watch (2006), p. 4.

4.1.2 International Aid Organizations and the Promotion of Schooling Across Both Secure and Insecure Zones in Conflict-Affected States

It is generally agreed that the international community did not provide Afghanistan with the necessary resources and assistance for security and re-construction soon after the fall of the Taliban rule and that became blatantly obvious as time progressed. What is occurring in more recent times since the fall of the Taliban and post 9/11, however, is that the international community has created and marketed something of a communal 'folie' or delusion. That delusion is that security is improved enough in most regions of the country that schoolchildren can now generally attend school safely. Clearly the high number and increasing number of school attacks in Afghanistan since 2004 and their occurrence in various regions in different provinces across the country suggests otherwise i.e., HRW reported 204 attacks on teachers, students and schools in Afghanistan from January 2005 to 21 June, 2006 as well as 17 assassinations of teachers and education officials in 2005 and 2006[30] and that "[international and national] forces had failed to provide the necessary security environment".[31]

Compounding further the lack of security for schools in Afghanistan is the reluctance of many aid organizations in Afghanistan to rely sufficiently or at all on Provincial Reconstruction Teams (PRTs are military units ranging in size from 80 to 300 personnel that include small numbers of civilians with experience in development work and/or diplomacy who work alongside the military unit on humanitarian projects with the intention being to win the popular support of the civilians in the area).[32] As previously discussed, international aid organizations are often reticent to work with PTRs fearing the actual or perceived militarization of their aid work:

> When military forces provide assistance to a civilian population during conflict, it is not for humanitarian purposes, but, rather, to further policies of their national governments, *provide force protection*, and meet their international legal obligations... (emphasis added)[33]

One could argue, however, that operating schools in insecure zones (i.e., UNICEF getting children into tents for schooling as soon as possible after a school attack in what is still a highly insecure area) is not in any sense a pure humanitarian mission any more than is the mission of the PTRs (i.e., PTRs providing security for aid and development projects thus combining humanitarian and more militaristic objectives relating to gaining popular support locally for the coalition war effort). The proposition advanced here is that international aid organizations supporting the

[30]Human Rights Watch (2006), p. 4.

[31]Human Rights Watch (2006), p. 106.

[32]Human Rights Watch (2006), p. 109.

[33]Dziedzic cited in Human Rights Watch (2006), p. 111.

operation of schools in insecure areas subject to the high probability of terror attacks compromises the most fundamental of all rights, the right to life and to physical and psychological security. It would appear then that international aid organizations and UN agencies have, in part at least, a bureaucratic agenda with a momentum of its own when it comes to education in regions plagued by conflict and systemic terror attacks. That agenda, one limited ostensibly to furthering the right to education, is generally viewed uncritically by the international community; stamped as it is with the 'good housekeeping seal' of political correctness. However, arguably part of the motivation of aid organizations in operating schools in particular zones *despite the security risks* appears to be one of self-interest in agency preservation. That argument is not lacking in credibility given that: (a) education projects receive huge international donor support; (b) such projects provide a ready raison d'être for the organization as well as (c) providing visible and tangible aid and development work that most in the international community regard as worthwhile in and of itself notwithstanding the security risks for schoolchildren and teachers attending at schools facing a high risk of an attack or repeated targeted terror attack.

4.2 Challenging the Legitimacy of School Attendance and Greater Access to Education as Indicia of Level of Overall Security in States Currently Immersed in the 'War on Terror'

The HRW 2006 report points out that systemic terror attacks on schools, schoolchildren, teachers and school allied staff fall into various categories of international crime under international humanitarian law:

> Attacks by the Taliban and other groups on students, teachers, and schools are not just criminal offenses. They are human rights abuses that infringe upon the right to freedom of education. *When committed as part of the ongoing armed conflict in Afghanistan, these attacks are serious violations of international humanitarian law, which are war crimes, as are acts and threats of violence with the primary purpose of spreading terror among the civilian population* (emphasis added).[34]

Thus, HRW in its 2006 report importantly implicitly acknowledges that children in Afghanistan are being sent to school in unsecured areas (with a resultant widespread high and increasing number of violations of international humanitarian law relating to organized terror attacks on education by the Taliban and other anti-government insurgent groups). Security for students, school teachers, allied staff and education aid workers then is grossly lacking in Afghanistan. Nevertheless, Human Rights Watch makes the following foundational and, on the view here,

[34]Human Rights Watch (2006), p. 112.

untenable recommendation in its 2006 "Lessons in Terror: Attacks on Education" report:

> Human Rights Watch urges that access to education be used as a key benchmark to measure the success of Afghan and international efforts to bring security to Afghanistan.[35]

Essentially then HRW is urging that schoolchildren be used as the proverbial "canaries in the coal mine". If the birds (canaries) die, then this indicates there are toxic fumes in the mine harmful to miners and the mine is not safe to enter. The implication is that the birds are expendable, the miners are not. Here, it appears it is the schoolchildren being treated by the national government and international community as if they were expendable vehicles for testing the overall level of security in the State. This as there appears to be a willingness to risk child deaths and grievous injury amongst schoolchildren compelled to attend schools despite the high risk of terror attack on these education sites and routes to these sites located in unsecured areas within the conflict-affected State.

Using education as an alleged key benchmark for improvements in security in Afghanistan translates into using as indicia of security, for instance, the number of schoolchildren attending school as well as the number of teachers teaching. This has led all too often to these children attending school despite an abysmal security situation and the high risk of a terror attack on the school or on the schoolchildren as they go to and from school. This heightened school attendance, opening of new schools and repair of damaged schools in hot terror zones in Afghanistan is importantly incentivized by the desire of the Afghan government and its international allies in the 'war on terror' to demonstrate to the international community that progress is being made in suppressing and eliminating the Taliban, other insurgents and the additional criminal element all responsible for undermining the security situation in Afghanistan. It is clear that whatever progress is being made toward re-stabilizing the country is largely a function of the huge financial investment of the donor countries as well as their investment of the blood of their sons and daughters fighting in the armed forces against the Taliban, Al-Qaeda and other opposition elements in Afghanistan.

It would appear that the urgency with which new schools are being built and damaged schools repaired despite a lack of adequate of security in many regions of Afghanistan may have more to do with the propaganda value of increased school attendance as an alleged sign of substantive progress in the 'war on terror'. The latter factor then being operative as opposed to any purely humanitarian interest in the education and the future well-being of the schoolchildren involved. In a sense, the children being sent to school at the behest of their parents, national government and international community in hot terror zones around the globe (i.e., despite the high probability of being victimized by a terror attack given the lack of adequate security) are essentially too often on what turns out to be *in effect* a suicide mission. That mission is one intended to spread the propaganda message that school

[35]Human Rights Watch (2006), p. 117.

attendance numbers allegedly are not being greatly adversely affected by the terror attacks on schools, school routes and directly on teachers and education personnel. The objective is to create the impression, to the degree possible, that there is some return to normal daily life in a reasonably secure environment thus countering the propaganda spun out by the Taliban and Al-Qaeda that the Afghan government and its Western allies are allegedly being defeated.

Thus, while it is the case that organized terror groups internationally are increasingly abducting children for use as suicide bombers,[36] the West and its allies in the propaganda 'war on terror' utilize their own unique version of what, in effect, may become a child suicide mission. The latter occurs then when children are sent to school in an active conflict zone infiltrated by terrorists despite there being inadequate security for the children at school or on the way to and from school with the result that certain of these children, as highly foreseeable, lose their lives or are gravely injured by a terror attack (all of which continues to this date).

This author argues in contradistinction to the 2006 HRW report that the benchmark for improvements in security in Afghanistan and other States currently undergoing conflict should be a direct measure such as, but not limited to: (a) reductions in the frequency of terror attacks and in the numbers of civilians killed or injured by terrorists, insurgents and other criminal elements; (b) the success rate in capturing and holding to account with due process perpetrators of the terror attacks and (c) a reduction in loss of life and injury to civilians as so-called 'collateral damage'. The aforementioned are the types of benchmarks of the security situation that are properly utilized as opposed to the number of schools opened and numbers of children attending regardless the actual security situation. The important point to acknowledge is that the emphasis on education as an alleged key benchmark for security has to date, in practice, *not* meant increased security for schools, schoolchildren, teachers, education officials and education aid workers in conflict areas. Quite the contrary, pressure from the national and local government in the conflict area, from U.N. bodies, and international aid organizations to open schools and increase school attendance even in areas that have poor or non-existent security and where there is a high risk of terror attacks on schools, students and educators has lead to large increases in death and injury to schoolchildren and adults associated with these schooling initiatives.

The Taliban began targeting civilians and schools and other civilian institutions in 2005 in part to increase their strategic propaganda position and to attempt to gain some tactical psychological advantage against the overwhelming armed opposition they were facing from the coalition forces.[37] Due in part to the complete destruction of schools or significant damage to education sites arising from various forms of terror attack (i.e., arson, mortar attack etc.) as well as shortfalls in international funding to build anew or repair schools in conflict zones globally, 50 per cent of Afghan basic education classes for schoolchildren are in fact held in tents or open

[36] O'Malley (2010), p. 15.

[37] Human Rights Watch (2006), p. 22.

air spaces which is not exactly ideal from a security perspective.[38] Further, the distance of the school in some rural areas from the community poses high risks to the children's security on the route to and from school:

> ...for many children in CAFS (conflict-affected fragile States), particularly girls, and children living in rural areas, school is often simply too far away and too unsafe to reach for fear of landmines, armed attacks, rape and abduction.[39]

What the HRW report 'Lessons in Terror' and the other NGO and UN reports concerning attacks on education tacitly if unintentionally acknowledge is that the opening of schools and the attendance of children at schools in Afghanistan is in reality an exceedingly poor benchmark for progress in security. This in that level of security as a correlate of school attendance is significantly confounded in CAFS by the degree of pressure from the government and international aid organizations operating in the region to: (a) send children to school notwithstanding inadequate security and (b) encourage and facilitate school attendance even subsequent to a terror attack where the school is still viable or where there is an alternate education site even if in the same area prone to terror attack. In Afghanistan, as discussed, the number of attacks on schools has increased dramatically since 2004 as have the number of students, and teachers injured or killed and this is the trend in a number of other conflict-affected States internationally as well.[40,41] Yet schools continue to be built and children encouraged to attend in highly unsecured zones within CAFS basically at their own risk. In fact, one is hard-pressed to know why 'ENTER AT YOUR OWN RISK' is not emblazoned on the door of schools in Afghanistan in locales with high terror activity and inadequate security for schools; especially when it comes to girls' schools which are so vigorously opposed by most of the Taliban as a matter of their group's stated philosophy pertaining to gender inequity:

> ...Between 2006 and 2007, 230 people died [in Afghanistan] from attacks on schools, students and education personnel, according to the Ministry of Education. In one incident, dozens of schoolchildren and five teachers were killed when they lined up to meet an MP Baghlan Province in November 2007. From 1 January, 2009 to 30 June, 2009, 123 schools were targeted by insurgents and 51 received threats, according to the Afghan Rights Monitor, citing figures from UNICEF. At least 60 students and teachers were killed and 204 wounded in security incidents in the same period (and since then, on 9 July 2009, 13 primary pupils were killed when Taliban forces detonated a bomb between two schools in Logar Province...[42]

This is not at all to dispute the fact that subsequent to a terror attack in a specific locale; especially if on a school, schools may close temporarily or permanently (i.e., in March 2009, 670 schools were closed in Afghanistan and as a result 170, 000

---

[38] Ellery (with Webley, K) (2010), p. 7.

[39] Ellery (with Webley, K) (2010), p. 7.

[40] Human Rights Watch (2006), p. 3–5.

[41] O'Malley (2010), p. 14–15, 21–23.

[42] O'Malley (2010), p. 173–74.

children were "denied an education".[43] Some international NGOs have chosen to withdraw to urban areas where there is more security,[44] but they frequently still have Afghan staff willing to go into the more insecure areas despite the high risk.

Whether schools close after a terror attack and if they do, for how long is determined by a myriad of interacting factors such as: (a) the extent of damage to the school and possibility for repair, (b) the ability of international aid organizations to enter the conflict zone to set up open air tents or other structures in the interim to serve as alternate sites for learning or to construct new school buildings, (c) the level of fear of the populace in sending their children to school where there is inadequate security given the incidence of terror attacks in the area, and d) the degree of pressure exerted on parents by the local government and international NGOs and other agencies working in the area to send the children back to school.

Thus, in regions of the world affected by Al-Qaeda, the Taliban or other organized well funded terror groups, there is no simple correlative relationship between level of security on the one hand and the opening of new schools, re-opening of repaired schools and school attendance on the other as there would be in States where there is at least a minimum adequate level of general security in the country. In fact, in some CAFS as the security situation deteriorates, the government accelerates its repair and reconstruction of schools and steps up its efforts to encourage parents to send their children to school despite their and their children's fears. This stepped up education initiative then after a terror attack is intended to counter the fact that parents are, subsequent to an attack on schools and/or schoolchildren and educators, reluctant to send their children to school and the understandable reality that the children themselves are generally fearful as well to return. The following statement from a parent describes the real and horrific risks parents are not uncommonly facing in attempting to educate their children in a State such as Afghanistan where education is a specific and highly visible target for terrorists:

> In Kandahar city, Human Rights Watch interviewed a mother who withdrew her three daughters from primary school after a girl in one daughter's class was kidnapped and killed. Her cousin's husband found the classmate's body ...the mother said "dead with all her books around her....I took them [the daughters] out [of school] and since then they have never gone back. They [the daughters] were afraid. They themselves didn't want to go". The mother emphasized that she thought "education was a good thing... [that] the girls [her daughters] are very smart ...that they are very interested [in learning]...We understand that school is good for the future. It's just the talk of the community, the threats that prevent us from allowing our girls to continue [in school]".[45]

The problem from an ethical and international humanitarian law perspective is that national governments in conflict-affected States and the international community hold an education development strategy out to be an effective form of counter-terror propaganda *even in the face of a general state of insecurity that*

---

[43]O'Malley (2010), p. 27.

[44]Human Rights Watch (2006), p. 9.

[45]Human Rights Watch (2006), p. 70.

normally should preclude school operation; at least in particular zones within CAFS.

The pressure is so intense on the Afghan government and its allies to communicate a message to the international community that Afghanistan has an alleged highly improved security situation, and is moving significantly toward normalization of that society, that schools have been re-opened or been constructed without due regard to the children's security. Another disturbing trend is that international aid organizations, as bureaucracies with their own financial and political vested interests in the education in fragile States enterprise, have at times facilitated the re-opening of schools previously threatened with, or actually attacked on condition that the schools are under the thumb of the Taliban:

> . . . negotiations to re-open 161 schools in southern Afghanistan that had remained closed due to the threat of attacks succeeded because they addressed the feelings [allegedly] shared by the community *and the armed opposition, the Taliban*, that schools were imposing alien (anti-Islamic) values (emphasis added).[46]

The problem is that the teaching of tolerance, freedom of thought and expression and respect for fundamental human rights as a mandated UNCRC (UN Convention on the Rights of the Child) aspect of the right to education is an improbability in essentially Taliban-controlled schools. Thus, while one can agree that teachings should not be anti-Islamic; so too they ought not denigrate any group (religious, language, ethnic, national etc.). Given the track record of the Taliban, however, spreading hatred and fear of all things and persons not Taliban-approved appears to be integral to the group's modus operandi. Of course, children in Afghanistan have no say in the matter of schools being subject to an organized terror group – the Taliban – as alleged 'quality control' managers of the curriculum (a fact that is inconsistent with the spirit of the UNCRC and especially article 12 of the Convention that accords children certain participation rights in accord with their maturity and age regarding decisions that profoundly affect their current lives and future. Thus, on the one hand, international NGOs such as UNESCO tout the importance of education as a vehicle for spreading understanding, tolerance and peace, and on the other, they appear, at times, to favour negotiating for schools staying open even if on condition that they be subject to the dictates of an organized terror group (i.e., as to curriculum, hiring of teachers etc.).

Contrary to the claims in the 2010 UNESCO report 'Education under Attack,'[47] it is dubious at best that operating schools under the authoritarian dictates of the Taliban is any indicia that significant proportions of the local community in fact concur with such a move. Further, it is here contended arguably *not* a sign of progress toward actual stabilization versus the mirage of stabilization that any school has reopened based on concessions to the Taliban contrary to what the 2010 UNESCO report suggests (unless of course normalization is defined as that which existed prior to the overthrow of the Taliban). Consider in regard to this point

[46]Human Rights Watch (2006), p. 29.

[47]O'Malley (2010), p. 54.

the following statement from the 2010 UNESCO report on Taliban terror attacks on education in Afghanistan:

> Afghanistan's' Minister of Education Farooq Wardak, appointed in late 2008, first encouraged religious and village leaders to mobilize support among local people for the re-opening of schools. He then invited influential local people from across the spectrum, including supporters of the opposition or anti-government elements such as the Taliban, for consultations to find out why schools have remained closed. Some objected to using the term "school"; others feared the curriculum or regulations were anti-Islamic. So the government allowed the word school to be changed to madrasa. It also permitted the communities to nominate a locally trained teacher of their choice [presumably one acceptable to the Taliban] to join the school's staff and ensure that nothing anti-Islamic was taking place... [48]

The above quote refers to facts that reveal a local and national government kowtowing to an organized terror group and ensuring that revisions are made to curriculum and teachers hired in accord with Taliban demands.

UNESCO and many other international human rights organizations and international and national NGOs don't seem to find such a strategy problematic from a children's human rights perspective. It would appear under such a scheme that *any* major change to the curriculum would be possible if made under the guise of removing something *purportedly* anti-Islamic. It would not seem that there are any constraints on what could conceivably be classed as 'anti-Islamic' by the teachers appointed in part or in whole to schools specifically to carry out the role of 'sanitizer of the curriculum' at those schools. It appears that the Afghan government and international NGOs as well as organs of the UN in negotiating and submitting to Taliban conditions for the reopening of schools are driven by the objective of schools operational and students attending at any cost for the reasons already discussed. It should not be forgotten that while it may be that there are certain schools reopened with the Taliban's blessing and functioning as a madrasa (religious school), these same Taliban continue to commit arson on and blow up schools that have not received the Taliban 'good housekeeping stamp' of approval thus killing and maiming the schoolchildren and teachers attending at the latter schools i.e., schools perceived to be supported by the Kabul administration and those that have been built and operated largely or completely through international relief efforts. Not infrequently, it continues in 2010 to be girls' schools that are an especially favoured target of the Taliban:

> Schools have been a prime target in the Afghan conflict and, in most affected provinces between 50-80% of schools have been closed due to either AGE attacks or so-called "night letters" ...threatening attacks on schools or on students or teachers...Girl students and girl's schools are particularly hard hit by these attacks ...Many communities remain affected and many girls are still precluded [by the Taliban and other insurgent Taliban supporters] from attending schools.[49]

---

[48]O'Malley (2010), p. 29–30.

[49]Office of the Special Representative of the Secretary -General for Children and Armed Conflict (2010), p. 10.

Further, it ought to be clear that while certain NGOs support and are involved in negotiation with the Taliban in non-urban areas in Afghanistan in the hope that this leads to the re-opening of schools and a reduction in terror attacks in that locale, this belies the fact that, at the same time, many international and national NGOs are highly dependent in the regions in which they operate on the security provided by the U.S. and its allies. The question must be asked: 'What is the alleged legitimacy in negotiating school re-openings with terrorists (i.e., the Taliban) who, in violation of international humanitarian and criminal law, have and continue, in various locales in the conflict-affected State in question, to deny schoolchildren the right to life, and to physical and psychological security?' (This based on the fact that the Taliban disapproves of the schools these children attend, or even the very fact that they wish to be educated as is the case in respect of girls).

In sum, while higher school attendance, more schools operational, more teachers properly trained etc. are indicators positively correlated with improved security in truly 'post-conflict' societies; this is not necessarily the case internationally in places that are not in fact in the post-conflict stage of development (i.e., States where the war on terror is still intense and ongoing as in Afghanistan for instance). This is apparent only when one takes accurate and full account of the number of school closings, the numbers of attacks on schools, students, teachers and other education personnel; all of which is inadequately monitored at present by the UN and by international NGOs.

What should be clear is that increasing school enrollment in provinces hard hit by terror attacks is *not* a sufficient counterbalance to the attacks on schools that cost children life or limb as well as kill or maim teachers, other school personnel and/or education aid workers. Yet, that thinking seems, in practice, to be reflected in the persistent education initiatives in areas that are highly insecure. That thinking which suggests that terror attacks on education are counterbalanced somehow by the re-opening of schools in the very same locale (which puts children again at high risk) is illustrated, for instance, by the fact that in the same paragraph of the February, 2010 Mission Report of the Special Representative of the Secretary-General for Children and Armed Conflict to Afghanistan which notes that 50 to 80 percent of the schools in the most conflict affected provinces in Afghanistan have been closed, there is reference to school re-openings:

> Schools have been a prime target in the Afghan conflict and, in most affected provinces between 50-80% of schools have been closed [due to attacks by terrorists and other insurgents]. . .The Minister of Education, H.E. Mr. Ghulam Farooq Wardak, informed the Special representative that the government has been able to re-open 223 schools in the last period out of a total of 673 schools closed due to insurgency, positively affecting 200,000 children and 3000 teachers.[50]

The unspoken and unfounded presumption in the quote immediately above (from the Special Representative of the Secretary-General for Children and Armed

[50]Office of the Special Representative of the Secretary -General for Children and Armed Conflict (2010), p. 10.

Conflict to Afghanistan 2010 Mission Report) is, on the analysis here, that these re-opened schools will not be attacked by the Taliban or other insurgents once more. Yet, there is no improved security situation to speak of at these schools. The Afghan police are not able to protect every such school given their paucity of numbers and training and perhaps even lack of enthusiasm for the task. Further, local so-called school protection committees are ill-equipped to fight the Taliban as are the few private security guards that may be guarding particular schools in certain locales. The frequency in certain provinces of terror attacks on education has been exceptionally high in recent years. For instance in 2009, it was reported that "In the province of Kandahar, the overall security situation is so bad that nearly half of all schools are closed some or all of the time".[51] Negotiations with the Taliban are a risky foundation for gambling with the lives of schoolchildren and, in any case, as discussed, school security on the Taliban's terms is likely to mean undermining the right to education in the broad sense as defined in the UN Convention on the Rights of the Child.[52]

Re-opening schools that have been closed previously due to terror attacks *without improving security* makes no sense from a strictly humanitarian perspective. However, it makes perfect sense as a counter-terrorism propaganda strategy intended to communicate to the international community the messages that: (a) development and modernization are purportedly unstoppable forces when backed by the West and its allies and the international community more generally via the donor monies contributed to international and national NGOs operating in CAFS (i.e., in the education sector), and (b) significant and steady progress toward development is allegedly being made such that the billions of donor monies are being well invested in developing and rebuilding a more modern Afghanistan. Thus, it is apparent that there is, at present, *a disconnect between level of security and education* in Afghanistan (as is the case in many other CAFS) in that any increase in school enrollment and/or school openings does *not* necessarily or generally indicate a better security situation (especially not insofar as education is concerned overall in that CAFS, or in particular provinces hard hit by organized terror campaigns mounted by various insurgent elements and organized terror groups). For that reason, it is entirely misleading and misguided, it is here argued in contrast to the suggestion of Human Rights Watch, to use education as a key benchmark for (improved) security in Afghanistan; i.e., to use education "to measure the success of Afghan and international efforts to bring security to Afghanistan"[53] At present, Afghanistan is not in a post-conflict stage of development where increases in the number of schools operational, and in school enrollment are actually likely to reflect concrete gains in stabilization. That is, these gains, if any, are undermined or even largely negated by the number of attacks on

[51] Glad (2009), p. 37.

[52] Convention on the Rights of the Child ratification status http://treaties.un.org/Pages/ViewDetails.aspx?src=TREATY&mtdsg_no=IV-11&chapter=4&lang=en (accessed 18 May 2010).

[53] Human Rights Watch (2006), p. 6.

education that cause these or other schools again to close temporarily or permanently and children and teachers to be killed or injured.

This author is wholeheartedly agreed with the Shura member in Uruzghan who stated: "If you build schools . . . it does not bring security. . ."[54] Indeed, where terror attacks are ongoing and intense in a locale, building or re-opening a school closed by previous insurgent attacks may, in those circumstances, in fact create more insecurity and jeopardize schoolchildren's safety further (as well as that of other civilians involved in education). International education aid interventions encouraging and facilitating school attendance in hot conflict zones with high terror activity within CAFS may thus inadvertently undermine development by exposing schoolchildren, teachers, and education aid workers to substantial harms and civilian education sites to unnecessary and significant risk of destruction:

> We already know there are strong correlations between fragility and low access and achievement in primary education-for instance, over half of children not in primary school worldwide are found in conflict-affected countries. Just as the World Bank has argued that provision of education, particularly for girls, is the single most effective intervention that countries can make to improve human development, the reverse is also true: ***attacks on primary schools, particularly girl's primary schools, and the degradation of the education system that results from persistent attacks and fear of attacks, are particularly damaging for development*** (emphasis added).[55]

Education is not a benchmark for security then in CAFS such as Afghanistan where the populace is experiencing intense systematic terror attacks perpetrated by various insurgents including organized terror groups. While some schools re-open or new ones are built; others close due to terror attacks. Note that there is no suggestion by national or international NGOs or the UN that the number of hospitals, religious institutions etc. built or operational in areas not adequately secured be used as a key benchmark for monitoring progress in security in CAFS. None would think of intentionally locating these facilities in locales without proper security or re-opening them if they were at high risk of imminent attack thus jeopardizing the staff and those receiving service at these facilities. Yet, this is precisely the case when it comes to schoolchildren and the basic education sector.

Parents are often left to make security assessments regarding whether it is safe to send their children to school at any particular time without access to adequate information on the constantly shifting security situation as it relates to education in particular locales with the CAFS. This problem was noted in a 2006 Human Rights Watch report and exists also currently. This in that there is inadequate monitoring and assessment of the changing security situation with respect to the threat to schools, students and teachers in particular locales. Further, what accurate information is available, if any, may not be accessible to parents:

---

[54] Azarbaijani-Moghaddam et al. (2008), p. 12.

[55] O'Malley (2010), p. 28.

> Without effective government or credible media that can track and speak definitively [and accurately] about the security environment, Afghan parents and students are forced to assess the risk based on rumours and incomplete information.[56]

Without accurate and sufficiently detailed information on the actual security situation in their particular locale and region, parents are vulnerable to persuasion regarding the alleged imperative to send their children to school at that time and not to delay or decline to send the children from then on subsequent to a terror attack on the school or on routes to and from school. That persuasion may come from parties that have, in no small part at least, their own interests at heart in maintaining high school enrollment (i.e., those parties being NGOs and other international organizations, representatives of local government etc.). National and international NGOs operating in the field in Afghanistan and in other conflict-affected States, as well as UN researcher/commentators on education in conflict-affected States, appear, in practice; though not in their rights rhetoric, to prioritize the drop in school enrollment following a terror attack as a problem from their perspective rather than the lack of security *per se*. This is reflected in the fact that the NGOs are keen to have the children return to school as soon as possible even after a recent terror attack on their school (once that school is repaired if damaged or re-opened after a temporary closing immediately after the terror attack) (or after a terror attack on a school in a neighbouring locale or subsequent to a recent threat of an imminent terror attack on their school or on a school in a neighbouring area) despite no substantive improvements in security. The international humanitarian aid staff most often lament the parent's reluctance to send their children back to school sooner rather than later (if at all) notwithstanding the fact that these staff are most often in all likelihood well aware of the ongoing lack of security for education in the area. Examples of this NGO sentiment which are likely not unrepresentative are reflected in the quotes below:

> The closure of a school is bound to have a ripple effect so that *many other schools close around [one affected school]* ***for no particular reason except that the school [the one affected school nearby] was burned***. When it [the school that suffered the terror attack] reopens, fewer girls come back, more boys. *This ripple effect magnifies the gravity of each attack and raises fears elsewhere* (emphasis added).[57]

The quote immediately above reveals that this NGO staffer finds it almost irrational that parents in schools in neighbouring areas to that where a school was burned would keep their children at home rather than take the risk of having their children caught in a terror attack at *their* school. The staffer also measures the gravity of the attack on one school in a particular area *in the first instance*, from his/her perspective, in terms of its impact on school enrollment at other schools. The staffer seems reluctant to acknowledge the parents' realistic fear that a terror attack on any school is a clear indicator of the severe and ongoing threat of terror attacks on schools, teachers and education staff almost anywhere and anytime in

[56]Human Rights Watch (2006), p. 76.

[57]Human Rights Watch (2006), p. 76.

that CAFS (i.e., as evidenced by the fact that even schools in urban areas previously thought to have been relatively secure have been attacked in Afghanistan).

Another NGO states:

> [The problem with nightletters] happened in Pol-e Khumri [near Kabul] last spring. And so many times in the southeastern provinces. . .*People cannot make decisions very easily*. For a month or two months you cannot see any children in school because they may fear very bad news from the people who distributed night letters [letters from the Taliban threatening terror attacks on schools, schoolchildren and teachers] or [who] attack or bomb the school. *For weeks you cannot expect to have children back in schools* (emphasis added).[58]

Again the NGO staffer's focus appears to be first and foremost on the drop in enrollment as the fallout from a terror threat (that threat delivered in the form of a 'night letter') and not on the need to recognize and address the genuine security risk facing schoolchildren, education staff and humanitarian education aid workers in the particular locale. The staffer then is indirectly downplaying the need and basic right of the parents to ensure their children's security as best they can by keeping them away from schools that are inadequately protected if they are protected at all. The sad fact is that while the international education aid community operating in CAFS that are still in the midst of conflict focus on increasing school enrollment with the hopes of improving children's access to and completion of a basic education (at least at the primary level), these humanitarian workers have not been able to effectively deal with the lack of security for basic education and systemic attacks on schools, students and school personnel:

> Addressing the systemic nature of conflict and violence in CAFS is often beyond the scope of the strategies and interventions of local, national and international agencies working in the field of education.[59]

It can readily be appreciated that a focus on education as an alleged measure of progress in security is particularly suitable for propaganda purposes for the Afghan and Western allied governments involved in the Afghan conflict opposing Al-Qaeda and the Taliban. This since attendance at schools and number of schools operational *despite an inadequate security situation* can be effectively manipulated by local and national government and international humanitarian organizations in Afghanistan (parents can be pressured/encouraged to send their children to school despite the lack of security with the issue being framed in terms of: (a) the need to act in the alleged best interest of the child, (b) the obligation to resist the terrorists, and to contribute to the future development of the country by ensuring the education of the next generation, (c) school attendance being interpreted as an alleged display of loyalty to the State etc.). Increased school attendance at the beginning of the school year *despite a lack of security* then effectively creates the *illusion* of progress in establishing better security. Moreover, increases in school enrollment at the beginning of the school year is misleading as an indicator of

---

[58]Human Rights Watch (2006), p. 76.

[59]Dryden-Petersen (2010), p. 43.

improvement in the security situation when not weighed against the drop out rate at primary and secondary school level in response to terror attacks and delivered threats of such attacks.

One can legitimately question the wisdom of certain national and international NGOs and international aid organizations supporting the notion of attempting to 'negotiate' with the Taliban and other insurgent groups on the security of particular schools. Such a high risk approach raises the possibility that much improved and stable school enrollment is the goal notwithstanding the risks to security of the students and staff and to the right to education (understood as defined under the Convention on the Rights of the Child.[60] The suggestions for improved security (see the quote below from a 2010 International Save the Children Alliance report for examples) are *all directed to increasing school enrollment first and foremost* and have, for the most part, not materialized as was previously discussed (i.e., the Afghan police are not generally protecting schools or investigating school attacks; a few security guards posted at a school on the occasion where this does occur are no match for the terrorists as is the case also with village school protection committees):

> *Continue to address* ***the issue of insecurity related to school enrollment and attendance*** including direct attacks on schools and school children as well as the general environment of insecurity that makes families uncomfortable in sending their children to school. Actions may include investment in guards for school buildings as well as to accompany children when walking to school, demining of all school areas, increased investment in perimeter walls and linkages with local police and security sector reform (emphasis added).[61]

Negotiation with the Taliban and other insurgent groups on schools as safe zones involves: (a) reliance on highly unpredictable parties that have been shown to be quite willing and capable of extreme violence perpetrated against children, and (b) parties that in the past have used school curriculum as a vehicle for garnering support for a terror movement. Unfortunately, some reports prepared for the international humanitarian aid community appear to fall into the trap of: (a) suggesting that making the Taliban the final arbiter of curriculum is something of a panacea for the security problem in Afghanistan as far as it relates to education and (b) essentially blaming the West for the violence perpetrated on schools, school-children and education personnel by suggesting (incorrectly on the view here) that NGO sponsored schools *are* anti-Islamic in their curriculum choices. Consider the following quote from a 2010 International Save the Children Alliance report:

> The Taliban Leadership Council has stated:
>
> Present academic curriculum is influenced by the puppet administration and foreign invaders. The government has given teachers in primary and middle schools the task to openly deliver political lectures against the resistance put up by those who seek independence... [U]se of the curriculum as a mouthpiece of the state will provoke the

---

[60]Convention on the Rights of the Child (entered into force 2 September 1990) http://www2.ohchr.org/english/law/crc.htm (accessed 22 May 2010).

[61]Dryden-Petersen (2010), p. 29.

people against it. If schools are turned into centers of violence, the government is to blame for it. . .

[The Save the Children Alliance report goes on to say the following]:As a direct result of curriculum choices, schools have been turned into centres of violence and focal points in Taliban resistance to the current government. Children thus attend school in fear, and many families decide not to allow children to go to school as a result of the danger. . . In this way, curriculum directly serves as a barrier to physically accessing schools.[62]

It is here contended in contrast that the responsibility for attacks on schools, schoolchildren, teachers and other education personnel lies fully and solely with the terrorists notwithstanding any real or perceived deficiencies in the curriculum of NGO or government sponsored schools in Afghanistan. Certainly there is no indication that NGO sponsored or government schools in Afghanistan implement curriculum or have done so in the past that is intended to promote anti-Islam sentiment or intolerance or violence. Schools have been "turned into centres of violence" because organized terror groups such as the Taliban have attacked them as a highly effective means of spreading terror.

The Special Representative of the UN Secretary General for Children and Armed Conflict reported in her February 2010 mission trip to Afghanistan that the security situation in Afghanistan has deteriorated since 2008 and that the Taliban and its non-state actor allies have begun to attack the UN and its partners (i.e., NGOs, international humanitarian organizations etc).[63] Children have increasingly become the victim of Taliban activity including being injured or killed by IEDs (improvised explosive devices), as the result of being caught in the crossfire, in the process of being used as 'human shields'[64] and being recruited as 'child soldiers' by the Taliban and other non-state armed insurgents (recruitment and use of children as a child soldiers, it will be recalled, is considered to be an attack on education as it aborts access to and completion of formal basic education).[65] In addition, there are documented cases of children being used by the Taliban as suicide bombers:

Children involved range from 13-16 years of age, and according to testimonies of failed bombers, have been tricked, promised money or otherwise forced to become suicide bombers. . .some children who have attempted suicide attacks have been heavily indoctrinated. . .some reports suggest that in the latest incidents of children used in bombings, they may not have been aware of what they were carrying, and explosives were set off remotely without their knowledge.[66] [note that the Special Representative also notes that some children have been placed at risk due to their recruitment and use by the Afghan National

[62]Dryden-Petersen (2010), p. 24.

[63]Office of the Special Representative of the Secretary-General for Children and Armed Conflict (2010), p. 4.

[64]Office of the Special Representative of the Secretary-General for Children and Armed Conflict (2010), p. 4.

[65]Office of the Special Representative of the Secretary-General for Children and Armed Conflict (2010), p. 5.

[66]Office of the Special Representative of the Secretary-General for Children and Armed Conflict (2010), p. 5.

> Police or Afghan National Army; this due allegedly to ineffective age determination procedures by these bodies rather than as a policy initiative][67]

4.3 The February 2010 Mission to Afghanistan of the Special Representative of the UN Secretary General for Children and Armed Conflict: Assessment of Security Issues in Relation to Education

There are at present an estimated 5 million children in Afghanistan out-of-school which represents 43 percent of the total school age population.[68] The Minister of Education suggested to the Special Representative that the government intended to provide Madrasa schools that still followed the government's basic curriculum guidelines and did not espouse violence. It is unclear whether such an approach will stem attacks on schools in Afghanistan given the fact that schools are a recognizable and accessible symbol of government especially in rural areas. There were 249 attacks against schools in August 2009 compared to 48 in July 2009 and 38 in September 2009.[69] Despite the increasing number of attacks on education in Afghanistan particularly in certain high risk areas, the Special Representative reported he would be "advocating . . .for education as a key bridge to peace in Afghanistan".[70] However, in the face of increased terror attacks on schools in Afghanistan, there has been little in the way of concrete suggestions for improving security for schools other than not to use schools as polling stations for elections (the latter practice tending to encourage terror attacks on schools). Another suggestion arising from the 2010 visit to Afghanistan of the Special Representative of the UN Secretary -General for Children and Armed Conflict was to promote the 'schools as safe zones' program with UNICEF as the lead organization:

> The Special Representative calls upon the Government of Afghanistan and the international community, guided by UNICEF, to expand the 'schools as zones of peace program' in the country, including community-based advocacy for greater access for girls.[71]

It is the case that negotiations with some village elders and religious leaders in Afghanistan in particular locales have led to an increased willingness to improve

---

[67] Office of the Special Representative of the Secretary-General for Children and Armed Conflict (2010), p. 5.

[68] Office of the Special Representative of the Secretary-General for Children and Armed Conflict (2010), p. 10.

[69] Office of the Special Representative of the Secretary-General for Children and Armed Conflict (2010), p. 10.

[70] Office of the Special Representative of the Secretary-General for Children and Armed Conflict (2010), p. 11.

[71] Office of the Special Representative of the Secretary-General for Children and Armed Conflict (2010), p. 11.

access to education for girls in those villages. NGOs have been able, in some limited instances, to convince those in power at the local level that educating girls is *not* in fact anti-Islamic.[72] However, at the same time, one might rightfully wonder whether the Taliban and other non-state armed groups intent on terror attacks on schools and perpetrating atrocities on civilians generally will be deterred by the NGO 'schools as safe zones' advocacy program. No doubt the 'schools as safe zones' program is useful in *genuinely* 'post-conflict' settings, or after a natural disaster, or when operating in a locale away from armed conflict such as in a refugee camp area located in a secure region. The feasibility of such a program operating in the midst of a zone where a terror group is highly active is highly dubious to say the least. A group such as the Taliban which systematically targets children for violent attack as a matter of official policy (i.e., uses children as suicide bombers, considers schoolchildren as a prime target for direct violent attack while they are at school or on their way to or from school especially with respect to girl schoolchildren,[73] uses children as 'human shields' for protection i.e., during an air strike[74] or uses children deliberately as human shields in other conflict situations in Afghanistan[75] etc.) and in most cases still precludes girls from attending school is a highly unlikely, and most importantly, unpredictable, unreliable partner in a 'schools as safe zones' initiative even should some of their contingents promise to participate at any point. Afghanistan is *not* a 'post-conflict' State to which models applicable in post-conflict States are readily generalizable if at all. In many areas of the country education aid is provided at considerable risk to the lives and safety of children, teachers and humanitarian aid workers.

Further, as previously mentioned, a problem exists in that while adults (i.e., teachers, education-related personnel such as bus drivers and education aid workers), in most instances, may be assumed to have made an informed, voluntary decision to assume certain security risks by their involvement in the education sector in a CAFS, the same cannot be said in regards to the schoolchildren. Hence, intentionally putting children in situations that are high risk in terms of potential physical and psychological harm coming to the children (i.e., having them attend schools located in the midst of an armed conflict/terror zone) is a violation of international humanitarian law. This reality cannot be masked by any 'sugar-coated' humanitarian rationales framed in terms of the children's right to education which right has *in effect* been improperly prioritized over the children's rights to life and general security of the person.

The Special Representative of the UN Secretary General for children and armed conflict reported after her February 2010 mission to Afghanistan that:

---

[72]Dryden-Petersen (2010), p. 43.

[73]Office of the Special Representative of the Secretary-General for Children and Armed Conflict (2010), p. 5 and p. 10.

[74]Schmitt (2010), p. 20.

[75]Office of the Special Representative of the Secretary-General for Children and Armed Conflict (2010), p. 4.

> The aggravated security conditions prevailing in the conflict-affected areas of the south, south-east, central and eastern regions [of Afghanistan] as well as in isolated areas of the north continue to hamper humanitarian aid delivery [including education aid as a component of the humanitarian aid emergency response]. *[The] UN Department of Safety and Security has designated 79 districts [in Afghanistan] as "extreme risk" that are inaccessible to program delivery by UN agencies.* Subsequently, UN agencies and NGOs have been restricting the scale and scope of their delivery assistance. *The World Food Programme, for example, has not been able to fully implement its "food for education program" which benefits approximately 1.5 million children daily [in Afghanistan] due to the deterioration of the security environment and the reluctance of road transport firms to risk attacks by AGE.* [the food for education program provides food to pre-school aged and school-aged children through the schools or preschool education programs in order to help boost enrollment, and foster good health and learning achievement. Many children are heavily dependent on the program as a major source of their daily food intake][76]
>
> *Furthermore, the protection of aid workers, especially national workers, has been compromised by threats, intimidation and attacks against them or [on] community leaders in areas they serve...*The Special Representative also visited Charhai Qambar IDP camp in west Kabul where many people have fled previous ongoing violence in Helmund province. The situation of the IDPs in this camp was of concern, as not all children were able to attend schools and families had very little support... (emphasis added)[77]

Note the difficulty as evidenced in the report by the UN Special Representative (and discussed in the quote immediately above) of providing education even in an IDP camp; a presumably 'safe school zone' as the term is used by UNICEF. In many of the regions in Afghanistan classified by the UN as 'extreme risk' or even so-called moderate risk areas (risk here referring to the risk of violence), the security issues should, but generally do not lead to safety matters taking precedence over education initiatives until *after* a threat of imminent attack or after an actual terror attack on education (i.e., it is not until there is a threat letter delivered or teachers and/or schools and/or schoolchildren have been attacked once more in the areas in question or members of the aforementioned civilian groups have been injured or killed that the school is closed temporarily at least). It should be understood that once an area is secure; there is no guarantee that it will remain thus as long as the general security situation in the country remains poor and on a downward spiral as in recent times appears to be more and more the case in Afghanistan. Note the use of food to lure families to send children to school even in the face of the security risks to the children and their families in doing so. Children should not have to risk their security in order to obtain food available for all intents and purposes mostly at school (*i.e., such basic relief should be available in a variety of contexts; especially for children and where security for those attending to obtain the food is given a high priority*). The use of food to boost school enrollment figures in places like Afghanistan that are still in the midst of intense armed conflict is thus a practice that raises serious ethical concerns.

---

[76]Global Food for Education Pilot Initiative http://www.fas.usda.gov/excredits/gffei.html (accessed 14 June 2010).

[77]Office of the Special Representative of the Secretary-General for Children and Armed Conflict (2010), p. 12.

Attending school in certain of the numerous higher risk areas in Afghanistan poses certain tangible and real threats to the safety of schoolchildren especially girls. Schools in such instances are not in fact the 'safe zones' that the international humanitarian aid community wishes them to be. Any incentive to lure children into these dangerous situations seems morally questionable. While food ought to be available to children whose families have decided they wish to send them to school, food should be equally available from the same humanitarian aid groups to out-of-school school-aged children insofar as it can, in practice, be delivered also out of the school context. One must concur, however, with the Special Representative of the UN Secretary-General on armed conflict and children that "Reaching and providing for children in the most conflict-affected areas of Afghanistan will continue to be problematic".[78] The dramatically increasing rate of attacks on education in Afghanistan demonstrate that in the face of the systematic terror campaign perpetrated by the Taliban and other insurgent groups "community-based security guarantees for the delivery of crucial humanitarian aid for children [including education aid]"[79] are not anywhere close to adequate to ensure the children's safety or the safety of the teachers, of other school personnel or of humanitarian education aid workers. The phrase "community-based security guarantees" or terms with the same meaning have become something of catch phrases in the humanitarian aid literature concerning the delivery of education aid in conflict-affected countries where the fighting is ongoing. That terminology masks the fact that attending school in certain areas in conflict-affected States such as Afghanistan constitutes a 'real and present danger' to children. This is the case despite the existence of any so-called "community-based security guarantees" offered by local villagers ill-equipped to defend against attacks by the Taliban and other insurgents should the school; its personnel or local village leaders for any reason curry disfavour with those violent groups. Note that: (a) "The number of *prevented* attacks [attributable to community-based school protection committees/groups] has been low according to the field research [conducted by Care International Afghanistan]; only 4% of respondents indicated that attacks had been prevented in the past" and (b) there was no consistent faith across provinces in Afghanistan in the police being willing and able to provide effective protection of schools with 16% of respondents even contending that police protection would likely instigate increased attacks on the schools (likely this latter group of respondents felt that having a police presence at schools would further reinforce the perception of schools as being symbols of the government and hence a viable high value target for attack by the insurgents).[80]

---

[78]Office of the Special Representative of the Secretary-General for Children and Armed Conflict (2010), p. 12.

[79]Office of the Special Representative of the Secretary-General for Children and Armed Conflict (2010), p. 12.

[80]Glad (2009), p. 3–4.

Afghanistan has not sufficiently emerged from conflict to allow for effective management of all aspects of the education system (security management, financial etc.). Afghanistan is one of the nine CAFS that have *not* been endorsed by a partnership of global donors in which donor monies are pooled and can be more readily available (the Education for All-Fast Track Initiative) as it has *not* been deemed a 'good performer' in terms of comprehensive strategic plans for the education sector.[81] Many international donors hold that "countries need stability in order to be considered safe for investment".[82] Afghanistan is still sadly a long way from what might be considered a stable country with strong civil institutions and effective government that can ensure the rule of law and adequate levels of security for education in all parts of the country and for society generally. For instance, at the time of writing, there has been another gas poisoning attack on schoolgirls in Afghanistan with the exposure occurring at the school in southwestern Afghanistan in Ghazni which is located about two hours drive from Afghanistan's capital Kabul. The teenage girls, about 50 in the latest incident, fell unconscious after smelling gas at the school. The senior provincial police officer Nawroz Al Mahmoodzada stated that: "It is again the same kind of attack to discourage girls from attending schools...It is very disturbing..."[83] The latest incident followed recent similar events in Kabul and northern Kunduz province.[84] While the Taliban, of late, have taken to denying responsibility for such gas attacks they are high on the list of suspects given that: (a) during their rule from 1996 to 2001; girls were not permitted to attend schools and (b) they have attacked schools, teachers and schoolchildren including girls on their way to or from school in the past.[85] It has been noted that attacks on schools in Afghanistan, such as gas poisoning attacks, appear correlated with the Taliban growing in strength in a particular locale as is the case in Kunduz province at the time of the recent gas poisoning attacks on schools i.e., in April and June 2010[86]: "Attacks like these spike in unison with the strength of insurgents".[87]

At present, there does *not* seem to be any insistence from the international humanitarian education aid community on adequate security as a *prerequisite* for education aid intervention as an emergency humanitarian response in any particular locale in Afghanistan (or in any other CAFS for that matter as well). Rather, the focus of the international humanitarian community appears more on documenting suffering than on avoiding it (i.e., by not carrying out education operations in areas where there is a considerable known risk of terror attack on schools and schoolchildren given the poor security situation and previous attacks in those locales). The

[81] Dryden-Petersen (2010), p. 12.

[82] Dryden-Petersen (2010), p. 14.

[83] Reuters (2010).

[84] Free Internet Press (2010).

[85] Free Internet Press (2010).

[86] Free Internet Press (2010).

[87] Khan (2010).

Special Representative of the UN Secretary-General on children and armed conflict followed suit by suggesting a system of "child violation alerts" among all battlefield entities that would keep the UN Monitoring and Reporting Mechanism partners informed of grave violations of children's basic rights.[88]While the latter reporting is of course important; it is no substitute for prevention of school attacks by ceasing to operate schools in zones that are at considerable risk of terror attack given received terror threats, the general lack of security in the particular locale; intractable opposition to girl's education by at least a powerful segment of the community despite the best efforts of humanitarian education aid workers to shift attitudes in this more conservative segment of the local population and other such factors. Without ensuring proper security as a pre-condition for operating a school in a particular locale, the international humanitarian aid community may in practice be unwittingly offering Afghani children in certain locales not educational opportunity, but rather a good opportunity to be killed or maimed.

It is an impressive advance for children's fundamental human rights in Afghanistan – even if only in principle at this point – that the Special Representative of the UN Secretary-General on children and armed conflict was able to obtain endorsement by the Afghan government of the idea that child protection provisions must be included in any peace agreement that ends the conflict in Afghanistan.[89] However, child protection in Afghanistan; as security itself more generally in that region, appears to be elusive. This is evidenced, for instance, by the pattern of attacks on schools by non-state actors which continues in earnest *following* the June 2010 Peace jirga held 2–4 June, 2010 between the Afghan government and various non-state actors. Taliban and other anti-government elements were welcome to attend peacefully if they wished to do so but were not formally invited to the aforementioned Peace jirga. Unfortunately, women were not involved in the planning of the event and had a very small representation there (50 out of 1400 available seats) all of which, in the view of many female rights activists in Afghanistan, does not bode especially well for a significant advance in the fundamental human rights of women and girls in Afghan society[90] notwithstanding any progress that has been made in this regard in the years since the end of Taliban rule. Consider also in respect of gender rights that terror attacks on girl's schools by the Taliban and insurgents have dramatically increased in recent years in Afghanistan.[91]

At present, there appears to be a largely futile approach to 'child protection' in Afghanistan in respect of ensuring schoolchildren's security insofar as it relies on appeals to the Taliban and other insurgent armed groups to end their attacks on schools and schoolchildren. There are instead, as discussed, an ever increasing number of school attacks by Taliban and antigovernment elements and attacks on

---

[88]Khan (2010) (citing Jennifer Rowell, head of advocacy for CARE International in Kabul).

[89]Office of the Special Representative of the Secretary-General for Children and Armed Conflict (2010), p. 14.

[90]Reuters (2010).

[91]Reuters (2010).

schoolchildren and teachers on their way to and from school or in other locations. The problem of school attacks is then exacerbated by the national and local government partnered often with NGOs placing Afghan children in harm's way by encouraging school attendance in various numerous locales across the country despite the lack of adequate security for education in those particular locales.

The Special Representative of the UN Secretary-General on children and armed conflict ends her February 2010 Afghanistan mission report with thoughts on the need for UN communications with the Taliban. Her comments in this regard appear unrealistically optimistic. The comments reflect a presumption that if the obligations regarding respecting children's right to security were communicated to the Taliban; it would have positive impact in terms of improving child protection for Afghan children:

> One major caveat to the advances made since her last visit is the difficulty for the UN to engage with non-state actors who commit violations against children . . .*It is critical that the UN communicate to them their responsibility to respect and comply with international law and to cease and desist on-going violations against children and to alert them on their responsibility to engage and to conclude action plans to bring these grave abuses to an end.* In this sense, the Special Representative hopes for a successful Peace Jirga . . .which would incorporate these elements for children. Peace remains the only hope for the future of Afghanistan and its children (emphasis added).[92]

There were, as it turns out, rockets sent in the way of the June 2010 peace conference participants' meeting place in Kabul with one landing just a few hundred meters away as well as three suicide attackers; one of whom managed to get just a few hundred meters from the tent where the Peace Jirga was being held. Fortunately, there were no casualties. However, these attacks on the June 2010 Peace Jirga likely shook even more the public's confidence in the government's ability to provide adequate security for the people generally given its inability to prevent these attacks despite the heightened security for the conference event; namely 12,000 troops in the streets providing security for the event.[93] This violent attack was the insurgents' own form of communication regarding the government's hopes for peace and improved security for civilians including children (an unjustifiable violent response regardless of any deficiencies that may or may not have existed in the organization and constitution of delegates of the June 2010 Peace Jirga). Given that schools are generally speaking a symbol of government; such events as the attack on the 2010 Peace Jirga do not bode well for the reliability of any so-called negotiated agreement with the Taliban and other anti-government elements for the security of schools, schoolchildren and education personnel in Afghanistan (as the increasing violence against Afghan schools, schoolchildren and teachers in recent months also attest).

---

[92]Office of the Special Representative of the Secretary-General for Children and Armed Conflict (2010), p. 15.

[93]Insurgents attack Afghan peace 'jirga' but cause no injuries http://www.montrealgazette.com/news/Taliban+suicide+squad+targets+Afghan+peace+jirga/3101687/story.html (accessed 17 June 2010).

One cannot but agree wholeheartedly with the sentiment expressed by the Special Representative that "Peace remains the only hope for the future of Afghanistan and its children".[94] In the meantime, schoolchildren must not be used as pawns in the counter-terrorism propaganda effort in the hopes to create the impression that: (a) school security is adequate (by a show of increased enrollment) or at least significantly and steadily improving across the country (when that is a dubious proposition at best); and that (b) increased attendance at school is a viable indicator of alleged significantly improved security generally across the various Afghan provinces (when in fact increased enrollment at the beginning of the year must be counterbalanced by the number of school closings and drop outs due to terror attacks and threat of terror attacks as well as against the number of students and school personnel injured or killed in their attempts to participate in the education system). There must be an end to the propagation of the unqualified 'feel-good' notion that in a CAFS such as Afghanistan where the terror campaign of insurgents is still very much active and ongoing, and security for schools inadequate, that schools are, generally speaking, a protective environment offering normality and stability in a sea of turmoil and armed conflict:

> *Schools are a fundamental component of building a protective environment for children under normal circumstances,* ***but this is particularly true during*** **[armed]** ***conflict***. They provide opportunities not only for learning and cognitive development, but are also vital elements of a child's psychosocial growth and welfare (emphasis added).[95]

While schools serving as a comparatively protective environment in a crisis may be feasible (depending on the specific situation) in a 'post-conflict' society, or after a natural disaster where: (a) an adequate level of basic security has been established and, (b) schools are not being targeted for violent attack, this is not the case in all CAFS as we have seen. Yet, the 'fourth pillar theory' regarding education as a humanitarian emergency response component is based on the presumption that education is by definition protective:

> Increasingly, education is being viewed as the 'fourth pillar', or a 'central pillar' of humanitarian response, alongside the pillars of nourishment, shelter and health services. *The key role of education as an institutional response and means of protecting children facing emergency has gradually becoming globally accepted and included in the UN cluster approach* (emphasis added)...[96]

Whether schools *during conflict* in a CAFS provide an environment stimulating learning and cognitive as well as psychosocial development is, of course, a moot point if the child is killed on the way to or from school or while receiving those education classes at school. In CAFS such as Afghanistan, we *cannot* start from the premise that schools are a fundamental component of building a protective

[94]Office of the Special Representative of the Secretary-General for Children and Armed Conflict (2010), p. 15.

[95]UNESCO (2010), p. 1.

[96]UNESCO (2010), p. 60.

environment given that security is inadequate for education in various regions within the country. Indeed, in many instances, schools are far from a protective environment in a CAFS but rather a magnet for terrorist violence:

> In Afghanistan, anti-government forces including the Taliban, their allies, common criminals and local warlords launch violent attacks against schools, students, teachers and administrators. Attacks include bombings of buildings, arson, targeted killings and acid attacks particularly on female students and teachers...Hundreds of teachers and students have been killed, and hundreds of schools have been forced to close. Girls are severely intimidated, and in Zabul, Uruzgan and Paktika provinces the numbers of girls attending lower secondary school has dropped to less than one per cent.[97]

Schools, especially easily identifiable schools (i.e., those located in separate buildings entirely dedicated to basic education) and those known to be poorly protected as well as girls' schools are, as discussed, targeted for terror attacks both due to their vulnerability and the high value symbolic nature of the target for terrorists. Yet, despite the fact that "Depending on the circumstances, *education during armed conflict can be a source of protection or of increased risk* as occurs when schools are attacked",[98] the international humanitarian education aid community continues to pursue increased school enrollment even where the security risks are tangible and excessive. Thus, in most instances, schools (whether in school buildings or alternate education sites) in Afghanistan and other CAFS still undergoing conflict close only when parents refuse to send their children to school and /or teachers refuse to attend due to the security risks or the school is severely damaged or destroyed (as opposed to closing due to proactive moves by government and NGOs to close schools where security is inadequate and there is a known significant risk of terror attack):

> ...official responses to the attacks on education in Afghanistan have been slow and lacklustre. Government and multinational agencies were reluctant initially to recognize the problem for fear of creating a sense of failure in reaching project goals and jeopardizing progress toward development.[99]

It is true that attention has begun to be focused on the issue of attacks on education in CAFS such as Afghanistan, and that there is at least a call for better monitoring by government and NGOs and international agencies of such attacks. However, at the same time, there has not been any slow down in government and NGOs encouraging school enrollment also in schools located in insecure areas. Insofar as NGOs are concerned, this suggests that the intent is still to attempt to show donors progress in development project goals and in practice do so even at the cost of children's security.

[97]UNESCO (2010), p. 245.

[98]UNESCO (2010), p. 61.

[99]UNESCO (2010), p. 246.

4.4 Revisiting the Topic of Community-Based Schools

In view of the dramatically increasing number of terror attacks in Afghanistan on schools; schoolchildren and teachers, the notion of community-based schools has gained popularity amongst the Afghan government officials and in the international education aid community serving Afghanistan (NGOs are often sponsors of such schools).[100] The notion appears to be that community-based schools (schools housed in a room or two of a private home or in existing community buildings especially mosques) may be at decreased risk of school attack. However, it should be recognized that: (a) such an alleged reduction in risk of school attack has not been empirically investigated in any formal sense[101] and (b) it is unclear whether a reduced comparative risk (supposing one exists compared to the risk of attack to schools situated in non-community facilities) would constitute adequate security given that the risk may still be significant. We are talking here, afterall, about a community-based school approach notwithstanding the fact that in 2010: "[The] UN considers half the country unsafe for road travel because of lack of security",[102] and where alliances between the Taliban and criminal elements have meant that even previously more secure areas in the north and west of Afghanistan have become increasingly insecure.[103]

It should be noted that locating community-based schools in mosques, for instance, is no guarantee of increased security as Taliban terrorists in Pakistan have shown themselves quite willing and able to attack mosques,[104,105] and such is not unheard of in Afghanistan as well[106]. Indeed, so-called 'night letters' warning not to educate girls are often posted by the Taliban in mosques in Afghanistan.[107] Should the community-based school situated in a mosque be perceived as: (a) supported in any way or to any extent by government (even though it may be NGO sponsored) or perceived as a symbol of foreign influence and interference in Afghanistan; or (b) promoting an inclusive education curriculum given that the mullah teaching at the community-based school has a more liberal view of education than does the Taliban (and has endorsed a curriculum that teaches about respect for basic human rights including gender equality consistent with notions of implementing the right to education under the Convention on the Rights of the Child)[108];

---

[100]UNESCO (2010), p. 246.

[101]UNESCO (2010), p. 246.

[102]UNESCO (2010), p. 247.

[103]UNESCO (2010), p. 248.

[104]The Christian Science Monitor (2010).

[105]India Vision (2010).

[106]APS Diplomat Recorder (2005).

[107]Human Rights Watch (2006), p. 45–46.

[108]Convention on the Rights of the Child ratification status http://treaties.un.org/Pages/ViewDetails.aspx?src=TREATY&mtdsg_no=IV-11&chapter=4&lang=en (accessed 18 May 2010).

or (c) providing something other than religious education within the highly restrictive constraints dictated by the Taliban, and/or (d) to be educating girls; it is at considerable risk of becoming an acceptable target from the perspective of at least large segments of the Taliban terrorist organization.

Note that at present: "95 per cent of the roughly 6 million registered students [in Afghanistan] attend government schools. Approximately 1.5 per cent attend Islamic schools (government registered madrasas), and close to 3 per cent attend community-based schools".[109] There are obviously great challenges in setting up community-based schools in rural and remote areas of Afghanistan including but not limited to: (a) difficulties in gaining local village support for the school (i.e., which school may in fact attract Taliban violence to the community), (b) problems in recruiting qualified teachers, and (c) issues pertaining to convincing village elders of the value of educating girls etc.

It would appear that there is no panacea for the problem of terror attacks on schools especially not in States not yet entering into or already entered into a 'post-conflict' stage. Community-based schools, while having some advantages in some instances (i.e., perhaps being less visible in certain cases where there is no building designated as a school building per se and requiring less travel time, if any, on dangerous roads for attendance[110] ; though girls would still likely be at risk just walking in a public place to a community or a government school)[111] -do not, for the reasons explained, ensure schoolchildren the minimum adequate level of security risk to which they, as all schoolchildren globally, are entitled. A marked shift to community-based schools may even result in a concomitant increase in terror attacks on such schools (as yet an empirical question). Community-based schools as a gathering place for students and teachers; are, afterall, also, as a result, potential high-value targets for terrorists. This, given the impact such an attack has in terms of effective undermining of the public's perception of progress by the government and its coalition partners in achieving stability and security in the region.

It has been noted that while community-based schools "increase children's enrollment, attendance and achievement significantly";[112] such schools may shift the burden of responsibility for schooling to communities and away from government. This shifting of the burden regarding education to the community then, the current author would suggest, may also include school protection when in fact local groups are ill-equipped to guarantee the security of schools from terror attacks. Given the factors here discussed, it is not at all clear that community-based schools will adequately mitigate the risk of terror attacks on schools; or that such schools will respond effectively in case of such attack. Yet, some have suggested that policy-makers "promote" community-based schools "given the alternative (no

[109]Burde (2010), p. 251.

[110]Burde (2010), p. 247.

[111]Burde (2010), p. 250.

[112]Burde (2010), p. 254.

education)".[113]: and, in part, based on the *hypothesized* "added benefit they [community-based schools] *may* bring to countering attacks".[114] This despite the fact that:

> *Claims about the benefits of community-based schools in relation to increasing children's safety and reducing attacks on education have yet to be empirically demonstrated.* In addition, optimism about the ability of community-based schools to reduce the numbers of attacks on students, teachers, and education personnel and on educational infrastructure should be tempered by a note about the infrastructure required to support them and the weaknesses of these schools on other accounts. . .when security deteriorates to the extent that it has in many parts of Afghanistan, it is impossible for NGO or Afghan government staff to access these regions. Programmes that require significant external support cannot survive in these conditions (emphasis added).[115]

Thus, the right to education is prioritized *above* the right to security of the person of the children also in respect of any community-based school initiative given the present circumstances in Afghanistan. In fact, there are indeed times when the alternative to having children put at high risk of being the victim of a terror attack must be taken (no education unless it can be delivered without the child's life and physical security generally being at significant risk). No party has the legal right under international humanitarian and human rights law, it is here contended, to downgrade the child's fundamental rights to survival and protection from serious physical and psychological trauma (such as occurs when schoolchildren are being intentionally encouraged or compelled to attend a school building or alternate education site likely to be targeted for a terror attack and which is highly vulnerable to such attack). Doing so, it can be argued, renders those responsible for the children's school attendance in such insecure circumstances in the midst of armed conflict co-perpetrators in the grave international crimes associated with any terror attack that does occur on the school site the children attend (just as commanders are culpable if they have the ability to save the lives of potential victims but either do nothing to prevent the grave harms, or actually facilitate the victims coming into harm's way). Notwithstanding the foregoing, however, the international education aid community, donor countries and CAFS such as Afghanistan are constantly seeking ways and means to ensure school attendance in the midst of armed conflict and despite the lack of adequate school security in many regions of the CAFS such as Afghanistan. Community-based schools, for instance, may be promoted when in fact should there be an imminent risk of terror attack, the school is left, for all intents and purposes, without adequate protection and without outside NGO or government assistance in the aftermath if the area remains insecure. As a result, the Afghan government and select international and national NGOs, in effect, continue to play Russian roulette with the lives of Afghan schoolchildren and others (i.e., education aid workers etc.) in the process of conducting what amount to field experiments on what might or might not work in terms

[113]Burde (2010), p. 254.

[114]Burde (2010), p. 254.

[115]Burde (2010), p. 258.

of : (a) avoiding terror attacks on schools and (b) recovering from terror attacks on a school such that schools or alternative education sites will be up and running again in the shortest feasible period to serve the schoolchildren whose education was interrupted by the previous attack (assuming of course that the area is once again deemed allegedly secure enough for NGO activity). Disturbingly, from the current author's point of view, there is even mention from some quarters promoting the idea of community-based schooling in Afghanistan of planning for anticipated terror attacks on community-based schools operating also in zones so insecure that NGOs could not reach them in the normal fashion:

> Humanitarian agencies would need to design creative ways to continue to support these schools in the event that they could not access them. *Starting new community-based schools* ***in conflict-ridden areas*** *will require insightful planning* (emphasis added).[116]

The suggestion is made by the current author then that operating schools (whether community-based, government or mosque schools etc.) in conflict-ridden areas where security cannot be adequately guaranteed constitutes a violation of international humanitarian, human rights and criminal law. It is unclear why children should in Afghanistan (or in any CAFS) be expected, and indeed in many instances required at the behest of parents and government; and encouraged by NGOs, to attend schools at high risk of terror attack given the school's location (some of those locations even including those considered out of bounds for NGOs and Afghan government staff based on the inability to provide the latter groups adequate security).

References

Agence France-Presse (2006) Attacks depriving 100,000 Afghan students: President (8 March 2006), cited in Human Rights Watch (2006), p 31

APS Diplomat Recorder (2005) Afghanistan –June 1-suicide bomber kills 19 in mosque (4 June 2005) http://www.thefreelibrary.com/AFGHANISTAN+-+Jun+1+-+Suicide+Bomber+Kills+19+In+Mosque.-a0133218120. Accessed 24 June 2010

Azarbaijani-Moghaddam S, Wardak M, Zaman I et al (2008) Afghan hearts, Afghan minds: exploring Afghan perceptions of civil-military relations (Research conducted for the European Network of NGOs in Afghanistan (ENNA) and the British and Irish Agencies Afghanistan Group (BAAG), p 12. http://www.humansecuritygateway.info/documents/ENNA_BAAG_Afghanistan_afghanheartsafghanminds.pdf. Accessed 29 May 2010

Burde D (2010) Preventing violent attacks on education in Afghanistan: considering the role of community-based schools (Chapter 13), cited in UNESCO (2010), p 251

Convention on the Rights of the Child Ratification Status (2011) http://treaties.un.org/Pages/ViewDetails.aspx?src=TREATY&mtdsg_no=IV-11&chapter=4&lang=en. Accessed 25 February 2011

Dryden-Petersen S (2010) Barriers to accessing primary education in conflict-affected fragile states: a literature review (A report written on behalf of International Save the Children

[116] Burde (2010), p. 258.

Alliance), p 43. http://www.savethechildren.org.uk/en/docs/Barriers_to_access_Literature_Review_Final.pdf. Accessed 3 June 2010

Ellery F (with Webley K) (2010) The future is now: education for children in countries affected by conflict (A report written for Save the Children UK), p 7 (downloadable from http://www.reliefweb.int/rw/rwb.nsf/db900SID/ADGO-85CQM2?OpenDocument&RSS20=18. Accessed 24 May 2010

Esfandiari G (2006) Afghanistan: militants are targeting schools, radio free Europe/radio liberty (22 February 2006)

Filkins D (2009) Afghan girls, scarred by acid, defy terror, embracing school. New York Times (14 January 2009). http://www.nytimes.com/2009/01/14/world/asia/14kandahar.html. Accessed 25 February 2011

Free Internet Press (2010) Gas attack on Afghan school girls (13 June 2010) http://freeinternetpress.com/story.php?sid=26063. Accessed 15 June 2010

Glad M (2009) Knowledge on fire: attacks on education in Afghanistan; Risks and measures for successful mitigation. (A study initiated and funded by the World Bank and carried out by CARE International in Afghanistan on behalf of the World Bank and the Afghan Ministry of Education), p 37 http://care.ca/ckfinder/userfiles/files/Knowledge_on_fire-attacks_%20schools.pdf. Accessed 18 May 2010

Human Rights Watch (2006) Lessons in terror: attacks on education in Afghanistan, vol 18, No 6 (C), p 101. www.hrw.org/reports/2006/afghanistan0706/index.htm. Accessed 18 May 2010

India Vision (2010) 73 killed as Pak Taliban attack Ahmadis' Mosques in Lahore (28 May 2010) http://www.indiavision.com/news/article/topnews/60156/ Accessed 24 June 2010

Khan AR (2010) What's behind the poisoning of Afghan girls (26 April 2010) http://www.aolnews.com/world/article/whats-behind-the-poisoning-of-afghan-schoolgirls/19454566. Accessed 15 June 2010

O'Malley B (2010) Education under attack (A report commissioned by Mark Richmond, Director, Division for the Coordination of United Nations Priorities in Education, Education Sector, UNESCO), p 54. http://unesdoc.unesco.org/images/0018/001868/186809e.pdf. Accessed 26 Apr 2010

Office of the Special Representative of the Secretary-General for Children and Armed Conflict (2010) Mission report on the visit of the special representative of the Secretary-General for children and armed conflict to Afghanistan (20–26 February 2010), p 10, downloadable at http://www.unhcr.org/refworld/docid/4c0e143b2.html. Accessed 11 June 2010

Reuters (2010) Afghan girls treated after suspected gas attack (Kabul, 12 June 2010) http://www.reuters.com/article/idUSTRE65B0PQ20100612. Accessed 25 October 2010

Sahim NM (2010) Radio free Europe. Illnesses at Afghan girl's school prompt poisoning fears (Wednesday May 19 2010). http://www.rferl.org/content/Illnesses_At_Afghan_Girls_Schools_Prompt_Poisoning_Fears/2024984.html. Accessed 19 May 2010

Salahuddin S, Shalizi H (2010) Scores of Afghan ill in third school poisoning. http://www.reuters.com/article/idUSTRE54A1IR20090512. Accessed 19 May 2010

Schmitt MN (2010) Human shields in international humanitarian law, Israel Yearbook of Human Rights, p 20

Shalizi H, Hamed M (2010) Reuters: Afghan girls hit again by suspected gas attack (Tuesday, 11 May 2010). http://www.reuters.com/article/idUSTRE64A1A720100511. Accessed 19 May 2010

The Christian Science Monitor (2010) Pakistani Taliban gunmen attack Pakistan mosques, kill at least 70 (28 May 2010) http://www.csmonitor.com/From-the-news-wires/2010/0528/Pakistani-Taliban-gunmen-attack-Pakistan-mosques-kill-at-least-70. Accessed 24 June 2010

UNESCO (2010) Protecting education from attack: a state-of-the-art review (UNESCO report in partnership with the Office of Her Highness Sheikha Mozah Bint Nasser Al-Missned of Qatar, UNESCO Special Envoy for Basic and Higher Education, p 15 http://unesdoc.unesco.org/images/0018/001867/186732e.pdf. Accessed 2 October 2010

Part III
Attacks on Education: Issues of Accountability for *Both* Sides in the ‘War on Terror’

Chapter 5
International Humanitarian Law and the Protection of Education in Conflict-Affected States

5.1 The Protected Status of Civilian Schools Under International Humanitarian Law

5.1.1 The Entitlement of Children to 'Special Protection' Under IHL and the Implications for the Protection of Civilian Schools from Attack and for the Absolute Prohibition on Their Use for a Military Purpose

Schools, as set out in customary practice regarding the rules of war and various conventions concerning the so-called 'civilized' conduct of armed conflict, are included in the general prohibition which exists, in most circumstances, against the targeting of civilian installations for attack. Attack of these civilian facilities is only permitted where there is a pressing 'military necessity' created by their use by the enemy for some significant military advantage. However, it is commonly held that under international law, school buildings *unoccupied* by civilians at the relevant time, unlike buildings with privileged status (civilian hospitals and most religious buildings), can be used for military objectives when there is a military necessity for doing so:

> The law of war equally forbids targeting [for attack] hospitals, religious buildings, schools and other civilian buildings unless they become justifiable military objectives. But ironically, it fails to equally protect these buildings from being ***used*** for such [military] objectives in the first place. *Under the law of war's privileges for civilian hospitals and most religious buildings, armed forces cannot use these buildings for military purposes-without exception. In contrast, the law of war's privilege for school buildings ambiguously allows military use based on necessity* (emphasis added).[1]

This section includes a challenge to the foregoing claim regarding the alleged less privileged status of civilian schools [hereafter referred to also simply as 'schools'] in comparison to that of civilian hospitals and most religious buildings during armed conflict in regards to a prohibited use for a military purpose even

---

[1] Bart (2010), p. 195.

S.C. Grover, *Schoolchildren as Propaganda Tools in the War on Terror*,
DOI 10.1007/978-3-642-17900-6_5,

under conditions of military necessity. That is, the contention is here advanced that unoccupied school buildings (and not just schools occupied by civilians and/or non-combatants) are precluded from use for a military purpose in all circumstances just as are most religious buildings and all hospitals and medical units (Note that the medical facilities serve a humanitarian purpose and treat the wounded or sick whenever the opportunity arises regardless of the latter's membership in any particular belligerent force –friend or foe). Were this not the case (were civilian school buildings that are normally dedicated to a civilian purpose lawfully available for use for a military purpose where there is deemed to be a compelling 'military necessity' for the same), it is here argued, the 'special protections' to be afforded to children under international humanitarian law would be but legal fictions (i.e., see "Protection of Children": Article 77(1) Protocol I additional to the 1949 Geneva Conventions: "The Parties to the conflict shall provide them [children] with the care and aid they require, whether because of their age or for any other reason").[2] Such would be the result in that the use of civilian schools for a military purpose, whether or not occupied by schoolchildren as well as armed forces, places all children at risk of harm. This it does by creating confusion for the enemy about which schools have or have not been converted to a military purpose thus putting any children still attending schools, or those living near schools at risk of grievous injury or death from attacks on schools. For that reason the use of civilian schools for a military purpose can also be considered a contributor to violence against schools during armed conflict and, in that sense, an alternate form of attack on a school in its own right.

The position articulated here that civilian schools have a 'privileged status' with regard to enjoying an absolute prohibition against their use for military purposes (even where there is a compelling military necessity and whether occupied by civilians and/or noncombatants or not) is thus contrary to the views of those who hold that:

> ... Protocol I [additional to the 1949 Geneva Conventions (API)] provides school buildings *only* with the general protections against being targeted that are given to all civilian buildings in Article 52. Moreover, Article 52 and 53 [of AP I] allow for military use of school buildings by expressing without limitation that schools may be converted into military objectives... Protocol I limits military use of schools only to the extent that civilians and noncombatants are present (emphasis added).[3]

The issue of just what Articles 52 and 53 of additional Protocol I to the 1949 Geneva Conventions (also hereafter referred to as API) imply (on the analysis here) about *the use of unoccupied schools* for military purposes will be discussed at length in a later section in this chapter. In that section, Articles 52 and 53 of API

[2] Protocol Additional to the Geneva Conventions of 12 August 1949, and relating to the Protection of Victims of International Armed Conflicts (Protocol I), 8 June 1977, entry into force 7 December 1978 [Article 77(1)]. http://www.icrc.org/ihl.nsf/full/470?opendocument. Accessed 28 June 2010.

[3] Bart (2010), p. 212.

will be shown to be quite consistent with a complete ban under IHL on the use of schools for a military purpose without exception.

In the context of the 'war on terror'; it is apparent that organized terror groups have no compunction regarding attacking schools. This is the case even where: (1) the terror group is fully cognizant of the fact that the school is a civilian object that has *not* been converted to a military purpose, and (2) whether or not children are still attending there or are present in the building at the time of the attack. However, this fact does *not* make the use of unoccupied civilian schools for a compelling military purpose by those fighting organized terror groups lawful under IHL in certain circumstances. This is the case, as explained, since doing so would obliterate the 'special protection' to be afforded children under IHL. More specifically, the use of unoccupied civilian schools for a military purpose under conditions of pressing 'military necessity' during armed conflict would reduce *children's* protection from a 'special protection' to the 'general protection' to be afforded any civilian (not engaged in the hostilities) during armed conflict. This would be the result in that unoccupied schools (civilian objects) would then not have the privileged protected status that prohibits their use for a military purpose under any scenario during armed conflict thus likely increasing considerably the risk for attack on schools that are occupied.

There is no authority under international humanitarian law, it is here argued, to treat children as having the identical status as adults in terms of the protections to be afforded them. Hence, children retain their right to 'special protection' even during times of pressing 'military necessity' and this fact: (1) confers on civilian schools a correlative protection from use for a military purpose without exception, and (2) sets out a higher standard for the school becoming the legitimate object of attack where it is suspected that the school has been converted to a military use. In regards to the standard required to launch an attack on a civilian school, there is a presumption of it being a civilian object (one that by its very nature is dedicated to a civilian purpose) and that presumption must prevail in cases of doubt. This emphasis on extreme caution in regards to launching an attack on a civilian school where there is any doubt regarding its status is evidenced by the fact that schools (along with houses or other dwellings and places of worship) are listed as an example of a building which must be presumed to be a civilian object unless proven otherwise as reflected in Article 52(3) of additional Protocol I

> ... Article 52(3) API [additional Protocol I to the 1949 Geneva Conventions] ... imposes a *presumption of civilian character in cases of doubt only with respect to objects which are 'normally dedicated to a civilian purposes' such as .... a school* (emphasis added).[4]

In contrast to the situation with civilian schools suspected of being military objectives (where the lingering doubt must be resolved in favour of *not* attacking); in regards to many other civilian buildings, the remaining doubt need not be resolved in favour of the building being regarded as a civilian object as long as

[4]Bart (2010), p. 212 [Article 52(3)].

everything feasible has been done in the circumstance to verify that the object is in fact a military objective.[5]

It is here argued then that while 'military necessity' when of an imminent, imperative nature may override the 'general protections' afforded civilians; this is *not* the case in respect of the 'special protections' to be afforded children in certain circumstances. For instance, as civilian elementary, middle and secondary schools are intrinsically linked to schoolchildren being at these schools or close by (there is an intimate nexus between schools and schoolchildren), schools of this nature benefit from: (1) special protection without limitation both as to use for a military purpose (i.e., no use of the school for a military purpose without exception), *and* (2) a higher than normal standard regarding determining a legitimate basis for attack (i.e., where there is any doubt as to whether the civilian school has been converted to a military purpose by the enemy; the lingering doubt must be resolved in favour of considering the school to be a civilian object).

5.1.2 Challenging Status Quo Interpretations of IHL on the Alleged Less Privileged Status of Civilian Schools

When civilian schools are used for military purposes, they then become vulnerable to lawful attack under international humanitarian law (IHL) based on alleged pressing 'military necessity' (lawful assuming the attacking force is a combatant force as defined under IHL). Unlawful attacks on schools by an enemy comprised of civilians organized into a terror group, as in Afghanistan, occur, however, regardless of whether the school is used for a civilian or military purpose by the opponents of the Taliban and other insurgents as the various NGO reports discussed previously attest. That much is clear. However, when it comes to what is considered lawful use of a civilian school during armed conflict, the clarity is no more. Rather, it appears that, in practice, States that adhere to IHL are quite contradictory in their positions on the legitimacy of the use of civilian schools for a military purpose during armed conflict:

> ... military use converts a school from a privileged site into a justifiable target for an opposing enemy [combatant force recognized under IHL]. Even more troubling, such use increases the likelihood that an opposing army will confuse converted and unconverted schools and wrongfully attack one that shelters children and other civilians [i.e., teachers, students, parents etc.] ***State practice paradoxically both opposes and accepts military use of schools during war***. The ongoing conflict in Iraq provides many examples. In 2003, the United States condemned Iraqi military commanders for employing school buildings and grounds as sites for artillery, materiel storage, and headquarters. Human Rights Watch noted that the Iraqi practice [of using schools for military purposes] directly contributed to the number of civilian casualties because those buildings became lawful targets for the coalition forces. The United States also denounced hostile insurgent forces for using school

[5]Henderson (2009), pp. 163–164.

> buildings as weapons caches and bases to launch attacks. Meanwhile, in northern Iraq, U.S. military commanders employed school buildings for military headquarters and command posts. Of note, American forces utilized school buildings that they characterized as abandoned or former schools while Iraqi and insurgent forces exploited ones that were still occupied by students (emphasis added).[6]

The fact that "State practice paradoxically both opposes and accepts military use of schools during war"[7] illustrates, it is here contended, that the use of civilian schools (whether occupied or unoccupied by civilians) for military purposes is not founded on any legally supportable, principled ground, but rather is a matter of State-calculated expediency. Further, in regard to the use of 'unoccupied' civilian schools for military purposes, note that just what constitutes a truly 'abandoned' or 'former' school building is often not as clear cut as some commanding officers might suggest. This is the case in that, for instance, children and teachers may 'abandon' a school building if they fear an imminent terror attack and not return for weeks or months depending on what military action ensues in the vicinity or neighbouring vicinity. However, they may never intend to permanently leave the school unoccupied by students and teachers in pursuit of the civilian purpose of education.

The current author then concurs that converting civilian schools to a military purpose may lead a combatant force that wishes to adhere to IHL to mistake unconverted schools for converted schools and lawfully attack in error. However, in what follows the propositions that: (1) the customary rules of war allow for the military use of *unoccupied* schools and that (2) IHL offers no protection in this regard will be further contested. The issue is of significance in the context of the war on terror even though the Taliban terrorists and Al-Qaeda have no hesitation in attacking any civilian installation to spread terror; including schools, religious and cultural facilities, hospitals and other non-school civilian buildings or sites whether occupied by civilians and/ or other noncombatants or not. Nevertheless, there is a need to clarify just what current IHL stipulates expressly or by implication about:

1. The lawful use, if any, of civilian schools for a pressing military purpose during armed conflict (i.e., whether unoccupied school buildings can be used for military purposes where there is a compelling military necessity or whether the IHL prohibition against such use during armed conflict extends also to unoccupied school buildings in all circumstances).
2. In what circumstances attacks on schools during armed conflict constitute a separable distinct international crime for which perpetrators can be held to account under international criminal law.
3. Whether civilians can under certain facts be considered to have participated in the commission of war crimes even when not part of an armed force and not directly engaged in combat. (We will consider this issue in respect of civilians such as politicians, members of national and international aid organizations and

[6]Bart (2010), pp. 195–196.

[7]Bart (2010), p. 196.

others who facilitate children and other civilians attending schools knowing that these schoolchildren and adult civilians are at considerable risk of being the victims of a terror attack while at the school or on their way to or from the school given the lack of security for education).

We will address all three of the above questions/issues in what follows in considering accountability for international crimes occurring during armed conflict and relating to: (1) the use of civilian schools for a military purpose, (2) terror attacks on civilian schools and (3) indirect complicity in attacks on education through certain intentional acts known to have the potential to further terrorist objectives.

5.1.3 Civilian Schools Used for a Military Purpose: The Intransgressible 'Principle of Distinction' Undermined

The view that civilians and/or non-combatants (members of the armed forces hors du combat, Red Cross personnel, army chaplains etc.) must be present in the civilian school in order that the school building be protected from use for a military purpose appears to be the current consensus reading of IHL on the matter of privileges to which the civilian school is entitled:

> Current international law does *not* provide most [civilian schools] with a direct, clear, and independent privileged status based on their inherent humanitarian nature or value to a people. Rather, *it protects schools against military use [and therefore becoming a lawful military objective for opposing forces and subject to lawful attack]* ***based solely on the presence of civilians and noncombatants [in the school]. It thereby focuses exclusively on the military attackers' obligations to discriminate in targeting.*** These indirect protections are anachronistic compared to the direct ones currently afforded to hospitals and religious buildings (emphasis added).[8]

The argument here, however, has been that under international humanitarian law, civilian schools without exception cannot lawfully be used for military purposes during armed conflict (as is the case also for civilian hospitals and most religious facilities). That is, schools cannot under IHL be used for a military purpose whether occupied by civilians and noncombatants or unoccupied by the same. We have already considered one key reason for this relating to the fact that since children have 'special protection' rights under IHL so, too, civilian schools, given their nexus to children, are also entitled to protection from military use without limitation. This as there is a grave risk, as explained, to the security of schoolchildren arising both from terror attacks on civilian schools, *and* from their use for military purposes whether occupied by civilians or not (given that the latter is a contributor to attacks on unconverted schools by the enemy as well).

---

[8]Bart (2010), p. 196.

The use of occupied *or unoccupied* civilian schools for military purposes, and the grave risk this poses to children, it is here argued, undermines not only children's IHL entitlement to 'special protection', but also arguably one of the most fundamental principles of IHL; namely the 'principle of distinction'. The 'principle of distinction' stipulates that a distinction must at all times be made in armed conflict between: (1) 'combatants' and (2) 'noncombatants' (the latter being a category of which 'civilians' are a subcategory with the other subcategories being those non-civilians who previously participated in combat but are now 'hors du combat' as well as medics, and chaplains). Violation of the principle of distinction, however, is in fact completely impermissible under IHL.

Before delving into the issue of the use of civilian schools for military purposes and the implications for the 'principle of distinction', let us be clear on a key point from the outset. *Any attack by an organized terror group* (i.e., the Taliban extremists, Al-Qaeda or other such organized terror group) against a school under any circumstance (whether or not there are civilians and/or other non-combatants present in the school, or whether the school is abandoned, or used as a cache for weapons or for any other military purpose by the opposing force etc.) is unlawful under international humanitarian law. Thus, terror attacks on schools perceived to be vehicles for counter-insurgency propaganda just by virtue of these schools being operational and having students attending and creating some sense of stabilization are also unlawful. This is the legal situation in that these organized terror groups are *not* combatants under IHL in the first instance (i.e., the terror groups are comprised of civilians engaging unlawfully in armed conflict with the State and its allies and, in addition, perpetrating international crimes including but not limited to the use of terror against civilians). Thus, attacks by organized terror groups on objects normally dedicated to civilian purposes (i.e., civilian schools); regardless whether these objects are or are not in fact being used for military purposes at the time, or whether there is a military necessity for the attack from the perspective of the terror group, violate international humanitarian law. The prime goal of such attacks is to spread terror amongst the civilian population and, hence, such attacks fall into the 'war crimes' category as opposed to legitimate military operation.

Let us again then consider the issue of the 'principle of distinction' and how it is undermined in the context of the war on terror. It has long been supposed that schools are protected from attack under IHL if they have civilians or non-combatants (i.e., the wounded and others hors du combat) occupying them. If schools are: (1) used for any military purpose by an armed force (such as to launch attacks etc.) thus endangering civilians present at or near the school, or (2) if an armed force uses the school to *shield* military operations given its location close to civilians; then culpability for any civilian causalities at the school, or near the school due to the enemy attacking that *converted* school is attributed to those who used the school for a military purpose and not to the attackers (supposing for the moment that the attackers are members of a lawful combatant force that adheres to IHL).[9]

[9]Solis (2010), p. 320.

("The presence or movements of the civilian population or individual civilians [such as at or near schools] shall not be used to render certain points or areas immune from military operations" [i.e., shall not be used to shield military operations]".[10] That is, the party to the conflict which *in the first instance* took actions to undermine the 'principle of distinction' by intentionally putting civilians at risk is held culpable for any civilian casualties in the scenarios described.

The Afghan government and its allies, of course, are *not,* as a matter of accepted policy or practice, using civilian schools occupied by civilians and/or noncombatants as a base from which to launch or support military attacks against the enemy. (The use of civilians or non-combatants in schools as 'human shields' (i.e., where the school has been converted to a military purpose by a terrorist group) is a violation of IHL under the customary rules of war and these civilians according to some legal scholars may be considered as "hostages" who have not lost their civilian status.[11] Recall also that all attacks by those who use a pattern and practice of terrorism in armed conflict (they systematically target civilians) are unlawful under international criminal law (i.e., the Rome Statute).[12] While the Afghan government and its allies do not use civilians and/or noncombatants in civilian schools as 'human shields'; the question arises as to whether they, nonetheless, are using civilians in schools for a military purpose. We turn to that question next.

5.1.4 The Use of Civilian Schools for Counter-Terrorist Propaganda as a 'Military Purpose': Negating the 'Principle of Distinction'

The focus in the following discussion is not on the attackers employing terrorism, but on the Afghan State and its allies in regard to their obligations under international humanitarian law regarding the protection of schools; both those occupied and unoccupied by civilians at the relevant time. The question is raised as to whether in the context of the 'war on terror', schools are, in a certain respect, being used for a military purpose by the Afghan government and its allies with the cooperation of the international humanitarian education aid community. This being the case though the 'military purpose' is other than the typical purpose of storing weapons or other military supplies in the school or using the school as a base for launching military

[10]Protocol Additional to the Geneva Conventions of 12 August 1949, and relating to the Protection of Victims of International Armed Conflicts (Protocol I), 8 June 1977, entry into force 7 December 1978. http://www.icrc.org/ihl.nsf/full/470?opendocument. Accessed 28 June 2010, Article 7.

[11]Schmitt (2010), p. 30.

[12]Rome Statute of the International Criminal Court (entered into force 1 July 2002). http://untreaty.un.org/cod/icc/statute/romefra.htm. Accessed 11 July 2010.

attacks etc. Put more specifically, 'are the defenders against organized terror groups in the context of the armed conflict in Afghanistan; namely: (1) the Afghan government and its allies (formally charged with the responsibility of protecting civilians), and (2) national and international NGOs (i.e., that sponsor many schools and prepare response plans for the prevention of attacks and rapid response strategies to attacks though holding no State responsibility for protecting schools) violating IHL by operating schools in Afghanistan in zones where schools have inadequate security?' That is, are the ostensible 'defenders' of schools in Afghanistan *themselves* unlawfully using schools for a 'military purpose' despite those schools being operational and housing civilians? In particular, are the ostensible 'defenders' of democracy and human rights using schools as part of a 'counter-insurgency strategy' that, in reality, violates IHL such that occupied schools are being used for an arguably 'military purpose'?

This author would reply 'yes' to the foregoing questions regarding the manner in which these defenders against organized terrorism are using occupied schools. This is to say that an unacceptable counter-insurgency strategy is being used in respect of basic education and schoolchildren. That counter-insurgency strategy involves the operation of schools also in high risk insecure zones (and not just secure zones) in Afghanistan where the children and teachers and other school personnel (civilians) present in the school (i.e., education aid workers, volunteer parents, village elders etc.) are at high risk of injury or death in a terror attack. The fact that these defenders would not restrict the operation of schools to areas where the State has at least minimally adequate control over security, and the rule of law is operative to some reasonable extent suggests a 'hidden agenda'. That hidden agenda is *not* concerned simply with schooling as a means to meeting individual rights entitlements to education, and education as a pathway to development in the country. Rather, that tacit agenda involves, it is here contended, the use of schools as a vehicle for counter-terrorist propaganda. More specifically, the following are intended to defeat the view that the terrorists are succeeding in de-stabilizing Afghanistan and halting development: significant numbers of schools operational, increased level of school enrollment, increased number of new schools opened and increased number of schools damaged by terror attacks repaired and opened anew, increased number of tent schools operating to replace schools damaged severely or destroyed in a terror attack etc.) That hidden agenda relating to 'counter-insurgency propaganda' is being operationalized via the basic education sector as described despite the risks that such a strategy entails to civilians (including child civilians students) who attend at the schools despite inadequate security.

Such an approach (operating schools during armed conflict even where there is inadequate security) is, it is advanced here, a violation of IHL and amounts to using schools for a military objective. 'Military objective' (as the term is used here) is defined in the context of Article 52(2) of Protocol I additional to the 1949 Geneva Conventions dealing with the protection of civilian objects. That provision reads as follows:

> Attacks shall be limited strictly to military objectives. In so far as objects are concerned, military objectives are limited to those objects which by their nature, location, purpose or

use make an effective contribution to military action and whose total or partial destruction, capture or neutralization, in the circumstances ruling at the time, offers a definite military advantage.[13]

Schools then, it is here contended, are operating as 'military objectives' when operating in an area that is not secure (i.e., where there is ongoing armed conflict and a high risk of a terror attack on the school). Their destruction has distinct propaganda value for terrorists in communicating that the general area where the school is located has not been stabilized by the Afghan government and its allies. In contrast, if the schools escape a terror attack and continue functioning; this provides a propaganda advantage for the Afghan State and its allies in suggesting that a civil life free of terror and authoritarianism is possible in Afghanistan and progress is being made in that direction.

Schools operating in such circumstances (within insecure zones in Afghanistan where school security is highly uncertain) are intended, by virtue simply of their being open and functioning, in point of fact first and foremost to provide a propaganda advantage over the enemy. Propaganda victories are an essential element in acquiring and retaining funding for military actions for the States involved in the 'war on terror'; in winning the commitment of the Afghan public and the international community to the effort to defeat the Taliban in Afghanistan and in obtaining aid monies for development work in that conflict-affected State Were it the case, in reality, that the primary interest of government officials and NGOs was that of developing the schoolchildren's potential and ensuring their future, the children would surely not be put in this situation of substantial risk to their personal security (by being encouraged to attend schools also where the area is not secured) as the latter is anathema to their potential well-being.

Any success achieved in counter-insurgency propaganda creates a degree of military advantage in respect of the propaganda battle that characterizes many internal conflicts; especially the so-called 'war on terror' which also, of course, has international dimensions. That success in this context, as discussed, involves creating the illusion of progress in securing areas that are in fact still insecure. The illusion of progress in achieving security in regions where this is in fact largely, or completely not the case, and in creating the perception that there is a return to a degree of normalcy in daily life, is created then in significant part by the operation of schools in those unsecured areas. Schooling, afterall, is symbolic of hope for the future, and the routine of daily life in what is supposed to be a secure environment. (This is not at all to suggest that progress is not being made in some areas within Afghanistan in terms of significantly weakening the terrorists and in gaining public support for their defeat). Schools thus are being used to send a counter-insurgency message simply by their being functional in the face of terror. They serve as a vehicle for the national government and its allies to send 'return propaganda fire'

[13]Protocol Additional to the Geneva Conventions of 12 August 1949, and relating to the Protection of Victims of International Armed Conflicts (Protocol I), 8 June 1977, entry into force 7 December 1978 [Article 52 (2)]. http://www.icrc.org/ihl.nsf/full/470?opendocument. Accessed 28 June 2010.

so-to-speak, to the Taliban and Al-Qaeda propaganda campaign; the latter waged via attacks on schools, schoolchildren, education personnel and education aid workers. The terrorists, further, broadcast anti-Afghan government and anti-Western propaganda via a host of media forums; for example, by way of online and televised 24 –h- media outlets; terrorist carefully crafted audiotapes, and videotapes containing threats, denunciations against the West, a call to others to join jihad against the West, and, at times, gruesome images of atrocities the terror group has perpetrated on certain of its victims. Interestingly, those videotapes of terror activities and civilian casualties distributed by terror groups to news outlets for consumption by the international public rarely, if ever, intentionally show the child victims of their attacks on education (i.e., so as to avoid alienating those in the international community from whom they hope to gain sympathy and support). Of late, as mentioned, the Taliban in Afghanistan has often not acknowledged its role in school attacks knowing full well that the local communities are well aware of the correlation between Taliban incursion into an area and a high incidence of terror attacks on education. In this way, the Taliban is able to: (1) induce extreme terror in local communities by threatening and/or destroying schools, and injuring or killing groups of schoolchildren and others associated with education, while at the same time (2) avoid the issue of having to provide any alleged justification for such acts of terrorism (for which there can be none); particularly as relates to grievously injuring or killing children.

The use of schools by national governments of CAFS such as Afghanistan and their allies as a key component in the counter-terrorism propaganda strategy (i.e., operating schools with minimal regard to security issues in order to create the impression of improved stabilization), in effect, obliterates the distinction between: (1) **schools used for a military purpose**: schools *without* either civilians (i.e., students and teachers etc.) or other noncombatants present in the building ('unoccupied schools') which are used to advance the military objectives of an armed force under conditions of pressing military necessity *versus* (2) **schools *not* used for a military purpose**: schools occupied by civilians (i.e., students and teachers or other non-combatants) and used for a humanitarian purpose (education, refuge etc.). In the instance discussed; occupied schools are being used for the military purpose of counter-insurgency propaganda thus: (1) putting schoolchildren and other civilians attending at the school in harm's way from a likely terror attack against an unprotected school; and (2) undermining the principle of distinction between civilian *versus* non-civilian objects.

To summarize then the dissemination of successful counter-insurgency propaganda is a 'military objective'. Schools operating in areas with a lack of security for the prime purpose of creating the illusion of State progress in stabilization of the area are tools in the attempt to achieve the military objective of successful counter-insurgency propaganda (the ultimate goal being the demoralization of the enemy and the winning of "the hearts and minds" of the Afghan people as well as the garnering of support for the war effort from the international community). There is then a blurring of the lines between what is and is not a school used for a 'military objective' since some schools with civilians present are being used for a military purpose though these civilians are not being used as human shields but rather as pawns in the counter-terrorism propaganda campaign. This situation then greatly erodes the principle of distinction between civilian and non-civilian objects. No longer is it the case then that all schools are civilian objects if only civilians and/or other noncombatants are present in the school (no armed forces, weapons or other military supplies in the school and no use of the schools for launching attacks or guiding or planning attacks on an armed enemy force). The latter is not the case then when schools are operating in insecure zones within the CAFS and children encouraged to attend despite the security risks in order that the school can be an effective part of a counter-insurgency propaganda effort. Furthermore, the children attending at the school must be considered as involuntary participants in any such counter-propaganda objective given their not being emancipated from parental control and the fact that their attendance at the school for the most part is at the behest of the State and the parents (i.e., there are coercive forces operative). It cannot be assumed that the children, in any case, fully appreciate the risks in attending at the school (i.e., many children do not cease attending at insecure school sites until one or more of their student colleagues and/or teachers are seriously injured or killed at school or on the way to and from school thus bringing the reality of the situation and the very tangible risks into stark relief). In a sense then the children are in a situation similar to a hostage in that they themselves generally did not intend to be exposed to the risk of terror attack based on a voluntary informed choice.

The question arises as to whether under IHL a school normally dedicated to a civilian purpose, but one which is now instead being used first and foremost for counter-insurgency propaganda purposes, qualifies as a legitimate military target/ objective for the enemy. The current author holds the view that attacks on schools (including attacks carried out to counter the propaganda benefits for the Afghan government and its allies of operational schools in both secured and unsecured areas of the country) are unjustified illegal attacks under IHL given that: (1) the 'military necessity' test is not met since the military advantages of such an attack, if any, are indeterminate at the time of the attack (it could bring a backlash from the community in fact due to the loss of civilian life as a result of premeditated terror acts and, hence, lose the attackers some of their support); (2) terror attacks are war crimes (3) there is a predicable significant loss of civilian life and injury to civilians to be expected as a result of the attacks on unprotected or poorly protected schools which, weighed against any potential propaganda advantage for the terrorists, must take priority and deter the attack (given that the right to life and security of the person is an inherent universal right of all civilians); (4) the Taliban and other insurgents are unlawful combatants that employ illegitimate tactics (i.e., terrorism perpetrated against civilians) such that any attack they carry out is a violation of IHL.

Arguably it is the case that schools, even though they may have students and teachers present and educational lessons ongoing, when used as part of the counter-terrorist propaganda campaign, have essentially lost their civilian status (i.e., they are no longer dedicated only to a humanitarian purpose as children's lives are being risked as well as that of other civilians in order to use schools for these propaganda purposes in unsecured zones). Further, civilians present in the school (students and teachers) in the process have arguably been transformed, without their knowledge necessarily or informed consent, into persons contributing to the armed conflict though not through contributing directly to the violence at least not in the usual sense (that is, the schools operating in insecure zones attract terrorist attack). This situation then erodes "the principle of distinction" (supported by the laws and customs of war and by international humanitarian treaty law) and the "principle of protection of the civilian population [as]... "intransgressible principles of international customary law".[14] The latter international humanitarian law principles define a modicum of civilized behaviour required of all parties to an international or non-international armed conflict regardless whether they are signatories to, or have ratified or acceded to the core international humanitarian law treaties.

In regards to the matter of the State's obligation (and the obligation of its allies participating directly in the conflict within that State's territory) to protect the CAFS civilian population during the armed conflict, it is clear that in respect of schools and their attendees, the States have *not* met their IHL obligations in this regard (to wit; the number of school attacks and civilian school-related deaths and casualties occurring while at the same time the State and its NGO partners are encouraging school attendance even without adequate security). When schools in insecure zones are closed at least temporarily in certain insecure zones in Afghanistan, it is most often it would seem because parents are afraid to send their children to school for a time after a terror attack while some teachers may also be too fearful to return immediately. Further, NGO, and international human rights organization policy makers and decision-makers also are too often, it would appear, willing to encourage school attendance despite the security risks. This fact is reflected also in the following quotes from a paper prepared as *the outcome document* of a 2009 exploratory seminar on international law and the issue of protecting schools in conflict- affected States hereafter referred to as 'the outcome paper' (the seminar participants included legal academics, a representative from the UN Office of the Special Rapporteur for the Right to Education; representatives from Human Rights Watch, Amnesty International, UNESCO, consultants with expertise regarding attacks on schools who have consulted for organizations such as UNESCO on the topic, and representatives from the Planning and Programming Directorate, Office of Her Highness Sheikka Mozah Bint Nasser Al-Missned). While the paper has a disclaimer suggesting that the views in the paper are not necessarily those of the organizational participants, at the same time, the paper is the outcome document of the seminar involving prominent representatives from these organizations. It is difficult thus to suppose that the organizational participants as organizations might hold radically different views than those expressed in the paper by their individual representatives though in certain instances this is, of course, possible.

[14]International Court of Justice Advisory Opinion on the Legality of Nuclear Weapons cited in *Prosecutor versus Kordic and Cerkez* (Appeals Chamber) Case No IT-95-14-2-A (17 December 2004) at pp. 16–17.

The outcome paper makes reference to: (1) children attending schools in the midst of armed conflict where security for the schools and for the children attending them is much less than adequate; and (2) implicitly also makes reference to various NGOs and international human rights organizations doing nothing to discourage school attendance despite there being inadequate protection for students, teachers and school buildings or for alternate education sites and where all of the foregoing are favoured targets for terror attacks. Rather, the onus is put on the children and teachers to work out ways to: (1) dodge armed forces' fire (sometimes via cooperation with combatant forces that adhere to IHL) and (2) prevent terror attacks or the consequences thereof. We thus find that the international human rights and humanitarian organization representatives participating in the aforementioned seminar on school attacks speak in the outcome document of trying to minimize collateral damage and prevent terror attacks. The reality is, however, that children in many areas within the CAFS still attend school with inadequate security provisions in the midst of the conflict and have no practicable way to avoid becoming victims of armed attack by either side in the conflict.

NGO, U.N. and State pleas as have been made to the Taliban terror group and other insurgents in Afghanistan to end their attacks on education and so the grievous harms done to students, teachers, other education personnel, humanitarian education aid workers and education facilities by these parties seem rather naïve. This is the case given that the agenda of organized terror groups is precisely to maximize such harms to innocents so as to destabilize the Afghan government; demoralize the Afghan people and dampen the West's enthusiasm for supporting the war on terror in Afghanistan.

Representative quotes from the aforementioned outcome paper on international law and attacks on education suggest that NGOs support continued school attendance in the midst of the armed conflict and despite inadequate security. In addition to rather futile pleas to the Taliban to end their attacks on schools and schoolchildren, on education personnel and on education aid workers; the seminar participants offer some optimistic suggestions for precautions that might help reduce the harm to civilians ('collateral damage') resulting from Western allied military operations:

> It might be possible for the military to improve its planning by seeking objective information from people knowledgeable about education in the area under attack. For instance, planners could minimize collateral harm [i.e., injuries and deaths of students and teachers and damage or destruction of school buildings etc.] by being given information on the likely movements of students and teachers (like the days and timings of classes, national examinations, vacations)...[15]
>
> In addition, educators and humanitarian workers can press upon soldiers the damage that their operations can do to students and their education. ... Planners and commanders are making subjective judgments about what is a reasonable trade –off between competing interests: this much civilian death and destruction is a reasonable price for achieving this

[15]Planning and Programming Directorate, Office of Her Highness Sheikka Mozah Bint Nasser Al-Missned. International law and the protection of education systems. In UNESCO (2010), p. 156.

> much of a military advantage. Education specialists, lawyers and other humanitarian workers can affect the trade-off judgments by actively engaging with military planners and their legal advisors.[16]

In addition, the quotes below from the aforementioned outcome paper reveal what some may characterize as a propaganda message regarding education and development which: (1) encourages children to continue to attend school in zones within CAFS where their security is at especially high risk if they do attend school and (2) attempts, in practice, to create the public perception in the international community that going to school (*even in the midst of armed conflict and without adequate security*) is 'healing' and that children are "resilient" enough to recover in most instances from the effects of war (i.e., in Afghanistan this would include having been the victim of a terror attack on the school and perhaps even seeing the school blown up or being burned to the ground as a result of arson or, in some instances, witnessing certain fellow students as well as teachers killed or maimed in the attack). There is in the quote that follows an over-generalization regarding the role of education (in respect of supporting individual children and society in their respective development goals) *from* the post-conflict societal context or a context involving specific areas within CAFS that are secure *to* a context where there is inadequate or virtually no security in the midst of armed conflict in a particular locale:

> Blowing up school buildings is an immediate loss of property, but that loss will lead to other losses. Children and young people still have resiliency even though they have been traumatized by war and insecurity, and being in school is important for helping them to cope, recover and develop. Moreover, education plays a leading role in preparing children and young people to earn a living, and to participate in the social, economic and political development of their country.[17]

To recap then, children must not be encouraged or compelled to attend school where their security is at grave risk in a terror zone. Encouraging and facilitating such school attendance in such circumstances, on the analysis here, violates international humanitarian law. Further, doing so must no longer be characterized as a humanitarian intervention focused on what is incorrectly and unapologetically characterized as 'relief', 'recovery', 'development' or 'reconstruction'. Having children attend school in the midst of an armed conflict where their security at school or on routes to and from school at particular locales within the CAFS is inadequately protected is rather, as we have discovered, intended first and foremost to serve bureaucratic self-interest and propaganda purposes.

The aforementioned outcome paper refers to: "[Military] Planners and commanders ... making subjective judgments about what is a reasonable trade-off between competing interests: "this much civilian death and destruction

---

[16]Planning and Programming Directorate, Office of Her Highness Sheikka Mozah Bint Nasser Al-Missned. International law and the protection of education systems. In UNESCO (2010), p. 156.

[17]Planning and Programming Directorate, Office of Her Highness Sheikka Mozah Bint Nasser Al-Missned. International law and the protection of education systems. In UNESCO (2010), p. 156.

is a reasonable price for achieving this much of a military advantage".[18] The question is asked here, however, whether the policy makers working for national and international NGOs and international human rights organizations, in practice, make somewhat of an analogous trade-off when they encourage school attendance in zones within CAFS that are not yet under government control, and despite the grave security risks school attendance in such an area entails. That is, are NGOs and international human rights organizations, with or without intent, in practice, operationalizing the following trade-off when they encourage school attendance despite inadequate security: "this much civilian death [of students, teachers, other education-related personnel and education humanitarian aid workers] and destruction [of schools] is a reasonable price for achieving this much of an advantage in promoting our development agenda and obtaining or sustaining international funding for our projects"?

When schools, by operating in an insecure zone, are used first and foremost to send a counter-insurgency propaganda message (regarding alleged stabilization and reclaiming of territory infiltrated by terrorists), they are not exclusively fulfilling a humanitarian objective (i.e., education of the populace). It is that humanitarian objective that is the foundational reason for their protection as a civilian object under IHL in the first instance. International humanitarian law stipulates explicitly that civilian objects shall not be the object of attack or of reprisals: "Civilian objects are all objects which are *not* military objectives...".[19] Civilians, particularly schoolchildren, used for counter-insurgency propaganda (thus having been encouraged to attend at school despite inadequate security) participate in this effort entirely unwittingly in most instances. Furthermore, teachers and individual frontline humanitarian education aid workers who put themselves at risk are generally dedicated primarily or often exclusively to education rather than to sending counter-insurgency propaganda messages. Yet, as explained, at the State and NGO organizational level; policy-makers and superior decision-makers do not necessarily have an exclusive focus on the educational and security interests of the children and all those civilians engaged in the education enterprise. Where the foremost objective of operating schools in the midst of armed conflict in particular locales is one of counter-insurgency propaganda, and this objective overrides prioritizing the safety of civilians, this is not only unjustifiable, but also a violation of international humanitarian law. This tact transforms a virtually unprotected civilian object into a valued military objective and places children and other civilians at high risk of injury or death. It is important to point out that attacks on schools to gain a propaganda advantage over those fighting the so-called 'war on terror' are not permissible under IHL since: (1) children are entitled to special protections under IHL as discussed *even if they are somehow being used/exploited*

[18] Planning and Programming Directorate, Office of Her Highness Sheikka Mozah Bint Nasser Al-Missned. International law and the protection of education systems. In UNESCO (2010), p. 156.

[19] Protocol Additional to the Geneva Conventions of 12 August 1949, and relating to the Protection of Victims of International Armed Conflicts (Protocol I) 8 June 1977, entry into force 7 December 1978. http://www.icrc.org/ihl.nsf/full/470?opendocument. Accessed 28 June 2010 [Article 52(1)].

for military purposes (as a child soldier, as a tool for counter-insurgency propaganda etc.), and (2) propaganda purposes are arguably an illegitimate basis under IHL for an attack that endangers the security of civilians even by a lawful combatant force (which the Taliban is not). Note that civilians are at increased risk of attack due to their education involvement both due to: (1) the lack of protection afforded the schools they attend and (2) the organized terror group's perceived need to shatter any illusion or hope of the State making substantive progress toward increased security.

5.1.5 More on the IHL Protection Guarantees for Civilians

Article 51 of Protocol I additional to the 1949 Geneva Conventions (concerned with international conflict) requires that civilians be protected insofar as possible from the dangers that are associated with military operations (as does Article 13(1) of Protocol II additional to the 1949 Geneva Conventions dealing with non-international conflicts *which uses the same text*):

> Art 51. - Protection of the civilian population
> 1. The civilian population and individual civilians *shall* enjoy general protection against dangers arising from military operations (emphasis added).[20]

When schoolchildren and teachers are used in the counter-terrorism propaganda campaign by being encouraged to attend schools despite woefully inadequate security for those schools, IHL is, as previously discussed, violated as a result. More specifically, on the analysis here, Article 13 of Protocol II is infringed in the context of a non-international conflict such as in Afghanistan. These civilians are actually being thrust directly into the "dangers arising from military operations" by the enemy (the terror group_ due to their being exploited as tools in counter-insurgency propaganda).

It is important that the point be emphasized that operating schools as part of a *development strategy* in zones where the conflict-affected State genuinely *does* have at least minimally adequate control over security, and the rule of law is adequately operational is *not* a violation of IHL. Though the operation of such schools in secure areas may send a useful counter-terrorist propaganda message as a side benefit; the operation of these schools in the latter locales is directed, in the first instance, to humanitarian objectives; namely education and societal development goals not military ones. Hence, the schools would be closed should security become an issue, and not reopened until the safety of the civilians attending there could be realistically and reasonably guaranteed. Schools operating in secure zones pose no increased security risk to the children and education personnel. This is unlike the

---

[20] Protocol Additional to the Geneva Conventions of 12 August 1949, and relating to the Protection of Victims of International Armed Conflicts (Protocol I) 8 June 1977, entry into force 7 December 1978. http://www.icrc.org/ihl.nsf/full/470?opendocument. Accessed 28 June 2010 [Article 51(1)].

situation where children and teachers are encouraged during armed conflict to attend at insecure education facilities (school buildings) or sites (open air schools, schools in tents, schools in community facilities etc.) that would be high value targets for terrorists due to the schools being regarded as an alleged symbol of foreign influence and/or of the national government. Thus, schools operating in areas within CAFS where the fighting is ongoing and intense and security inadequate may serve primarily (military) propaganda functions rather than education objectives. This being reflected in the risks with children's safety the powers that be are prepared to take by encouraging children to attend schools in particular locales where there is no adequate security.

5.1.6 Non-Governmental Actors and Their Potential Culpability Under IHL for Indirectly Facilitating Terror Attacks on Education

It is the view advanced here that NGOs and international human rights organization personnel operating in CAFS such as Afghanistan have a direct responsibility, along with the delegates of the State and its State allies (i.e., politicians, members of the armed forces and their commanders) under IHL, to: (1) do what they can to ensure that schools are in fact safe and stay safe from terror attacks; and (2) discourage school attendance at any school where the safety of students and teachers cannot be adequately guaranteed in the context of the armed conflict. Violations of these IHL obligations, it is here contended, may trigger potential prosecution by the International Criminal Court for those responsible which may include also: (1) nationals of States Parties to the Rome Statute and (2) persons operating in the jurisdiction of a State Party to the Rome Statute (i.e., Afghanistan). Thus, although the U.S. has not itself ratified the Rome Statute, it is the case that the actions in Afghanistan (a State party to the Rome Statute) of U.S. nationals (as members or administrators of American or international NGOs or human rights organizations) where these violate IHL; potentially fall under the jurisdiction of the ICC.

On the analysis here then NGO and human rights organization personnel (whether at the administrative policy/decision-making level or frontline level) *who encourage children to attend schools that are: (1) known to be insecure and located in a zone with high terror activity and (2) hence ripe for a highly likely and foreseeable targeted terror attack* could be potentially be considered (depending on the totality of the facts in the particular case) by the International Criminal Court (ICC) as indirectly complicit in the 'war crime' of terrorism (intentional systemic targeted attacks on civilians and civilian objects; in this case schoolchildren and education-related personnel including education aid workers and schools respectively). This complicity arises then due to these parties facilitating the objectives of terrorists by *intentionally and knowingly* encouraging schoolchildren and education-related personnel to be placed at high risk of grievous harm due to terror attacks. It is *not* necessary, it is suggested, as an element of the international crime of facilitating terrorism that the NGO and human rights workers directly intended or wished to further the objectives of the Taliban or other insurgents; only that they were aware that their intentional acts (encouraging and facilitating children's attendance at unsecured schools) had a high probability of doing so.

With respect to the issue of potential culpability of members of the international human rights and humanitarian community for violations of IHL, note that it is a common but erroneous presumption that private or non-governmental actors (such as are members of national or international NGOs and human rights organizations) that do not have a close relationship with an armed group cannot be held culpable for violations of international humanitarian law:

> International humanitarian law does *not* regulate the conduct of private actors who do not have a sufficiently close link to an armed group. Moreover, it does not place any clear obligations on the parties to a war, in their capacities as warring parties, to protect the public from private actor violence [i.e., to protect against the complicity of national and international human rights and humanitarian aid workers in terrorist violence against education as a result of their encouraging children to attend schools operating in insecure locales subject to a foreseeable high risk of targeted terror attacks on education]. By contrast, a state does have an implied duty to protect educators and students from attacks by private actors. . . [21]

Consider that these national and international human rights and humanitarian education aid interveners are operating, in many respects, at the behest of, and/or in partnership with and/or with the financial support of the national government and international donor governments that are parties to or signatories of the Rome Statute (i.e., Afghanistan acceded to the Rome Statute 10 February 2003, the United Kingdom ratified the Statute 4 October 2001 etc.).[22] In some instances, they also work with small contingents of the armed forces of these donor states who are providing some time- limited security for education and other development work (in Afghanistan these combination small military-development units are referred to as 'provincial reconstruction teams')

> The PRTs [provincial reconstruction teams] are small military units (ranging in size from 80 to over 300) *incorporating a small contingent of civilians with a development or diplomatic background with a mandate to carry out development and humanitarian projects in a "hearts and minds" campaign* to win over the local population and extend the writ of the central government (emphasis added).[23]

In the latter instances (i.e., involving PRTs), one might argue that those private actors (NGO personnel and other education aid interveners "do . . . have a sufficiently close link to an armed group" such that "international humanitarian law does . . . regulate

[21]Planning and Programming Directorate, Office of Her Highness Sheikka Mozah Bint Nasser Al-Missned. International law and the protection of education systems. In UNESCO (2010), p. 157.

[22]Coalition for the International Criminal Court (2009).

[23]Human Rights Watch (2006), p. 109.

[their] conduct".[24] However, even aside from the issue of whether or not there is a close link between the private actors (personnel from national or international human rights or humanitarian organizations) and the armed forces of one of the warring parties in a particular CAFS (that is, whether or not the civilians doing humanitarian work are part of a unit that includes soldiers etc.), there is still a strong case to be made that the conduct of private actors *is* directly regulated by international humanitarian law in certain circumstances during armed conflict. That is, the actions and decisions of private actors (i.e., NGO frontline workers, and policy and practice decision-makers) during armed conflict are directly regulated by IHL, it is argued here, wherever these actors are in the position to facilitate the violation of IHL which may or may not actually cause harm to civilians or others (where substantial harms do occur, the IHL violations involved may reach to the level of a 'grave crime' under IHL). Solis, a legal expert on the law of armed conflict comments on the issue of the potential culpability of private actors under IHL thus:

> . . . the provisions of the laws and customs of war are addressed not only to combatants and to members of the state and other public authorities, *but to anybody who is in a position to assist in their violation* (emphasis added).[25]

Solis provides a case example of the fact that the conduct of civilian private actors is directly regulated by international humanitarian law in times of armed conflict. That example is the 1946 British Military Court conviction of Bruno Tesch and one other in 'the Zyklon B case'. These civilian defendants (private actors) were convicted for facilitating Nazi 'war crimes' in violation of IHL by providing the poison gas from their privately owned factory (gas normally used for legitimate domestic purposes) for use to murder allied nationals imprisoned in Nazi concentration camps: "The Military Court acted on the principle that *any civilian who is an accessory to a violation of the laws and customs of war is himself [or herself] also liable as a war criminal* (emphasis added)".[26] It could conceivably arise then (based on the responsibility of private actors to abide by IHL where their actions would make a difference as to whether IHL violations are committed); that humanitarian education aid personnel would be prosecuted by the ICC (assuming the other Court jurisdictional criteria were also met) for contributing to IHL violations. This might occur, for instance, if these private actors (NGO personnel) directed or implemented a policy or practice wherein schoolchildren were encouraged and assisted to attend school in a CAFS in unsecured locales where there was a known and foreseeable high risk of targeted terror attacks on the schools or on the routes to and from school. Where such attacks materialized (with or without resulting significant loss of life and injury to the civilians at the school); the offense would not just include complicity in an intended terror act, but complicity with an actual terror attack thus increasing the gravity of the crime to yet a higher level. In such instances then responsibility for the IHL

---

[24]Planning and Programming Directorate, Office of Her Highness Sheikka Mozah Bint Nasser Al-Missned. International law and the protection of education systems. In UNESCO (2010), p. 157.

[25]Solis (2010), p. 335.

[26]Solis (2010), p. 335.

violations would lie with: (1) the private actors (i.e., NGO personnel) even though they were not associated with any armed group and with (2) the donor countries that funded these private actors (NGOs) for these activities despite not ensuring that the activities of these humanitarian organizations in the education sector complied in all respects with the requirements of IHL (State culpability would, of course, have to be handled in a forum other than the ICC; perhaps the International Court of Justice should an inter-State complaint be launched. The latter is unlikely; however, as generally the national government of the CAFS is partnered with the NGOs and supported by the international community in facilitating school attendance even when security is inadequate in an effort to create the illusion of significant development progress despite the internal ongoing armed conflict).

It is here contended that international aid community responsibility to protect schools, schoolchildren, education personnel and frontline humanitarian education aid workers importantly includes, among other things, not operating schools in zones where security is not adequate for the schools nor encouraging attendance at any insecure school (whether NGO sponsored or other community-based school, a government school or religious school). To do otherwise is, on this analysis, to be interpreted as using schoolchildren, their teachers and other education-related personnel (as well as frontline humanitarian education aid workers) as pawns in what can be considered a specific type of military purpose. That military purpose, as explained, involves using the operation of schools as part of the counter-terrorist propaganda campaign (one component in a counter-insurgency strategy) intended to convince the populace in the region, and the international community, of *alleged* substantial progress in stabilization of various regions in the country in which terrorists have been active. Notwithstanding recent NGO and UN reports on school vulnerability to terror attack and calls for better security, there is, in the current author's view, a relatively cavalier disregard *in practice* for the attendant risks to the civilians involved (students, teachers etc.) considering the continued operation of these schools in the knowledge that they have grossly adequate security. Consider, for instance, in this regard that the outcome paper previously referred to makes the statement that: "Deadly attacks on teachers and students go to the heart of our subject matter",[27] while, at the same time, contending that "*... a state must take steps to realize the right to education during war and insecurity* [and] has a legal duty to take all reasonable steps to stop students and teachers from being attacked, *and to maintain and repair education services despite whatever violence the country is undergoing* (emphasis added)".[28] It is here contended in contrast that: (1) the right to life (which includes also (a) the protection from grievous injury due to the violence associated with armed conflict and the specific targeting of education by insurgent forces or (b) so-called 'collateral damage' to education –students,

[27]Planning and Programming Directorate, Office of Her Highness Sheikka Mozah Bint Nasser Al-Missned. International law and the protection of education systemsIn UNESCO (2010), p. 167.

[28]Planning and Programming Directorate, Office of Her Highness Sheikka Mozah Bint Nasser Al-Missned. International law and the protection of education systems. In UNESCO (2010), p. 169.

teachers and schools-caused intentionally or unintentionally due to an attack on another prime target) takes priority over the right to education in times of war and great insecurity if and when the security of students and teachers cannot be adequately guaranteed in any particular education setting and that (2) taking all "reasonable steps" to protect students and education personnel from attacks includes suspending education in settings where their safety is at considerable risk such as at schools likely known to the insurgents (government or non-government schools or alternate education sites) which are situated in specific conflict-ridden areas within Afghanistan where security has not been established.

While the outcome paper (prepared in relation to the 2009 seminar on international law and the protection sponsored by Planning and Programming Directorate, Office of Her Highness Sheikka Mozah Bint Nasser Al-Missned) holds that: IHL law and the Rome statute is *inapplicable* to private actors (i.e., which would include then also private actors such as NGO personnel who facilitate the harms that arise from attacks on education by striving to have education services delivered despite the high security risks), the current author holds the view that IHL and the Rome Statute *are* applicable. Further, the outcome paper holds that the State has the duty to take all reasonable steps to continue to implement the right to education despite there being ongoing violence and insecurity in the country:

> Children, youth and adults always possess a human right to education. *The state's obligations to fulfil this right continue through peace and war, acting in accordance with the standard of proportionality (or reasonableness)* (emphasis added).[29]

It should be recognized in assessing the claims in the above quote that nothing in IHL expressly states or implies that the 'right to education' should take priority over the right to security (i.e., right to life and protection from harms) as is, in effect, occurring in some locales in CAFS such as Afghanistan. That is, 'the standard of proportionality (or reasonableness)' with regard to the implementation of the right to education is not met when schoolchildren are encouraged to attend unsecured schools in the midst of hot or low-level combat regions within a CAFS. When IHL makes reference to children accessing education, in contrast, there is a presupposition of pre-existing adequate security for the children and education personnel. For example, Article 24 of the Geneva Convention IV makes reference to the obligations of the parties to the conflict to ensure the well-being of children orphaned or separated from their parents which includes providing an education consistent with the children's cultural traditions. This article refers to essentially a 'post-conflict' situation and emphasizes the obligation to care and protect the child civilians and provide education. The article is premised on children having their security needs met by the occupying power:

> Art.24. The Parties to the conflict shall take the necessary measures to ensure that children under fifteen, who are orphaned or are separated from their families as a result of the war, *are not left to their own resources, and that their maintenance, the exercise of their religion*

[29]Planning and Programming Directorate, Office of Her Highness Sheikka Mozah Bint Nasser Al-Missned. International law and the protection of education systemsIn UNESCO (2010), p. 171.

> *and their education are facilitated in all circumstances*. Their education shall, as far as possible, be entrusted to persons of a similar cultural tradition (emphasis added).[30]

Article 78 of Protocol I additional to the 1949 Geneva Conventions (international conflicts) refers to the right to education of children evacuated from a conflict area for their own security:

> *Whenever an evacuation occurs* pursuant to paragraph 1, each child's education, including his religious and moral education as his parents desire, shall be provided while he is away with the greatest possible continuity (emphasis added).[31]

The right to education articulated in Article 4(3) of Protocol II additional to the 1949 Geneva Conventions (non-international conflicts) under the subtitle of "Humane Treatment" (as with Article 78 referring to education in Protocol I) must be read in the context of the rest of the article which refers to providing children with adequate care and meeting their security needs:

> *Children shall be provided with the care and aid they require, and in particular:*
>
> (a) *they shall receive an education*, including religious and moral education, in keeping with the wishes of their parents, or in the absence of parents, of those responsible for their care;
> (b) all appropriate steps shall be taken to facilitate the reunion of families temporarily separated;
> (c) children who have not attained the age of fifteen years shall neither be recruited in the armed forces or groups nor allowed to take part in hostilities;
> (d) *the special protection provided by this Article* to children who have not attained the age of fifteen years shall remain applicable to them if they take a direct part in hostilities despite the provisions of subparagraph (c) and are captured;
> (e) measures shall be taken, if necessary, and whenever possible with the consent of their parents or persons who by law or custom are primarily responsible for their care, to *remove children temporarily from the area in which hostilities are taking place to a safer area within the country and ensure that they are accompanied by persons responsible for their safety and well-being* (emphasis added).[32]

The current author holds then that the 'right to education' under IHL importantly presupposes and incorporates the right to be educated in an *effectively secure* education setting (i.e., such that children would be discouraged, for instance, from attending school where schools are not adequately protected from terror attack if IHL is to be respected). The notion of the State having the obligation to do everything practicably feasible to have children attend school even during conflict

[30]Convention (IV) relative to the Protection of Civilian Persons in Time of War. Geneva, 12 August 1949. http://www.icrc.org/web/eng/siteeng0.nsf/html/genevaconventions. Accessed 13 July 2010.

[31]Protocol Additional to the Geneva Conventions of 12 August 1949, and relating to the Protection of Victims of International Armed Conflicts (Protocol I), 8 June 1977, entry into force 7 December 1978. http://www.icrc.org/ihl.nsf/full/470?opendocument. Accessed 28 June 2010 (Article 78).

[32]Protocol II Additional to the Geneva Conventions of 12 August 1949, and relating to the Protection of Victims of Non-International Armed Conflicts, 8 June 1977. http://www.icrc.org/web/eng/siteeng0.nsf/html/genevaconventions. Accessed 13 July 2010.

(as suggested in the aforementioned outcome paper), and in a circumstance where children's security could have been better protected by their *not* attending unsecured schools in the midst of the violence, is, it is here argued, inconsistent both with: (1) the right to education and (2) with IHL obligations. Hence, IHL violations are committed where all necessary and feasible precautions for ensuring schoolchildren's safety are not taken since the international human rights and humanitarian representatives and national and local politicians of the CAFS appeal for continued school attendance despite the ongoing violence and lack of security for the schools in particular regions within the country. These are IHL violations for which private actors (such as NGOs) may potentially be culpable due to their facilitating the war crime of terrorism (depending on their specific role, if any, in knowingly and intentionally exposing schoolchildren to the high risk of violence from targeted terror attacks against education). Culpability for additional grave IHL violations (i.e., complicity in the infliction of severe physical and mental suffering) may also result where children and others at the school or on their way to or from school are injured or killed due to a targeted attack on education after being encouraged to attend an unprotected school by members of the national and/or international human rights/humanitarian community doing development work in the region and/or or by government officials rather than being instructed to stay home until and unless the school could be adequately secured.[33]

In this author's view, the standard for the State duty to protect life (which extends also to non-state actors including private actors such as NGO personnel if they are in the position to affect whether or not, and to what extent IHL is violated) is higher than simply a standard of 'reasonableness'. Rather, the standard is to do all that is feasible and necessary to implement measures that will protect life and prevent harm coming to civilians (i.e., students and teachers etc.). Certainly, those who would encourage school attendance despite the lack of security in the area and the high risk of a targeted terror attack on schools in that particular locale are not, on the view here, meeting the latter higher standard for the 'duty to protect'. Thus, when it is stated in a paper included in a 2010 UNESCO report (see the quote from the report below) that school should continue even in an armed conflict situation involving "hot fighting" zones and "general insecurity"; such a proposition must, on the view advanced here, be rejected as inconsistent with the requirements of international humanitarian law. Those IHL requirements presuppose that adequate security is in place for education and stipulate that complicity in the intentional violation of the protected civilian right to life during armed conflict is a grave international crime. In the case of schoolchildren also then the right to life and to security of the person supersedes the right to education and any requirement or expectation by the State and its partners in the non-governmental NGO sector that the children ought to risk their lives or well-being to attend school:

---

[33]Planning and Programming Directorate, Office of Her Highness Sheikka Mozah Bint Nasser Al-Missned. International law and the protection of education systems. In UNESCO (2010), p. 171 (chart).

> ... each state has the responsibility to promote the right to life and the right to education...
> ... the ministry of education will have a major role to play in making education as safe as possible, ***and in taking steps to ensure continuity of education despite hot and low-level fighting and general insecurity***.[34]

The phrase "making education as safe as possible" in the quote above does *not* connote necessarily that the level of security provided to schoolchildren is adequate to effectively protect the children's right to life and to physical and psychological integrity at school or on the way to and from school. This is the case given that education is to continue "despite hot and low-level fighting and general insecurity" according to government officials and their national and international NGO partners. Thus, making schools 'as safe as possible' *in these circumstances* may be to provide a grossly inadequate level of security. Certainly, schoolchildren have not been adequately protected in CAFS such as Afghanistan as evidenced by the casualty rate due to targeted terror attacks on schools and school routes. In Afghanistan, further, the Ministry of Education, as discussed, takes the position that the responsibility for school security, is beyond its jurisdiction and capability in the context of the ongoing intense armed conflict. Yet, government education officials and NGOs continue to stress the importance of attending school despite legitimate serious security concerns. The children are then in these contexts at risk of being attacked i.e., by Taliban or Al-Qaeda inspired terrorists and even of being taken as human shields or abducted for use as suicide bombers. [This author concurs with those who view civilians used as human shields (i.e., teachers and students controlled by terrorists occupying their school) as 'hostages'. Where these hostages are forced into participating in the hostilities, they may under IHL lawfully come under attack as a result but they should be viewed as persons who should be spared if at all possible and feasible given the circumstances (note that the taking of hostages is a violation of IHL as per Article 4(2)(c) of Additional Protocol II and Common Article 3(1)(b) to the 1949 Geneva Conventions).[35] Child suicide bombers this author would argue are also not culpable being akin to child soldiers who have been exploited and manipulated in various ways or compelled more directly to engage in violence].

Given the high and increasing numbers of attacks on school buildings, alternative education sites and on schoolchildren, teachers, other education personnel and humanitarian aid workers in Afghanistan, as in several other high conflict CAFS, the international community has finally been forced to address the issue of school security. However, the chances that national governments and the international humanitarian education aid community will seriously consider and address how *they* might be greatly contributing to the problem of school terror attacks in the first instance (i.e., by operating schools in particular locales despite the inadequate security in those specific areas thus inviting terror attacks) may in fact be low. This because when it comes to discussion in the international community regarding

---

[34] Planning and Programming Directorate, Office of Her Highness Sheikka Mozah Bint Nasser Al-Missned. International law and the protection of education systems. In UNESCO (2010), p. 176.

[35] Schmitt (2010), p. 30.

attacks by organized terror groups on schools in Afghanistan (and in other CAFS still in the midst of the fighting), the focus is almost always exclusively on the culpability of the attackers. The presumption is that the 'defenders' of education (the Afghan government and its allies, NGO school sponsors, international human rights and humanitarian aid organizations operating in the field etc) are *not* using the schools for military purposes and hence are not responsible in any way for the terror attacks. It has here been argued, however, that operating a school in an insecure zone where it is at considerable risk of a targeted terror attack, and, in so doing, risking the lives and well-being of children and education personnel, serves primarily a counterterrorism propaganda military purpose in violation of IHL rather than a humanitarian education purpose. Encouraging and facilitating schoolchildren and education personnel attending dedicated school buildings or alternative education sites that are not secure (thus putting them at high risk of death or injury) is, it has been here contended, *not* exempt then from being considered as conduct which violates IHL.

It should be a matter of great concern to the international community that children and teachers are still attending at schools in Afghanistan (and in other CAFS) that are highly insecure; often with the encouragement and support of representatives from the national and international human rights and humanitarian community as well as from officials at all levels of the CAFS and its allies. Rather, than guaranteed security for education in CAFS such as Afghanistan being in place in those regions of the country where the children currently do attend school, it appears that the students and teachers and frontline humanitarian education aid workers at risk of attack can only wrap themselves in the dubious protective armour of 'rights rhetoric' (as voiced by the international humanitarian and human rights community representatives regarding the right to education in conflict-affected fragile States).

Schools in insecure zones within CAFS (regardless of where those schools are housed i.e., in separate school buildings, open air venues, tents, community buildings used for multipurpose etc.) must, it is here argued, be afforded 'special protection'. The latter requires then an absolute prohibition on the use of schools for what can be considered the 'military purpose' of creating counter-insurgency propaganda (or their use for any other military purpose). This responsibility to afford schools guaranteed security flows from the IHL obligation on the State, and on public officials and private actors (such as NGO personnel) to afford schoolchildren protection from armed attack (i.e., since, as explained previously, using schools for counter-insurgency propaganda purposes makes schools an attractive terror target thus placing schoolchildren and other civilians involved with basic education directly in harm's way). Unfortunately, it is virtually impossible to guarantee the security of all schools or school routes in insecure regions within Afghanistan. It should thus be noted in respect of the issue of school security in Afghanistan that most schools in Afghanistan are likely insecure. This since 83 percent of schools are located in dispersed rural areas and 65 percent of the students enrolled in school are attending these schools in various provinces.[36] It is simply

[36]Burde (2010), p. 251.

impossible for Afghan security forces and their allies to devote the necessary resources to protecting these often hard-to-reach schools scattered as they are throughout the provinces; many of which are still experiencing heavy fighting and a general state of insecurity. Further, the context of the war on terror poses very specific problems since the modus operandi of organized terror groups is to defy IHL. Thus suggestions, if implemented, such as having an international universal symbol to designate educational buildings[37] may help avert some collateral damage in attacks by forces that adhere to IHL, but, at the same time, such a symbol would serve as something of a 'bull's eye' targeting aid for organized terror groups comprised of Taliban and/or Al-Qaeda that do not abide by IHL.

5.1.7 The Privileged Protected Status of Civilian Schools: Safeguarding Tangible and Intangible Cultural Property/Heritage

(a) *Community-Based Schools and the Protection of Cultural Property During Armed Conflict*

Using community-based schools in Afghanistan, as advocated by some NGOs and academics[38] and housing them in mosques, for instance, despite the absence of at least minimally adequate security, risks harm to religious buildings. By indirectly contributing to attacks on religious buildings by encouraging NGO sponsored community-based schools in mosques, NGOs may potentially be held liable for complicity in damage to, or destruction of religious buildings which category of civilian building has a special protected status under IHL i.e., Article 16 of Protocol II additional to the 1949 Geneva Conventions concerning "Protection of Cultural Objects and Places of Worship:

> Art 16. Protection of cultural objects and of places of worship: Without prejudice to the provisions of the Hague Convention for the Protection of Cultural Property in the Event of Armed Conflict of 14 May 1954, it is prohibited to commit any acts of hostility directed against historic monuments, works of art or places of worship which constitute the cultural or spiritual heritage of peoples, and to use them in support of the military effort.[39]

Further, some of these community-based schools may be housed in religious buildings that may have enormous significance historically and/or in terms of the group's cultural heritage. Those that facilitate schools being housed in such structures

[37]Planning and Programming Directorate, Office of Her Highness Sheikka Mozah Bint Nasser Al-Missned. International law and the protection of education systems. In UNESCO (2010), p. 174.

[38]Burde (2010), p. 251.

[39]Protocol Additional to the Geneva Conventions of 12 August 1949, and relating to the Protection of Victims of Non-International Armed Conflict (Protocol II), 8 June 1977 http://www.icrcorg/ihl.nsf/FULL/475?OPenDocument. Accessed 2 July 2010 (Article 16).

despite: (1) the general insecurity in the region, and (2) the known increased risk of terror attack on the building as an education site, can be held, on this analysis, also to be violating IHL in that regard. That is, humanitarian aid workers, as well as the CAFS governments that approve their education work in unsecured regions of the CAFS, may potentially be held to be complicit in facilitating the damage to, or destruction of religious or other buildings that may be highly culturally significant and even iconic buildings of great symbolic importance to the local populace, or to humanity generally. As a result, both the State and the individual private (non-governmental) actors responsible for putting these buildings at risk of terror attack as an education site may be guilty of certain violations of IHL (i.e., IHL provisions that require that anyone in a position to set the conditions that would facilitate or encourage attacks on such buildings refrain from dong so).

Note that the 1954 *Hague Convention for the Protection of Cultural Property in the Event of Armed Conflict*,[40] by implication, provides special protection to those relatively small number of exceptional school buildings that have great historic and/ or symbolic cultural significance to a people or to humanity (i.e., what might be considered 'heritage sites'):

> ... some school buildings receive additional protection based on their cultural value pursuant to the 1954 Hague Convention for the Protection of Cultural Property in the Event of Armed Conflict. . . .[41]

Where certain buildings (which may or may not be religious buildings) are classed as 'cultural property' under the 1954 Hague Convention, and are *not* legitimate military objectives, they are afforded special protection under the law of armed conflict (i.e., under certain conventions such as the 1954 Hague Convention dealing with cultural property). That protection would render an attack on such culturally and/or historically distinctive (unconverted) civilian buildings a violation of IHL. This would be the case regardless whether the damage to, or destruction of the building resulted from a targeted attack or one that was not targeted but could have been avoided. The use of such historically and/or culturally significant buildings for a military purpose; namely, as part of the counter-insurgency propaganda strategy that involves operating schools in those buildings despite inadequate security (as a show of the purported return to normalcy); puts these buildings at great risk of damage or destruction from terror attacks. Those responsible for placing and operating an NGO-sponsored or other school in buildings fitting the 1954 Hague Convention definition of 'cultural property', and doing so despite the insecure situation and hot fighting zone; indirectly contribute to the damage to, or destruction of such civilian objects (and/or the death or injury to the civilians attending there, or in the proximity of these buildings). For knowingly placing these buildings and the civilians at greatly increased risk of attack in this way; those responsible for locating the schools at such sites may be potentially liable for

[40]1954 Hague Convention for the Protection of Cultural Property in the Event of Armed Conflict. http://www.icrc.org/IHL.nsf/FULL/400?OpenDocument. Accessed 26 June 2010.

[41]Bart (2010), p. 211.

complicity in 'war crimes' under IHL which involve both the damage and destruction of protected civilian objects and persons.

(b) *Article 4 of the 1954 Hague Convention Regarding the Protected Status of Cultural Property: Implications for the Protected Status of Schools*

Some scholars writing on the law of armed conflict suggest that it is only the small number of school buildings with significant historic and/or cultural importance that are protected from military use in times of pressing military necessity when unoccupied by civilians (i.e., the contention being then that most unoccupied 'ordinary' civilian school buildings can be lawfully used for military purposes such as launching armed attacks where there is a compelling military necessity). These scholars reference Article 4(1) of the 1954 Hague Convention regarding 'special protection' for certain property; including buildings defined as 'cultural property', but maintain that most school buildings are exempted from the protections afforded by Article 4(1) of the Hague Convention:

> **Article 4: Respect for cultural property**
> 1. The High Contracting Parties undertake to respect cultural property situated within their own territory as well as within the territory of other High Contracting Parties by refraining from **any use** of the property and its immediate surroundings or of the appliances in use for its protection for purposes which are likely to expose it to destruction or damage in the event of armed conflict; and by refraining from any act of hostility directed against such property [when assumed to be civilian objects].[42]
> ("But it [the 1954 Hague Convention] does not specifically include school buildings in its definition of cultural property and thus [its protection guarantees] would not apply to most schools").[43]

As will be discussed here shortly; certain other international humanitarian law experts; including some justices (who served on an international criminal tribunal at the trial level dealing with unlawful use of a school during armed conflict) hold quite a different view. They, as does the current author, consider that civilian schools do fall into the category of protected 'cultural property' due to their significant educational/humanitarian purpose whether or not the multi-purpose building housing the school or the school building (dedicated only to education) itself has some special historic or iconic symbolic cultural significance to the immediate community or to humanity in general.

It is contended here then that protecting civilian schools, including unoccupied schools, from: (1) terror attacks, and (2) from use for a military purpose even where there is a pressing military necessity for such use (a use which would increase the risk of attack on the school by the enemy) is implicitly incorporated into IHL provisions regarding the need to protect cultural heritage. This is evident given the fact that civilian schools are cultural objects. Apart from family and community contributions to informal education about culture and tradition, school is a place which is central to

---

[42] 1954 Hague Convention for the Protection of Cultural Property in the Event of Armed Conflict. http://www.icrc.org/IHL.nsf/FULL/400?OpenDocument. Accessed 26 June 2010 (Article 4).

[43] Bart (2010), p. 211.

the task of transmitting cultural heritage (i.e., through formal education) and is, therefore, a highly significant institution for society. Thus, for this reason also, school buildings located in the midst of armed conflict and left unoccupied by civilians need to be protected and preserved so that they can be used for an education function once more when security is restored (as is recognized in IHL). The special protected status of schools (which this author argues already exists under IHL) is essential in accomplishing this. Unoccupied separate ordinary school buildings or community-based buildings housing schools dedicated to civilian education purposes and closed due to terror attacks or other targeted attacks or due to the risk of becoming collateral damage, as well as any other education sites at such risk, are entitled under IHL then to special protection against both armed attack and use for a military purpose. Schools thus provide a key cultural function in society which underlies their special protected status regarding attack and use for a military purpose. This IHL 'special protection' of schools is essential as: (1) the development of the young through schooling is vital to the survival of the particular society and its culture, and (2) the possibility for education is greatly facilitated through the availability of adequate instructional facilities (housing books, labs, and other educational tools etc.).

Schools through their humanitarian education function are linked to the intangible aspects of cultural heritage that are protected under IHL via special protection status provisions. Note in this regard that the Trial Chamber of the International Criminal Tribunal for the Former Yugoslavia (ICTY) in *Prosecutor versus Kordic and Cerkez* affirmed the view (also expressed by the current author) that 'special protection' is to be afforded schools as 'cultural property' under the 1954 Hague Convention and certain other conventions over and above the 'general protection' due all civilian buildings. That is, the Trial Chamber in *Prosecutor versus Kordic and Cerkez* held that schools are entitled to special protection from use for a military purpose without exception while, in contrast, civilian buildings under the 'general protection' provision are protected from use for a military purpose only if there is no pressing military necessity:

> 359. Article 1 of the Cultural Property Convention lists numerous types of cultural property for protection in the form of "movable or immovable property of great importance to the cultural heritage of every people", "buildings whose main and effective purpose is to preserve or exhibit the movable cultural property", and "centres containing a large amount of cultural property"...
>
> 360. *The Trial Chamber notes that educational institutions are undoubtedly immovable property of great importance to the cultural heritage of peoples* in that they are without exception centres of learning, arts, and sciences, with their valuable collections of books and works of arts and science. The Trial Chamber also notes one international treaty which requires respect and protection to be accorded to educational institutions in time of peace as well as in war. [fn 490: Protection of Artistic and Scientific Institutions and Historic Monuments, known as "Roerich Pact", 15 April 1935, Art.1. Currently 11 American States are parties thereto] (emphasis added).[44]

[44]*Prosecutor versus Kordic and Cerkez* (International Tribunal for the Prosecution of Persons Responsible for Serious Violations of International Humanitarian Law Committed in the Territory of the Former Yugoslavia since 1991, Trial judgment of 26 February 2001). http://www.unhcr.org/refworld/topic,4565c22538,4565c25f449,41483e9be,0.html. Accessed 15 July 2010.

Indeed, the statute of the ICTY includes a provision at Article 3(d) that makes it clear that seizure of a civilian school violates the laws or customs of war (i.e., that provision makes no reference to the unlawfulness having to be connected to a lack of pressing military necessity for the seizure). In addition, educational institutions are mentioned at Article 3(d) of the ICTY Statute along with buildings and sites known to have the higher level special protection in regards to use for a military purpose:

Article 3: Statute of the ICTY

Violations of the laws or customs of war

The International Tribunal shall have the power to prosecute persons violating the laws or customs of war. Such violations shall include, but not be limited to:

...

(d) ***seizure of***, destruction or wilful damage done to institutions dedicated to religion, charity and ***education,*** the arts and sciences, historic monuments and works of art and science [where these are presumed to be civilian objects without a military purpose] (emphasis added).[45]

The Appeals Chamber of the ICTY in *Prosecutor versus Kordic and Cerkez* disagreed with the Trial Chamber in the same case on whether schools were entitled to 'special protection' as opposed only to the 'general protection' due all civilian buildings. The Appeal Chamber disputed the notion that all educational buildings meet the criteria for being classed as 'cultural property' under the 1954 Hague Convention. Relying on the commentary of the International Committee of the Red Cross regarding Article 53 of Additional Protocol I to the Geneva Conventions, the Appeal Chamber maintained that *only* objects of significance to humanity generally; unique in character and closely tied to the history and culture of a people could be considered to be 'cultural property'.[46] However, the Appeal Chamber provided no explanation in its judgment as to why schools should be specifically mentioned in Article 3(d) of the ICTY statute (in regard to the prohibition under IHL of seizure or wilful damage) along with objects particularized due to their entitlement to 'special protection' as cultural objects i.e., historic monuments, works of art etc. which by their nature reflect the cultural or spiritual heritage of a people. The current author thus, with respect, views the *Kordic and Cerkez* ICTY Appeal Chamber exclusion of schools from the concept of 'cultural property' to be unsupported in law.

There is no doubt that there exist heritage sites that have situated there objects of importance to humanity given their unique and iconic historic/cultural meanings (or the environmental site in itself may be considered cultural/heritage property).

---

[45]Statute of the International Criminal Tribunal for the Former Yugoslavia [Article 3(d)]. http://www1.umn.edu/humanrts/icty/statute.html. Accessed 16 July 2010.

[46]International Tribunal for the Prosecution of Persons Responsible for Serious Violations of International Humanitarian Law Committed in the Territory of the Former Yugoslavia since 1991 *Prosecutor versus Kordic and Cerkez* (Appeals Chamber) Case No IT-95-14-2-A (17 December 2004) at para. 92. http://www.icty.org/x/cases/kordic_cerkez/acjug/en/cer-aj041217e.pdf. Accessed 2 July 2010.

However, so-called "ordinary" schools (operating in buildings of no particular distinction or repute) are also of vital importance to humanity since a quality education for all children; one grounded in respect for human rights is a force for peace and unity and a contributor to the spiritual heritage of peoples. Further, the uniqueness of the ordinary school derives from the uniqueness of the particular children it serves and the potential in those students to make a contribution to society and perhaps to humanity more generally that their schooling helps actualize. All civilian schools then, on this analysis, qualify as 'cultural property' entitled under IHL to special protection.

While Article 3(d) of the ICTY Statute sets out that seizure of a civilian school is a violation of the Statute, one of the defendants in *Prosecutor v Kordic and Cerkez* was charged, among other things, with ordering the use of a school for a military purpose; namely using the school as a detention centre for civilian hostages. Dario Kordic and Maio Cerkez; the former a leading politician; the latter a commander of a brigade in the Bosnian Croat military, were both involved in the effort to eliminate Bosnian Muslims from Central Bosnia from 1992-1993 and the attempt to establish the region (the Lasva Valley and surrounding area) as home exclusively to one ethnic group; the Bosnian Croats. In the process, numerous grave international crimes were committed for which each of these men (along with other defendants) were variously held accountable by the International Criminal Tribunal for the Former Yugoslavia (ICTY). For instance, Dario Kordic had ordered that detention facilities be set up for Bosnian Muslims including at the Dubravica School. The detention centre was a component supporting the attack on the municipality where the school was located and the ethnic cleansing effort there. About 350 Muslim civilians were illegally detained at the school including men, women and children. The Trial Court also made a finding of fact that the detainees were told that if the fighting were to come near the school, they (the civilian hostage detainees) would be blown up along with the school. Thus, the case of *Prosecutor v Kordic and Cerkez* includes a civilian school being seized and used for a military purpose in violation of international law (i.e., Article 3 of the ICTY Statute). The Appeal Chamber concluded on this point as follows:

> . . . the Appeals Chamber finds that a reasonable Trial Chamber could have concluded that unlawful confinement of civilians and imprisonment (Counts 21 and 22 for Kordic) occurred in Dubravica Elementary School.[47]

In *Prosecutor v Kordic and Cerkez*, a school normally dedicated to a civilian education purpose was used for a military purpose (the unlawful confinement of civilians), but can there be any lawful use of a school for a military purpose during armed conflict? We have already considered that even unoccupied schools are

---

[47]International Tribunal for the Prosecution of Persons Responsible for Serious Violations of International Humanitarian Law Committed in the Territory of the Former Yugoslavia since 1991 *Prosecutor versus Kordic and Cerkez* (Appeals Chamber) Case No IT-95-14-2-A (17 December 2004) at para. 594. http://www.icty.org/x/cases/kordic_cerkez/acjug/en/cer-aj041217e.pdf. Accessed 2 July 2010.

entitled to 'special protection' *without exception* against use for any military purpose based on various factors including but not limited to: (1) the 'special protections' that are afforded to children under IHL and (2) the adverse implications that use of an unoccupied school for a military purpose would have on: (a) the safety of children who live near the school (given that the school would now be at high risk of attack), and on (b) the likelihood of the State being able to meet the developmental needs of the children which, among other things, necessitates their being able to access education (the adverse effect arising due to the high risk that the school would be significantly damaged or destroyed if it became a military objective thus necessitating its closing and interrupting the children's education in the short and even long-term) and (3) the special protected status of schools as 'cultural objects' that cannot be used for a military purpose even where there is military necessity.

We turn next to a more detailed consideration of those provisions in IHL that some academics claim support the notion that unoccupied civilian schools (meaning schools unoccupied by civilians and/or other noncombatants) during armed conflict may be used for a military purpose where there is deemed to be and is a pressing military necessity for such use. The interpretation that will here be offered of those IHL provisions, in contrast, leads to the opposite conclusion. That conclusion is namely that unoccupied (as well as occupied) civilian schools are protected without limitation from military use during armed conflict.

5.1.8 Examining the Implications of Articles 52 and 53 of Protocol I Additional to the 1949 Geneva Conventions for the Unqualified Protection of Civilian Schools Against Military Use During Armed Conflict

The common interpretation regarding the protection against military use afforded *unoccupied* civilian school buildings during armed conflict (buildings with no special historic/cultural symbolic significance) is that: (1) it is not more than exists for most other civilian buildings not occupied by civilians and/or non-combatants, and (2) allegedly *less* than that for hospitals, and most religious buildings which are *never* permitted to be used for military purposes under IHL (even in cases of pressing military necessity and whether occupied or unoccupied by civilians and/or noncombatants). The protection for ordinary civilian school buildings against military use then (under what is here considered an erroneous interpretation under IHL) is highly restrictive and derives from the presence of civilians and non-combatants in the building. That is, the contested proposition is that unoccupied ordinary civilian schools (buildings that allegedly are not cultural objects according to some scholars) can be used for a lawful military purpose when there is a compelling military necessity:

> The later Geneva Conventions of 1864, 1929 and 1949 . . . exclusively concern an attacking force's choice of targets and *do not create an independent privileged status that might prohibit attacking and defending armed forces from using school buildings for military purposes. Ultimately, they provide no more protection for school buildings than exist generally for all civilian buildings under the 1907 Hague Convention* (emphasis added).[48]

It has been suggested by some scholars of the law of armed conflict that there is a lack of clarity in the text of IHL treaties regarding: (1) what constitutes a civilian educational facility (i.e., given that some buildings are used for several purposes; education being only one of these) and, hence, it is unclear whether any higher standard of protection is due such buildings compared to other civilian buildings (even if that standard is not as high as that to be afforded to religious buildings, cultural objects such as museums and medical facilities); (2) how long a building must be dedicated in part or in whole to education to be considered an education facility deserving (if at all) of higher standard of protection both from attack and from use for a military purpose; (3) whether non-use of a school building for education purposes for any significant length of time negates any special protection of that building against military use where there is a military necessity; and (4) whether civilian school buildings have a privileged status regardless of whether or not currently occupied by civilians and engaged *at the time* in providing education or other humanitarian services (i.e., such that civilian school buildings cannot be attacked unless they become a lawful military target through the use that the enemy has made of the building for a military purpose).[49] However, the general consensus amongst scholars on the laws of armed conflict on the issue of the protection of schools during armed conflict (a consensus view which the current author contests) appears to be that there is currently *no* IHL prohibition against the use for lawful military purposes of *unoccupied* civilian school buildings (although Judge Advocate General's Corps, Gregory Raymond Bart and many other scholars of the law of armed conflict who hold the consensus view would like to see such a prohibition explicitly incorporated into the conventions on the laws of war and become part of customary practice).

The notion that there is no protection for unoccupied civilian schools against use for a military purpose where there is a compelling military necessity is based, according to Judge Advocate General's Corps, Gregory Raymond Bart and some other scholars, on Articles 52 and 53 of Protocol I additional to the 1949 Geneva Conventions:

> Articles 52 and 53 [of Protocol I addition to the 1949 Geneva Conventions] allow for military use of school buildings by expressing without limitation that schools may be converted into military objectives . . . Article 52 . . . states that religious and school buildings are normally dedicated to civilian purposes but creates a presumption in case of doubt whether "a place of worship . . . or a school, is being used to make an effective contribution to military action". This language therefore recognizes that armed forces may conceivably use any unoccupied civilian buildings for military purposes, especially those near combat

[48]Bart (2010), p. 211.

[49]Bart (2010), p. 211.

> areas ... *Article 53 limits the application of this language in the case of religious buildings by expressly prohibiting their military use. But Protocol I contains no limitation of its application in the case of school buildings.* Accordingly, Article 52 acknowledges that unlike religious buildings, no independent prohibition exists against military use of [unoccupied] school buildings i.e., converting them into military objectives (emphasis added).[50]

The current author respectfully contests the aforementioned proposition that Articles 52 and 53 of Protocol I Additional to the 1949 Geneva Conventions lay the groundwork for lawful use for a military purpose during armed conflict of school buildings that are *unoccupied* by civilians or other noncombatants where there is a compelling military necessity. Before we consider this issue further, note that although Protocol I refers to international conflicts, most of its provisions are regarded as customary laws of war.[51] Hence, the same humanitarian principle would, if it is incorporated into Protocol I additional to the 1949 Geneva Conventions, no doubt be applicable also to non-international conflicts such as that in Afghanistan currently. Nothing in what follows, however, should be interpreted as an argument against the value of clarifying these issues further in IHL (i.e., clarifying that civilian schools cannot, in any circumstance, whether or not occupied by civilians and/or other noncombatants, be lawfully used for military purposes in times of armed conflict).

Let us reconsider then the meaning and intent of Article 52(3) of Protocol I additional to the 1949 Geneva Conventions which states:

Art 52. General Protection of civilian objects

1. *Civilian objects* [those that at the relevant time were not converted to use for a military purpose and/or objects that would not create a military advantage if totally or partially destroyed, captured or neutralized] shall not be the object of attack or of reprisals**.** Civilian objects are all objects which are not military objectives as defined in paragraph 2.
2. *Attacks shall be limited strictly to military objectives.* In so far as objects are concerned, military objectives are limited to those objects which by their nature, location, purpose or use make an effective contribution to military action and whose total or partial destruction, capture or neutralization, in the circumstances ruling at the time, offers a definite military advantage.
3. *In case of doubt whether an object which is normally dedicated to civilian purposes, such as* a place of worship, a house or other dwelling **or *a school,*** *is being used to make an effective contribution to military action, it shall be presumed* ***not*** *to be so used* (emphasis added).[52]

Article 52(3) of Protocol I refers to doubts about whether or not the enemy is in fact using for a military purpose a school normally dedicated to a civilian purpose (thus turning the school into a legitimate military objective). The doubt (as to whether the school is in reality a legitimate military objective) which is referred to

---

[50] Bart (2010), p. 212.

[51] Dinstein (2004), p. 11.

[52] Protocol Additional to the Geneva Conventions of 12 August 1949, and relating to the Protection of Victims of International Armed Conflicts (Protocol I), 8 June 1977, entry into force 7 December 1978. http://www.icrc.org/ihl.nsf/full/470?opendocument. Accessed 28 June 2010 (Article 52).

in Article 52(3) can arise in various ways, including but not limited to: the presence of what appear to be civilians and/or noncombatants in the school and/or confusion over whether there are military supplies at the school or whether counterattacks have been launched from the school (where the school may or may not also be occupied by civilians and/or other noncombatants) etc. There may be uncertainty in the 'fog of war' as to: (1) whether civilians and/ noncombatants are being unlawfully used as 'human shields' by an enemy armed force occupying the school for a military purpose. (In cases where civilians and/or noncombatants are being used as 'human shields', this does not under IHL, as previously discussed, automatically preclude an attack on the school if there is a compelling military necessity for such an attack; though, if possible, harms to the civilians being held as human shields are to be minimized by the attacking force); (2) whether the school is being used *exclusively* for a civilian purpose (education) or other non-military humanitarian purposes as well (i.e., such as a place of refuge for civilians and for other noncombatants such as wounded soldiers hors du combat at the relevant time thus precluding a lawful attack); or (3) whether enemy belligerents and/or their local village supporters have taken control of the school and it is in fact being used for some non-humanitarian purpose at that time thus permitting a lawful attack on the school.

Any doubt regarding whether a school has become a military objective is, according to Article 52(3) Protocol I, to be resolved in favor of *not* attacking. That is, the bias with regard to (civilian) schools where there is doubt is in favor of considering the school *not* to be a military objective/target. The combatant force in adhering to IHL thus must meet a higher standard in determining that the school in question is a military objective and can be lawfully attacked than would be the case for most other civilian objects not listed in Article 52(3) (i.e., factories). (Hospitals or medical units; cultural and religious objects also enjoy this higher standard of protection from attack in cases of doubt and are dealt with in separate Articles of Protocol I and/or various other conventions).

Hence, the specific inclusion of schools in the list in Article 52(3) Protocol I concerning the *special caution* that must be taken in deciding whether or not to attack a building normally dedicated to a humanitarian, non-militaristic use (i.e., education) where there is doubt about the object's civilian status at that time is significant. This special caution to be applied to ordinary civilian school buildings regarding launching attacks on those schools in cases of doubt as to the status of the buildings at the time (i.e., status as non-legitimate military targets) is stipulated in Article 52(3) Protocol I likely since: (1) civilian schools are normally non-military objects and are essential to the society (i.e., they are valued 'cultural objects'), and, for that reason, any doubt as to their status as civilian objects at a particular point in time during armed conflict must be resolved in favor of *not* attacking, and (2) civilian schools cannot generally be considered legitimate military objectives/targets based on their nature and location per se. (This is unlike the situation for certain other categories of civilian objects such as bridges. Bridges, for instance, by their very nature, and often due to their special location, could make a *unique* effective contribution to the military effort. Hence, doubt as to certain bridges actually being a lawful military objective/target may therefore be more readily resolved in favor of an attack. Thus, a lower standard is applied regarding the lawfulness of attack on this category of civilian object (bridges) than is to be employed under IHL regarding an attack on civilian schools in cases of doubt). This higher standard applied for attacks on schools normally dedicated to a civilian purpose (in cases of doubt regarding their status) reflects the special importance of schools to society as cultural objects.

The general presumption underlying Article 52(3) is then that schools generally will not be, and are likely not being used for a military purpose, and thus, in most instances, need not be attacked as there would be no military advantage in doing so. That presumption in any particular instance where there is doubt must, according to IHL, be disproved (rebutted) with convincing substantive empirical evidence before an attack on the civilian school would be considered lawful under IHL (that is, convincing concrete evidence must be available that the school *is* actually a lawful military objective/target since it is being used by the enemy for a military purpose that provides the enemy with a significant military advantage). It may be inferred then that there is also a general prohibition implied under Protocol I Article 52(3) on the use of even unoccupied schools for a military purpose. This in the recognition that such use makes schools a likely target for attack; something Article 52(3) makes clear should be avoided if at all possible.

Attacks on unoccupied schools, afterall, are likely to have highly adverse consequences for an IHL protected class (the civilian population) since:

1. Schools are generally close to civilian dwellings such that an attack on a school, even if unoccupied, is likely to cause considerable collateral damage to civilians and civilian objects which are located in close proximity to the school.
2. Damage or destruction of schools, even if unoccupied at the time of the attack, causes special harm long-term to children; a vulnerable group entitled to special protection under IHL (i.e., interruption of their education, traumatization etc.) That special protection for children under IHL incorporates within it, on the analysis here, also a higher standard of protection for schools than exists for many other civilian buildings against use for a military purpose. That higher standard of protection for schools involves: (a) prohibiting their use for a military purpose without limitation as well as; (b) a higher standard regarding attack on a school where there is both doubt as to whether or not the school is a legitimate military objective, and whether an attack is justified also on other necessary grounds (i.e., whether or not there is in fact a pressing imminent military necessity for the attack involving the need to block the enemy's significant military advantage deriving from the enemy's use of the school for a military purpose).

Article 52(3) of Protocol I thus, on the view expressed here, reinforces the principle that, according to IHL, parties to an armed conflict are prohibited, without exception, from use of civilian schools for a military purpose even if the schools are unoccupied.

Furthermore, the principle is established under IHL that even in times of occupation of a territory by a foreign State /or non-State foreign or internal belligerent armed force; certain key buildings such as hospitals and schools shall continue to be used exclusively for the humanitarian purposes for which they are normally dedicated. This principle is reflected, for instance, in Article 14 of Protocol I additional to the Geneva Conventions with respect to civilian medical units as follows:

Art 14 - Limitations on requisition of civilian medical units

1. The Occupying Power has the duty to ensure that the medical needs of the civilian population in occupied territory continue to be satisfied.
2. The Occupying Power shall not, therefore, requisition civilian medical units, their equipment, their materiel or the services of their personnel, so long as these resources are necessary for the provision of adequate medical services for the civilian population and for the continuing medical care of any wounded and sick already under treatment.
3. Provided that the general rule in paragraph 2 continues to be observed, the Occupying Power may requisition the said resources, subject to the following particular conditions:

   (a). that the resources are necessary for the adequate and immediate medical treatment of the wounded and sick members of the armed forces of the Occupying Power or of prisoners of war;
   (b). that the requisition continues only while such necessity exists; and
   (c). that immediate arrangements are made to ensure that the medical needs of the civilian population, as well as those of any wounded and sick under treatment who are affected by the requisition, continue to be satisfied.[53]

Likewise, Article 78(2) of Protocol I (more indirectly) establishes the same principle that civilian schools and the education service they provide are not to be directed to military purposes. Hence, if children are evacuated to a safer part of the country, for instance, and are schooled there, *the school cannot be used for military purposes* (such as would be indoctrination of the children into the occupier's cultural traditions or recruitment of the children into the occupier's armed force): "Whenever an evacuation occurs pursuant to paragraph 1, *each child's education, including his religious and moral education as his parents desire*, shall be provided while he is away with the greatest possible *continuity*" (emphasis added).[54] Article 78(2), hence, emphasizes the obligation of both warring parties to ensure that children can pursue their normal course of civil education studies in a secure environment (civil school) as a protected civilian group. Destruction of, significant damage to, or use of unoccupied civilian schools for a military purpose is not consistent with that humanitarian education objective.

Contrary to the consensus view, it is here contended that there is nothing in Article 52(3) of Protocol I additional to the 1949 Geneva Conventions that sets out the general principle that use of occupied *or unoccupied schools* for military

[53]Protocol Additional to the Geneva Conventions of 12 August 1949, and relating to the Protection of Victims of International Armed Conflicts (Protocol I), 8 June 1977, entry into force 7 December 1978. http://www.icrc.org/ihl.nsf/full/470?opendocument. Accessed 28 June 2010 (Article 14).

[54]Protocol Additional to the Geneva Conventions of 12 August 1949, and relating to the Protection of Victims of International Armed Conflicts (Protocol I), 8 June 1977, entry into force 7 December 1978. http://www.icrc.org/ihl.nsf/full/470?opendocument. Accessed 28 June 2010 [Article 78(2)].

purposes (i.e., under conditions of pressing military necessity during armed conflict or during occupation) conforms to the requirements of international humanitarian law. This author states this knowing full well that Western forces also, at times, have used *unoccupied* schools for military purposes and have held out such use as allegedly being consistent with what is permissible under IHL under certain limited circumstances.

5.1.9 The Rome Statute and the Protection of Civilian Schools in Armed Conflict: Interpreting Article 8

Articles 8(2)(b)(ix) and 8(2)(e)(iv) of the Rome Statue under the title "War Crimes" refers to the fact that intentional *attacks* on civilian buildings normally dedicated to education (except where the building is a legitimate military objective under IHL as when used for military purposes by the enemy) constitute a 'war crime'. Hence, this international crime is classified in the Rome Statute under 'Other serious violations of the laws and customs applicable in... armed conflict, within the established framework of international law' occurring in the context of international and non-international conflicts respectively as follows:

> **Article 8 (2)**
> **War Crimes**
> **(b) Other serious violations of the laws and customs applicable in *international armed conflict*, within the established framework of international law, namely, any of the following acts:**
> 8(2)(b)(ix) Intentionally *directing attacks* against buildings dedicated to religion, ***education***, art, science or charitable purposes, historic monuments, hospitals and places where the sick and wounded are collected, *provided they are not military objectives* (emphasis added).
> **(e) Other serious violations of the laws and customs applicable in *armed conflicts not of an international character*, within the established framework of international law, namely, any of the following acts:**
> (8)(2)(e)(iv) Intentionally *directing attacks* against buildings dedicated to religion, ***education***, art, science or charitable purposes, historic monuments, hospitals and places where the sick and wounded are collected, *provided they are not military objectives* (emphasis added).[55]

It is important to recognize that it is significant that education buildings are listed in Articles 8(2)(b)(ix) and 8(2)(e)(iv) of the Rome Statute along with other 'cultural objects' that have 'special protection' against attacks (such as "buildings dedicated to religion, ... art, science or charitable purposes, historic monuments, hospitals and places where the sick and wounded are collected, provided they are not military objectives [that is, provided these objects/ buildings have not been converted to

[55]Rome Statute of the International Criminal Court (entered into force 1 July 2002), http://untreaty.un.org/cod/icc/statute/romefra.htm. Accessed 11 July 2010 [Articles 8(2) (b)(ix) and 8(2)(e)(iv)].

military use thus making them lawful military objectives/targets for attack]".[56] The latter objects/structures (cultural objects of special significance serving an important humanitarian objective such as hospitals and medical units) are also mentioned in the Protocols additional to the Geneva Conventions and other international humanitarian law instruments as having special protection *without limitation* (that is, even in times of military necessity) *from use* for a military purpose. Thus, a viable interpretation is that, according to the Rome Statute, schools, whether occupied or not, also enjoy the same high standard of absolute protection against use for a military purpose without exception as do the other examples of note listed in Article 8(2)(b)(ix) (and the analogous Article 8(2)(e)(iv) respecting non-international armed conflict) referring to special protection from attack for these objects (i.e., making it a war crime to attack these objects when they are being used for their normal essential civilian humanitarian purpose). Was this not the case, school buildings likely would be especially vulnerable to lawful as well as unlawful attack given: (1) their susceptibility under normal circumstances to attack (that vulnerability to attack is evidenced, for instance, by the high rate of such attacks in recent years in CAFS internationally), and (2) their potential adaptability as structures for use for a military purpose (a feature not distinctive to school buildings) putting these facilities at an even higher risk of attack; thus effectively negating their special protection guaranteed under Article 8 of the Rome Statute.

The aforementioned Article 8 provisions of the Rome Statute then identify and name *particular* buildings/objects as entitled to special protection from attack when the buildings/objects are used for their usual purpose and the named buildings include education buildings (i.e., civilian schools) which are universally recognized as dedicated to humanitarian civilian purposes.

Note that daycare facilities and pre-school facilities are, on the analysis here, also regarded as dedicated to educational/developmental humanitarian purposes and the buildings where they are housed are, therefore, also to be classed as civilian education buildings in part or in whole.

Where a belligerent force converts a *civilian* school to use for a military purpose, it is *that* force and not the attacking force that is culpable of an IHL violation (a war crime) concerning an intentional attack on a school (a building normally dedicated to a civilian use); one with special protection guaranteed under IHL against attack (as reflected in, for instance, the application of a higher standard for resolving the doubt as to a school's status before attack on the school can be considered lawful under IHL).

Stipulating that education buildings in particular under IHL enjoy a special protection against intentional attack (along with the other examples given in Article 8(2)(b)(ix)) of the Rome Statute is then but one side of a coin where the other side –a prohibition *without limitation* against the use of schools for a military

[56]Rome Statute of the International Criminal Court (entered into force 1 July 2002), http://untreaty.un.org/cod/icc/statute/romefra.htm. Accessed 11 July 2010 [Articles 8(2) (b)(ix) and 8 (2)(e)(iv)].

purpose -is essential to protecting against such attacks in the first instance. Article 8 (2)(b)(ix)) of the Rome Statute, therefore, imposes by implication, as Rowe notes, certain special obligations on the belligerents:

> ... Rome Statute, art. 8(2)(b)(ix) recognizes that if buildings dedicated to education are used in such a way that they become military objectives ... their right to be protected from attack will be lost. ***The effect of this is to impose an obligation on those taking part in the armed conflict not to use such a building so as to make it military objective by their adversary*** (emphasis added).[57]

Rowe, however, (as is clear from the entire context of his comments in his paper as a whole) is referring to a general obligation on both warring parties not to use schools for military purposes *if at all possible and reasonable* in the circumstance (i.e., where there is no compelling military necessity) since to do otherwise is to make schools (according to IHL) legitimate military targets for attack for the adversary. Thus, he holds that seizure of a school during an armed conflict (and presumably, *on his view*, use for a military purpose) *is* permissible if there is an imperative urgent military necessity.[58] Rowe refers to Articles 8(2)(b)(xiii) and 8 (2)(e)(xii) of the Rome Statute (see below) as alleged support for the notion that schools can be seized and used for a military purpose where there are exigent military needs for the same (presumably since Article 8 endorses the notion of attacks on protected objects as lawful if these objects have been converted to a military use thus, by implication, envisioning such use). *The a priori question to be answered, however, is whether or not such use of a school for a military purpose in the first instance is lawful under IHL.* It will be argued in what is to be discussed here that humanitarian considerations *outweigh* military objectives when it comes to the question of the use of civilian schools (on the analysis here; privileged protected buildings) for a military purpose (such that such use is, in the first instance, and thereafter unlawful under IHL *without exception*).

The articles of the Rome Statute which Rowe relies on to suggest that schools can be used for a military purpose under conditions of pressing military necessity read as follows:

> **Article 8 (2)**
> **War Crimes**
> **(b) Other serious violations of the laws and customs applicable in *international* armed conflict, within the established framework of international law, namely, any of the following acts**
> 8(2) (b) (xiii) Destroying *or seizing* the enemy's property *unless* such destruction or seizure be *imperatively demanded by the necessities of war* (emphasis added);
> **(e) Other serious violations of the laws and customs applicable in armed conflicts *not* of an international character, within the established framework of international law, namely, any of the following acts:**
> 8(2)(e)(xii) Destroying *or seizing* the property of an adversary *unless* such destruction or seizure be *imperatively demanded by the necessities of the conflict* (emphasis added);

---

[57]Rowe (2010), pp. 179–193 (footnote 35 at p. 186).

[58]Rowe (2010), pp. 179–193 (footnote 35 at p. 186).

> (f) Paragraph 2 (e) applies to armed conflicts not of an international character and thus does not apply to situations of internal disturbances and tensions, such as riots, isolated and sporadic acts of violence or other acts of a similar nature. It applies to armed conflicts that take place in the territory of a State when there is protracted armed conflict between governmental authorities and organized armed groups or between such groups.[59]

The current author takes the position, however, that the justification in the Rome Statute for *seizing* schools (those normally dedicated to a civilian purpose) under an "imperatively demanded"... "necessities of the conflict" rationale will *not* arise unless: (1) the adversary is *already* using the building for a military purpose (and has thus, under IHL, *unlawfully* converted the school to a military objective in the first instance); and/or (2) the objective is to prevent any use (or further use) of the school for a military purpose. On this analysis then, *seizure* of a school does *not* imply that it can lawfully be used for a military purpose by the armed party that does the seizing or any other. Were this constraint not operative, there would, in practice, be little or no protection for any civilian school against use for a military purpose given that an *alleged* argument can be made, in most instances, for the pressing military strategic benefit of using school buildings for a military purpose. This is particularly true given the realties of the war on terror which often involve fierce firefights and combat at close quarters in the midst of concentrations of civilians; of their dwellings and other civilian buildings and facilities such as schools. However, it is here argued that civilian schools [unconverted schools] whether occupied or unoccupied are entitled, as 'cultural objects', to special protection both from attack and in regards to use for a military purpose; the latter *without limitation*. Thus, neither their nature (as civilian schools); purpose (humanitarian and cultural); nor location can be used to attack or use the school for a military purpose even where this would create a military advantage.

The seizure of a school, just as with an attack on a school, is permissible then, on the analysis here, only if and when the school has been used for a military purpose by the adversary in the first instance. Once seized from the enemy, however, the school must be protected from continued use for a military purpose though, in practice, this often does not occur in the theater of the armed conflict (for reasons, on the view here, with respect, which include a misapprehension of IHL on the issue of prohibitions on the use of education buildings for military purposes).

The 'special protection' from attack guarantee under article 8(2)(b)(ix) of the Rome Statute for "buildings dedicated to religion, *education*, art, science or charitable purposes, historic monuments, hospitals and places where the sick and wounded are collected"[60] cannot thus be dissected from the necessary corollary of an *unqualified* special protection for these particular buildings/objects against use for a military purpose. That is, the 'special protection' for schools from attack is

[59]Rome Statute of the International Criminal Court (entered into force 1 July 2002), http://untreaty.un.org/cod/icc/statute/romefra.htm. Accessed 11 July 2010 [Articles 8(2)(b)(xiii) and 8 (2)(e)(xii)].

[60]Rome Statute of the International Criminal Court (entered into force 1 July 2002), http://untreaty.un.org/cod/icc/statute/romefra.htm. Accessed 11 July 2010 [Article 8(2) (b) (ix)].

essentially negated where there is no 'special protection' *without limitation* (i.e., even where there is an alleged compelling military necessity for such use) against use for a military purpose which would make these privileged buildings highly vulnerable to attack.

5.1.10 The Protection of Civilian Schools in Armed Conflict: More on the Implications of Article 53 of Protocol I Additional to the 1949 Geneva Conventions

Recall also that Protocol I additional to the 1949 Geneva Conventions at Article 53 (regarded as setting out customary law of armed conflict) makes it clear that the use of 'cultural objects' and places of worship for military purposes is a violation of IHL:

> **Art 53. [Special] Protection of cultural objects and of places of worship**
> Without prejudice to the provisions of the Hague Convention for the Protection of Cultural Property in the Event of Armed Conflict of 14 May 1954, and of other relevant international instruments, it is prohibited:
> (a) to commit any *acts of hostility* directed against the historic monuments, works of art or places of worship which constitute the cultural or spiritual heritage of peoples [assuming these have not been converted to a military use];
> (b) ***to use such objects in support of the military effort;***
> (c) to make such [civilian] objects the object of reprisals (emphasis added).[61]

It has previously been argued here that civilian schools belong to the category 'significant cultural objects' (as was held, it will be recalled, also by the Trial Chamber of the ICTY in *Prosecutor versus Kordic and Cerkez*) and, therefore, enjoy a special protected status *over and above* the level of 'general protection' afforded most other civilian buildings. Hence, on the analysis here, civilian schools are protected from use for a military purpose even in times of military necessity. As mentioned previously, a civilian education building generally will become a military objective ripe for attack not due to its very nature or location, which normally offers no unique intrinsic military advantage, but due to its having been converted to a military use. Thus, for this reason also, the belligerent force that would convert a school to such a use and so make the school a potential target for attack is solely responsible for it becoming a military objective in the first instance and any civilian casualties that result. Such a force using a school for a military purpose can be said to be violating IHL which requires that civilians and civilian objects be protected rather than endangered, and that civilian schools be afforded special protection without exception also against their use for a military purpose.

[61]Protocol Additional to the Geneva Conventions of 12 August 1949, and relating to the Protection of Victims of International Armed Conflicts (Protocol I), 8 June 1977, entry into force 7 December 1978. http://www.icrc.org/ihl.nsf/full/470?opendocument. Accessed 28 June 2010 (Article 53).

5.1.11 Use of Unoccupied Civilian Schools for a Military Purpose and the Issue of 'Human Shields'

The use of a school (normally dedicated to a civilian purpose) for a military purpose (whether in times of military necessity or at other times) then converts that school to a military objective/target and endangers civilians at the school and/or in its vicinity as well as civilian objects proximate to the school as well as the school itself. It can be argued that the use of schools for military purposes, even if unoccupied by civilians and/or non-combatants, still in some key respects amounts, *in effect*, to the use of human shields. This is the case given the fact that there is normally a close proximity of civilians to schools and, therefore, a considerably increased risk to their safety when unoccupied schools are used for military purposes and, hence, become a likely target of armed attack. This close proximity of schools to a concentration of civilians then may, depending on the specific circumstances, help to some extent to shield the armed force occupying the school or supplies stored at the school from attack (assuming the armed force that has the potential to attack is intent on minimizing civilian casualties in accord with the requirements of international humanitarian law). It is not surprising then that belligerents who do not adhere to, or respect IHL, show a pattern and practice of using buildings for military purposes that include those situated close to or in the midst of the civilian population such as schools:

> During the Gulf War, a cache of Iraqi Silkworm surface-to-surface missiles were discovered inside a school *in a densely populated Kuwait City area* ... During Operation Allied Force, the Yugoslav armed forces reportedly used churches, *schools*, and hospitals to shield troops and equipment against NATO airstrikes (emphasis added)[62]

For the reason also of the potential significant harmful impact on civilians and civilian buildings near the unoccupied school, Protocol I additional to the 1949 Geneva Conventions is properly interpreted, it is suggested, as giving: (1) special protection to schools (unoccupied or occupied) from attack except in cases of military necessity, and (2) special protection against use for a military purpose (i.e., protection of civilian schools from use for launching attacks, for operating a command centre, storing weapons etc.), whether or not occupied by civilians and/or noncombatants, and *even in times of military necessity*. That is, the humanitarian value of civilian schools outweighs any military necessity justification for their use for a military purpose. Combatants or unlawful civilian belligerents (as are members of organized terror groups) using an empty school building for a military purpose; not only place all schools, including those that have not been converted for military purposes, at increased risk of attack (given the difficulty that may exist in determining which schools have or have not been converted to a military purpose), but also endanger civilians and civilian objects that are normally housed close to schools:

[62]Waxman (2005), p. 21 (footnote 44). Cited in Henderson (2009) at pp. 194–195.

> ... the perpetrator can no longer control the result of an... attack once launched; thus the mere undertaking of such an ... extremely dangerous attack [on a school where unjustified by military necessity such as an attack on a school dedicated to civilian humanitarian objectives] would be penalized for good reasons [the risk to civilians in the school or in close proximity to the school and to other civilian objects close by].[63]

Note also that violations of Articles 51 and 52 of Additional Protocol I to the 1949 Geneva Conventions do *not* contain a "result provision". That is, civilians and/or other noncombatants (i.e., fighters 'hors du combat' taking refuge in the school) do *not* need to be killed or injured in order for an attack on a civilian school to be potentially considered unlawful under international humanitarian law (as when the attacked school had *not* in fact been used for a military purpose). This, by implication, points to the fact that schools have intrinsic humanitarian value for the society separate and apart from whether or not civilians or other noncombatants may be present there. Therefore, attacking a school, even when all civilians and other non-combatants have fled the school (i.e., for fear of an imminent attack on the school) and it is *unoccupied*, is still a violation of IHL (though it will constitute a grave violation only if there is extensive damage or destruction to the building or the loss of life or injuries that result from the attack (i.e., whether so-called 'collateral damage' to life and property, or instead intentional damage/destruction of life and property, depending on the specific objectives of the perpetrators of the attack).

Civilian schools thus have an *ongoing* intrinsic cultural and humanitarian value to society recognized under IHL which entitles them to 'special protection' over and above the right to protection arising only as a function of the presence of civilians and other non-combatants at the site at any particular time. This is reflected in the fact, for instance, that IHL prohibits an attack on the school should there be any doubt regarding whether or not the school has in fact lost its civilian object status (i.e., the school may be *unoccupied* and there may be *suspicion* that the enemy is using it to store supplies, but this would not be a sufficient basis for a lawful attack). Thus, combatants and other belligerents (including organized armed civilian insurgents such as terrorists) have no right under IHL, which assigns special protection to schools, to convert these buildings, even if unoccupied, to military use under any circumstances. Acknowledgement of and adherence to this IHL principle, and prosecution for transgressions, would, it is expected, greatly reduce the possibility of attacks on schools justified in terms of 'military necessity'.

---

[63]International Tribunal for the Prosecution of Persons Responsible for Serious Violations of International Humanitarian Law Committed in the Territory of the Former Yugoslavia since 1991 *Prosecutor versus Kordic and Cerkez* (Appeals Chamber) Case No IT-95-14-2-A (17 December 2004) at para 62. http://www.icty.org/x/cases/kordic_cerkez/acjug/en/cer-aj041217e.pdf. Accessed 2 July 2010.

5.1.12 Lessons Embedded in Article 52(3) of Protocol I on Whether Unoccupied Civilian Schools May be Lawfully Used for a Military Purpose

It is common that legal scholars in the field of the law of armed conflict maintain that Article 52(3) of Protocol I stands for the proposition that unoccupied schools may be lawfully used for military purposes where there is an imminent pressing military necessity. Hence, combatants have taken these understandings/interpretations of IHL to the field. For instance, Judge Advocate Bart states:

> Human Rights Watch explained in detail that Iraq's use of hospitals and mosques violated international humanitarian law by failing to honor the special privileged status of these sites. Yet the report's section on protected sites did not mention the Iraqi's improper military use of [civilian] schools [both occupied and unoccupied].[64]

Judge Advocate Bart thus takes this Human Rights Watch report's lack of mention or discussion of the Iraqi's use of unoccupied schools for military purposes as unlawful as alleged evidence that the correct view is that IHL does *not* prohibit the use of unoccupied school buildings for military purposes. He states:

> The current law of war contains no clear prohibition against the armed forces using school buildings for military purposes, *as long as civilians and noncombatants are not present* (emphasis added).[65]

However, the Human Rights Watch (HRW) report may have simply been focused on the forces of Saddam Hussein making military use of civilian buildings where civilian and noncombatants were more likely to have taken refuge and sought help and sanctuary (such as at hospitals and religious sites) where noncombatant casualties would likely have been high, and not on buildings perhaps more likely to be unoccupied by civilians during the fighting such as schools. We cannot conclude then from the lack of any mention or discussion in the HRW report of those forces using unoccupied schools for a military purpose as unlawful that HRW holds such use to be consistent with IHL. Even if this were the position of HRW, this would not in itself be sufficient to make such an interpretation of IHL valid.

Bart highlights the fact that Article 53(b) of Protocol I prohibits the use of religious buildings for military use without exception and the fact that schools are *allegedly* not listed as another such example in Article 53. He cites this as alleged evidence that *unoccupied* schools can purportedly be used for military purposes; at least when there is a pressing "military necessity" to do so. However, recall that, for instance: (1) schools are listed along with places of worship as specially protected against seizure (and hence use for a military purpose as well presumably) in certain international instruments such as the Statute of the ICTY (Article 3); (2) schools are grouped together with "buildings dedicated to religion, art, science or charitable

[64]Bart (2010), p. 213.

[65]Bart (2010), p. 213.

purposes, historic monuments, hospitals and places where the sick and wounded are collected" in Article 8 of the Rome Statute as being entitled to special protection from attack (unless there is military necessity) thus implicitly acknowledging a prohibition against their use for a military purpose in the first instance which would potentially necessitate such an attack; and (3) schools arguably are 'cultural objects' (for the reasons previously discussed) and, hence, would fall, on that basis, under the special protection entitlements provided to such objects by Article 53 Protocol I with respect to protection from use for a military purpose also under conditions of military necessity. Thus, the protection of schools against use for a military purpose without exception *is* in fact articulated in Article 53 Protocol I additional to the Geneva Conventions, it is here argued, since schools are incorporated into the category of 'cultural object'.

Consider also that Article 53 Protocol I additional to the Geneva Conventions lists various specific objects *as examples* of 'cultural objects'. For instance, under Article 53(a): "it is prohibited to commit any acts of hostility directed against the historic monuments, works of art or places of worship which constitute the cultural or spiritual heritage of peoples". That these can be interpreted as just examples and not a definitive, exhaustive list of cultural objects is evident from the fact that Article 53(b) goes on to stipulate that it is prohibited: "... to use *such* objects in support of the military effort"; while Article 53(c) stipulates that it is a violation "to make *such* objects the object of reprisals" (emphasis added)". That is, provisions (b) and (c) of Article 53 Protocol I do not refer to "*these*" *or* "*those*" objects (those specifically listed in Article 53(a)) as being protected from use for a military purpose and from reprisals). The reference rather to "such objects" can be reasonably interpreted to allow such special protections without limitation against use for a military purpose to be extended to other cultural objects as well that "constitute the cultural or spiritual heritage of peoples". It has here been argued that *unconverted* civilian schools (whether occupied by civilians and other non-combatants or not) are also covered by the special protection under IHL without exception against use for a military purpose accorded significant cultural objects.

Further, it should be noted that Article 53 of Protocol I additional to the Geneva Conventions states that it is not the definitive provision regarding what buildings are to be protected from attack and from use for a military purpose without exception (i.e., The preamble to the text of that article states "Without prejudice to the provisions of the Hague Convention for the Protection of Cultural Property in the Event of Armed Conflict of 14 May 1954, and of other relevant international instruments").[66] Thus, the text of Article 53 in and of itself would, in any case, not provide a sufficient legally supportable basis for holding that unoccupied civilian schools are excluded from protection against use for a military purpose without limitation. In any case, for the reasons discussed, the current author contends that

[66] Protocol Additional to the Geneva Conventions of 12 August 1949, and relating to the Protection of Victims of International Armed Conflicts (Protocol I), 8 June 1977, entry into force 7 December 1978. http://www.icrc.org/ihl.nsf/full/470?opendocument. Accessed 28 June 2010 (Article 53).

Article 53 of Protocol I does in fact prohibit use of unoccupied (or occupied) civilian schools for a military purpose without exception.

5.1.13 Additional Considerations Regarding IHL and the Prohibition on the Use of Civilian Schools for Military Purposes

Consider also that most schools are in residential areas and are often neighborhood schools. For instance, in Afghanistan most schools are in rural villages amidst villagers' dwellings, while the more centrally located schools, of which there are fewer, are located in urban areas with larger civilian populations. Hence, in Afghanistan as elsewhere using even unoccupied school buildings for military purposes would place military objectives (i.e., civilian schools converted to a military purpose) close to the civilian population including children in violation of, for instance, Article 51 of Protocol I additional to the 1949 Geneva Conventions (and a parallel Article in Protocol II additional to the 1949 Geneva Conventions; Article 13(1)). Article 51 of Protocol I, it will be recalled, states in part:

> The civilian population and individual civilians shall enjoy general protection against dangers arising from military operations . . .[67]

There is a high risk as explained, of 'collateral damage' (death and injury to civilians living close to schools, including children; the latter being a group entitled to special protection) when unoccupied schools are used for a military purpose. This then would lead to an infringement of the requirement under IHL that the parties to the armed conflict do everything feasible to reduce such a risk of 'collateral damage'. Article 51 (Protocol I) and Article 13(1)(Protocol II) then set up a requirement of using sites for military purposes that are as far way from collections of civilians as possible in the circumstance and as required under IHL. This then would generally preclude unoccupied schools being legitimate candidates for military use in times of significant and urgent military necessity especially given their proximity to child civilians living in the neighborhood; a civilian group that enjoys special protection under IHL (and, on the analysis here, due to the special protection to be accorded to civilian schools).

Consider also that Article 53 (Protocol I) and Article 16 (Protocol II) additional to the Geneva Conventions: i) prohibiting attacks on unconverted places of worship which are dedicated to a civilian purpose, and ii) banning without limitation the use of such buildings for military purposes during armed conflict, may have been premised also on the assumption that such buildings would serve to provide various

[67]Protocol Additional to the Geneva Conventions of 12 August 1949, and relating to the Protection of Victims of International Armed Conflicts (Protocol I), 8 June 1977, entry into force 7 December 1978. http://www.icrc.org/ihl.nsf/full/470?opendocument. Accessed 28 June 2010 (Article 51).

types of humanitarian aid and *sanctuary* during armed conflict. The protection clauses concerning hospitals and places of worship in Protocols I and II may thus have been premised more clearly also on the notion of protecting the civilian and/or noncombatants attending there during armed conflict for humanitarian aid and sanctuary. This interpretation is consistent with the fact that: "The 1977 Protocol . . . expands the prohibition against military use to include most religious buildings *independent of their historic or cultural value* (emphasis added)".[68] Hospitals and religious buildings can be considered to be buildings/facilities that are likely to take on an extra importance in times of armed conflict in providing service to civilians and noncombatants in terms of sanctuary. These are building sites normally dedicated to humanitarian functions; therefore, in the usual course, considered to be neutral and not a threat to either side. Hospitals and places of worship are not normally officially "closed" in times of conflict and strife, but rather hospital and religious personnel at these respective sites traditionally seek to serve the populace throughout turbulent times to the extent possible. Civilians and other noncombatants then are likely to seek medical treatment, and/or other humanitarian aid and/or solace and refuge at hospitals and religious buildings in great numbers during armed conflict:

> The protection of [civilian] hospitals *from targeting and military use* was acknowledged as linked to the safety of wounded and sick persons. And the protection of religious buildings from targeting and some from military use was acknowledged as *linked to the safety of pilgrims and persons seeking special refuge* (emphasis added).[69]

The unqualified prohibition against use for a military purpose of hospitals and religious buildings meant further that the civilians and/or noncombatants using these facilities in times of armed conflict would be better protected, in law at least, from being used as human shields and from injury or death as collateral damage in an attack. It is not surprising thus, given the implication for the safety of civilians and other noncombatants during armed conflict, that these categories of building (i.e., hospitals and places of worship) should be highlighted in Protocols I and II additional to the 1949 Geneva Conventions as deserving of not only protection from attack (except in cases of exceptional military necessity); but also against use for a military purpose without limitation. The highlighting in IHL of an unqualified protection for hospitals and places of worship against use for a military purpose (i.e., even where there is military necessity) was and continues to be importantly premised on the expected high use of these facilities for aid and sanctuary by civilians and other noncombatants during times of armed conflict. The protection of these facilities then relates to the Protocol I and II protection of civilians from harm due to military operations as much as from their importance to a community or a people in terms of the cultural or spiritual heritage they represent.

Schools, it has here been argued, are also entitled to this 'special protection' given: (1) the special protections to be afforded to children under IHL, and the adverse effects on the latter should civilian schools be attacked or, in times of

[68] Bart (2010), p. 209.

[69] Bart (2010), p. 214.

military necessity, or any other time, be used for a military purpose whether occupied by civilians and/or noncombatants or not and (2) and the importance of schools as a vehicle for transmission of local and indeed global culture/heritage to the next generation. The question arises then as to why the drafters of the Protocols additional to the 1949 Geneva Conventions did not make it more clear that schools are also protected from military use even where there is military necessity, and regardless whether occupied or unoccupied by civilians and/or noncombatants as is the case for instance for civilian hospitals, medical units, and places of worship. In answering that question, consider that the drafters of the Protocols additional to the Geneva Conventions would, in all likelihood, have expected that schools located *in insecure combat zones* would be 'officially closed' during armed conflict: (1) for the protection of the children and teachers (an assumption that sadly is often, in fact, in recent times *not* the case in CAFS such as Afghanistan as we have seen; with the end result being hundreds of terror attacks on schools and children being gravely injured and killed along with education personnel and other civilians), and closed (2) due to the anticipated inability of the government centralized education administrative system to function during the armed conflict. It is, afterall, a rather recent phenomenon that a State party to an armed conflict and its international State allies would: (1) use schools (more specifically school enrollment numbers, numbers of schools operational etc. also *in zones not yet secured*) as a tool in the propaganda war against its enemy as is occurring in the context of the war on terror, and, hence, (2) continue to operate schools located in the midst of intense conflict zones. These civilians then in Afghanistan and in other CAFS (i.e., students, teachers, other education personnel and humanitarian education aid workers) attending schools without adequate security, as has been documented in innumerable reports by high profile international UN and NGO organizations, are at grave risk of being used as human shields by terrorists and/ or of being injured or killed as a result of a terror attack on the school such as a bombing or arson.

The suggestion here then is that had the drafters of the Protocols additional to the 1949 Geneva Conventions envisioned that schools would be allowed to operate as educational institutions during armed conflict *despite the lack of security* for these buildings (as is the case in Afghanistan and many CAFS), they might have included in the Protocols a separate provision highlighting the absolute prohibition on the use of civilian schools for a military purpose (such as was incorporated for civilian hospitals and religious buildings). However, given that: (1) the drafters of Protocol I did *not* likely expect that civilian schools in CAFS would continue to offer schooling despite their high vulnerability to attack, and would thus be occupied by civilians even during armed conflict, and given the fact that (2) the provisions against the use of hospitals and religious buildings for a military purpose in the Protocols are in fact derivative of the expected presence of civilians at those facilities even during armed conflict; no separate clause specifically mentioning *only* schools and a prohibition without exception against their *use f*or military purposes was included in the Protocols (though, as has been here discussed, schools are included as entitled to special protection as 'cultural objects' under the additional protocols).

Other provisions of the Protocols, by implication, provide the same protection for both occupied and unoccupied schools i.e., Article 51 (Protocol I) and Article 13 (1) (Protocol II) which refer to the requirement that civilians not be placed in harm's way by military operations. Using an unoccupied school for a military purpose is just such a 'military operation' that would substantially increase the risk of collateral damage given that schools are located in the midst of the civilian population. Similarly, hospitals and ordinary religious buildings (buildings that do not generally have a special historic or iconic cultural significance) are generally located in the midst of a civilian area and dedicated to important humanitarian functions.

Note that medical personnel, as per internationally recognized professional medical ethics codes, are required also to treat the enemy wounded if they are delivered into their care. Hence, military medical units also receive special protection from attack if exclusively used for humanitarian medical purposes and enjoy protection against use by the enemy for a military non-medial purpose even in times of military necessity. This author would hold that buildings are civilian if used for a humanitarian purpose. However, some legal scholars such as Henderson hold that military medical units, while entitled to 'special protection' from a targeted attack or use for a military purpose, are still technically 'military objectives' with the consequence that they do not enjoy the same consideration when estimating how to reduce collateral damage.[70] The current author thus is disagreed with Henderson on the latter contention.

An unqualified ban on the use for military purposes of hospitals and religious buildings is essential, just as with civilian schools, in: (1) reducing the risk of attack and injury to civilians and other noncombatants attending at these sites; (2) reducing the risk of collateral damage to civilians and civilian objects that are highly likely to be situated near these sites; and (3) preserving these buildings so important to the community which are expected to be dedicated in the normal course to humanitarian (education) purposes and upholding respect for human rights and diversity. In regards to the latter point, the IHL protection of certain civilian cultural objects for the purpose of upholding respect for human rights and diversity and promoting peace is particularly relevant to civil institutions dedicated to education.

5.1.14 More on Schools as Cultural Objects That Serve Important Humanitarian Purposes

It is important to appreciate that there has been an evolution in the notion of 'cultural heritage' and, hence, in what constitutes a 'cultural object' since the entry into force of the Protocols additional to the Geneva Convention. That evolution in the notion of 'cultural heritage' leads to the conclusion that schools are

[70]Henderson (2009), pp. 195–196.

entitled under IHL to an unqualified special protection from use for a military purpose: (a) whether occupied or unoccupied by civilians and/or other noncombatants at the time, and (b) whether or not such use would provide a military advantage to the force that seizes and uses the school for a non-humanitarian purpose. The evolution in the concept of 'cultural heritage' has been described thus:

> The exceptionalism originally afforded cultural heritage in international humanitarian law arose from its perceived significance to humanity through its advancement of the arts and sciences, and knowledge. By the mid-twentieth century, and the rise of human rights in international law, this rationale was recalibrated to emphasise its importance to the enjoyment of human rights and promotion of cultural diversity. This shift in rationale manifested itself most clearly in the articulation and prosecution of war crimes, crimes against humanity and genocide. *Cultural heritage and its protection was no longer based on its exclusivity but its intrinsic importance to people and individuals, to their identity and their enjoyment of their human rights.* It has become fundamental in establishing cases of violations of international humanitarian law and international criminal law, and assessing the claims of victims of gross violations of human rights. Furthermore, this shift in rationale has been reinforced with a broadening notion of cultural heritage in the late twentieth century. *No longer confined to tangible heritage like monuments, sites and works of art of exceptional importance to all humanity, cultural heritage encompasses the intangible and the ephemeral, like language, traditional knowledge, songs, dance, deemed significant by a group (not necessarily a state)*(emphasis added).[71]
>
> As the reach of international humanitarian law was extended to noninternational conflicts with the emergence of human rights in international law, the provisions relating to cultural heritage were likewise extended. This development together with the recalibration of other international humanitarian law and human rights provisions has reinforced the *interdependence of the protection of cultural heritage (tangible and intangible) and the effective enjoyment of human rights by individuals and groups* (emphasis added).[72]

Civilian schools then are dedicated to the humanitarian purpose of promoting and transmitting the intangible elements of cultural heritage (i.e., language and cultural identity, the people's history and sociology, knowledge regarding global politics and human rights etc.) and as such are entitled under current IHL to 'special protection' as cultural objects over and above that normally given to civilian objects (i.e., schools whether occupied by civilians or unoccupied are entitled to protection not only from attack except where the school has been converted to a military purpose, but also protection, without exception, against use for a military purpose). In this regard, consider that the 'right to education', as understood under the UN definition in the CRC (Article 29),[73] is vital to respect for human rights and tolerance. Thus, schools are intended to promote cultural heritage in a manner that is protected under IHL (i.e., schools may serve a particular minority group using that group's language as the language of instruction in some or all classes; and bring children from various ethnic groups together while respectfully teaching about and honouring diverse cultural traditions in the region). On this analysis, all

[71]Vrdoljak (2009), p. 1.

[72]Vrdoljak (2009), p. 4.

[73]UN Convention on the Rights of the Child Adopted (entry into force 2 September 1990). http://www2.ohchr.org/english/law/crc.htm. Accessed 18 May 2010) (Article 29).

school buildings dedicated to a civilian humanitarian purpose would be entitled to special protection, whether occupied or not, and whether or not the building has some specific historic or special iconic symbolic cultural significance. This being the case since civilian schools are, by definition, devoted to the transmission of culture, and knowledge of peoples and, hence, are inevitably concerned with fundamental human rights relating to the right to cultural identity, respect for all peoples, the right to access information, to participate in society (by being schooled and learning at school various skills and knowledge vital to societal participation as an adult) and the like.

It is here contended that where a school is used to foster hate toward a minority group or any other identifiable group and/or used to recruit child soldiers, child suicide bombers etc. that school is already been used for a military purpose. Technically, this puts the children and teachers in the latter schools at risk of lawful attack under IHL as a legitimate military objective/target. However, democratic States are: (1) reluctant to attack any schools normally dedicated to a civilian purpose and occupied by civilians which are not at that precise time directing fire against the armed forces of that State or its allies and (2) loathe to attack any school occupied or not (although this has occurred in cases where the attacking State has maintained that the school was a legitimate military objective under alleged conditions of pressing military necessity as defined under IHL). For instance, HRW has accused (rightly or wrongly) Israel of unlawfully destroying certain unoccupied schools, amongst certain other civilian objects, allegedly without a legitimate military purpose, during 'Operation Cast Lead' which took place in Gaza from 27 December 2008 to 18 January 2009.[74]

5.1.15 IHL and the Use of Schools for Propaganda Purposes

Note that Article 24, 1949 Geneva Convention IV, according to the Commentary of the International Committee of the Red Cross on Article 24, establishes the principle that schools are *not* to be used for religious or political propaganda purposes by a party to an armed conflict:

> The idea of education must be understood in its broadest sense as including moral and physical education as well as school work and religious instruction. ***The Article specifies that this task [education] is to be entrusted, as far as possible, to persons of the same cultural tradition as the parents. That provision is most important. It is intended to exclude any religious or political propaganda*** *designed to wean children from their natural milieu; for that would cause additional suffering to human beings already grievously stricken by the loss of their parents* (emphasis added).[75]

[74]Human Rights Watch (2010), p. 3.

[75]International Committee of the Red Cross Commentary on Article 24 Geneva Convention IV. http://www.icrc.org/ihl.nsf/COM/380-600028?OpenDocument. Accessed 17 July 2010.

This principle prohibiting the use of education for propaganda purposes by a party to an armed conflict, on the current author's analysis, would seem generalizable also to the situations of schools used by terrorists or their supporters to spread terror ideology as the same values and respect for human rights are in jeopardy without such protection against such a use. Likewise, the operation of schools by a democratic State (partnered with national or international NGO with a humanitarian/human rights mandate) where it is known that the school is at high risk of terror attack is a situation, it is here argued, where the school is serving a military counter-terrorism propaganda function more so than a humanitarian one, or at least a dual function that includes a military propaganda purpose. Such a situation then violates IHL; for instance, the basic values regarding the protection of children during armed conflict that underlie Article 24, 1949 Geneva Convention IV.

5.1.16 Use of an Occupied or Unoccupied Civilian School for a Military Purpose as Unlawful Under IHL

The absolute prohibition on using hospitals and religious sites for a military purpose is intended to help reduce the possibility that the site will be attacked as a military objective. With the special prohibitions on use for a military purpose of these particular civilian buildings being explicitly expressed in the Protocols additional to the Geneva Conventions, the hope likely was that doubts would be less likely to arise as to these sites being non-military objectives not suitable for attack (at least for those potential attackers that adhere to IHL).

Civilians schools can only be attacked for reasons of 'military necessity' if considered in the first instance to be a military objective (i.e., due to their use for military purposes by enemy armed belligerents). As schools are 'cultural objects' devoted to humanitarian purposes important to the transmission of various intangible elements of cultural heritage, and to fostering respect for human rights (i.e., educational institutions are categorized as such in the Rome Statute Article 8(2)(b)(ix) and 8(2)(e)(iv)), it is here contended, that the *use* of school buildings for a military purpose (whether occupied or unoccupied by civilians and/or other noncombatants) is a violation of international humanitarian law. This is reflected in the fact, for instance, that it is the very violation of IHL by the opposing force (their use of schools for a military purpose) that permits the lawful lifting of the usual stringent prohibitions on endangering civilians and cultural objects (the latter normally dedicated to civilian purposes). Note that citizen casualties in such attacks, whether in the targeted school or in the vicinity; as well as damage to civilian objects in the area, is required to be minimized to the extent possible. Indeed, wanton reckless damage and destruction of civilian objects and reckless killing or maiming of civilians are 'war crimes' even in the context of an attack that was lawful in the first instance given military necessity. These prohibitions against endangering civilians and civilian objects are the hallmark of IHL.

Another example of the *lawful* suspension of the normal IHL protections for civilians and civilian objects (based on *unlawful* conduct by the enemy *in violation of the rules of war*) is the right of attack on civilians who are at the time participating in the armed hostilities since doing so is unlawful for civilians except in very limited circumstances such as that of a national popular uprising.

Put another way, civilian schools, like hospitals and places of religious worship are normally considered to be "undefended" buildings used for neutral humanitarian civilian purposes and, hence, not subject to attack. It is only when that neutrality becomes compromised through unlawful use of a civilian school for military purposes that an attack on the school building (unoccupied or occupied by civilians and /or other non-combatants) is lawful under IHL. Thus, a lawful attack (under IHL) on schools, places of worship and hospitals (whether occupied or unoccupied by civilians and/or noncombatants) is the indicia of loss of protected' status for these buildings due in the first instance to *unlawful use* of these buildings normally dedicated to essential civilian purposes (i.e., an 'unlawful use' being a 'military purpose' in this instance). If belligerents could, at any time, lawfully use unoccupied civilian schools for a military purpose (as has been generally claimed by most legal scholars on the laws of war as well as commanders in the field), then the designation *in particular* of (civilian) schools along with "buildings dedicated to religion, . . . art, science or charitable purposes, historic monuments, hospitals and places where the sick and wounded are collected" (in Article 8(2)(b)(ix) of the Rome Statute) as buildings normally immune from attack as undefended 'cultural/ civil objects' would be largely meaningless. This would be the case just as would a prohibition from attack on the other buildings listed in Article 8(2)(b)(ix) of the Rome Statute (i.e., hospitals and buildings dedicated to religious purposes) be meaningless if *they* were *available* for lawful military use in times of military necessity (a possibility expressly prohibited in the protocols additional to the 1949 Geneva Conventions) even if never having been converted away from their humanitarian purpose.

It is here contended thus that the IHL prohibition without exception against military use of hospitals and places of worship (i.e., even in times of military necessity) applies also to civilian schools. This is, for instance, clearly the implication of the elevated protection against attack accorded civilian schools in the Rome Statute article 8(2)(b)(ix) as a building devoted to an essential humanitarian function. The protection against attack for civilian schools in the context of an international armed conflict is listed in a separate article (Article 2(b)(ix)) in the Rome Statute from that regarding the protection from attack for civilian buildings more generally which is articulated at Article 8(2)(b)(ii) in term of a prohibition against "Intentionally directing attacks against civilian objects, that is, objects which are not military objectives". This suggests that schools (along with the other objects listed in Article 2(b)(ix)) have an intrinsic highly important cultural and humanitarian significance entitling them to protection based on more than the mere fact that they are normally dedicated to civilian purposes. (Note that Article 2(e)(iv) of the Rome Statute regarding non-international conflict has the same wording as Article 2(b)(ix)).

This interpretation (that under IHL there must be *unlawful* conduct by the armed adversarial force before civilian buildings or persons can be endangered through an attack) is further supported by the fact that in those circumstances where civilian structures have persons *lawfully* defending their humanitarian activities (an action that cannot be classified as a military use of the building); they cannot, under IHL, be lawfully attacked. Thus, Article 13 of Protocol I additional to the 1949 Geneva Conventions sets out this principle with examples of conduct that is not unlawful and would *not* justify an attack on a civilian object such as a civilian hospital or medical unit:

Art 13. Discontinuance of protection of civilian medical units

1. The protection to which civilian medical units are entitled shall not cease unless they are used to commit, outside their humanitarian function, acts harmful to the enemy. Protection may, however, cease only after a warning has been given setting, whenever appropriate, a reasonable time-limit, and after such warning has remained unheeded.
2. *The following shall* ***not*** *be considered as acts harmful to the enemy:*

   (a). *that the personnel of the unit are equipped with light individual weapons for their own defence or for that of the wounded and sick in their charge;*
   (b). *that the unit is guarded by a picket or by sentries or by an escort;*
   (c). *that small arms and ammunition taken from the wounded and sick, and not yet handed to the proper service, are found in the units;*
   (d). *that members of the armed forces or other combatants are in the unit for medical reasons.*[76]

Lawful attack on a structure normally dedicated to civilian purposes is fundamentally based then on 'military necessity' that implies, at the outset, that the civilian structure has lost its civilian status due to its ***unlawful*** use and, therefore, it has become a legitimate military objective. Thus, using an unoccupied (or occupied) civilian school for a military purpose such as launching attacks against an enemy force is, on the analysis here, an unlawful use as evidence by the fact that it results in the school losing its protected status against attack. However, when civilians in the school defend themselves against attack with light individual weapons, this is not a violation of IHL and thus would not render the school a legitimate military objective subject to lawful attack. Likewise, the personnel of a medical unit defending themselves and the wounded and sick in their charge with light individual weapons is *not* sufficient to have the medical unit lose its protected civilian status (see Article 13, Protocol I cited above).

[76]Protocol Additional to the Geneva Conventions of 12 August 1949, and relating to the Protection of Victims of International Armed Conflicts (Protocol I), 8 June 1977, entry into force 7 December 1978. http://www.icrc.org/ihl.nsf/full/470?opendocument. Accessed 28 June 2010 (Article 13).

5.1.17 The Martens Clause and Its Application to the Issue of Protection of Unoccupied Civilian Schools from Attack or Use for a Military Purpose

Since schools are considered in the Rome Statute to have a special protected status as institutions serving important humanitarian functions; there is, it is here contended, a general prohibition against the use of civilian schools for a military purpose in times of armed conflict even if the buildings are unoccupied by civilians or other non-combatants. That is, there is no authority under IHL to remove the special protected status of civilian schools as important humanitarian institutions through such military use i.e., no authority under IHR to blur the distinction between civilian and non- civilian school buildings. Were such a prohibition against use of schools for a military purpose not in place, adversaries would often be unsure whether any particular school was or was not amongst those converted to a military purpose. The consequence would then be to put schools at considerably increased risk of attack despite the high value to the society of educational institutions. Use of civilian schools for a military purpose thus undermines the cardinal rule of IHL requiring a distinction be made, and readily recognizable not only between civilians and combatants, but between civilian and non-civilian objects (military and non-military objectives/targets). Further, use of civilian buildings for a military purpose, even if unoccupied, knowingly puts civilians in the proximity of the building at serious risk of harms from military operations as discussed. There is nothing in IHL that allows a belligerent force to *itself* create the military necessity for that force or the enemy force to attack that civilian building i.e., by using a building for a military purpose thus making it vulnerable to attack by the adversary, or, for example, the same armed party as used it blowing it up since it had been found out by the enemy and contained sensitive materials or weapons that that party did not want to fall into the hands of its enemy). Such military use of civilian schools is thus unlawful use that suspends IHL protection of those buildings and the protection for any civilians or noncombatants in them where there is military necessity for an attack (i.e., where there would be a substantial military advantage in damaging or destroying the military objective; namely the school).

Henderson makes the point that a lawful attack on a non-human target (i.e., a building such as a school) must have some military advantage meaning that it "will directly or indirectly weaken the military capability of the enemy".[77] He maintains thus that "an object cannot be attacked [lawfully under IHL] just because damaging or destroying that object will contribute to the political or strategic goals of the armed conflict".[78] This author is in agreement on this point with Henderson and applies this thinking to the issue of attacks on civilian schools. For instance, as discussed, terror attacks on civilian schools do not contribute to a weakening of the

[77] Henderson (2009), p. 43.

[78] Henderson (2009), p. 43.

military capability of the enemy but rather undermine the political popularity of the government in power and its international backers given their inability to provide security to such vital societal institutions as schools. Henderson also makes the point that IHL treaties generally set out prohibitions against violence rather than permissions and he argues that all is permissible in armed conflict except if specifically prohibited in IHL.[79] However, as Henderson himself concedes, certain authorizations for military action are explicit in the treaty, others implicit in IHL.[80] Therefore, we must conclude that certain prohibitions may also be implicit and flow from others that are made explicit in the treaty such that one cannot conclude that all is permissible in armed conflict unless expressly prohibited in an IHL treaty. The current author has argued that the prohibition under IHL against the use of civilian schools for a military purpose is, to some extent, in some international treaties, such an implicit prohibition that flows from several others that are expressly articulated. In this regard consider also the Martens Clause which states:

> Until a more complete code of the laws of war is issued, the High Contracting Parties think it right to declare that in cases not included in the Regulations adopted by them, populations and belligerents remain under the protection and empire of the principles of international law, as they result from the usages established between civilized nations, *from the laws of humanity and the requirements of the public conscience* (emphasis added).[81]

This author interprets this clause to mean that should a necessary prohibition be omitted from an IHL treaty for whatever reason, or not expressly stated, this cannot be used as a basis for violating the laws of humanity. This author would argue that the omission of an *express* and unqualified prohibition against the use of schools for a military purpose during armed conflict in the additional protocols to the 1949 Geneva Conventions represents a case to which the Martens Clause is applicable. This is the case since the use of civilian schools for a military purpose during armed conflict (whether occupied or unoccupied by civilians) places civilians, including children, at risk of grave harm by increasing the risk of attack on a target in the midst of civilian population (as well as increasing the risk of damage to and/or destruction of school and other buildings that serve a critical humanitarian function). Thus, use during armed conflict of civilian schools for a military purpose violates "the laws of humanity and the requirements of public conscience" to use the terminology of the Martens Clause. Put differently the Martens Clause can be interpreted as follows:

> At its most restricted, the Clause serves as a reminder that customary international law continues to apply after the adoption of a treaty norm. A wider interpretation is that, as few international treaties relating to the laws of armed conflict are ever complete, the Clause provides that *something which is not explicitly prohibited by a treaty is not ipso facto*

---

[79]Henderson (2009), pp. 38–39.

[80]Henderson (2009), p. 39.

[81]Ticehurst (1997).

> *permitted. The widest interpretation is that conduct in armed conflicts is not only judged according to treaties and custom but also to the principles of international law referred to by the Clause* [i.e., principles relating to the laws of humanity and the requirements of the public conscience].[82]

Thus, the Martens Clause appears to be quite relevant to the problem of the legality or illegality under IHL of the use of unoccupied civilian schools for military purposes where there is compelling military necessity during armed conflict. The argument here is then that: (1) such military use of a civilian school violates implicit prohibitions in treaty law (IHL); and (2) the fact that an explicit prohibition against such use may or may not be included in particular treaty law does not mean "ipso facto" that such military use of unoccupied civilian schools is permitted.

On the importance of the Martens Clause the ICRC stated the following:

> Both the Geneva Conventions of 1949 and the two Protocols additional thereto of 1977 restated the Martens Clause. Furthermore, the 1977 Diplomatic Conference which led to the drafting of Additional Protocol I underlined the continuing importance of the Martens Clause by moving it from the preamble, where it first appeared in the 1973 draft, to a substantive provision of the Protocol. *Undoubtedly, therefore, the Martens Clause is still relevant.* This was confirmed by Nauru, stating that "... the Martens Clause was not an historical aberration. Numerous modern-day conventions on the laws of war have ensured its continuing vitality". (emphasis added).[83]

Note also that according to "the ICJ's [International Court of Justice] Advisory Opinion... the Martens Clause is a customary rule and is therefore of normative status".[84] According to Judge Shahabuddeen of the ICJ "the Martens Clause is not simply a reminder of the existence of other norms of international law not contained in a specific treaty- *it has a normative status in its own right* and therefore works independently of other norms".[85] The ICRC states:

> It appears that, when determining the full extent of the laws of armed conflict, *the Martens Clause provides authority for looking beyond treaty law and custom to consider principles of humanity and the dictates of the public conscience* (emphasis added).[86]

It is here argued then that the 'laws of humanity' and the 'dictates of public conscience' require that civilian schools be regarded as safe havens for children that must thus be protected from attack whether occupied by civilians and other non-combatants or not. This then implies a correlative prohibition *without exception* on the *use* of civilian schools for military purposes during armed conflict (i.e., even in conditions of alleged pressing and urgent military necessity).

---

[82]Ticehurst (1997).

[83]Ticehurst (1997).

[84]Ticehurst (1997).

[85]Ticehurst (1997).

[86]Ticehurst (1997).

5.1.18 More on the Basic 'Principle of Distinction', 'Military Necessity' and the Scope of IHL Protection for Civilian Schools

Were there no prohibition on the use of unoccupied civilian schools for a military purpose during armed conflict, as is generally claimed is the case, the IHL protection against *any* school becoming a military objective would, in practice, be extraordinarily weak. This given that a belligerent force could lawfully convert an unoccupied civilian school to a military purpose simply on the purported grounds of alleged 'military necessity' anytime this rationale was advanced by a commander. It would then be extraordinarily difficult to discern if and when this had taken place. In a close combat situation, as in the war on terror, where the Taliban and Al-Qaeda use not only human shields, but also occupied and unoccupied civilian buildings as shields, there would be few civilian buildings (including unoccupied schools) that could not be said to potentially provide some military advantage to Afghan forces and their allies were they seized and converted to the latter's own military purpose.

Note that the argument made here is that the lawfulness of an attack on a school building due to 'military necessity' (i.e., where the school has *already* been converted to a military purpose), does *not* at all imply lawfulness in regards to *converting* an unoccupied civilian school into a 'military objective' in the first instance by using it for a military purpose hence endangering civilian lives in (i.e., hostages) or near the school. The two situations, it is here contended, are not at all parallel in a key respect relating to the basic IHL "principle of distinction":

1. A lawful attack based on military necessity, and launched on a school as a military objective, is an attack on a school that has *already* been converted by the enemy from use for a civilian purpose to a military one. The attack at that specific time then is on a military *not* a civilian object. *Such an attack, therefore, does not undermine the IHL basic principle of distinction between civilian and non-civilian (military) objects.* (Should the building return to having a civilian purpose, it could not longer be lawfully attacked).
2. However, when a school which is dedicated to civilian purposes is taken over, based on military necessity, for the very purpose of *converting* its use to a military purpose, this constitutes a form of attack also. It is an attack that does violence to the basic IHL 'principle of distinction' (i.e., such action blurs the distinction between civilian versus non-civilian (military) objects by eliminating the building's original civilian status and confusing the enemy regarding which school buildings have or have not been converted to a military purpose).

Hence, on the analysis here, converting a civilian school (occupied or unoccupied) to a military purpose, even where there is military necessity, constitutes a violation of IHL since: (1) doing so erodes the principle of distinction; (2) civilian schools enjoy 'special protection' under IHL from use for a military purpose since children, who are entitled to 'special protection', under IHL, are at high risk of adverse consequences from such a conversion of schools (injury and death when unoccupied schools in their area become military objectives as well as denial of the right to education) and (3) as recognized in Article 2(b)(ix) of the Rome Statute, civilian schools serve a highly important humanitarian cultural function just as do "buildings dedicated to religion, art, science or charitable purposes, historic monuments, hospitals and places where the sick and wounded are collected";[87] resulting in 'special protection' from attack that presupposes also, on the analysis here, protection without limitation from use for a military purpose.

Article 48 of Protocol I additional to the Geneva Conventions (an article that has the status of customary law) establishes by implication, it is here argued, that any act which intentionally blurs the distinction between military objectives/targets and civilian objects (i.e., buildings used for a military purpose versus those used for a civilian purpose such as education) is a violation of IHL. Those who convert a civilian school to a military purpose during armed conflict generally make efforts to conceal that conversion from the enemy thus: (1) sabotaging the 'principle of distinction' which is a fundamental rule in the international customary law of armed conflict (by intentionally attempting to create confusion for the adversary about which are or are not civilian objects) and, hence, (2) undermining the effective operation of Article 48 of Protocol I which reads as follows:

> **Article 48: Basic rule [Protocol I additional to the 1949 Geneva Conventions]**
> *In order to ensure respect for and protection of the civilian population and civilian objects*, the Parties to the conflict *shall at all times distinguish* between the civilian population and combatants and between civilian objects and military objectives and accordingly shall direct their operations only against military objectives (emphasis added).[88]

Taking over an unoccupied or occupied civilian school and converting it to a military purpose does not, for the reasons explained, constitute "ensuring respect for and protection of . . . civilian objects".[89] It is relevant to note in the context of this discussion that neither Protocol I nor Protocol II additional to the 1949 Geneva Conventions refers to a potential lawful military use of unoccupied civilian schools based on military necessity (whereas lawful *attack* against objects normally dedicated to civilian purposes, where there is military necessity, is provided for in the aforementioned IHL instruments). Further, the Martens Clause (which *is* included

---

[87] Rome Statute of the International Criminal Court (entered into force 1 July 2002), http://untreaty.un.org/cod/icc/statute/romefra.htm. Accessed 11 July 2010 [Article 8(2) (b)(ix)].

[88] Protocol Additional to the Geneva Conventions of 12 August 1949, and relating to the Protection of Victims of International Armed Conflicts (Protocol I), 8 June 1977, entry into force 7 December 1978. http://www.icrc.org/ihl.nsf/full/470?opendocument. Accessed 28 June 2010 (Basic Rule: Article 48).

[89] Protocol Additional to the Geneva Conventions of 12 August 1949, and relating to the Protection of Victims of International Armed Conflicts (Protocol I), 8 June 1977, entry into force 7 December 1978. http://www.icrc.org/ihl.nsf/full/470?opendocument. Accessed 28 June 2010 (Basic Rule: Article 48).

in the aforementioned Protocols), as discussed, reveals that the fact that these Protocols do not include an explicit prohibition on converting civilian schools to a military purpose, does *not* at all affirm that such military actions are lawful under IHL.

5.1.19 The IHL Criteria for Military Necessity as Involving Only Lawful Measures

It is the case that the protection of civilians and civilian buildings under IHL is not absolute. For instance, collateral damage to civilian buildings is anticipated in armed hostilities (though the obligation is to always minimize such harm to the extent possible even where attacks are permissible under IHL). Notwithstanding the foregoing, however, it is here contended that neither belligerent party may under IHL intentionally itself create the conditions which undermine the protection normally afforded civilian buildings dedicated to important humanitarian functions (i.e., schools) by converting these occupied or unoccupied civilian buildings to a military purpose. Once the former civilian object is functioning as a military one, however, attacks on that building will likely meet the criteria of 'military necessity' under IHL (that is, if there is no doubt about the building being a military objective, and the attack on it is measured so as to minimize, as much as is feasible, given the military mission and context, any wanton reckless and militarily unnecessary damage to civilians, or to the converted building so that if not destroyed, it may one day be returned to a civilian purpose). Such attacks on a military objective are lawful as they do not violate the principle of distinction (they are attacks on converted buildings that are now functioning with a clear military purpose).

The important implication of the foregoing is that there can be no alleged lawful takeover and use of civilian schools for a military purpose *in the first instance* based on 'military necessity'. Hence, such a takeover or seizure *cannot* be upheld as legally supportable under IHL in *that* instance. This is the case since 'military necessity' arises only in relation to lawful measures:

> The rule of military necessity was defined in the Lieber Code, and later adopted by the ICRC, as "the necessity of those measures which are indispensable for securing the ends of war, ***and which are lawful*** according to the modern law and usages of war" [the laws and customs of war]. In other words, ***military necessity cannot be used as an excuse to violate explicit IHL provisions*** because the requirements of military necessity [i.e., the balance that must be struck between humanitarian and military concerns] have already been incorporated into IHL rules [such as the requirement, on the analysis here, that *privileged* civilian buildings such as schools enjoy a high standard of protection from attack as well as protection without limitation against conversion of their use to a military purpose] (emphasis added).[90]

---

[90]Human Rights Watch (2010), p. 110.

Converting an unoccupied or occupied civilian school to a military objective is an unlawful measure since it blurs the distinction between privileged protected buildings providing a key humanitarian service to a group entitled to special protection (children) on the one hand; with military objects on the other. There is, however, a limitation that sets out that 'military necessity' justifications must be based on lawful acts that, for instance, *at a minimum* do not blur the distinction between *privileged* civilian buildings such as schools dedicated to a humanitarian educational purpose versus buildings used for a military purpose (military objectives that do not enjoy protection). (That privileged status of civilian schools is reflected in the fact, for instance, that the Rome Statute under Article 8 has a separate "stand alone" article (article 8(2)(b)(ix)) concerning the protection of schools and other buildings of special importance to humanitarian functions such as hospitals and places of worship among others. That is, the protection of schools is not subsumed under Article 8(2)(b)(ii) "Intentionally directing attacks against civilian objects, that is, objects which are not military objectives".[91]

It is interesting to note in regards to the issue of the special protected status of schools that following the adoption of UK legislation that allows for domestic prosecution of international crimes (as defined under the statute of the ICC [International Criminal Court]), the United Kingdom updated its *Manual of the Law of Armed Conflict*. That update reflected the *privileged* status of civilian schools and the protection to be afforded these buildings under IHL against *both* attack and use for a military purpose:

> The United Kingdom's Manual of the Law of Armed Conflict... has been recently updated following the adoption of implementing domestic legislation for the ICC. The updated manual includes specific references to the protection of education buildings. In addition to clearly stating that attacks on school[s] are unlawful unless being used for military purposes, the manual also expounds clear rules that commanders can follow in other situations. **The manual even determines that the 'use of a *privileged* building for an *improper* purpose is a 'war crime' traditionally recognized by the customary law of armed conflict' and provides as an illustration *the use of a school* as a sniper's post** [use for a military purpose where the school may or may not be occupied by civilians at the time]" **The manual also lists the land and buildings of institutions dedicated to education as property which, even if they belong to the state, should be treated as private property, and that the seizure, destruction, or damage of them is forbidden** (emphasis added).[92]

The IHL constraint on the use of 'military necessity' as a justification for undermining humanitarian considerations is, as explained here, a prerequisite for the proper and lawful implementation of Article 48 of Protocol I of the Geneva Conventions which stipulates that "the Parties to the conflict shall at all times distinguish between the civilian population ... [versus] combatants and civilian

---

[91]Rome Statute of the International Criminal Court (entered into force 1 July 2002), http://untreaty.un.org/cod/icc/statute/romefra.htm. Accessed 11 July 2010 [Article 8(2)(b)(ii)].

[92]Sheppard (2010), p. 130.

objects . . . [versus] military objectives".[93] Article 48 of Protocol I, it is here argued, sets out a legal obligation under IHL not only that privileged civilian objects such as schools be protected from attack when not contributing to the adversary's military effort but also that: (1) the parties to an armed conflict not use any privileged building such as a civilian school normally dedicated to a civilian purpose and convert it for use to a military purpose (which inevitably also renders that property vulnerable to attack and blurs the distinction between privileged civilian objects and military objectives); or (2) exact reprisals on buildings that at some time in the past were converted to a military purpose but now once more are functioning as civilian buildings (arguably such reprisals also blur the distinction between civilian and military objects). Note that the prohibition against punitive attacks; 'reprisals', is contained in Article 52(1) of Protocol I additional to the 1949 Geneva Conventions).[94]

"Military necessity incorporates the fundamental legal obligation . . . [of] distinguishing military objectives from civilian objects"[95] and, on the analysis here, *also the legal obligation not to contribute to the blurring of that distinction for the enemy* (such as occurs when civilian schools are converted to a military use during armed conflict). This author is thus in accord with Human Rights Watch that: "The concept of military necessity . . . rejects measures that . . . violate the rules of war. . . ".[96] It has been argued here that using a civilian school for a military purpose during armed conflict in fact violates the rules of war by blurring the distinction between *privileged* civilian objects and military non-civilian objects such that the enemy becomes uncertain which schools have been converted to a military use and which have not. Thus, converting a civilian school to a military use during armed conflict, it is here contended, constitutes a war crime in that it undermines the IHL principle of distinction.

That doubts could arise in regards to the status (civilian versus military) of various objects (such as buildings) was anticipated and is reflected, as previously discussed, in Article 52 (3) of Protocol I additional to the 1949 Geneva Conventions[97] (which discusses how such doubt is to be resolved in regards to whether or not to attack certain types of buildings such as schools). However, it is here contended that there is an IHL obligation not to create the basis for such doubt in

---

[93]Protocol Additional to the Geneva Conventions of 12 August 1949, and relating to the Protection of Victims of International Armed Conflicts (Protocol I), 8 June 1977, entry into force 7 December 1978. http://www.icrc.org/ihl.nsf/full/470?opendocument. Accessed 28 June 2010 (Basic Rule: Article 48).

[94]Protocol Additional to the Geneva Conventions of 12 August 1949, and relating to the Protection of Victims of International Armed Conflicts (Protocol I), 8 June 1977, entry into force 7 December 1978. http://www.icrc.org/ihl.nsf/full/470?opendocument. Accessed 28 June 2010 [Article 52(1)].

[95]Human Rights Watch (2010), p. 110.

[96]Human Rights Watch (2010), p. 110.

[97]Protocol Additional to the Geneva Conventions of 12 August 1949, and relating to the Protection of Victims of International Armed Conflicts (Protocol I), 8 June 1977, entry into force 7 December 1978. http://www.icrc.org/ihl.nsf/full/470?opendocument. Accessed 28 June 2010 [Article 52(3)].

the first instance, and, in particular, not to do so with respect to privileged buildings such as schools that are so vital to the well-being of the children and the community.

In sum then "While the rule of military necessity grants military planners considerable autonomy about the appropriate tactics for carrying out a military operation, this autonomy remains subservient to the laws and customs of war".[98] One of those laws and customs-the principle of distinction-for the reasons explained; *precludes* the use of civilian schools for military purposes during armed conflict even where such use might make a significant contribution to the planned military actions and provide some significant military advantage.

The fact that reprisals are prohibited under IHL against civilian property that was *in the past* used for a military purpose indicates that under IHL buildings normally dedicated to civilian purposes are presumed to have a civilian status during armed conflict *unless proven otherwise* (that is, unless there is concrete evidence *at that precise time* of their having become a military objective due to their use at the relevant time for a military purpose). Under IHL (more specifically Article 52(3) of Protocol I additional to the 1949 Geneva Conventions),[99] all residual significant doubts as to the status of privileged buildings such as schools is, as was discussed, to be resolved in favor of regarding the object as a civilian one.

It is here contended that in Afghanistan the principle of distinction is undermined to varying extents and ways by *both sides* in the war on terror in regards to schools. The Afghan government operates government schools and permits the operation of NGO -sponsored schools situated in insecure areas where these schools have inadequate protection if any at all. This, it has been argued here, constitutes use of civilian schools as propaganda tools in the war on terror (a military use) intended to create the public perception that the insurgents are being roundly defeated and normalcy and stability is returning to the conflict-affected State. At the same time, the Taliban and other insurgents perpetrate unlawful targeted attacks on civilian schools in Afghanistan (schools still dedicated to a civilian humanitarian function; namely education). Such attacks do not accord with the principle of military necessity which is grounded in the laws of humanity; nor are they a proportionate response to schools used in part as propaganda tools. Such attacks are essentially propaganda messages intended to spread terror and inflict maximal injury and death upon innocent civilians including children. In any case, terrorists are not (lawful) combatants, but rather civilian belligerents perpetrating war crimes (inflicting intentional suffering) and crimes against humanity (i.e., such as when they attack schools; part of a "systematic attack directed against ... [a]civilian

[98]Human Rights Watch (2010), p. 110.

[99]Protocol Additional to the Geneva Conventions of 12 August 1949, and relating to the Protection of Victims of International Armed Conflicts (Protocol I), 8 June 1977, entry into force 7 December 1978. http://www.icrc.org/ihl.nsf/full/470?opendocument. Accessed 28 June 2010 [Article 52(3)].

population" which is listed under Article 7 of the Rome Statute as a crime against humanity).[100]

It is the significant humanitarian purpose of the facility (i.e., civilian hospitals and religious buildings), or in some exceptional cases also its symbolic or iconic cultural significance, that under IHL affords it special protection from attack. This is evidenced by the fact that as per Article 19 of the Fourth Geneva Convention, civilian hospitals cannot be lawfully attacked for treating the wounded or ill who are members of the potential attacker's adversarial forces (namely noncombatants at the hospital who are hors du combat due to injury or illness).[101] Schools, too, are privileged humanitarian institutions deserving of such unqualified protection against attack and use for a military purpose (as here is argued already exists under IHL). The humanitarian civilian status of schools is clearest when: (1) schools are used as part of a development strategy for the society with schools operating only in zones with adequate security where they can fulfill their education mandates (as opposed to serving also a counter-insurgency propaganda goal that involves the schools operating regardless of security concerns), and (2) where the school has become a refuge during armed conflict for civilians and other noncombatants taking cover and/or receiving humanitarian aid there.

5.1.20 The Hague Convention Article 56 and Its Implications for the Protection of Civilian Schools

Article 56 of the Hague Convention (IV) Respecting the Laws and Customs of War on Land and Its Annex: Regulations Concerning the Laws and Customs of War on Land, 18 October 1907 prohibits the seizure of educational facilities, and by implication then, on the view here, also the use of school buildings (occupied or unoccupied) for military purposes without exception. Arguably, this ban against the seizure of property dedicated to humanitarian purposes such as educational institutions has become a general custom of war for any party exercising any degree of military authority in any part of the territory of the adversary and not just an obligation regarding occupation by a belligerent:

> **Article 56 Hague Convention IV**
>
> *The property of municipalities, that of* ***institutions dedicated to*** *religion, charity and* ***education****, the arts and sciences,* ***even when State property, shall be treated as private property.***

---

[100] American NGO Coalition for the International Criminal Court Terrorism and the International Criminal Court: The worst terrorist crimes are covered by the Rome Statute. www.amicc.org/docs/terrorism.pdf.

[101] Commentary of the International Committee of the Red Cross on Article 19 of the Fourth Geneva Convention cited in a Harvard Program on Humanitarian Policy and Research (International Humanitarian Law Research Initiative) document. http://www.ihlresearch.org/opt/pdfs/qaprotection.pdf. Accessed 1 July 2010.

> ***All seizure of***, destruction or wilful damage done to institutions of this character, historic monuments, works of art and science, is forbidden, and should be made the subject of legal proceedings (emphasis added).[102]

Note that schools are ***not*** considered, on the interpretation of the International Committee of the Red Cross (ICRC) of Article 56 of Hague Convention IV, to be included in the *exceptions* to the prohibition against the seizure and use of public property (whether occupied or unoccupied by civilian and/or noncombatants which exception applies to "items that can be used for military purposes").[103] This then implies that schools cannot under IHL be lawfully used for a military purpose during armed conflict.

Schools, *even where they are public property* as are most schools, are to be treated as if they were private property according to the ICRC commentary. This provision thus elevates the protected status of civilian schools to a higher than average level compared to most other civilian buildings/objects. Thus, the use of civilian schools for a military purpose during armed conflict violates the rule that they are to be treated as if private property and ignores the fact that they have a special protected status. Civilian schools then are publically funded buildings (though some may be privately funded as well by NGOs etc.) with a privileged status *regarding their use* whether occupied by civilians or not and regardless of the necessities of war. This is evident in the ban on seizure of schools since seizure would most frequently involve the intent to use the school for a military purpose. The ICRC states in interpreting Article 56 of the Hague Convention:

> Property used for religious purposes, for charity, ***education,*** or the arts and sciences, ***must be treated as private property*** even if it belongs to the State. Here the law is quite clear. It is ***forbidden to seize***, destroy or willfully damage such property... (emphasis added)[104]

Article 23 (d) of the Hague Convention IV stipulates that it is a violation of the *laws and customs of war*: "To destroy or seize the enemy's property, unless such destruction or seizure be imperatively demanded by the necessities of war".[105] Thus, in any armed conflict (international or non-international), there is a 'general prohibition' against attack upon property located in enemy territory or its seizure *where there is no military necessity* and regardless whether either of the belligerents is an occupying power or not. However, we have already discovered that military necessity is *inapplicable* to the notion of the seizure and use of civilian schools for a military purpose for the reasons explained i.e., it would undermine the principle of

---

[102]International Conferences (The Hague), Hague Convention (IV) Respecting the Laws and Customs of War on Land and Its Annex: Regulations Concerning the Laws and Customs of War on Land, 18 October 1907 (Article 56). http://www.unhcr.org/refworld/docid/4374cae64.html. Accessed 20 July 2010.

[103]International Committee of the Red Cross (2002), p. 11.

[104]International Committee of the Red Cross (2002), p. 11.

[105]Convention (IV) respecting the Laws and Customs of War on Land and its annex: Regulations concerning the Laws and Customs of War on Land. The Hague, 18 October 1907 [Article 23(d)]. http://www.icrc.org/ihl.nsf/INTRO/195?OpenDocument. Accessed 4 July 2010.

distinction for property dedicated to a humanitarian objective that is vital to the cultural fabric and success of the community. This fact is acknowledged, as mentioned previously, for instance, in the updated war field manual for UK forces on the laws of armed conflict.

One key factor in favor of such a prohibition against use of civilian schools for a military purpose is that schools, along with most places of worship and civilian hospitals, are too central to the cultural and spiritual life of the community to be exposed to potential attack as a consequence of their being converted from a humanitarian mission to use for a military purpose. Schools may also play a key role during armed conflict serving the humanitarian needs of the local populace if allowed to function as a 'safe haven' for children and youth (a scenario that has not been possible to date in the high conflict zones within Afghanistan). The destruction of school buildings (consequent to their use for a military purpose and attacks by the opposing forces based on alleged "military necessity") would severely interfere with the State's ability to ensure the educated populace so critical to the State's development and economic competitiveness. In that respect, schools too are vital to the society's survival.

5.1.21 Further Issues Regarding the Protected Status of Civilian Schools Against Use for a Military Purpose During Armed Conflict

Henderson, writing on the contemporary law of military targeting, maintains that schools do *not* have special protection status under IHL which would prohibit their use for military purposes where there is military necessity. However, at the same time, he maintains that schools nonetheless "attract special attention" as objects to be avoided as 'collateral damage' wherever possible (i.e., whether or not there are civilians and/or noncombatants present in the school or the school is entirely unoccupied).[106] This customary practice during war to avoid, wherever and whenever possible, having schools damaged collaterally, even when those schools are unoccupied, is based on recognition of the special significance of schools to the society. Consider that this "special consideration" given to civilian schools (reflected in the efforts to avoid such schools becoming 'collateral damage') is but one side of the coin where the other side has to be a customary practice of avoiding converting schools normally dedicated to a humanitarian purpose to a military purpose (since the latter would make the school more vulnerable to attack by the opposing forces). The latter obligation, as mentioned, is now acknowledged by the UK.

The 'special consideration' for civilian schools regarding protection, as has here been discussed, has been articulated in the Rome Statute at Article 8 as a privileged

[106]Henderson (2009), pp. 194–195.

status for schools (which thus places limitations on their lawful use during armed conflict). It has here been contended then that in fact IHL does already incorporate unqualified prohibitions on the use of schools for military purposes during armed conflict based on the recognized special value of schools and education to society (the protection extends then to both school buildings occupied by civilians and to unoccupied school buildings and regardless of the necessities of war). It is precisely the recognized essential value of schools to society which underlies the so-called "special consideration" by commanders of forces that adhere to IHL in assessing whether a school should be exposed to the risk of being part of the 'collateral damage' in an attack on another site.

While it has been noted here that the conflict in Afghanistan is best characterized as a non-international conflict, Protocol I additional to the Geneva Conventions (dealing with international conflicts) which has attained the status of customary law; nonetheless offers some insight into what protections are to be afforded *particular* civilian buildings such as schools during armed conflict. The International Committee of the Red Cross (ICRC) in its commentary on Protocol I additional to the Geneva Conventions makes the observation that "... even in contact areas [i.e., between the parties to the armed conflict] there is a presumption that civilian buildings located there [i.e., civilian schools] are not used by armed forces, and consequently it is prohibited to attack them unless *it is certain* that they accommodate enemy combatants or military objects" [thus creating the military necessity for an attack].[107] The general presumption to which the ICRC refers in its foregoing commentary on Protocol I (i.e., the presumption that armed forces will normally not occupy civilian buildings such as schools even where they are located at the frontlines of the combat) must logically be based on a general understanding that such use is prohibited. This general prohibition against using civilian buildings for a military purpose is essential in that innumerable civilian buildings could provide some significant immediate military advantage if used for a military purpose. Commanders then could then easily make claims as to military necessity in their use and erode the principle of distinction with regard to civilian versus military objects as previously discussed. The latter is particularly true in the context of the so-called 'war on terror' where fighting is often at close quarters in civilian areas and the terrorists are using human civilian shields as well as civilian buildings such as schools and other buildings normally dedicated to civilian purposes as shields. Indeed, Article 52(3) of Protocol I implicitly relies on that general understanding of a prohibition against the use of civilian buildings for military purposes by requiring that any doubts about whether an object is a civilian object or a military objective must be decided in favor of the presumption that its use is for a civilian purpose. What is of note is that *civilian schools* are particularized in that article along with places of worship and dwellings as: (1) civilian buildings entitled to

[107]Commentary of the International Committee of the Red Cross on Protocol I additional to the 1949 Geneva Conventions. http://www.icrc.org/ihl.nsf/WebList?ReadForm&id=470&t=com. Accessed 10 July 2010.

a high level of protection and (2) entitled to application of the *rebuttable* presumption that they have *not* been used for a military purpose unless there is substantive convincing evidence to the contrary. This then reflects the importance that IHL puts on the protected status of civilian schools.

While there is no exhaustive list as to what qualifies quintessentially as a civilian object in Protocol I additional to the Geneva Conventions, Article 52(3) of Protocol I, as mentioned, does provide a few key examples: "... a place of worship, a house or other dwelling or a school".[108] The ICRC points out that there was long debate about whether a list of civilian objects and military objectives should be given in Protocol I, but in the end the drafters decided on listing only the three especially important examples of civilian objects in Article 52(3) which included schools. It would make no sense then to assume that the same armed force that would abide by Article 52(3) of Protocol I and resolve any doubt as to status of a school in favor of presuming it to be a civilian object unless there were concrete evidence otherwise; would then themselves use that building (i.e., a school) for a military purpose thus putting the buildings at risk of attack by the enemy. Similarly, Protocol II additional to the Geneva Convention at Article 13[109] by holding that civilians not be placed in harm's way due to military operations would also preclude use of civilian schools for military purposes (i.e., give the proximity of schools to civilian dwellings and the local populace.).

The ICRC has noted that belligerents' idea of what constitutes a military objective/target [ripe for attack] *prior* to the drafting of Protocol I "differed considerably, depending on whether the territory concerned was their own, enemy territory or territory of an ally occupied by enemy forces".[110] At present, the issue of whether IHL as it now stands permits the *use* of unoccupied civilian school buildings for military purposes during armed conflict (i.e., *controversy* as to whether unoccupied civilian schools can be legitimately converted to a military use where there is alleged military necessity) has not been brought to the fore or much discussed. Rather, many prominent Western scholars on the laws of armed conflict (who are also high ranking officers in the armed forces) seem to hold the consensus view that currently unoccupied schools can be used for military purposes. One wonders if they would hold the same view/give the same interpretation were the fighting in their home country.

---

[108]Protocol Additional to the Geneva Conventions of 12 August 1949, and relating to the Protection of Victims of International Armed Conflicts (Protocol I), 8 June 1977, entry into force 7 December 1978. http://www.icrc.org/ihl.nsf/full/470?opendocument. Accessed 28 June 2010 [Article 52(3)].

[109]Protocol Additional to the Geneva Conventions of 12 August 1949, and relating to the Protection of Victims of Non-International Armed Conflict (Protocol II),), 8 June 1977, entry into force 7 December 1978 (Article 13). http://www.icrc.org/ihl.nsf/full/470?opendocument. Accessed 28 June 2010.

[110]Commentary of the International Committee of the Red Cross on Protocol I additional to the 1949 Geneva Conventions, http://www.icrc.org/ihl.nsf/WebList?ReadForm&id=470&t=com. Accessed 10 July 2010, p. 631.

This author, as discussed, disputes the contention that civilian schools under IHL do not *currently* have an independent privileged status that exists: (1) even when the building is unoccupied and (2) affords these buildings, in theory at least, special protection from both attack and use for a military purpose regardless the military exigencies at the time. There is, however, in any case, movement toward the view in the international legal community that civilian schools *should* be entitled to such a privileged status covering protection also against use for a military purpose since:

> *Just like hospitals and religious buildings, schools occupy a unique role in civilian communities.* Schools are centers of education, shelter, and activity for children; facilitators of democratic expression through voting and peaceful assembly; and sources of civic pride. As such, they are often the first public structures built in new communities or settlements and are arguably more important to a community's future growth and development than other civilian buildings such as museums, sports facilities, libraries, or even a city hall. *Thus, as a matter of policy, schools merit a . . . privileged status similar to that afforded to hospitals and religious buildings that prohibits their military use because of their inherent educational, and therefore humanitarian, value to society* (emphasis added).[111]

5.2 Prosecuting Armed Perpetrators of Attacks on Education *and* Those Who Intentionally Allow Schoolchildren to Become Easy Targets for Terrorists

Injuries and deaths of civilians due to terror attacks on schools; especially when involving high numbers of schoolchildren, or the use of the children at the school as human shields, are acts that tend to engender in the international community deep resentment toward the attackers; at least for these specific acts. Ironically, those responsible for encouraging schoolchildren to attend particular schools despite: (1) the inadequate security in the zones where the schools are situated and (2) the high risk of a targeted terror attack on these schools; have, to date, largely escaped any questions of accountability posed by a concerned global public and/or the international media. This is the case even when terror attacks on these unprotected schools do in fact occur and many children are killed or maimed. In contrast, when Afghan forces and their allies launch an attack on any military objective for reasons they consider meet the criterion of 'military necessity' (setting aside the issue of whether or not their assessment is accurate), and that operation unintentionally causes significant civilian casualties (so-called 'collateral damage'), there is generally an outcry from the international media and the public:

> After all, images of dead and injured civilians transmitted across a globalized media (which often pays little heed to the military rationale of an operation) can make it appear as if the attacker has mounted inhumane operations.[112]

---

[111] Bart (2010), p. 215.

[112] Schmitt (2009), p. 22.

It would appear that the potential for a degree of *perceived* culpability of the Afghan government and its allies, as well as of the international education aid community operating in Afghanistan, for casualties resulting from having schools operating where there is inadequate security is negated by propaganda. That propaganda concerns the State and international aid community's Afghan development strategy which includes greatly improved access to education regardless the risks to the schoolchildren's security in attending schools in particular insecure zones within the country. Actual culpability arising due to the aforementioned parties encouraging school attendance even where the security is known to be wholly inadequate is thus not addressed and there is no accountability on *this* score. All blame/responsibility for the harm is directed rather to: (1) the insurgent attackers for carrying out an act of hostility which violates IHL and to (2) the children who attended school for being in the right place (for an education) at the wrong time. Consequently, those who facilitated the placing of the children in harm's way of a terror attack, knowing full well the high risk for such an attack in those locales at the time, are wrongfully held blameless for what potentially could amount to a 'war crime' as previously discussed (depending on the specifics in each case). As Sheppard states "Important first questions when arguing for accountability for an attack on education are to consider who is to be held accountable and where".[113] Where: (1) national and international NGOs and human rights organizations intervene to provide humanitarian education aid, (2) states internationally back these groups through funding, and (3) national Ministries of Education insist (such as in Afghanistan) on carrying on education services in the midst of high or low-level armed conflict *where security is grossly substandard*, the question of accountability for the civilian child and other civilian victims of terror attacks on education has to date not been addressed. This "free pass" given to the aforementioned groups on their possible indirect role in facilitating the civilian deaths and casualties that result when a school is attacked, or when students, teachers and other education workers are attacked directly on the way to or from school must be abandoned. Instead, the conduct of school authorities, public officials and NGOs in encouraging and facilitating school attendance in terror zones with inadequate protection for education must be scrutinized with respect also to their potential culpability under IHL for war crimes in this regard.

State and NGO rights rhetoric concerning the Afghan population's entitlements to education and development has served as a sleight of hand maneuver. That maneuver then has distracted the international audience and misdirected its attention away from considerations regarding the children's need and right for security of the person and entitlement to survival and protection from all forms of physical and mental violence as the first priority under IHL (that right taking priority over the right to access education which, in any case, presupposes a secure education environment in the first instance).

[113]Sheppard (2010), p. 126.

It is here argued that while all non-military objects deserve protection; they deserve increased protection in accord with the value of these objects for the society, *and* the risks to civilians should these non-military objects (i.e., school buildings; houses) be attacked or used for a military purpose. Further, the current author contends that: (1) the foregoing basis for the 'special protection' status of certain non-military objects is already incorporated into current IHL and that (2) schools are recognized in IHL as deserving special protection *both* from attack (unless there is military necessity involved) *and* from use under any circumstance for a military purpose (i.e., the special protection status of schools deriving both from the value of schools to the society, and the risk to civilians attendant on the use of schools for military purposes whether occupied or unoccupied). Unfortunately (from the point of view of this author at least), this has not been the interpretation of current IHL adopted by certain international criminal courts in respect of any absolute prohibition on the use of civilian schools for military purposes as has here been discussed (i.e., as evidenced by the *Kordic and Cerkez* ICTY *Appeal* Chamber judgment).[114]

5.2.1 The 'Grave Breaches' Versus the 'Serious Violations' Designation of War Crimes Under IHL: Implications for the Protection of Schools and Schoolchildren

There is currently no international law that *explicitly and expressly* designates: (1) armed attacks on civilian schools where there is *no* military necessity, or (2) (without exception) their use for a military purpose *both* as a *grave* breaches of the 1949 Geneva Conventions (as opposed to implicitly or directly categorizing one or both of these actions as *serious violations* of the laws and customs of war akin to other unlawful attacks on civilian objects). For instance, as discussed, Article 8 (2b) (ix) of the Rome Statute designates attacks on education facilities where there is no military necessity as a *serious violation* of the laws of war; a 'war crime'. However, it should be understood that terror attacks on civilian schools are intended to inflict intense gratuitous suffering and also involve persecution of children (an identifiable class of vulnerable persons). Hence, such attacks are covered, it is here contended, also under Rome Statute Article 7(f) (concerning torture) and 7(h) (concerning systemic persecution) and dealing with the grave offense of 'crimes against humanity' (which cannot be rationalized in terms of military necessity in any case). Furthermore, it should be recognized that the systemic and widespread campaign of terror by the Taliban and other insurgents in Afghanistan against education (including, in part, as it does both attacks on civilian schools and their use-occupied

[114]International Criminal Tribunal for the Former Yugoslavia *Prosecutor versus Kordic and Cerkez* (Appeals Chamber) Case No IT-95-14-2-A (17 December 2004). http://www.unhcr.org/refworld/topic,4565c22538,4565c25f449,41483e9be,0.html. Accessed 15 July 2010.

and unoccupied- for a military purpose so as to undermine the principle of distinction and inflict intense suffering on civilians) meets the Rome Statute definition of 'torture' under Article 8(2)(a)(ii); a grave war crime; and one which cannot be rationalized in terms of military necessity.

The designation ('grave breach') would categorize the war crimes involving terror attacks on schools, or (without limitation) their use for a military purpose (which undermines the principle of distinction) as international crimes that under IHL require prosecution of perpetrators as part of any remedy, or the complete remedy if the adjudicated outcome is to be just. This would allow the international community, through the International Criminal Court (ICC), or via a special international criminal tribunal, to assume jurisdiction where the State refuses, or is unable for some reason, to prosecute those responsible for perpetrating these international crimes within its territorial jurisdiction. (The latter assuming other jurisdictional criteria are also met such as, for example, in relation to the ICC, that the crimes occurred after the entry into force of the Rome Statute in that particular State Party to the Rome Statute, or there was a referral of the situation giving rise to the case by the UN Security Council to the ICC regarding a non-State party to the Rome Statute where the crimes occurred after the Rome Statute came into force etc.). It would also allow for universal criminal jurisdiction such that another nation State which captures such perpetrators would have jurisdiction to prosecute should the perpetrator's home State decline or be unable to do so.

Finally, consider the level of suffering being inflicted on the children of Afghanistan and its systematic nature due to *both sides* to the conflict, *in practice*, not fully assigning schools and schoolchildren the special protected status to which they are entitled. That is: (1) the terrorists unhesitatingly perpetrate terror attacks against schools, schoolchildren, educational personnel and humanitarian education aid workers while (2) the Afghani government and its Western government allies, as well as the international NGO contingent and UN bodies and delegates operating in the field, place Afghan children in harm's way by encouraging and facilitating their school attendance in insecure zones that are hot beds of terror activity and where schools and school routes are not adequately protected. Both sides in the conflict (the 'war on terror') then are using schoolchildren as a means for communicating propaganda messages regarding their respective alleged progress in meeting their own military objectives (and in the case of the Afghan government and its allies; also propaganda respecting their development objectives which are characterized as inseparable from their military objectives).

The level and extent of the mental and physical suffering involved for schoolchildren in Afghanistan (and in many other CAFS), both in the short and long-term, due to attacks on schools and to the use of schools for a military purpose justifies, it is here argued, designating: (a) attacks on civilian schools where there is no immediate and compelling military necessity and/or the attack is part of a terror campaign, and (b) use of civilian schools for a military purpose under any circumstance as 'grave breaches' of international humanitarian law. Afterall, schoolchildren are entitled under IHL to special protection over and above the protection accorded other civilians. That special protection guarantee demands that civilian schools be regarded as 'safe havens' for children and teachers and allied education workers (including education aid workers), and that the IHL and international criminal law reinforce such a norm which will, hopefully, in time reach the level of a customary practice of war.

Note that the proposition that use without exception of schools for a military purpose be designated a 'grave breach' of IHL is an extension of Bart's original valuable proposal to provide civilian schools 'special protected' status such as is given to hospitals and religious buildings and certain other sites where such use would be considered a 'serious violation' of the 1949 Geneva Conventions. It is beyond the scope of this book to consider whether the use of hospitals and religious buildings and other specially protected sites for a military purpose should constitute grave breaches rather than serious violations of IHL as defined, for instance, in the Rome Statute).[115]

5.2.2 *Individual States' Handling of Accountability for International Crimes Involving Attacks on Education or Unlawful Use of Civilian Schools for a Military Purpose*

With regard to individual States' handling of the issue of war crimes involving unlawful attacks on schools or unlawful use of schools for a military purpose, there is often: (a) no recognition of any special protected status for schools and (b) no designation of such acts as specific stand alone war crimes:

> ... since the war crimes legislation in many countries has not been updated to reflect developments in international law such as the Rome Statute and the statute of the International Criminal Tribunal for the Former Yugoslavia (ICTY), attacks on schools [and presumably also use of a school for a military purpose where there is no urgent pressing military necessity] often have to be subsumed into broader crimes such as attacks on civilian objects or other catch-all war crime categories.[116]

In Bosnia-Herzegovina, the State Court of that nation in 2008 found Pasko Ljubicic guilty of war crimes during the Bosnian war. As a senior officer of the military police of the Croatian Defense Council, he was found responsible for, among other war crimes, using a military police unit to attack a village which attack involved, in part, burning a Muslim primary school. Under the Bosnian indictment for his war crimes, there was no separate charge listed for his attacks on schools rather "this crime appears to have been subsumed within [his] war crimes charges for attacks on civilian objects and the destruction and looting of property".[117] Thus, specific charges under the Rome Statute or ICTY or other international criminal

[115]Rome Statute of the International Criminal Court (entered into force 1 July 2002), http://untreaty.un.org/cod/icc/statute/romefra.htm. Accessed 11 July 2010.

[116]Sheppard (2010), p. 129.

[117]Sheppard (2010), p. 129.

tribunal statute concerning illegitimate attacks on education or unlawful use of schools for a military purpose during armed conflict are (depending on the current state of the law in that domestic jurisdiction) often abandoned as separate stand alone crimes if and when the case is transferred to the domestic courts. This serves to undermine the gravity of the violations *against child civilians in particular* of such attacks on education (operationalized as unlawful attacks on schools *and* the unlawful use of schools for a military purpose). It may also, as Sheppard rightly points out, significantly decrease the likelihood of perpetrators being held accountable for specific acts of terrorism against schools (such as unlawful attacks on schools, or unlawful use of a school for a military purpose):

> ... when countries fail to introduce definitions of international crimes into domestic law, *efforts to prosecute such crimes can be hampered*, even though prosecutors may be able to frame international crimes, such as war crimes, in terms of domestic equivalents. *Using domestic criminal law offenses in this way... may fail to fully capture the nature and gravity of the offense*[as when war crimes involving attacks on education or use of a civilian school for military purposes are subsumed under other international crimes defined in the domestic statute rather than being treated as stand alone international crimes].[118]

Sheppard also suggests that under national law, statutes of limitations may apply thus hindering or preventing prosecution of attacks on education.[119] However, it is here suggested in contrast, (as to the issue of statutes of limitations under domestic law) that international law (whether the customary law of armed conflict, or formalized codified law such as the Rome Statute) *supersedes* domestic statutes of limitations where grave international crimes have been committed (i.e., where these offences were considered international crimes under the 'law of civilized nations' [to borrow a phrase from the European Convention on Human Rights Article 7(2)[120]] at the time they were committed.

There are also recent examples of what happens when schools are, *in practice*, essentially not regarded as having a special protected status and a loose standard is applied for determining whether attacks on particular unoccupied schools are legitimate under IHL:

> ... the ICTY Prosecutor noted that Human Rights Watch found generally reliable the Federal Republic of Yugoslavia's (FRY) White Book report of civilian casualties, which included allegations that the NATO bombing campaign destroyed or damaged many schools in Yugoslavia. Further... the United Nations Children's Fund (UNICEF) estimated that forty-five percent of Kosovo's schools were severely damaged or destroyed and that 668 out of 1000 needed significant repairs.[121]

---

[118]Sheppard (2010), p. 130.

[119]Sheppard (2010), p. 130.

[120]European Convention on Human Rights [Article 7(2)]. (originally entered into force 9 March 1953). Text amended by the provisions of Protocol No. 14 (CETS No. 194) as from the date of its entry into force on 1 June 2010. Available at the Council of Europe Website. http://conventions.coe.int/treaty/Commun/QueVoulezVous.asp?NT=005&CL=ENG.

[121]Bart (2010), p. 214.

Clearly there is a need for greater regard to existing IHL provisions on the issue of the protected status of schoolchildren, schools and the education enterprise as a whole (as well as a need to consider if and how IHL can be clarified and improved in terms of the protection it affords education and schoolchildren).

5.2.3 The Worsening Plight of Schoolchildren in Afghanistan

A recent report (at the time of writing of this book) on civilian casualties in Afghanistan; is an authoritative report sponsored by the United Nations Assistance Mission in Afghanistan (UNAMA) covering the period 01 January to 30 June 2010.[122] UNAMA regards the conflict in Afghanistan as non-international and one which obligates all the parties to the conflict, including non-State parties, at a minimum, to adhere to the standards of Common Article 3 of the 1949 Geneva Conventions and the customary laws of armed conflict. The UNAMA holds, in addition, that "several rules in the Geneva Conventions and the Additional Protocols are part of customary international law".[123] The UNAMA report indicates that "Among those killed or injured by the Taliban and other AGEs [anti-government elements] were 55 per cent more children than in 2009, along with six per cent more women".[124] Staffan de Mistura, Special Representative of the Secretary-General, states:

> *Afghan children and women are increasingly bearing the brunt of this conflict.* They are being killed and injured in their homes and communities in greater numbers than ever before (emphasis added).[125]

Clearly, children are not being adequately protected in Afghanistan as is the case also particularly for women and female children. In Afghanistan, schools (whether self-contained buildings, open air sites or buildings used for mixed purposes) and the routes to and from school remain prime areas for terrorists targeting children for armed attack. Rosy scenarios contemplating negotiating with the Taliban and other insurgents for the lives and safety of schoolchildren are inconsistent with the reality of the increasing and relentless brutality of the situation as it concerns children.

> Analysis by [the] UNAMA Human Rights Unit identified two critical developments that increased harm to civilians in the first six months of 2010 compared to [the same period in] 2009: AGEs [anti-government elements] used a greater number of larger and more

---

[122]United Nations Assistance Mission in Afghanistan (2010).

[123]United Nations Assistance Mission in Afghanistan (2010), p. 6.

[124]United Nations Assistance Mission in Afghanistan. Featured News: Afghan civilian casualties rise 31 per cent in first six months of 2010. http://unama.unmissions.org/Default.aspx?tabid=1741&ctl=Details&mid=1882&ItemID=9955.

[125]United Nations Assistance Mission in Afghanistan. Featured News: Afghan civilian casualties rise 31 per cent in first six months of 2010. http://unama.unmissions.org/Default.aspx?tabid=1741&ctl=Details&mid=1882&ItemID=9955.

sophisticated improvised explosive devices (IEDs) throughout the country; and, *the number of civilians assassinated and executed by AGEs rose by more than 95 per cent and included public executions of children...* [i.e., on June 10, 2010, a boy of seven was hanged in Sanjin region, Helmund Province after the Taliban accused him of spying for the government].[126] This intensified pattern of assassinations and executions reinforced the widespread perception of Afghan civilians that they are becoming more and more the primary target in this period of conflict", said Staffan de Mistura, Special Representative of the Secretary-General.[127]

Three quarters of all civilian casualties were linked to Anti-Government Elements (AGEs), an increase of 53 per cent from 2009. At the same time, civilian casualties attributed to Pro-Government Forces (PGF) decreased by 30 per cent compared to the first half of 2009.[128]

The UNAMA also noted that as the intense fighting spread in the first six months of 2010, civilians actually experienced a decreased presence of government security forces and were provided less protection than previously.[129] It is noteworthy that nowhere in the recommendations of the UNAMA[130] is there mention of the international humanitarian/human rights law obligation on the Afghan State and its allies and all other actors (including NGOs, UN organizations) to stop encouraging parents to send their children to school in zones known to have inadequate security to protect against terror attacks (this putting the children at grave risk). This being the case despite the fact that many of the children killed or injured by the Taliban and other AGEs are targeted for these harms while at school or on the way to or from school. During the 2010 period covered by the UNAMA report:

Night letters, disseminated by AGEs [anti-government elements] warning teachers and pupils not to attend schools were distributed in the southern, southeastern, central and northern regions of Afghanistan. On 29 February, the head of a girl's school in Puli-Khumri, the provincial capital of Baghlan, received threat letters, allegedly from the Taliban, warning her to close the school otherwise her children would be killed. UNAMA HR has documented cases where IEDs were placed on routes used, particularly by female students, to walk to school, resulting in casualties.[131]

Despite Taliban credible threats of attacks on education, and the innumerable actual terror attacks on schools, and schoolchildren (and the risk of aerial bombardment of civilian schools by allied forces as part of collateral damage because the school is right or wrongly thought to be a legitimate lawful target under IHL having allegedly been used for a military purpose), schools in insecure zones within Afghanistan are generally not closed until and unless an adequate security situation

---

[126] United Nations Assistance Mission in Afghanistan (2010), p. 29.

[127] United Nations Assistance Mission in Afghanistan (2010), p. 6.

[128] United Nations Assistance Mission in Afghanistan. Featured News: Afghan civilian casualties rise 31 per cent in first six months of 2010. http://unama.unmissions.org/Default.aspx?tabid=1741&ctl=Details&mid=1882&ItemID=9955.

[129] United Nations Assistance Mission in Afghanistan (2010), p. 14.

[130] United Nations Assistance Mission in Afghanistan (2010), pp. 16–17.

[131] United Nations Assistance Mission in Afghanistan (2010), p. 29.

is established in the areas surrounding the school (including on the routes to and from school) and at the school site:

> AGEs attacked educational facilities, and harassed and intimidated teachers and students. As a result, *schools* were destroyed or *closed either on a semi-permanent or temporary basis*, denying educational opportunities for thousands of children, particularly in the southern, southeastern, northern and central regions (emphasis added).[132]

Indeed, it would appear that schools in zones within Afghanistan that have ongoing abysmal security are: (1) closed on a so-called 'semi-permanent' basis (whatever that means) only when they are so damaged by an attack, that considerable time, money and resources are required to restore the school to an operational level or (2) closed temporarily until the schools not badly damaged can be repaired and/or parents can be convinced to send the children to school once more and teachers are willing to return. While the UNAMA discusses accountability, there is no mention of holding to account Afghan government officials and their individual partners (i.e., NGO personnel etc.) for encouraging school attendance even in insecure zones with the predictable outcome of a certain number of schoolchildren, teachers and education humanitarian aid workers being killed or injured at some of these school sites or in their vicinity.

It is striking that while improvised explosive devices (IEDs) are amongst the most prominent and deadly weapons of choice for the Taliban and AGEs in Afghanistan (40% of the civilian deaths in Afghanistan in the first six months of 2010 were attributable to IEDs),[133] the government and its allies, as well as the international humanitarian community operating to assist civilians there, have not sought to ensure that children attend school only when there is no longer a threat of IEDs on the route to or from school or on the school grounds or vicinity. This is in direct contradiction to the objectives of the global effort to protect children from explosive landmines in other armed conflict or post-conflict contexts. For instance, the 'Ottawa Convention on the Prohibition of the Use, Stockpiling, Production and Transfer of Anti-Personnel Mines and on Their Destruction (1997)' preamble begins with the following words:

> Determined to put an end to the suffering and casualties caused by anti-personnel mines, that kill or maim hundreds of people every week, mostly innocent and defenceless civilians and especially children. . . and have other severe consequences for years after emplacement . . . [134]

Similarly the 'Convention on Cluster Munitions' (2008) also draws attention to the suffering caused to children by explosive devices:

> *Determined* to put an end for all time to the suffering and casualties caused by cluster munitions at the time of their use, when they fail to function as intended or when they are abandoned,

---

[132]United Nations Assistance Mission in Afghanistan (2010), p. 29.

[133]United Nations Assistance Mission in Afghanistan (2010), p. 19.

[134]Ottawa Convention on the Prohibition of the Use, Stockpiling, Production and Transfer of Anti-Personnel Mines and on Their Destruction (1997). http://www.un.org/Depts/mine/UNDocs/ban_trty.htm. Accessed 29 Aug 2010.

> *Concerned* that cluster munition remnants kill or maim civilians, including women *and children* ... (emphasis added)[135]

Yet, in Afghanistan the suffering caused by IEDs for schoolchildren is indirectly, though unintentionally, facilitated by the Afghan government and its allies as well as by high profile humanitarian and human rights organizations encouraging school attendance despite knowing of the woefully inadequate security situation in various zones where schools are located and in the surrounding areas.

It is widely known by military commanders in Afghanistan, the Afghan government and its allies and representatives of international human rights and humanitarian organizations working there that for the Taliban and other insurgents, Afghanistan's schools are a prime valued though unlawful military target. *Schools located in insecure zones then are very much to be considered at the frontline of terror operations for the Taliban and other AGEs (anti-government elements).* As a consequence, under international humanitarian law, the State and its allies have a legal obligation to remove schoolchildren (as well as teachers, education-related personnel and education aid workers) from the vicinity of what the Taliban and other AGEs have designated as military objectives. Allowing children to attend school in these insecure zones is akin to allowing children to attend school in a vulnerable U.S. military encampment which is a high value Taliban military objective.

The failure in Afghanistan of the State and its international allies to ensure the removal of schoolchildren from schools and from the vicinity of schools where security is inadequate (knowing that schools and the route to and from school are high value terror targets for the Taliban and other AGEs) constitutes a violation of: (a) Additional Protocol II Article 13 which states that: 'the civilian population and individual civilians shall enjoy a general protection against the dangers arising from military operations' and of (b) Additional Protocol II Article 4(3)(e) which states in part: 'measures shall be taken... to remove children temporarily from the area in which hostilities are taking place to a safer area within the country and ensure that they are accompanied by persons responsible for their safety and well-being'.[136] While it may not always be necessary or practicable to remove children to another part of the country in Afghanistan, sending children to schools that are located in unsecured areas and, hence, become terror targets is certainly in direct contradiction to the spirit and intent of Additional Protocol II Article 4(3)(e) (which is directed to ensuring the safety of children caught up in armed conflict). These obligations under Protocol II (which many scholars hold have attained the status of customary law) arguably fall not only to the States and non-States armed parties to the conflict, but also to the international humanitarian/human rights community personnel working in Afghanistan who, although not parties to the conflict; through their

[135]Convention on Cluster Munitions (2008) entered into force 1 August 2010. http://www.clusterconvention.org. Accessed 29 Aug 2010.

[136]Protocol Additional to the Geneva Conventions of 12 August 1949, and relating to the Protection of Victims of Non-International Armed Conflicts (Protocol II), 8 June 1977. http://www.icrc.org/ihl.nsf/FULL/475?OpenDocument. Accessed 29 Aug 2010.

actions significantly impact the safety and well-being of child civilians (school-children) and education-related workers.

Recall also the previous discussion regarding the responsibility of private actors (such are NGO personnel) to uphold IHL, at a minimum, as expressed in Common Article 3 of the Geneva Conventions.[137] The principle of keeping civilians out of harm's way to the extent possible in armed conflict can be considered as customary law (i.e., reflected in Common Article 3 of the Geneva Conventions) binding all those in a position to foster humane treatment of civilians, and prevent them grievous harm. To meet these obligations is to abide by the principles of humanity; a term articulated in the Martens Clause.[138]

References

Bart GR (2010) The ambiguous protection of schools under the law of war: time for parity with hospitals and religious buildings. In: UNESCO (2010) Protecting education from attack: a state-of-the-art review, pp 195–225. http://unesdoc.unesco.org/images/0018/001867/186732e.pdf. Accessed 25 June 2010

Burde D (2010) Preventing violent attacks on education in Afghanistan: considering the role of community-based schools, Chap. 13, pp 245–259. In: UNESCO (2010) Protecting education from attack: a state-of-the-art review. http://unesdoc.unesco.org/images/0018/001867/186732e.pdf. Accessed 26 June 2010

Coalition for the International Criminal Court (2009) Rome statute ratification chart by region. http://www.iccnow.org/documents/RATIFICATIONSbyRegion_21_July_20091.pdf. Accessed 2 July 2010

Dinstein Y (2004) The conduct of hostilities under the law of international armed conflict. Cambridge University Press, Cambridge

Henderson I (2009) The contemporary law of targeting: military objectives, proportionality and precautions in attack under Additional Protocol I. Martinus Nijhof, Leiden

Human Rights Watch (2006) Lessons in terror: attacks on education in Afghanistan, vol 18, no 6 (C). www.hrw.org/reports/2006/afghanistan0706/index.htm. Accessed 12 July 2010

Human Rights Watch (2010) I lost everything. Israel's unlawful destruction of property during 'Operation Cast Lead'. http://www.hrw.org/node/90334. Accessed 29 Oct 2010

International Committee of the Red Cross (2002). The law of armed conflict: belligerent occupation. http://www.icrc.org/Web/eng/siteeng0.nsf/htmlall/5P8EX4/$File/LAW9_final.pdf. Accessed 6 July 2010

Rowe P (2010) The application of international humanitarian law to attacks on education in armed conflict. In: UNESCO (2010) Protecting education from attack: a state-of-the-art review. http://unesdoc.unesco.org/images/0018/001867/186732e.pdf. Accessed 13 July 2010

Schmitt MN (2009) Human shields in international humanitarian law. Columbia J Transnatl Law 47:17–59. http://www.marshallcenter.org/mcpublicweb/MCDocs/files/College/HShlds-Schmitt.pdf. Accessed 1 July 2010

Schmitt MN (2010) Human shields in international humanitarian law. Isr Yearb Hum Rights:30 www.marshallcenter.org/mcpublicweb/MCDocs/.../HShlds-Schmitt.pdf. Accessed 10 July 2010

[137]Common Article 3 of the 1949 Geneva Conventions. http://www.icrc.org/ihl.nsf/WebART/365-570006. Accessed 29 Aug 2010.

[138]Ticehurst (1997).

Sheppard B (2010) 'Painful and inconvenient': accountability for attacks on education. In: UNESCO (2010) Protecting education from attack: a state-of-the-art review, pp 125–146. http://unesdoc.unesco.org/images/0018/001867/186732e.pdf. Accessed 25 February 2011

Solis GD (2010) The law of armed conflict: International humanitarian law in war. Cambridge University Press, New York, p 320

Ticehurst R (1997) International committee of the red cross commentary on the martens clause. http://www.icrc.org/web/eng/siteeng0.nsf/html/57JNHY. Accessed 18 July 2010

UNESCO (2010) Protecting education from attack: a state-of-the-art review, pp 147–178. http://unesdoc.unesco.org/images/0018/001867/186732e.pdf. Accessed 11 July 2010

United Nations Assistance Mission in Afghanistan (2010) Afghanistan: midyear report on protection of civilians in armed conflict 2010. UNAMA, August 2010. http://www.humansecuritygateway.com/showRecord.php?RecordId=33534. Accessed 28 Aug 2010

Vrdoljak AF (2009) Cultural heritage in human rights and humanitarian law. In: Ben-Naftali O (ed) Human rights and international humanitarian law. Oxford University Press, Oxford. http://works.bepress.com/ana_filipa_vrdoljak/15. Accessed 6 July 2010

Waxman M (2005) International law and the politics of urban air operations (for the RAND corporation). http://www.rand.org/publications/MR/Mr1175. Accessed 25 February 2011

Chapter 6
Schoolchildren Knowingly Placed at Risk of Terror Attack: The Complicity of High Profile Human Rights Gatekeepers

In this chapter, we begin by examining the applicability to the plight of Afghanistan's schoolchildren of a model regarding the role of international high profile human rights gatekeepers in vetting or not vetting certain grievances as legitimate international human rights issues. The question addressed is why the fact that children are still attending at unsecured schools in the midst of intense armed conflict in Afghanistan is not viewed as: (a) a grave violation under international humanitarian law (treaty and the customary law of armed conflict) of their fundamental right to security of the person as civilians, and as (b) an infringement of their right under IHL to special protection as children in times of armed conflict. Rather than attendance at schools in high risk terror zones in Afghanistan being viewed as a potential violation of children's fundamental human right to life and survival, school attendance under these conditions has been classified by international high profile human rights gatekeepers as an outcome consistent with humanitarian education aid relief (such as occurs in natural disaster or other emergency situations unrelated to armed conflict). Indeed, the global community has, *in practice*, come to perceive education as a priority for Afghan children *superseding* their right to security. We will focus primarily on the role of international humanitarian/human rights organizations in fostering, along with the national government, school attendance in unsafe locales within Afghanistan while framing such activity as humanitarian in nature. We will also address the lack of accountability for such actions.

Bob proposes a framework which explains "the human rights movement adopting new rights".[1] By human rights movement Bob is referring to "NGOs, international organizations, state bureaucracies, foundations, journalists, individuals, and others who work, sometimes together in networks, sometimes in competition with one another, to promote ideals and values denominated in international law as 'human rights'".[2] The so-called 'new rights' at issue include among others, according to Bob, those rights "codified but allotted few resources by the rights movement".[3] It is suggested here that although the right of child civilians to security in times of armed

[1]Bob (2009), p. 2.
[2]Bob (2009), p. 2.
[3]Bob (2009), p. 3.

S.C. Grover, *Schoolchildren as Propaganda Tools in the War on Terror*, 221
DOI 10.1007/978-3-642-17900-6_6, © Springer-Verlag Berlin Heidelberg 2011

conflict is extremely well-established in international treaty and customary law, that principle is *not* being adequately or fully implemented as applied to schoolchildren in the context of the war on terror. That is, the right of schoolchildren not to be intentionally placed in harm's way by being sent to schools that are inadequately secured in an armed conflict situation such as in Afghanistan is considered a 'non-issue' by high profile human rights gatekeepers (i.e., well known national and international human rights and humanitarian organizations). This is not to say that NGOs and others in the international humanitarian/human rights community are not beginning to discuss ways to better secure schools and better protect children on the way to and from schools. Rather, it is to suggest that the notion of keeping schools that cannot be properly secured closed until such time as that situation can be fully remedied is not, in practice, the tact that is taken in Afghanistan nor in several other conflict-affected States. Rather, the objective of the government and the international humanitarian community, as has here been previously discussed, has been to get schools up and running as soon as possible *despite the ongoing security threat* which may or may not be imminent in any particular instance, but has been, to date, always unpredictable, and, of late, much more likely than in the past few years. That is, schools are operating in very insecure locales within Afghanistan almost as if it were a 'post-conflict' situation which it is not.

Bob suggests that: (a) high profile international human rights gatekeepers determine in large part whether an issue will be regarded as a legitimate human rights concern and that (b) States most often follow their lead in this regard.[4] As international humanitarian/human rights organizations have a vested interest financially, politically and in terms of their profile in providing and facilitating educational services, they are unlikely to classify children attending school despite grossly inadequate security (as is occurring in some parts of Afghanistan) as an unacceptable practice from a humanitarian/human rights law perspective. The indicia of this is the fact that the international humanitarian/human rights movement continues to be heavily involved in ensuring children in Afghanistan attend school across the country regardless of the inadequate security situation in any particular zone within that jurisdiction.

The generally impoverished Afghan parents living in remote villages in that country have not been in a position to communicate their grievances in regard to their children having been injured or killed at school, or on the way to or from school. At the same time, these parents were generally under the impression that the children would be provided proper security in attending school. International journalists have devoted little if any attention to this issue. When international journalists have covered stories such as gas poisonings of girl schoolchildren in Afghanistan, or children horribly disfigured by terrorists throwing acid in their faces, or children killed or losing limbs or suffering other devastating injuries in arson or bombing attacks on their school; the focus has been exclusively on the attackers. Attention has *not* been focused also on those largely responsible for facilitating and encouraging the children's school attendance in the first instance

[4]Bob (2009), p. 2.

despite the security concerns (i.e., government education and other officials and NGO personnel). This is the case despite the fact that the aforementioned parties generally have knowledge of the lack of school security and the *foreseeable* potential consequences of school attendance under these circumstances for the safety of the children.

In covering stories of the schoolchildren who have become the victims of terror attacks in Afghanistan, targeted simply and solely because they do attend school, international journalists have most often articulated the story as one concerning the courage of the children in attending school in such a perilous circumstance, and of their parents for taking that risk with their youngsters. The journalists have rarely, if ever, considered whether these parents in fact were cognizant of precisely how abysmal the security situation would be for their children in attending school. Instead, these youngsters killed or injured by the Taliban or other insurgents while attempting to attend school and young schoolgirls, their faces disfigured by a terrorist acid attack, are essentially being depicted as the West's or democracy's voluntary "child soldiers" or "little warriors" acting on their own initiative in the fight against terror. This, rather than being described as having been duped into risking life and limb to attend school by the reassurances and encouragement offered by the government and humanitarian education workers (when in reality their security was at extreme risk in particular locales within the country). These victims of a realized terror attack are thus used as symbols of inspiration and determination in the struggle to defeat the terrorists.

When an individual wishes to obtain a basic education, the underlying assumption generally is that he/she will live long enough that it will pay dividends in terms of securing a better quality of life for that individual in future (and by extension for the society as a whole). One can understand then the urgency that humanitarian organizations, the Afghan government and its allies feel in returning children to school as soon as possible after a terror attack on the schoolchildren and/or the school often leading to a return when the security situation is still precarious. To delay the return to school until security is assured is apparently assessed by the Afghan government and its allies, and representatives of the international humanitarian community operating in Afghanistan, as equivalent to sending a message to the Afghan public at large and the international community that hope for success in the war on terror and in the possibility of stabilization of the security situation and development is lost; at least for a time. The latter explanation of the incentive for the rush to operate schools even in inadequate security situations in various locales within Afghanistan is in contrast then to the status quo interpretation focused as it is on an alleged concern for the educational welfare of the children. That concern seems considerably less credible if one is knowingly exposing the children to a high risk of death or grievous injury from a potential but probable terror attack on education (at their school or on the route to or from school) as is occurring in Afghanistan and several other conflict-affected States.

The schoolchildren, fresh faced and excited about school before being victimized by the all too often occurring terror attack, fulfill a symbolic function in the war on terror similar to that served by Shirley Temple in World War II; an idealized child symbol of the presumed infinite enthusiasm for life, and resilience of the general populace and its alleged optimism regarding the ultimate victory to be had by anti-terrorist forces.

The current book is, in part, an attempt both to: (a) bring an international high profile to the grievances of parents in Afghanistan who have had children injured or killed due to lack of security for school attendance and to (b) make a plea for accountability of all parties responsible for facilitating the attendance of schoolchildren in Afghanistan also in specific locales within various provinces in the country where schools are unsecured and routes to and from school are at a significant risk of terror attack. It is an attempt to counter the explicit and implicit education-related anti-terrorist propaganda messages communicated to the Afghan people and the international community by: (a) the Afghan government and its Western allies and (b) the international human rights/humanitarian community operating in Afghanistan; both using schoolchildren as tools in that effort (where school attendance is used as an erroneous marker for alleged progress in the security situation). The unchallenged use of schoolchildren for such a propaganda purpose in the war on terror has proven to be, as we have seen, a significant contributor to: (a) perpetuating the pattern of sending children to school also in unsecured zones within Afghanistan and (b) the consequent ever increasing number of child deaths and injuries relating to terror attacks on education.

6.1 The Six Grave Violations of Children's Fundamental Human Rights During Armed Conflict and a Significant Omission

The relatively recent phenomenon of national and international NGOs, and human rights/humanitarian aid organization workers and State governments and their allies as well as UN agencies encouraging schoolchildren to attend schools even in insecure zones within conflict-affected States such as Afghanistan (where the school is known to be highly vulnerable to armed attack) has been largely deemed a 'non-issue' for the international human rights/humanitarian community. This is reflected, in part, by the fact that facilitating and encouraging attendance at schools known to be highly vulnerable to terror attack has *not* been deemed one of the six grave violations against children's fundamental human rights during armed conflict (violations identified by the UN Secretary General's Special Representative for Children and Armed Conflict and explicitly acknowledged by that Office to be 'war crimes'). The six grave violations against children identified by the Special Representative include the following:

Killing or maiming of children;
Recruitment or use of children as soldiers;
Attacks against schools or hospitals;
Denial of humanitarian access for children;

Abduction of children;
Rape and other grave sexual abuse of children[5]

The objective of the Special Representative on Children and Armed Conflict in identifying these six grave violations and having them monitored and reported to the UN Security Working Group was: (a) to have the UN Security Council consider occurrence of these grave violations against children as themselves indices of a threat to peace and security; and (b) to have the UN Security Council take account of these violations in its deliberations regarding what should be the Security Council response to specific threats to peace.[6] The focus insofar as basic education and armed conflict is concerned has been entirely on the armed groups doing the attacking to the complete exclusion of those groups facilitating the schoolchildren becoming easy targets for terror attack. *Attacking a school*, is listed by the Office of the Special Representative of the UN Secretary General for Children Affected by Armed Conflict as one of the six grave violations for which: (a) perpetrators should be better held accountable and (b) which violation should be monitored and reported to the UN Security Council (communicated to the UN Working Group on Children and Armed Conflict and to the relevant Security Council sanctions committees). It has here been argued, however, that those responsible for facilitating such attacks on schoolchildren by: (a) encouraging and facilitating school attendance at schools known to be inadequately protected and (b) travel to and from school along routes known to hold a substantial risk of being the target of terror attack, have also committed a grave violation against children that implicates international criminal law as well as international human rights and humanitarian law. They, too, then have potentially committed a *grave violation* of children's basic human right to life and security. This would include then not just State government officials among others but also NGO and UN personnel. While the UN staff normally have immunity from all civil and criminal liability, it is here contended that as such intentional acts that place children at a known increased risk of harm from a terror attack is beyond the UN Charter jurisdiction, UN personnel involved in such acts are not immune from potential criminal prosecution or civil liability for the same.

6.2 The Response of High Profile Gate-Keepers to Attacks on Education

Though "the number of attacks on schools, teachers and students has been rising since 2000, and increased sixfold between 2003 and 2006",[7] the UN Security Council has paid scant attention to the issue of attacks on schools and on schoolchildren other than as relates to recruitment of child soldiers:

[5]Office of the Special Representative to the UN Secretary General for Children Affected by Armed Conflict Ending the six grave violations against children in conflict http://www.un.org/children/conflict/english/themostgraveviolations.html (accessed 3 September 2010).

[6]Coomaraswamy (2010).

[7]Human Rights Watch (2009), p. 2–3.

> Although the [UN] monitoring and reporting mechanism [for the six grave violations against children] documents six grave violations against children, in practice, violations other than recruitment and use of child soldiers [i.e., attacks on schools and schoolchildren trying to attend school] have received only superficial attention. The disparity can be seen clearly from the following: since the beginning of 2008, the [UN] Secretary-General has issued 9 country reports on children and armed conflict, and the Security Council working group has issued 10 separate sets of conclusions on individual situations. These 19 documents included a total of 141 separate recommendations related to the recruitment and use of child soldiers, but only 18 recommendations on sexual violence and only 6 related to [targeted] attacks on education [i.e., attacks on schools for the purpose of destroying the school and maiming and killing schoolchildren and education personnel. *Note that recruitment of children as child soldiers also aborts or interferes with children's education as does sexual violence perpetrated upon the child, thus both also constitute attacks on education*]. Seven of the 19 documents include no recommendations on either sexual violence [against children of whom girl schoolchildren are at an especially high risk from those who oppose the education of females] or attacks on education, even in situations where the Secretary-General has described rates of sexual violence as "alarming" and where attacks on schools have also been cited.[8]

It would appear then that the United Nations Security Council Working Group mandated to address the six grave violations against children affected by armed conflict has, in effect, undermined the perceived severity of the terror threat to schoolchildren and schools. Further, the lack of attention paid to attacks on schools by the Working Group has detracted from the perceived urgency with which strategies must be developed to reduce the terror threat to education for these schoolchildren. This appears to be the predictable result of the United Nations also using education as a propaganda tool to tout alleged improvements in security and development in various conflict-affected States overwhelmed by insurgent terror activity. (Note that the 'UN Working Group on Children and Armed Conflict' emphasis on child soldiers, their recruitment and use in various roles (spies, sexual slaves to the armed unit, fighters directly involved in combat, scouts that clear landmines, cooks and messengers etc.) has resulted in some success in negotiations with States to end such exploitation though the practice continues unabated in some regions. However, little progress has been made in most conflict-affected States in regards to ending attacks on education in its various other forms.

The problem of attacks on education (attacks on schools, schoolchildren, education personnel and education aid workers), however, requires, more so perhaps than does the issue of child soldiers, addressing also the role of *democratic* governments in facilitating such a grave violation against the right of children to security of the person. This in that, as we have discovered through our inquiry here, democratic States are willing and anxious to ensure children's attendance at school in conflict-affected States even where there is a substantial risk to the child's survival or well-being physically and psychologically arising from high probability

[8]Office of the Special Representative to the UN Secretary General for Children Affected by Armed Conflict Ending the six grave violations against children in conflict http://www.un.org/children/conflict/english/themostgraveviolations.html (accessed 3 September 2010).

terror attacks targeting education. It is noteworthy that the annual reports to the UN Security Council by the Secretary General on Children and Armed Conflict:

> presents certain statistics but the main thrust of the reporting is *incident based reporting with an attempt to identify perpetrators where possible*. This specific incident and perpetrator focus makes this a unique report in the UN system, especially as it is presented as the report of the Secretary-General (emphasis added).[9]

There is then the attempt to identify specific incidents and individual perpetrators regarding the six grave violations including 'attacks on schools' (i.e., the identity of the commanders who gave the order to attack and those who carried out the mission, those responsible for the policy to perpetrate terror attacks on schools etc). What has been highlighted here, however, is the need for a broader view of who is responsible for the maiming and killing of schoolchildren in such terror attacks on education and for the damage to or destruction of schools. That broader view would involve recognition that: (a) those who encouraged and facilitated the children's attendance at school despite knowledge that the particular school sites in question were left unprotected against terror attack, as were the routes to and from school, also contributed to these terror attacks at those particular locations and, therefore (b) they are also possible perpetrators of the grave violation of children's basic human right to life and security of the person. An acknowledgement of this reality would require also identifying as possible perpetrators particular government officials, and the national and international humanitarian education aid/human rights organization representatives and workers who facilitated and encouraged school attendance despite knowing of the high risk of terror attack in the specific situation and at the particular locale within the conflict-affected State. The same is true for any Afghan government or non-government security personnel or Western military commander or private security firm personnel worker or United Nations organization representatives (perhaps in conjunction with development workers), who encouraged school attendance knowing full well that sufficient and ongoing security for the school, the school children, education personnel and humanitarian education aid workers could not and/or would not be provided. The fact is that various UN representatives and those from diverse aid organizations have also not, in practice, generally demanded adequate security for educational activities *prior to* children being allowed to attend school.

The countries of origin of these international humanitarian education aid workers facilitating school attendance despite security concerns are those same Western countries providing significant donor support to the war on terror as well as to the development effort in CAFS such as Afghanistan. These facts would suggest that political motives may, in large part, be an explanation for the fact that those who encourage and facilitate school attendance in conflict-affected States, even in particular locales where security cannot be adequately provided, have, to date, not also been classed as possible perpetrators of a grave violation of children's human right to survival and to physical as well as psychological security. It is time

[9] Coomaraswamy (2010).

long over due, however, that all those who directly, or indirectly (as described) contribute to the killing and maiming of schoolchildren knowing the risks inherent in the children attending school in the particular circumstance be held fully accountable under international law including international criminal law. The Rome Statute under it General Principles of Criminal Law Part 3, provision 3(d), in fact, considers as perpetrator also any person who:

> *In any other way contributes to the commission or attempted commission of such a crime* [i.e., a war crime] by a group of persons acting with a common purpose. *Such contribution shall be intentional and shall either:*
>
> (i) Be made with the aim of furthering the criminal activity or criminal purpose of the group, where such activity or purpose involves the commission of a crime within the jurisdiction of the Court; ***or***
>
> (ii) *Be made in the knowledge of the intention of the group to commit the crime* (emphasis added)[10]

In this instance, the actions of those who *intentionally* encouraged and facilitated school attendance in various locales within Afghanistan where there was a *known* high and ongoing risk of terror attack, it is argued, fall under principle 3(d) (ii). That is, these individuals intentionally and knowingly contributed to increasing the risk of grave harm to children by positioning them as easier targets for terrorists knowing full well that their actions could further the goal of the terrorists (i.e., to maim and kill schoolchildren and the civilians-teachers, education aid workers and others-associated with the children's schooling). This increased potential of harm to the schoolchildren was created by congregating the children at recognizable school buildings, or multi-purpose buildings known to also house schools, or at open air school sites, and by encouraging and facilitating the children's travelling along unsecured routes to and from school. This encouragement and facilitation of school attendance at unsecured sites was "made in the knowledge of the intention of the group [i.e., the Taliban and other insurgents within Afghanistan] to commit the [international] crime [namely; terror attacks on child civilians and civilian objects; both constituting war crimes]".[11] NGOs such as Human Right Watch, Save the Children, UNICEF and others have not, however, so far addressed their own possible contribution to successful terror strikes on schools, schoolchildren and education-related workers resulting from encouraging and facilitating school attendance despite the high risk of terror attack. Rather, they speak of the need for the Security Council to mandate UN country teams to negotiate with terrorists and other armed groups to cease and desist in all forms armed attacks against education. They recommend:

> expand the scope of dialogue with parties to the armed conflict to achieve concrete, measurable action plans that address all grave violations against children, including ... attacks on education... plans [that are] time bound and include key benchmarks, including

[10] Rome Statute of the International Criminal Court (entered into force 1 July, 2002) http://untreaty.un.org/cod/icc/statute/romefra.htm (accessed 4 September 2010).

[11] Rome Statute of the International Criminal Court (entered into force 1 July, 2002) http://untreaty.un.org/cod/icc/statute/romefra.htm (accessed 4 September 2010).

> the development of clear policies prohibiting ... attacks on schools, and other violations against children; measures to communicate "zero-tolerance" policies throughout the chain of command; and transparent accountability measures that include clear sanctions against any members who violate the policy.[12]

The reality is, however, that as long as the Afghan government and its allies and the international humanitarian/human rights community, in practice, endorse and facilitate school attendance despite inadequate security (notwithstanding their simultaneous calls for better security), the Taliban and other insurgent group terror attacks on education will continue and even escalate. This the evidence on incidence trends regarding attacks on education collected by international humanitarian organizations and other independent bodies has borne out.

It is noteworthy that despite the inordinate level of suffering caused by attacks on schoolchildren and schools for the children and their families and the conflict-affected community and nation as a whole, the UN Security Council working group that concerns itself with possible sanctions regarding the six grave violations against children has not referred information on attacks on schools or any of the other violations to the International Criminal Court.[13] This means that those individuals who have facilitated or encouraged school attendance in insecure zones where such attendance put the children at risk of grievous harm from armed attack will not be held accountable under international criminal law. This is the case as individual States whose own delegates were complicit in this way (i.e., in the Taliban or other insurgents committing the war crime of attacking schools and civilians associated with the education enterprise in Afghanistan or other conflict-affected States) are unlikely to prosecute, or to exercise universal criminal jurisdiction over those nationals of other States who are also guilty of making the same indirect contribution to the success of terror attacks on education.

A further problem with the current UN Security Council monitoring of education-related grave violations against children is that, as Human Rights Watch notes, the grave violation directly mentioning education refers only to attacks on schools even though:

> Attacks on education do not only include attacks on infrastructure, but also attacks against teachers and students themselves (including on their way to and from school), the use of schools for military purposes, and harassment and threats against teachers, parents and students intended to suppress school, attendance.[14]

It is as if the failure to mention attacks perpetrated directly on schoolchildren helps divert attention away from the grievous consequences of children attending schools in CAFS in locales that are unprotected and situated in the midst of an intense conflict zone; having been encouraged to do so by government officials, NGO and UN personnel. The destruction of or damage to school buildings per se is much less emotion-provoking than consideration of the high numbers of child

---

[12]Human Rights Watch (2009), p. 4.

[13]Human Rights Watch (2009), p. 4.

[14]Human Rights Watch (2009), p. 7–8.

deaths and injuries resulting from terror attacks on unprotected or inadequately protected schools and school routes.

In addition, Human Rights Watch notes that the UN Security Council working group dealing with the grave violation of attacks on education more often called upon parties to the conflict to *investigate* allegations of such abuse and hold any perpetrators accountable as opposed to demanding an end to these violations and considering prevention strategies.[15] The 2009 Human Rights Watch Report then rightfully raises serious doubts about the adequacy of the UN Security Council Working Group's response to attacks on education in various high conflict States. Predictably, however, there is no explicit and specific mention in the report of the need to interrupt school attendance until security can be reasonably assured for the schoolchildren and education personnel attending schools in a CAFS. Rather, there is, as usual in such NGO reports, mention of the need for what is vaguely described as "early warning systems" and a non-specific reference to preventive measures in regards to attacks and decreasing harms to students:

> In some countries, attacks on schools or teachers are preceded by threats, warning letters, or increased presence of armed groups in the area [as is certainly the case in Afghanistan]. Governments and UN country teams should establish early warning systems to track such threats in order to devise response strategies that attempt to prevent actual attacks and protect students.[16]

It would appear that there is a great reluctance to do the most obvious thing and that is, to stop sending children in conflict-affected States plagued by terror activity to unsecured schools along unsecured routes. That is the most proactive preventive strategy available as 'dialogue' with the Taliban and Al Qaeda elements to end attacks on education have been unsuccessful on the whole. One simply cannot imagine Western parents being expected to rely on so-called 'early warning systems' which are supposed to trigger as yet undefined preventive measures to keep their schoolchildren safe. Predictably, the 2009 Human Rights Watch Report articulates a perspective, as with other NGO reports, that unjustifiably appears to place the survival, and safety of children as a lesser priority compared to their right to access education (as short-lived as that access to education may be if the children are killed or grievously injured in a terror attack on the school or on the route to or from school):

> Government and relevant agencies should put in place advance rapid response systems so that ***when attacks occur*****, schools are rebuilt (if possible), and destroyed educational materials replaced,** ***so that children can return to school as quickly as possible***. This could involve ***the creation of a special emergency fund for the immediate rebuilding of damaged schools*** (emphasis added).[17]

The focus then seems to be on returning children to school as quickly as possible after a terror attack on education. That is, as soon as school buildings can be

[15]Human Rights Watch (2009), p. 6.

[16]Human Rights Watch (2009), p. 8.

[17]Human Rights Watch (2009), p. 8–9.

repaired or built anew; student desks and teacher equipment provided; or tents or other materials for an open air school provided, and destroyed educational learning materials replaced as well as parents persuaded to allow their children to return to school. After a terror attack on education then the objective of the State government and its allies and the humanitarian education aid sector is to return children to school as soon as possible, in effect, for all intents and purposes placing them precisely where they can once more become an easy target for terrorists. Children who luckily survived the preceding attack unscathed may not be so lucky the next time. In contradictory fashion, the same aforementioned 2009 Human Rights Watch report recommends home-based or distance-learning alternatives when insecurity prevents children from attending at school. However, if security of schoolchildren were truly the top priority; then school reconstruction and the building of new schools would not be on the agenda until an adequate security situation was reasonably assured instead of immediately after a terror attack; the latter being the recommendation of Human Rights Watch and other NGOs. Hence, when NGOs refer to sending children back to school 'as soon as possible'; they seem to be referring to the time lapse until the school is in operational shape once more post a terror attack, or a new school is completed, or materials accessed for an open air school, and parents convinced once more to send their children back to school. The security situation so soon after a terror attack would, however, generally not yet have improved enough to eliminate the considerable risk to students of death or injury correlated with school attendance.

Criminal culpability under international criminal law, on the view here, as discussed, may thus also arise from the intentional actions of certain members of the international humanitarian/human rights community and national government in encouraging and facilitating the operation of unsecured schools, and school attendance at these institutions. This is the case given the known foreseeable increased risk to civilians (i.e., schoolchildren, teachers, other education personnel and humanitarian education aid workers) of death or grievous bodily injury resulting from a terror attack. It is important to understand that criminal culpability in this instance does *not* require a specific motive to further the military objectives of the terrorists (which potentially would be an act of treason under domestic law). Rather, criminal culpability under international criminal law in this context requires only that: (a) actions were intentionally taken that foreseeably would advance the objectives of the terrorists to harm civilians, and (b) those actions were taken with full knowledge of the potential increased risk to civilians that would in fact arise as a result of those actions (in this case, facilitating and encouraging school attendance despite knowing of the extremely inadequate security at the school and on the routes to and from school). Such actions as the aforementioned are a potential violation (depending on all the facts of each case), it is here contended, of the customary laws of armed conflict and of the Additional Protocol II to the 1949 Geneva Conventions which has also attained the status of customary law (Afghanistan ratified Protocol II additional to the Geneva Conventions November 10, 2009). In addition, these actions; namely sending children to unsecured schools and along unprotected routes to and from school in active terrorist zones, facilitates the terrorists committing "violence to life and person..." and hence potentially constitutes complicity in the violation of provision 1(a) of Common Article 3 of the Geneva Convention (again depending on the specific fact pattern in each case). Further, intentionally placing children at such risk by sending them to school when security is inadequate is potentially to be complicit also in the terrorists' degrading treatment of children constituting an affront to their personal dignity. Thus, it would appear that the schoolchildren are being treated by both sides in the 'war on terror' as if they were expendable tools in the propaganda contest between the parties to the armed conflict.

6.3 Eric H. Holder, Jr. (Attorney General) et al. v. Humanitarian Law Project et al.: The Question of Potential Culpability of NGOs in Allegedly Facilitating Terrorist Objectives

Let us explore now a recent U.S. Supreme Court (USSC) case which addresses the relatively novel question of the potential criminal culpability of humanitarian organizations and their employees where their actions and/or polices or practices *in effect* allegedly facilitate the objectives of terrorists. We will first consider the judgment in the case and then the relevance of the case to the issue of accountability of NGO organizations and individual personnel for encouraging and facilitating school attendance knowing that this put the children and education personnel at high risk of victimization in a terror attack directed against education.

The USSC case in question is *Eric H. Holder, Jr., Attorney General, et al. v. Humanitarian Law Project et al.*[18] Our interest in this case in the context of the present inquiry is not first and foremost whether or not the U.S. federal statute challenged in the case is or is not constitutional. Rather, our interest is in questions larger than the constitutionality or lack of constitutionality of a particular U.S. federal statute per se; namely: 'What activities constitute giving material support and resources to terrorist groups in furtherance of their objectives; military and political? Does the person accused need to have known that their conduct was likely to further the group's terror objectives and/or does the person need to have this specific intent before they can be considered to have unlawfully provided material support and resources to the terror group and be subject to prosecution as a result?'

The plaintiffs in *Holder* (who were U.S. citizens and U.S. organizations) challenged the constitutionality of an aspect of the U.S. federal law the 'Antiterrorism and

[18] *Eric H. Holder, Jr., Attorney General, et al. v. Humanitarian Law Project et al.* US Supreme Court 561US___(2010) http://www.oyez.org/cases/2000-2009/2009/2008_08_1498 (accessed 4 September 2010).

Effective Death Penalty Act' ("AEDPA"). Section 303 of the AEDPA stipulated that it is a crime for U.S. nationals and others residing in the U.S. to 'provide material support or resources' to groups designated by the U.S. Secretary of State as foreign terrorist organizations. This is the case even if the support or resources directed to the designated foreign terror group were intended to further the *nonviolent* activities of that group. The plaintiffs held that section 303 of the AEDPA was unconstitutionally vague and they sought an injunction to block enforcement of that section. The District Court found in favor of the plaintiffs and found section 303 unconstitutionally vague, and this was upheld on appeal by the U.S. Court of Appeals, Ninth Circuit. Hence, the U.S. Congress enacted the 'Intelligence Reform and Terrorism Prevention Act' ("IRTPA") which amended the 'Antiterrorism and Effective Death Penalty Act' ("AEDPA"). The IRTPA (a) stipulated that it is a crime to *knowingly* 'provide material support or resources' to groups designated by the U.S. Secretary of State as foreign terrorist organizations (even if the support or resources directed to the designated foreign terror group were intended to further the nonviolent activities of that designated group), and (b) added terms to the statute that more precisely defined what was meant by providing "material support or resources" namely, among other things "training", "expert advice or assistance", "personnel", and "service".[19]

The question considered by the USSC in the case was: "Are provisions of the AEDPA (amended) which prohibit providing 'any ... service ... training [or] other specialized knowledge' to designated foreign terrorist organizations unconstitutionally vague?"[20] By a majority vote of 6 to 3, the USSC held that in terms of the application of the statute in the case at bar (that is, considering the specific type of support and resources the plaintiffs were planning to provide to the designated foreign terror groups in this instance), section 303 of the AEDPA (as amended) was *not* constitutionally vague. The designated terror groups at issue were the Kurdistan Workers' Party (PKK) and the Liberation Tigers of Tamil Eelam (LTTE).

The three dissenting judges agreed that section 303 of the AEDPA was *not* unconstitutionally vague. However, the dissenting judges *disagreed* that the plaintiffs could be criminally prosecuted for furthering the lawful political objectives of the designated foreign terror groups.[21]

---

[19] *Eric H. Holder, Jr., Attorney General, et al. v. Humanitarian Law Project et al.* US Supreme Court 561US___(2010) http://www.oyez.org/cases/2000-2009/2009/2008_08_1498 (accessed 4 September 2010), Dissenting Opinion, p. 1.

[20] *Eric H. Holder, Jr., Attorney General, et al. v. Humanitarian Law Project et al.*,US Supreme Court 561US___(2010) http://www.oyez.org/cases/2000-2009/2009/2008_08_1498 (accessed 4 September 2010).

[21] *Eric H. Holder, Jr., Attorney General, et al. v. Humanitarian Law Project et al.*,US Supreme Court 561US___(2010) http://www.oyez.org/cases/2000-2009/2009/2008_08_1498 (accessed 4 September 2010).

6.3.1 Dissenting Opinion of Justice Breyer, with Whom Justices Ginsburg and Sotomayor Join Dissenting

The dissenting judges held that if the U.S. humanitarian groups wished to work with the designated terror groups to teach them how to file grievances to the UN and advocate for their 'organization's' lawful political objectives; this speech should not be prohibited nor should their freedom of association with the designated terror group exclusively for this purpose since:

> ... the Government has *not* met its burden of showing that an interpretation of the statute [the AEDPA] that would prohibit this speech-and association-related activity serves the Government's compelling interest in combating terrorism. And I [Justice Breyer, joined by Justices Ginsburg and Sotomayor] would interpret the statute as normally placing activity of this kind outside its scope.[22]
>
> The plaintiffs, all United States citizens or associations, now seek an injunction and declaration providing that, without violating the statute, they can (1) train members of [the] PKK on how to use humanitarian and international law to peacefully resolve disputes; (2) engage in political advocacy on behalf of Kurds who live in Turkey; (3) teach PKK members how to petition various representative bodies such as the United Nations for relief; and (4) engage in political advocacy on behalf of Tamils who live in Sri Lanka.[23] (internal quotes omitted)

The Dissenting judges in the case held that the U.S. Federal government was interfering with First Amendment rights (freedom of speech) of the humanitarian aid workers since the activities the plaintiffs proposed engaging in with the designated terror groups were comprised of: "communication and advocacy of political ideas and lawful means of achieving political ends" and the content of that speech involved the subject of "using international law to resolve disputes peacefully or petitioning the United Nations, for instance [and hence constituted]... political speech".[24]

6.3.2 Analysis of the Dissenting Opinion

One can argue, however, that until and unless the designated terror groups cease and desist from all terror activity and denounce violence, working with these groups

---

[22] *Eric H. Holder, Jr., Attorney General, et al. v. Humanitarian Law Project et al.* US Supreme Court 561US___(2010), http://www.oyez.org/cases/2000-2009/2009/2008_08_1498 (accessed 4 September 2010), Dissenting Opinion, p. 1.

[23] *Eric H. Holder, Jr., Attorney General, et al. v. Humanitarian Law Project et al.* US Supreme Court 561US___(2010), http://www.oyez.org/cases/2000-2009/2009/2008_08_1498 (accessed 4 September, 2010), Dissenting Opinion, p. 2.

[24] *Eric H. Holder, Jr., Attorney General, et al. v. Humanitarian Law Project et al.* US Supreme Court 561US___(2010), http://www.oyez.org/cases/2000-2009/2009/2008_08_1498 (accessed 4 September 2010), Dissenting Opinion, p. 2–3.

for any purpose (even if intended for lawful objectives) unjustifiably serves to legitimize the group and, by implication, in the perception of at least a segment of the international community, endorses even the violent activity of the group. While it is correct, as pointed out by the dissenting judges in *Holder*, that the plaintiffs were not seeking to "solicit a crime",[25] at the same time, one might hold that by legitimizing the designated terror group which has killed and maimed innocent civilians and continues to do so, plaintiffs are in fact "likely to incite or produce [further] imminent lawless action" in furtherance of those organizations objectives. This given that supporters of the terror groups will have received the message that Western NGOs are prepared to endorse their political objectives perhaps in large part due to the lengths the terror group members are prepared to go to in achieving them (i.e., acts of extreme violence). Violence then is viewed by the terror groups and their supporters as an effective tool in communicating that desperation which will garner support and empathy from international humanitarian organizations. Thus, this author, in contrast to the dissenting opinion in *Holder*, contends that "the plaintiffs' speech to these organizations" is indeed "incitement"[26] to commit additional terrorist acts as it tends very often to embolden terror organization members and supporters in that direction. This is the case given that violence has garnered the terrorist group attention and 'material support and resources' from the West (in the Holder case instance in the form of training in advocacy, moral support for their political cause etc.).The First Amendment right of freedom of association, furthermore, was never intended by the framers of the U.S. Constitution to afford persons the opportunity to be directly or indirectly be complicit in facilitating violence. Yet, this is the case, it is here contended, when terror groups are unwittingly legitimized via communications with NGOs and refuse to denounce violence as an organization and refrain from all violence as a group.

When one compares the situation in *Holder* with that of humanitarian organizations working in Afghanistan, consider that the latter also often advocate communication with the Taliban and other insurgents:

> The CARE study in Afghanistan recommends that where potential attackers are known, community leaders might *consider engaging in preventative negotiations with them to try to reach agreement on continuing education locally*. But it warned that this option must not be taken lightly and *only local leaders would know if it was appropriate, might achieve the opposite effect or would be beyond their reach.*
>
> At an international expert seminar, "Protecting Education from Attack", hosted by UNESCO in Paris in September 2009, *it was argued that the efficacy of attempting to challenge armed groups to end attacks on education and comply with international humanitarian law would depend on the motives and structure of such groups.* If they are seeking international recognition as a potential government in waiting, they might be more

[25] *Eric H. Holder, Jr., Attorney General, et al. v. Humanitarian Law Project et al.* US Supreme Court 561US___(2010), http://www.oyez.org/cases/2000-2009/2009/2008_08_1498 (accessed 4 September 2010), Dissenting Opinion, p. 4.

[26] *Eric H. Holder, Jr., Attorney General, et al. v. Humanitarian Law Project et al.* US Supreme Court 561US___(2010), http://www.oyez.org/cases/2000-2009/2009/2008_08_1498 (accessed 4 September, 2010), Dissenting Opinion.

> cooperative; but many parties to conflict are made up of semi-autonomous factions with different levels of discipline and different levels of will to comply. ***Where the objective is to terrorize the civilians or drive an ethnic group out of a region,*** *the task [of attempting to convince insurgents to end attacks on education]* ***will be considerably more difficult*** (emphasis added).[27]

It should be noted, however, that in the quote immediately above that there is an acknowledgement at least that such communication with terror groups that have not, as a criminal organization, denounced violence 'might achieve the opposite effect or would be beyond their reach'. In the instance of Afghanistan, this is also the case i.e., communication with the Taliban or other insurgents for the purpose of attempting to negotiate schools as safe havens may in fact lead directly or indirectly to increased school attacks. The Taliban terrorists have to date not renounced violence as a group and, at present, as an organization, have not indicated that they are interested in peaceful co-existence or power sharing with various mainstream political entities in Afghanistan. Rather, the Afghan Taliban terrorists currently seek to impose their own dictatorial restricted vision of Afghanistan which denies gender equity and resists development. Hence, negotiating for the safety of schools with the Taliban terrorists and other groups in Afghanistan continuing a campaign of terror and their local supporters does not overall appear feasible. What then of the notion of continued attempts by NGOs to negotiate school safety directly with insurgents and their supporters? Let us turn again to the USSC *Holder* case and consider the issue of 'free speech' as it relates to communication with terror groups.

In *Holder*, the Dissenting USSC justices held that the issue they sought to address was one of balancing an individual's First Amendment rights of freedom of speech and freedom of association (in communicating with a terror organization so designated by the U.S. federal government as well as most of the Western States) on the one hand, and national security interests in the context of international terror on the other.[28] Justice Breyer writing for the dissenting justices in *Holder* stated: "To put the matter more specifically, precisely how does application of the statute to the protected before us activities [criminal prosecution for communicating with the terrorist group (free speech) to teach them peaceful advocacy skills, how to communicate with the United Nations etc] help achieve that important security-related end?"[29] With respect, this author would contend that by not demanding and requiring as a precondition of communication with the designated terror group that the group cease all terror activity (and that this end to the perpetration of violence be verified by the appropriate independent international body) the terror group is

---

[27]O'Malley (2010) p. 124.

[28]*Eric H. Holder, Jr., Attorney General, et al. v. Humanitarian Law Project et al.* US Supreme Court 561US___(2010) http://www.oyez.org/cases/2000-2009/2009/2008_08_1498 (accessed 4 September 2010), Dissenting Opinion, p. 6.

[29]*Eric H. Holder, Jr., Attorney General, et al. v. Humanitarian Law Project et al.* US Supreme Court 561US___(2010) http://www.oyez.org/cases/2000-2009/2009/2008_08_1498 (accessed 4 September 2010), Dissenting Opinion, p. 7.

reinforced in their use of violence by receiving an audience with highly respected Western NGOs, and international attention in this way. The more appropriate questions may be: 'Why must NGOs and humanitarian aid organizations seek to communicate with designated terror groups: (a) *prior to* these groups denouncing violence and demonstrating their commitment in this regard, and (b) while the groups are still actively engaged in committing acts of terror. That is, 'why should the latter tact be taken as opposed to undertaking a communication process regarding schools and their safety in the context of peace negotiations?' The question arises as to whether allowing such communication as previously described in *Holder* (and as here discussed regarding attempted negotiation for safe schools) involving NGOs and humanitarian aid groups communicating with terror groups inadvertently legitimizes the terror group. This would appear to be a strong possibility especially if the terror group continues to pursue violence (whether or not alongside other potential more peaceful means of achieving their political aims which they might adopt) and such communications are nevertheless ongoing. It would seem that there is a compelling national security interest of the State in insisting on non-communication with groups that engage in ongoing terror and advocate the use of terror as a means to attain their political objectives.

The majority of the Court held in *Holder* that (1) providing the type of support and resources to the designated terror groups which the plaintiffs intended (training members of the PKK on how to use humanitarian and international law to peacefully resolve disputes; (2) the humanitarian groups engaging in political advocacy on behalf of Kurds who live in Turkey; (3) teaching PKK members how to petition various representative bodies such as the United Nations for relief; and (4) engaging in political advocacy on behalf of Tamils who live in Sri Lanka would free up resources for the terror group which could then be directed to their ongoing terror activity. The Dissenting justices, however, held that:

> There is no obvious way in which undertaking advocacy for political change through peaceful means or teaching the PKK and LTTE, say, how to petition the United Nations for political change is fungible with other resources that might be put to more sinister ends in the way that donations of money, food, or computer training are fungible. It is far from obvious that these advocacy activities can themselves be redirected, or will free other resources that can be directed, towards terrorist ends.[30]

This author would argue, however, that the inevitable legitimization of designated terror groups via such communication with humanitarian organizations as proposed in *Holder* serves an essential international propaganda function for the terror groups. This built-in propaganda advantage deriving from communications with Western NGOs (here regarding peaceful means for advancing the terror groups political agenda) allows designated terror groups potentially to focus on perpetrating fewer but more major and deadlier terror attacks with heavier civilian casualty

---

[30]*Eric H. Holder, Jr., Attorney General, et al. v. Humanitarian Law Project et al.* US Supreme Court 561US___(2010) http://www.oyez.org/cases/2000-2009/2009/2008_08_1498 (accessed 4 September 2010), Dissenting Opinion, p. 8.

tolls for maximum global attention and effect. There is perhaps even an incentive in these circumstances to try and create the illusion of the group being a major force to reckon with by perpetrating more major terror attacks (as opposed to smaller more random and widespread attacks) to boost the significance of the group in the eyes of the international community and place the group, in their own estimation at least, in a better bargaining position in petitioning bodies such as the United Nations with their demands.

The majority in the Holder case, as does this author, refers to the issue of inadvertently legitimizing terror groups by communicating with them:

> the Government says that the plaintiffs' proposed activities will "bolster a terrorist organization's efficacy and strength in a community" and "undermine this nation's efforts to *delegitimize and weaken* those groups. In the Court's [majority] view, too, [in *Holder*] the Constitution permits application of the statute to activities of the kind at issue [i.e., prohibiting communication with the designated terror groups for the purposes at issue in *Holder*] in part because those activities could provide a group that engages in terrorism with "legitimacy". *The Court suggests that, armed with this greater "legitimacy", these organizations will more readily be able to obtain material support of the kinds Congress plainly intended to ban—money, arms, lodging, and the like* (emphasis added).[31]

Thus, the majority opinion in Holder held that not all communication with terror groups was banned just that which in some way facilitated the group's terror activities and objectives. In this regard, the majority held that:

> speaking, writing, and teaching aimed at furthering a terrorist organization's peaceful political ends could "make it easier for those groups to persist, to recruit members, and to raise funds[32]

However, the dissenting justices in *Holder* held that:

> . . . this 'legitimacy' justification cannot by itself warrant suppression of political speech, advocacy, and association". *Speech, association, and related activities on behalf of a group will often, perhaps always, help to legitimate that group*. Thus, were the law to accept a "legitimating" effect, in and of itself and without qualification, as providing sufficient grounds for imposing such a ban, the First Amendment battle would be lost in untold instances where it should be won. Once one accepts this argument, there is no natural stopping place (emphasis added).[33]

The problem of inadvertently legitimizing a terror group through communication with the group (even about humanitarian objectives or peaceful and lawful political objectives) can be avoided, however, as discussed, by deferring such

---

[31] *Eric H. Holder, Jr., Attorney General, et al. v. Humanitarian Law Project et al.* US Supreme Court 561US___(2010) http://www.oyez.org/cases/2000-2009/2009/2008_08_1498 (accessed 4 September 2010), Dissenting Opinion, p. 9–10.

[32] *Eric H. Holder, Jr., Attorney General, et al. v. Humanitarian Law Project et al.* US Supreme Court 561US___(2010) http://www.oyez.org/cases/2000-2009/2009/2008_08_1498 (accessed 4 September 2010), Dissenting Opinion, p. 10.

[33] *Eric H. Holder, Jr., Attorney General, et al. v. Humanitarian Law Project et al.* US Supreme Court 561US___(2010) http://www.oyez.org/cases/2000-2009/2009/2008_08_1498 (accessed 4 September 2010), Dissenting Opinion, p. 10.

communication until such time as the group, in principle and in practice, rejects and ceases violent activity. The same effort not to lend legitimacy to terror groups in the context of the conflict-affected State of Afghanistan then would require that NGOs, United Nations bodies and human rights/humanitarian aid groups operating in Afghanistan end their advocacy for communicating with the Taliban terrorist element and other violent insurgents as long as these latter groups persist in their terror campaign (i.e., stop their push for local community persons or even NGO personnel themselves to communicate with these terrorist groups directly or through intermediaries for the purpose of attempting to negotiate safe schools and protect communities from all insurgent violence until and unless these particular groups cease their terror activities). The current author takes the view that negotiating with terror groups about schooling concerns whilst those groups are still actively engaged in ongoing terror activity does lead to incitement of further violence by implicitly legitimizing the group and all that it represents. This is especially the case since terrorist groups are defined first and foremost precisely by their acts of terror. Hence, when high profile NGOs communicate with terror groups to help them further the group's political agenda in a lawful way (as was proposed by the plaintiffs in *Holder*), this does amount to 'coordinating' with that terror group; not just about the group's peaceful initiatives, if any, but tacitly and inadvertently also in sending the propaganda message that the designated terror group allegedly deserves endorsement despite its ongoing terror campaign.

The dissenting justices in the aforementioned USSC case noted that a significant part of the reasoning of the majority in *Holder* in ruling against the plaintiffs and finding the plaintiff's wish to teach the designated terror groups at issue advocacy skills and how to deal with the United Nations and use international law to advance their political cause was founded:

> on the ground that peaceful negotiations might just buy time . . . , lulling opponents into complacency. ... And the PKK might use its new information about the structures of the international legal system . . . to threaten, manipulate, and disrupt (internal quotes omitted).[34]

The dissenting justices on this key point comment:

> What is one to say about these arguments—arguments that would deny First Amendment protection to the peaceful teaching of international human rights law on the ground that a little knowledge about the international legal system is too dangerous a thing; that an opponent's subsequent willingness to negotiate might be faked, so let's not teach him how to try? What might be said of these claims by those who live, as we do, in a Nation committed to the resolution of disputes through deliberative forces (internal quotes omitted).[35]

---

[34]*Eric H. Holder, Jr., Attorney General, et al. v. Humanitarian Law Project et al.* US Supreme Court 561US___(2010) http://www.oyez.org/cases/2000-2009/2009/2008_08_1498 (accessed 4 September 2010), Dissenting Opinion, p. 13.

[35]*Eric H. Holder, Jr., Attorney General, et al. v. Humanitarian Law Project et al.* US Supreme Court 561US___(2010) http://www.oyez.org/cases/2000-2009/2009/2008_08_1498 (accessed 4 September 2010), Dissenting Opinion, p. 13.

The above comment of the dissenting justices in *Holder* seems eminently reasonable in the abstract, but arguably not so reasonable in the context of the designated terror groups at issue *ongoing terror campaigns* while they are learning about international law and the international legal system. Given the reality of the designated terror groups' failure to denounce terrorist acts, their alleged interest in the UN and the international legal system is highly suspect to say the least. Further, we must also consider the fact that these designated terror groups have committed and continue to commit grave human rights violations thus calling into question their interest in and potential commitment to international human rights and humanitarian law as well as the customary laws of armed conflict.

Importantly, Justice Breyer (and the other two justices of the USSC joining him in his dissent in *Holder*) suggested the following remedy to the alleged unconstitutionality of the statute challenged by the plaintiffs which statute bars communication with designated terror groups regarding strategies for peaceful advocacy and the workings of the international legal system and what is needed to negotiate that system:

> I believe that a construction that would avoid the constitutional problem is fairly possible. In particular, I would read the statute as criminalizing First-Amendment protected pure speech and association only *when the defendant knows or intends that those activities will assist the organization's unlawful terrorist actions. Under this reading, the Government would have to show, at a minimum, that such defendants provided support that they knew was significantly likely to help the organization pursue its unlawful terrorist aims* (emphasis added).[36]

Consider then Justice Breyer's suggestion regarding the standard for deciding whether an NGO or humanitarian group is providing material support and resources to terror groups as such a standard might apply in the context of conflict-affected Afghanistan, and national and international NGOs and United Nations organization frontline workers and policy-makers: (a) advocating and engaging in communication with the Taliban and other insurgents directly or through local community intermediaries (i.e., regarding making schools safe havens protected from the armed conflict etc.) whilst the group is still committing terror attacks in the same or other regions of the country; and at the same time (b) NGOs encouraging and facilitating the sending of children to school even in highly insecure zones within Afghanistan and the high risk of terror attack on the school and on the schoolchildren at school or on their way to or from school. It appears fair to say that in the case of both of these NGO activities, the humanitarian organizations *know* that they (the activities) are "significantly likely to help the [terror] organization pursue its unlawful terrorist aims".[37]

---

[36] *Eric H. Holder, Jr., Attorney General, et al. v. Humanitarian Law Project et al.* US Supreme Court 561US___(2010) http://www.oyez.org/cases/2000-2009/2009/2008_08_1498 (accessed 4 September 2010), Dissenting Opinion, p. 17.

[37] *Eric H. Holder, Jr., Attorney General, et al. v. Humanitarian Law Project et al.* US Supreme Court 561US___(2010) http://www.oyez.org/cases/2000-2009/2009/2008_08_1498 (accessed 4 September 2010), Dissenting Opinion, p. 17.

Communicating with the terror group's local leaders despite the group's ongoing terror tactics assists the terror group in furthering its 'military' objectives by legitimizing the group in the eyes of the local community. Such communication with the terror group despite the group not denouncing violence, furthermore, confers tremendous power on the terror group. This it does by sending the message (correct or incorrect) to the local and international community that the West is helpless in the face of terror and not in a position to make communication with the terror group contingent on the group stopping its terror campaign locally and throughout the country. More specifically, encouraging and facilitating the sending of children to school even when the children are at high risk of terror attack in attending (given the failure of the Taliban as a group to renounce violence) furthers the terror groups' objectives in killing and maiming children by making them easier targets. Absent a verifiable renunciation in practice of violence by the Taliban as an organization; communications with that terror group regarding safe schools is an inadequate basis to send children to school as soon as possible after a terror attack (as is the apparent objective of numerous high profile national and international NGOs, and aid organizations in Afghanistan and as is promoted by various UN bodies as evidenced from the reports here cited).

Encouraging and facilitating school attendance in a CAFS (in areas experiencing intense fighting between the parties): (a) based on purported guarantees from a terror group that schools will be regarded as safe zones, (b) without ensuring the protection of the children, and (c) when that terror group has not renounced violence as a general policy and practice of the group; poses a grave risk to the children's lives and safety. That activity, therefore, on the analysis here, potentially meets Justice Breyer's standard for deciding when an activity provides material support and resources to terror groups. This in that the NGOs and other humanitarian/human rights groups know full well that this action (encouraging and facilitating school attendance where security is in fact not assured) is "significantly likely to help the [terror] organization pursue its unlawful terrorist aims". The dramatically rising number of Afghan schoolchildren killed or maimed while attempting to attend school or while at school and the number of schools attacked and damaged or destroyed is testament to the fact that encouraging and facilitating school attendance without adequate security "helps the terror organization pursue its unlawful terrorist aims".[38] There is, furthermore, incontrovertible evidence that NGOs know the risks of pushing for school attendance even without adequate security (as they do) in zones with high levels of terror activity within a conflict-affected State such as Afghanistan. NGOs advocating and facilitating communication with the Taliban terror group and other insurgents whilst the group is still attacking schoolchildren and schools elsewhere and/or in the specific locale in question is an unreliable strategy. It is a tact that puts children at high risk of

[38] *Eric H. Holder, Jr., Attorney General, et al. v. Humanitarian Law Project et al.* US Supreme Court 561US___(2010) http://www.oyez.org/cases/2000-2009/2009/2008_08_1498 (accessed 4 September 2010), Dissenting Opinion, p. 17.

death or injury should the parents be persuaded to send the children to school based only on the reassurances from local government officials and NGO personnel of the wisdom of doing so and promises, if available, from the terror group to exclude schools and schoolchildren from the armed conflict.

Returning now for the moment to the Holder case, Justice Breyer for the dissenting justices states:

> **A person acts with the requisite knowledge if he is aware of (or willfully blinds himself to) a significant likelihood that his or her conduct will materially support the organization's terrorist ends** (emphasis added).[39]

Any such activity is *not* protected by free speech or free association guarantees in the opinion of the USSC in *Holder* both with respect to the majority and dissenting opinion.[40]

The current author then (applying the standard of the dissenting justices in *Holder* and notions of the basis for individual criminal culpability in the Rome Statute) maintains, for the reasons here previously explained, that the representatives of international and national human rights/humanitarian aid groups, NGOs and personnel from certain UN bodies operating in Afghanistan potentially do meet the standard for unlawfully "providing material support and resources" to a terror group (something which can finally be decided only on the totality of the facts in any particular instance). The aforementioned parties, it is contended, provide 'material support and resources' to the Taliban terrorist element and to other insurgents in Afghanistan committing acts of terror when these organizations:

(a) Encourage and facilitate school attendance in high terror zones without adequate security knowing full well this will likely further the objectives of the terrorists by making the schoolchildren easy, accessible, high value targets. (It could be argued that the plight of Afghan schoolchildren in terms of their victimization by terrorists targeting education is the poster case illustrating national and international humanitarian/human rights workers 'willfully blinding' themselves as to how certain of their activities in Afghanistan; namely encouraging and facilitating school attendance in all regions of Afghanistan even where security is inadequate, will significantly increase the likelihood of the terrorists achieving their objectives; here the killing and maiming of child and other civilians); and
(b) Communicate about schooling directly or through an intermediary with the Taliban and other insurgents that continue to embrace violence as a strategy and continue to perpetrate atrocities on schoolchildren and other civilians throughout Afghanistan with such communication serving then to legitimize

---

[39] *Eric H. Holder, Jr., Attorney General, et al. v. Humanitarian Law Project et al.* US Supreme Court 561US___(2010) http://www.oyez.org/cases/2000-2009/2009/2008_08_1498 (accessed 4 September 2010), Dissenting Opinion, p. 17.

[40] *Eric H. Holder, Jr., Attorney General, et al. v. Humanitarian Law Project et al.* US Supreme Court 561US___(2010) http://www.oyez.org/cases/2000-2009/2009/2008_08_1498 (accessed 4 September 2010), Dissenting Opinion, p. 18.

the terror group to a degree. As to the latter point, it has been noted even within the international humanitarian community that "aid [in whatever form] can [in certain instances] legitimise the values of war and positions of warmongers (implicit ethical messages)".[41] (Communicating with the Taliban terrorists and other insurgent groups in Afghanistan that have not renounced terrorism may mean but a short respite, if any, from the violence directed against schoolchildren and education personnel. Afterall, the terrorists hold virtually all the cards given the Afghan government's difficulty in the circumstance in monitoring and predicting terrorist attacks. Further communicating with the Taliban about what basic school curriculum is acceptable to that group amounts to 'coordinating' with a terrorist group to further their military/political objectives i.e., re-establishing Afghanistan as a State ruled by the iron hand of the Taliban.)

The current author is in accord with the view that:

> foreign organizations that engage in terrorist activity [i.e., the Taliban , Al Qaeda etc.] are so tainted by their criminal conduct [violating also international humanitarian law] that any contribution to such an organization facilitates that conduct [i.e., terrorist groups are virtually defined by their terrorist acts; not any peaceful activities they may also engage in; the latter in the hopes of assuaging the public's outrage and in an attempt to sanitize their image somewhat.][42]

Justice Breyer points out in *Holder* that in U.S. criminal law statutes (as it is here suggested is also the case in all democratic countries) there is incorporated:

> a mens rea requirement to all of the subsequently listed elements of the crime... the defendant would have to know or intend [for the offence of providing material support or resources to a terrorist group] (1) that he is providing support or resources, (2) that he is providing that support to a foreign terrorist organization, and (3) that he is providing support that is material, meaning (4) *that his support bears a significant likelihood of furthering the organization's terrorist ends* (emphasis added).[43]

On the analysis here, it is contended that the individuals associated with human rights/humanitarian organizations (national and international human rights/humanitarian aid workers as well as NGO and UN personnel) operating in Afghanistan potentially meet the four criteria listed above regarding *mens rea* for the international crime of aiding and abetting terrorists (in this case, due to their intentionally placing child civilians and schools in Afghanistan at high risk of terror attack by encouraging and facilitating school attendance despite knowledge of the inadequate

---

[41] Department for International Development (2010). Working effectively in conflict-affected ad fragile situations (Briefing Paper "Do no harm")(March, 2010) Available for download at http://www.comminit.com/en/node/312064/3083 (accessed 7 September 2010).

[42] *Eric H. Holder, Jr., Attorney General, et al. v. Humanitarian Law Project et al.* US Supreme Court 561US___(2010) http://www.oyez.org/cases/2000-2009/2009/2008_08_1498 (accessed 4 September 2010), Majority Opinion, p. 4.

[43] *Eric H. Holder, Jr., Attorney General, et al. v. Humanitarian Law Project et al.* US Supreme Court 561US___(2010) http://www.oyez.org/cases/2000-2009/2009/2008_08_1498 (accessed 4 September 2010), Dissenting Opinion, p. 18.

security provisions to allow this to be done safely and the foreseeable risk of attack). There is no need in order to meet the *mens rea* criteria for the aforementioned war crime that the culpable individuals who encouraged and facilitated the risking of Afghani children's lives in this way (i.e., frontline workers and/or decision-makers at the upper echelons of the human rights/humanitarian and UN organizations) need to have preferred or intended to support the terrorists violent objectives; only that they had knowledge that their conduct likely would further those objectives (i.e., given the high risk of a terror attack on unprotected occupied schools).[44] Certainly, it can be presumed that the humanitarian/human rights community operating in Afghanistan would prefer there to be no schoolchild casualties due to the armed conflict and terror attacks in that State. It is only necessary, however, that those culpable were prepared to take the risk of terror attack on schoolchildren and schools by encouraging and facilitating school attendance even without adequate security (i.e., in order to be in a position, for instance, to claim alleged progress in development work and maintain the support of international donor countries and the international public for their development initiatives).

As to the issue of what is meant by 'material support' to a terror group, we turn to Justice Breyer's useful explanation:

> That word [material support] can mean being of a physical or worldly nature, but it also can mean being of real importance or great consequence.[45]

In the situation of conflict-affected Afghanistan; NGOs, Afghan government officials and others encouraging and facilitating school attendance even without adequate security provide 'material support' in terms of something of great importance to the Taliban terrorists and other insurgents as opposed to tangible physical resources such as money, weapons, technical equipment, personnel etc. The 'material support', in this instance, is the opportunity for the Taliban and other insurgents to more easily systematically strike at child civilians and spread maximum terror amongst the general civilian population as well as the chance to undermine the population's faith in the government's attempts to reestablish security and public services. On the analysis here then knowingly giving 'material support' to a terrorist group can include a potentially wide range of activities depending on the specific context. The scope of the term cannot be arbitrarily delimited in advance of considering the individual unique conflict situation where such alleged 'material support' was provided.

The humanitarian/human rights group frontline workers and policy and decision-makers group are then, on the analysis here, potentially prosecutable under international criminal law should such cases be referred to the International Criminal Court

---

[44]*Eric H. Holder, Jr., Attorney General, et al. v. Humanitarian Law Project et al.* US Supreme Court 561US___(2010) http://www.oyez.org/cases/2000-2009/2009/2008_08_1498 (accessed 4 September 2010), Dissenting Opinion, p. 18.

[45]*Eric H. Holder, Jr., Attorney General, et al. v. Humanitarian Law Project et al.* US Supreme Court 561US___(2010) http://www.oyez.org/cases/2000-2009/2009/2008_08_1498 (accessed 4 September 2010), Dissenting Opinion, p. 18–19.

(ICC) (the NGOs allegedly committed these acts leading to grave violations of children's fundamental right to life and security of the person in the jurisdiction of a State Party to the Rome Statute. (Note that Afghanistan ratified the Rome Statute 10 February, 2003).

6.4 Humanitarian/Human Rights Rhetoric as a Smokescreen for Non-Humanitarian Objectives?

It is high time that the international human rights/humanitarian community come to grips with the fact that certain of their actions in particular situations can cause grave harm and that their human rights/humanitarian mandate does *not* ensure that their actions are always in the best interests of the victimized civilians they wish to serve. Humanitarian/human rights 'talk' must not be successfully used to misdirect the international community regarding the increased risk of harm to children in Afghanistan resulting from the NGOs and others urging school attendance even in the midst of woefully inadequate security in various regions and communities within Afghanistan. This would not be the first time that human rights/humanitarian rhetoric has been used as an alleged justification for conduct in the context of armed conflict that was supposed to be *entirely* directed to better safeguarding the security of the children caught up in the conflict situation but, in fact: (a) involved also non-benevolent self-serving organizational motives and (b) involved conduct which, in some respects and instances, placed the children at considerably higher risk of harm from the armed conflict than had the humanitarian group not intervened. One example as described and analyzed by Starns and Parsons,[46] involves the evacuation of 1,500,000 British children from their urban homes to the rural countryside in Britain and to locations outside the country prior to the outbreak of WW II in 1939. This large scale evacuation took place over a period of three days. Certainly, evacuation of child civilians from an armed combat zone, as was previously discussed, is consistent with the requirements of international humanitarian law. In this regard, recall Article 4(3)(e) of Protocol II Additional to the Geneva Conventions:

> (e) measures shall be taken, if necessary, and whenever possible with the consent of their parents or persons who by law or custom are primarily responsible for their care, to *remove children temporarily from the area in which hostilities are taking place to a safer area within the country and ensure that they are accompanied by persons responsible for their safety and well-being* (emphasis added).[47]

---

[46]Starns and Parsons (2002), p. 266–278.

[47]Protocol II Additional to the Geneva Conventions of 12 August 1949, and relating to the Protection of Victims of Non-International Armed Conflicts, 8 June 1977 http://www.icrc.org/web/eng/siteeng0.nsf/html/genevaconventions (accessed 7 September, 2010).

However, as Starns and Parsons[48] explain, despite the exclusively humanitarian rationales offered by the then incumbent government of Britain for this mass evacuation of children from their British urban area homes just before WWII began; the motives underlying the evacuation were not in fact entirely humanitarian. The aforementioned authors explain as follows:

> Conventional accounts of evacuation history [relating to the evacuation during the WW II period of one million and one- half British children to the British countryside and abroad] have portrayed the British government as one which initiated evacuation schemes merely in order to protect children from the horrors of war. Yet despite this assumption, there were other, more pressing concerns which directed evacuation policy. *Children also became an integral part of the British war effort* (emphasis added).[49]

The evacuations then were motivated by State interests first and foremost. This is illustrated by the fact, for instance, that though advisors from the British Air Ministry had warned the British government at the time not to evacuate the children to the eastern counties of Britain due to anticipated heavy fighting there (the main thrust of the air and sea attack would be targeted on this area), that advice was not heeded by the government.[50] Starns and Parsons comment as follows on this historical fact:

> *Why then in view of previous advice, was a decision taken [by the British government] to send children into* ***known*** *danger areas?* The answer to this question was quite simple, and underpinned the whole of the government's evacuation policy. Evacuation was not simply about moving [child] civilians from dangerous areas to places of relative safety; it was about 'the dispersal of the population,' and meeting essential wartime demands. The evacuation of children liberated more women for work in munitions factories. *Propaganda played on the fears of parents and argued that children would be healthier and stronger in the country [rural countryside].* Mothers in particular were portrayed as being irresponsible if they did not consent to the [voluntary] evacuation of their children. Evacuation was also considered to be a vital component in lifting military morale ... propaganda films [at the time] which supposedly included the views of ordinary British soldiers [stated] that "if we know our children are safe we will fight better". *Both the need to utilize women in essential war industries and the need to maintain military morale were driving forces behind the evacuations of children. Therefore the whole evacuation process was not merely about providing safe areas for civilians...* ***Certainly, government officials did not consider the safety of children to be of prime importance*** ... **[i.e., children evacuated to the eastern counties in Britain arguably actually saw more of the armed conflict than would have been the case had they stayed in their urban dwellings**; the placements were not investigated and some children were abused in their new homes where they billeted with strangers 'caring' for them. Furthermore, evacuating some of the children abroad was viewed in no insignificant measure as a means of conserving supplies for those who were of fighting age while the children were viewed as "useless mouths". It was also hoped that the plight of the child evacuees to the U.S. might garner sympathy for the British plight and encourage American material support for the British war effort] (emphasis added).[51]

[48]Starns and Parsons (2002), p. 266–278.

[49]Starns and Parsons (2002), p. 266.

[50]Starns and Parsons (2002), p. 267.

[51]Starns and Parsons (2002), p. 264–269.

Strikingly, when it came to evacuating children overseas some British officials who endorsed the scientifically invalid theories of eugenics saw the evacuees as a means of preserving the so-called British line should there be a German occupation. They proposed that the children be selected for evacuation abroad using various criteria that were intended to allegedly screen for the brightest and genetically healthiest (these children then being expected to procreate as adults and return to conquer the Germans should Britain be overtaken). The Admiralty was not consulted on the plan to evacuate children overseas, but when so informed later, advised the British government that it could not ensure the safety of the ships that were evacuating these children:

> *[In addition] unknown to parents, a few ships carried troops and war material along with [child] evacuees and were obvious targets for enemy action. Most convoys of ships carrying evacuee children were torpedoed at some point during their journey*, most of these were towed back to Britain. Three ships sank ... the SS City of Benares was torpedoed on September 17, 1940 and seventy-seven children were killed (emphasis added).[52]

In the same way, it is here contended that encouraging and facilitating school attendance in Afghanistan in situations where it is well known that security for schools and routes to and from schools at particular locales in that conflict-affected country cannot be reasonably assured, does *not* likely constitute wholly humanitarian-motivated conduct. In fact, the conduct arguably (depending on all the aggravating and mitigating factors in any specific circumstance) potentially shows a reckless disregard for the safety and well-being of children. In the latter instance, the intent of State government officials (and/or NGO and UN personnel on the ground in Afghanistan), in large part, is to use children as propaganda tools in the effort to demonstrate to international donor countries and the international public generally alleged substantive progress in NGO, and UN development work and purported significant improvements in re-stabilization of the country. Evidence of that progress is purported to be properly measured in terms of indicia such as number of schools operational and improvements in school enrollment.

Compare this with the example of the evacuation of British children to the rural counties in that country during WWII described above. Those evacuations, in some situations, as explained, arguably served primarily State interests while putting the children's safety at greater risk. Propaganda was also used to urge parents to send their children to these rural evacuation sites with the government reassuring the parents the children would be safe there when this was not necessarily the case. In Afghanistan, similarly, children are often being used as propaganda tools in the so-called 'war on terror'. Having children attend school despite the security risks; and as soon after a terror attack on the school as possible; is directed to boosting the morale of the population regarding alleged progress in re-stabilization of the country. Further, parents in Afghanistan are being urged (pressured?) to fight the Taliban symbolically by sending their children to school despite any realistic security concerns they might have.

---

[52]Starns and Parsons (2002), p. 269.

It would appear that the international community would prefer to assume that democratic State governments and the international aid community, in all instances, seek only to protect children in times of armed conflict (be that in the context of a non-international or international armed conflict). Clearly, however, in Afghanistan and other conflict-affected countries children's security has taken a back seat to the State's and the international humanitarian community's self-interest to the extent that schoolchildren are being encouraged and supported to attend schools when the children's security is at high risk in doing so. This situation then, it is here contended, does *not* meet the minimum standard for education in emergency situations espoused by the 'Inter-Agency Network for Education in Emergencies' (INEE) self-described as: "an open global network of practitioners and policy-makers working together to ensure all persons the right to quality education and a safe learning environment in emergencies and post-crisis recovery".[53]

Consider that Minimum Education Standard 2 of the INEE states:

> Learning environments are secure and safe, and promote the protection and the psychosocial well-being of learners, teachers and other education personnel.[54]

As a subset of minimum standard two, the following are amongst those factors that must be in place to meet the standard

> Access routes to the learning environment are safe, secure and accessible for all;
> Learning environments are free from military occupation and attack[55]

Clearly, more often than not, at least in some regions of Afghanistan, access routes to and from school are *not* safe and learning environments are *not* free from terror attack. Yet, schoolchildren are encouraged to attend school as soon as possible after a targeted terror attack against education once schools are operational again. References to the latter objective are made in various NGO reports and in statements made by high Afghan government officials as previously discussed. Note also that parents in Afghanistan are generally unable to provide home schooling due to the high rates of illiteracy in the adult population, while having a teacher come to a home-based school (assuming one would be available which is often a dubious proposition) may in itself pose risks to the family dwelling and all the children attending at the home school. There are then no easy solutions to the problem of terror attacks on education in a CAFS. The reality is that in some instances of intense terror activity in a particular locale within Afghanistan; it may not be possible to deliver education in a safe and secure environment. Yet, the State government as well as NGOs and humanitarian education aid organizations intervening in the education sector in Afghanistan do not always make access to education contingent on the ability to provide a safe learning environment thus failing miserably to meet the key *minimum* standards for education in emergencies advocated by the INEE.

---

[53]Inter-Agency Network for Education in Emergencies' (INEE) (2010) at (Mission Statement).

[54]Inter-Agency Network for Education in Emergencies' (INEE) (2010) at p. 61.

[55]Inter-Agency Network for Education in Emergencies' (INEE) (2010) at p. 61.

6.5 Combined Development-Military Tactics and the Consequences for School Security

In August 2008, three education sector aid workers in Afghanistan who were affiliated with the International Rescue Committee (IRC) were murdered by the Taliban. They had been driving on the road to Kabul in a vehicle clearly marked IRC. The IRC workers had been working in the area to improve access to education for disabled children. It should be noted that the IRC had worked in Afghanistan for twenty years at the time of the killings and so was well known by the populace there.[56] There is a general perception that in Afghanistan, and in other conflict-affected States, particularly in the last 10 years, there has been a significant increase in attacks on humanitarian workers including education aid workers.[57] When it comes to protection strategies for international humanitarian aid workers "one widespread institutional response to the increase in security concerns has been the practice of 'remote management', whereby international NGO personnel work at a distance from the conflict area and rely on national staff and local NGOs to maintain the operations".[58] This means essentially when it comes to education aid work, that those amongst the most responsible for the practice of encouraging and facilitating school attendance despite inadequate security do so while they themselves are at a safe distance from the conflict. Remote management runs the risk of decreasing local acceptance of the organization and its work.

Since the Bush administration, humanitarian aid has increasingly been viewed by State governments; the U.S. and other members of the Organization for Economic Cooperation and Development, as integral to foreign policy. Such aid is designed, in part, to sway locals in the direction of supporting the forces that oppose terrorist insurgent groups.

Members of the OECD are amongst the richest donor governments when it comes to international humanitarian aid.[59] It has been said that:

> When all is said and done, the only protection humanitarian actors have is the clarity of their image. Both coalition forces and the majority of aid actors have seriously abused this image in Afghanistan [i.e., since certain humanitarian aid organizations coordinate with troops and private security firms in order to operate in insecure zones rather than withdrawing when security is inadequate for their operations; and specialized small military units which include civilian NGO development experts also exist in Afghanistan. The latter, provincial reconstruction teams engage in small reconstruction efforts such as repairing roofs that are normally handled exclusively by humanitarian aid groups.], thus perpetuating a deadly confusion between humanitarian organizations and political-military institutions.[60]

---

[56]Novelli (2010), p. 71–96.

[57]Novelli (2010), p. 74.

[58]Novelli (2010), p. 81.

[59]Polman (2010), p. 129.

[60]Polman (2010), p. 132 (citing Fabrice Weissman, Research Director of MSF Foundation, Medicins Sans Frontieres (Doctors Without Borders), Paris.

It has also been noted that many NGOs in Afghanistan "placed themselves at the service of the UN Assistance Mission in Afghanistan and of the interim government" (the new Afghan government that took office subsequent to the fall of the Taliban). This, too, it has been suggested, has contributed to the perception (correct or not) that humanitarian organizations operating in Afghanistan are often tied up with the political and military objectives of the government and its Western allies.[61]

Clearly, Afghanistan and Iraq are strategically important countries for the West politically and militarily, and this may help explain the fact that "in 2006 Iraq and Afghanistan accounted for over 60 percent of all aid to severely conflict-affected countries".[62] However, humanitarian education aid work is framed in the consciousness of the international community and in the public information campaigns of national and international humanitarian organizations as completely neutral humanitarian aid intervention. Afterall, it is true that access to education is a vital development concern and that "at least half of the world's out-of-school children are located in conflict-affected and post-conflict countries".[63] Humanitarian aid to basic education in conflict and non-conflict-affected States increased from 747 million U.S in 2000 to 2.8 billion by 2006.[64] Further, aid to conflict-affected areas of the world and to education development initiatives in these countries has increased significantly over the last decade and this trend likely will continue as "international development organizations, rather than working around wars and conflicts, have learnt how to work within them, and along side them".[65]

This substantial increase in aid to basic education results, in part, from the perception that education fosters development and peace which no doubt is generally true in a wide range of contexts. However, such is not necessarily the case where at least the minimum level of adequate security does not prevail. In that regard, what has been discussed here is the fact that when children's security is *in practice* considered secondary, as it is in Afghanistan, to the objectives of maintaining donor funding and ensuring school attendance in virtually all security circumstances (despite claims to the contrary by humanitarian aid organizations), then such education aid work is also tied up with politics and organizational bureaucratic self-interest. Such an approach to education aid is relatively new as has here been pointed out previously. Furthermore, the entire concept of aid to conflict zones and to education within those ongoing conflict areas is a new approach as is reflected in the conduct of the UN in respect of its changing pattern of humanitarian intervention:

> During the Cold War, although UN intervention was relatively uncommon, when it did take place it was on the basis of agreed ceasefire or clear peacekeeping arrangements. UN agencies did not attempt to operate in the context of an ongoing conflict. The ad hoc UN

[61]Polman (2010), p. 133.

[62]Novelli (2010), p. 84.

[63]Novelli (2010), p. 86.

[64]Novelli (2010), p. 86.

[65]Novelli (2010), p. 86.

> resolutions that have made negotiated access possible, however, send a different signal. The new paradigm, while not condoning conflict, now appears to accept that political instability is an unfortunate reality in the South. Unable to prevent internal war, the West has resigned itself to *finding ways of working within ongoing crises and managing their symptoms* (emphasis added).[66]

Humanitarian educational intervention in hot conflict zones which involves ensuring children's school attendance despite the security threat, on the view here, sets up a double standard for the children of the developing world who live in conflict-affected States. That is, a standard is set up which, in effect, holds that the children of conflict plagued States (i.e., Afghanistan) can be properly expected to risk their security to attend school in order that the State and the humanitarian education aid sector can meet its mandated development targets. Intervening in conflict zones to provide education aid where school security is lacking may, in fact, create an incentive for terror attacks on education. This is the case in that education facilitated or sponsored by Western humanitarian groups and the UN is viewed by terrorists as a vehicle for spreading Western ideology and winning over the populace. There is in fact some acknowledgement in the international aid community that intervening in conflict zones invites increased attacks on humanitarian education aid workers involved with providing or helping to provide educational services (the same is true of course, as we have seen, in regards to the increase in attacks on schools, schoolchildren, teachers and other education-related personnel).

It appears that there is in the international humanitarian community a tacit acceptance of 'collateral damage' associated with education aid intervention in conflict-affected States where the fighting is still intense and ongoing (i.e., death and injury inflicted on humanitarian education aid workers). This is evidenced in the comment below:

> This is not to say that that the international community accepts the normality of war, but that increasingly it has come to some kind of accommodation with conflict and instability and to attempting to provide certain basic goods and services therein. *By doing so, it has by default increased the risk of attacks on those people that deliver these services* [humanitarian aid workers] (emphasis added).[67]

What the current author has been discussing in this book is the tacit, legally and morally insupportable acceptance by the international community, and the international humanitarian community in particular, of schoolchildren as 'collateral damage' in the context of humanitarian educational interventions in conflict zones. Schoolchild casualties at school or on the way to or from school in Afghanistan have become somewhat of a normative expectation. Note that the term 'collateral damage' is generally used in the context of unintended, but expected unavoidable civilian casualties associated with certain military operations. The term is used here unconventionally, and for effect, to refer to unintended but expected and unavoidable child casualties associated with humanitarian education aid interventions in

[66]Novelli (2010), p. 86.

[67]Novelli (2010), p. 86–87.

highly insecure conflict zones (where security for schools and schoolchildren cannot be adequately provided and there are frequent targeted terror attacks on education). Those humanitarian interventions are viewed by NGOs as key components in the attempt to fight terrorism by offering the people a chance at a better future through various development initiatives.

All this is *not* to say that this 'collateral damage' involving schoolchildren being killed or injured is not lamented by the international humanitarian aid community and the international community at large, or that there is no wish to reduce these child casualties. Rather, it is to say that the State government and humanitarian education aid sector in CAFS such as Afghanistan are not prepared, it appears, to suspend children's access to education for any appreciable time until the children's security can be more reasonably assured. This is evidenced by the fact that attacks on education in Afghanistan continue to rise dramatically[68] as do the schoolchild casualties as has been here discussed; with these children being targeted simply for their attempting to pursue an education perceived as sponsored by the West for its own interests. There is an acceptance then by the international community of significantly higher numbers of child casualties due to increased terror attacks on education as retribution for education aid intervention in the conflict zone. That acceptance of schoolchild deaths and injury is evidenced by the fact that humanitarian education aid workers and national government officials operating in conflict zones such as Afghanistan are too often prepared to have children attend school without adequate security with the *foreseeabl*e high risk of child deaths and grievous injury; both physical and psychological, ensuing at some point due to a targeted terror attack on education (sometimes even forewarned with i.e., night letters).

Encouraging and facilitating school attendance in highly insecure zones within conflict-affected countries such as Afghanistan invites the blurring of the distinction between humanitarian and military policy. Such a practice places children at high risk of terror attack. Should an attack eventuate, this in turn often has implications for counter-insurgency actions and for the ongoing propaganda battle associated with the so-called 'war on terror' which arguably helps fuel further violence. Education in this context then is not a vehicle for promoting peace contrary to the rights rhetoric used to couch justifications for encouraging school attendance in unsecured zones within the CFS (as in Afghanistan). Such rights rhetoric does *not*, furthermore, accord with the reality of intentionally risking the security of children, education personnel and humanitarian education aid workers in the context of educational activities that are unprotected from terror attack. Hence, while development initiatives (including humanitarian education aid intervention) are often perceived as a part of an effective counter-insurgency strategy, in fact, as we have seen, such intervention in conflict zones without adequate security can on the contrary stimulate terror attacks, engendering more fear and panic in the general populace and thus bolstering the perceived power of the insurgents.

[68] Novelli (2010), p. 90.

> ***Clearly in the case of Afghanistan, education has become a central battleground in the war, intensifying dangers that all education personnel and students face there... The dilemma for education aid workers is that counterinsurgency and counterterrorism strategies of the Western powers become the major perceived rationale for educational interventions.*** While activities [of education aid workers] remain largely the same, their discursive representation means that they [national and international education aid workers operating in Afghanistan] can be interpreted as part of the 'war effort'. (emphasis added)[69]

The intractable and potentially deadly dilemma for the schoolchildren of Afghanistan is that they are expected to attend school even where conditions are highly hostile to the education enterprise (i.e., in highly insecure locales within the CAFS where the Taliban wish to deny access to education perceived as sponsored by the West and not vetted by the terror group and where the right of girls to access education is denied in any case).

Note that education for girls in Afghanistan has emerged as a key contested area symbolizing the tension between the pressures for development versus the dictates of the Taliban as to what ought to be an acceptable societal status quo regarding gender power relations. Some have even suggested that "Educational provision (particularly for girls) became a key discursive justification for the military intervention in Afghanistan".[70] In many respects, in Afghanistan as in many other fragile States, education in the midst of conflict and a lack of security has become a means to achieving adult agendas that have much to do with State interest and the bureaucratic self-interests of humanitarian aid organizations attempting to placate donors, and less and less to do with the best interests of the children. Tragically, such an approach serves to facilitate the objective of terrorist insurgents who increasingly find that targeting schools, schoolchildren, education personnel and humanitarian education aid workers has high propaganda value.

References

Bob C (ed) (2009) The international struggle for new human rights. University of Pennsylvania Press, Philadelphia, p 2

Coomaraswamy R (Under-Secretary General and Special Representative of the Secretary-General for Children and Armed Conflict) (2010) The Security Council and children and armed conflict: an experiment in the making. Public lecture at the Centre for Human Rights in Conflict, University of East London School of Law (12 April 2010). http://www.un.org/children/conflict/english/12-apr-2010-the-security-council-and-caac.html. Accessed 4 Sept 2010

Human Rights Watch (2009) Taking the next step: strengthening the [UN] Security Council's response to sexual violence and attacks on education in armed conflict, p 2–3. Available for download from http://www.hrw.org/en/news/2009/04/20/taking-next-step. Accessed 31 Aug 2010

[69] Novelli (2010), p. 91.

[70] Novelli (2010), p. 90.

Inter-Agency Network for Education in Emergencies (INEE) (2010) Minimum standards for education: Preparedness, response, recovery. http://www.ineesite.org/uploads/documents/store/Minimum_Standards_2010_eng.pdf. Accessed 25 February 2011

Novelli M (2010) Political violence against education sector aid workers in conflict zones: a preliminary investigation into the possible link between attacks and the increased merging of security and development policy in UNESCO. Protecting education from attack: a state-of-the-art review, p 71–96. http://unesdoc.unesco.org/images/0018/001867/186732e.pdf. Accessed 8 Sept 2010

O'Malley B (2010) Education under attack (a report commissioned by Mark Richmond, Director, Division for the Coordination of United Nations Priorities in Education, Education Sector, UNESCO), p 124. http://unesdoc.unesco.org/images/0018/001868/186809e.pdf. Accessed 26 Apr 2010

Polman L (2010) War games: the story of aid and war in modern times. Viking, London, p 129

Starns PE, Parsons ML (2002) Against their will: the use and abuse of British children during the Second World War. In: Marten J (ed) Children and war: a historical anthology. New York University, New York, pp 266–278

Chapter 7
Concluding Remarks

7.1 A Summary

Children in many conflict-affected regions globally, such as Afghanistan, are attending schools or informal education sites which are unsecured settings despite the fact that this makes them a high value and very likely target for terror attack as has here been discussed. These children, in fact, are often attending school despite the lack of anything approaching adequate security. This is occurring largely at the urging of: (a) local and national government officials, (b) national and international humanitarian aid and human rights organizations with operations in the conflict-affected State, and (c) indirectly by the encouragement of the US military and its allies working in tandem with international aid organizations to implement small reconstruction projects carried out by a select number of PRT (provincial reconstruction teams) units designated to build and repair schools among other projects. This concluding chapter begins with a summary of just some of the international law violations implicated when children are encouraged and supported in attending at schools in armed conflict zones despite the risk to their security. This discussion is then followed by consideration of (a) the basis for State and NGO responsibility for such violations; (NGOs' being accountable under international humanitarian law despite NGOs not being signatories to treaties where such law has attained the status of customary law) and (b) whether the UN or its organs can be held accountable for their contribution to encouraging and facilitating children attending schools in unsecured areas where they are put directly in harm's way due to the armed conflict. Also addressed in what follows is the potential civil liability and criminal culpability of individuals working for or having worked for the State, UN bodies and/or NGOs which individuals are responsible for the policy and decision-making that supports the ongoing practice of sending children to school in high conflict unsecured areas in Afghanistan such that the children's survival and well-being is at stake. Finally, we conclude with (a) consideration of how attacks on education involve all six grave violations against children during armed conflict identified by the UN Special Representative for Children and Armed Conflict and (b) a call for ending the practice of encouraging and facilitating school attendance even in highly insecure zones within Afghanistan and other CAFS where the

S.C. Grover, *Schoolchildren as Propaganda Tools in the War on Terror*,
DOI 10.1007/978-3-642-17900-6_7, © Springer-Verlag Berlin Heidelberg 2011

children and other civilians associated with the education enterprise are at high risk of terror attack.

Encouraging and facilitating school attendance, perhaps even many times pressuring parents to send their children to school despite the fact that: (a) the schools, teachers and students are targeted for terror attack in these active conflict regions, and (b) security for the schools and for the routes to and from school are inadequate; constitutes potential complicity, it is here argued, in the violation of Common Article 3 of the Geneva Convention[1] and Protocol II additional to the 1949 Geneva Conventions (guaranteeing protection for civilians)[2] which has attained customary law status according to legal experts. Thus, not only the State governments involved bear international responsibility for this conduct which potentially constitutes a grave violation of the children's basic human rights (depending on the unique fact pattern in each case), but also the international aid community. This includes also UN agencies operating in the region which, it is here argued, do not enjoy immunity when they exceed the jurisdiction of the UN Charter as in this case. Though the NGO humanitarian aid and UN organizations are, of course, not belligerents in the conflict, they, by facilitating and encouraging school attendance in unsecured zones, are nonetheless inadvertently advancing a prime terrorist objective knowing that this was the risk (i.e., that terrorist objective being to kill or cause grievous injury to schoolchildren, teachers, other education personnel and humanitarian aid workers). In so doing, the international aid community is, it is argued, potentially 'aiding and abetting' the commission of 'war crimes' [i.e., the targeting for armed attack by terrorists of child civilians and of others not involved in the combat and the destruction of certain civilian infrastructure (schools)].

The 'aiding and abetting' of an international crime arises in that the individuals representing the international aid community possess the sure knowledge that when children attend school in a region without adequate security, and one plagued by systemic terrorist attacks directed toward schools and schoolchildren and teachers, the children are at high risk of harm. Intentionally facilitating the children attending school under these circumstances thus, on the view here, amounts to degrading and inhuman treatment of the children in violation of their basic human right under international humanitarian and human right law to dignity and security of the person. That is, should the children become the victims of a terror attack, this would cause them great mental suffering, and more often than not also severe physical suffering. Further, the children very often attend school filled with fear and trepidation; not knowing when the next terror attack on education in their region will come, but often confident it will come. This runs counter to the spirit of the Geneva Convention provisions (covering both international and non-international

[1]Common Article 3 of the 1949 Geneva Conventions http://www.icrc.org/ihl.nsf/WebART/365-570006 (accessed 9 September, 2010).

[2]Protocol II Additional to the Geneva Conventions of 12 August 1949, and relating to the Protection of Victims of Non-International Armed Conflicts, 8 June 1977 http://www.icrc.org/web/eng/siteeng0.nsf/html/genevaconventions (accessed 9 September, 2010).

conflicts) that stipulate that children, to the extent possible, should be removed from high conflict areas and, in all instances, be provided with adequate protection during armed conflict. The latter principle has arguably now become an international customary norm.

This international humanitarian law obligation to provide for the protection of children during armed conflict is then contravened when children are made to be visible, accessible high value targets for attack as occurs when children attend school without adequate security during ongoing armed conflict in areas plagued by intense terror activity. The child protection obligation under IHL is articulated, for instance, in the following Geneva Convention provisions[3]:

ARTICLE 17: Convention (IV) relative to the Protection of Civilian Persons in Time of War. Geneva, 12 August 1949

The Parties to the conflict shall endeavour to conclude local agreements for the removal from besieged or encircled areas, of ... children

Protocol Additional to the Geneva Conventions of 12 August 1949, and relating to the Protection of Victims of Non-International Armed Conflicts (Protocol I), 8 June 1977

ARTICLE 77 – Protection of children (Protocol I)

1. Children shall be the object of special respect and shall be protected against *any form of* indecent assault ... (emphasis added) [arguably facilitating attacks on child civilians by sending then to school in unsecured locales in a conflict-affected State is failing to protect children from a form of indecent assault-terrorist attack- that offends the child's human dignity] (emphasis added).

ARTICLE 78 – Evacuation of children (Protocol I)

1. No Party to the conflict shall arrange for the evacuation of children, other than its own nationals, to a foreign country except for a temporary evacuation *where compelling reasons of the health or medical treatment of the children or, except in occupied territory,* ***their safety****, so require*. Where the parents or legal guardians can be found, their written consent to such evacuation is required... (emphasis added)

It should also be recalled that Protocol I Additional to the 1949 Geneva Conventions sets out the principle, according to the International Committee of the Red Cross, that education is not to be used for propaganda purposes:

ARTICLE 78 – Evacuation of children (Protocol I)

2. Whenever an evacuation [from the direct conflict area] occurs ... each child's education, including his religious and moral education as his parents desire, shall be provided while he is away with the greatest possible continuity.

Protocol I requires 'continuity' in education consistent with the child's cultural traditions and normal educational experience should the child be evacuated from an area with intense fighting. This principle concerning the prohibition against using education for propaganda purposes during armed conflict, being as it is part of Protocol I, also may be considered to have attained the status of customary law.

---

[3]Provisions of International Humanitarian Law (specifically the Geneva Conventions and Additional Protocols 1 and 2) relevant to children http://www.essex.ac.uk/armedcon/story_id/000312.html (accessed 8 September, 2010).

In the context of the war on terror, it is here suggested, it is *not* curriculum content that is being used for propaganda purposes by the Afghan government, and its allies and the international humanitarian presence in Afghanistan though the Taliban claim the opposite. Rather, it is the very fact of school attendance despite inadequate security that serves a vital propaganda purpose for the Afghan government and its allies as well as the international humanitarian education aid community operating in Afghanistan by creating the illusion of highly significant progress toward stabilization and development. It is argued by the current author that in the context of an armed conflict, the use of education for a propaganda purpose (involving sending children to school despite the inadequate security situation) is also prohibited under Protocol I (customary law). This is the case given that such a practice also violates children's fundamental human right to psychological and physical security, and survival and fuels violence.

It can further reasonably be argued that national and international humanitarian/ human rights NGO personnel, and representatives of various UN organizations (subsidiary bodies), with the consent and acquiescence of the Afghan government, in encouraging and facilitating school attendance despite the inadequate security situation, where sooner or later suffering to children arising from a terror attack is not only possible but highly probable, constitutes complicity in the violation of the 'United Nations Convention Against Torture and Other Cruel, Inhuman or Degrading Treatment or Punishment' (article 16)[4] (ratified, for instance, by Afghanistan 1 April, 1987 and by the United States 21 October, 1994).[5]

Note that as the prohibition against inhuman and degrading treatment is a *jus cogens* customary norm, intentional conduct which knowingly facilitates a terror group according civilians such treatment is itself an international crime for which non-governmental actors can also potentially be held directly responsible under international human rights and humanitarian law. NGO personnel then, it can be argued, are also bound by the aforementioned torture treaty which codifies customary law.

The Convention in question reads as follows at Article 16:

ARTICLE 16: United Nations Convention Against Torture and Other Cruel, Inhuman or Degrading Treatment or Punishment

1. Each State Party shall undertake to prevent in any territory under its jurisdiction other acts of cruel, inhuman or degrading treatment or punishment which do not amount to torture as defined in article I, when such acts are committed by or at the instigation of *or* with the consent or acquiescence of a public official or other person acting in an official capacity. In particular, the obligations contained in articles 10, 11, 12 and 13 shall apply with the substitution for references to torture of references to *other forms of cruel, inhuman or degrading treatment* or punishment.

[4]United Nations Convention Against Torture and Other Cruel, Inhuman or Degrading Treatment or Punishment entered into force 26 June 1987 http://www2.ohchr.org/english/law/cat.htm.

[5]United Nations Convention Against Torture and Other Cruel, Inhuman or Degrading Treatment or Punishment, ratifications http://treaties.un.org/Pages/ViewDetails.aspx?src=TREATY&mtdsg_no=IV-9&chapter=4&lang=en (accessed 9 September, 2010).

2. The provisions of this Convention are without prejudice to the provisions of any other international instrument or national law which prohibits cruel, inhuman or degrading treatment or punishment or which relates to extradition or expulsion (emphasis added).

One can argue that the parents and other family members of the schoolchildren are the indirect victims in all this; their not uncommonly having been pressured by local government and the international aid organizations and UN organs to send the children to school despite inadequate security.

Children then are being used as propaganda tools in the war on terror in Afghanistan by the Afghan government, and their allies and certain national and international NGOs and UN bodies which encourage and facilitate school attendance without adequate security such that the children's right to life and well-being is being treated as if secondary to their right to access education. This situation then does not meet the criteria for implementing the children's 'right to education' as articulated in the Convention on the Rights of the Child which right cannot be dissociated from the CRC articles guaranteeing survival and security of the person.[6] Neither does attending school in unsecured terror zones meet the minimum standard for education in conflict-affected regions set out by the 'Inter-agency Network for Education in Emergencies'.

So desperate are some NGOs to ensure that children attend schools allowing the NGOs to better fulfill their mandates and have something to demonstrate in the way of alleged progress in their donor-supported development initiatives, that these NGOs have advocated meeting at least some Taliban demands as to: (a) curricular content and (b) running of schools in the hopes of negotiating *the promise* of schools as safe havens immune from armed terror attack. The 2010 UNESCO report "Education Under Attack" states:

> in Afghanistan, at least, attacks on education can be reduced if the community *and even the Taliban* are given more of a sense of ownership of education and their fears of external imposition of schools and/or alien values are addressed (emphasis added).[7]

While some schools may have been reopened on this basis, at least for a time, it is unclear that the children are learning about peace and tolerance (a requirement of implementing the right to education under the Convention on the Rights of the Child) when a terror group is orchestrating the running of the school behind the scenes. The Taliban 'ownership' of schools comes with strings attached including authoritarian dictates, for instance, regarding exclusion of girl's from education. At the same time, the Taliban are perpetrating an ever increasing number of terror attacks on schools in Afghanistan as has been discussed (as well as in Pakistan). The Afghan government, in some instances, has agreed to sanitized curriculum content and placement of locals on school councils serving an oversight function for the Taliban to ensure curriculum content is agreeable to the terror group and does not serve alleged Western interests.

---

[6]Convention on the Rights of the Child (entered into force 2 September, 1990) http://www2.ohchr.org/english/law/crc.htm (accessed 22 May, 2010).

[7]O'Malley (2010), p. 116.

The government and national and international NGOs have also encouraged school attendance as soon as new schools can be built or made operational again after a terror attack without any appreciable improvement in the level of security which would ensure the children's protection at school and on the way to and from school. NGOs and UN organizations have also touted as feasible reliance on the occasional Taliban or insurgent promise not to attack schools and thus urge sending children to school in perilously unsecured environments based on such promises. These Taliban 'promise makers', to the extent that they exist, are the very people who continue to perpetrate poison gas attacks on girls' schools, recruit children as suicide bombers, launch school attacks with some regularity, and have recently hanged children they have accused of being spies for the government and its allies. Essentially then negotiating with the Taliban regarding allowing children to safely attend school prior to that terror group renouncing violence amounts to playing Russian roulette with the lives of Afghan schoolchildren. It should not be forgotten for example that:

> Pakistan's negotiations with various Taliban incarnations in Southern and Northern Waziristan and Swat resulted in intolerable threats to the Pakistani state, people, and the international community.[8]
>
> In his communiqués, Mullah Omar has repeatedly indicated that discussions of negotiations in the West and Kabul indicate that the will of the Afghan government and NATO is breaking and urged his followers to fight all the harder.[9]

By engaging in actions while knowing full well that these provide significant support to terrorists in meeting their deadly objectives (i.e., encouraging and facilitating school attendance without adequate security, and advocating 'negotiations' with the Taliban terrorists and other insurgents though these armed groups have not renounced violence as a strategy for their organization as a whole thus legitimizing the terror group), the international education aid community operating in Afghanistan has arguably constructively made itself, through its delegates, a party to the armed conflict and abandoned, to a large extent, its purported neutral humanitarian status. As the Rome Statute makes clear in articulating the legal principle underlying *individual criminal responsibility* for war crimes and other international crimes, one need not him or herself (i.e., NGO or government frontline worker or superior) have the specific intent or objective of aiding and abetting the commission of an international crime (i.e., a war crime) in order to be complicit in its commission. Rather, it is sufficient if one knows that his or her conduct (encouraging and facilitating school attendance in unsecured terror zones) is likely to significantly further the likelihood of that crime being committed by a known group (i.e., the Taliban) with the objective of committing the crimes (war crimes involving terror attacks on schoolchildren and other civilians involved with education and on civilian schools):

---

[8] Felbab-Brown (2009), p. 1.

[9] Felbab-Brown (2009), p. 3.

Article 25: Rome Statute

Individual criminal responsibility

3. In accordance with this Statute, **a person shall be criminally responsible and liable for punishment for a crime within the jurisdiction of the Court if that person**:

. . .

(d) ***In any other way contributes to the commission or attempted commission of such a crime by a group of persons acting with a common purpose*** [here the Taliban and other insurgents]. ***Such contribution shall be intentional*** [purposively encouraging and facilitating school attendance knowing security is inadequate] and shall ***either:***

(i) Be made with the aim of furthering the criminal activity or criminal purpose of the group, where such activity or purpose involves the commission of a crime within the jurisdiction of the Court; ***or***

(ii) ***Be made in the knowledge of the intention of the group to commit the crime;*** [knowing the intention of the Taliban to perpetrate terror attacks on schoolchildren, education personnel, and humanitarian education aid workers and on dedicated civilian school buildings and open air and other education sites, NGO and State government personnel still encourage and facilitate school attendance in unsecured areas where the risk of a targeted attack on education is extremely high] (emphasis added).[10]

On the point of 'aiding and abetting' a terror group, see also the previous discussion of the judgment in United States Supreme Court in *Holder*[11] on providing 'material support' (i.e., meaning significant support as opposed to physical resources) to a terror group.

7.1.1 The Organizational Accountability of NGOs, States and the UN and Its Organs for Violations of International Law

7.1.1.1 Holding National and International NGOs and UN Agencies Accountable

NGO, as the term is used here, refers to organizations that are non-profit, non-governmental organizations, national or international in character, which pursue humanitarian objectives, do not promote or use violence and have a certain organizational structure and often, though not always, have a legal personality that is based on statute.[12] In recent years, NGOs have gained greatly in power and influence globally and have increasingly intervened in conflict-affected States (i.e., regarding educational aid delivery) while the conflict is still ongoing. However, NGOs have largely escaped any question of their accountability for any harm

[10]Rome Statute of the International Criminal Court (entered into force 1 July, 2002) http://untreaty.un.org/cod/icc/statute/romefra.htm (accessed 9 September, 2010).

[11]*Eric H. Holder, Jr., Attorney General, et al. v. Humanitarian Law Project et al.* US Supreme Court 561US___(2010) http://www.oyez.org/cases/2000-2009/2009/2008_08_1498 (accessed 4 September, 2010).

[12]Lindblom (2010), p. 344.

they may have inflicted through their interventions in States experiencing ongoing conflict:

> As a consequence of the considerable number, resources, and political role of non-governmental organization (NGOs), the demands for their accountability are increasing. The NGO sector attracts large amounts of international funding ... and their role is powerful both locally and transnationally. The possibility of holding NGOs legally responsible for their conduct is only one aspect of the larger question of their accountability.[13]

NGOs, national and international, when responsible for wrongdoing that violates international human rights or humanitarian norms, must, on the view here, be held accountable. They must properly be held accountable both as organizations and in respect of the NGO personnel involved in the violations of international human rights/humanitarian law where these occur. When NGOs commit wrongful acts under international law; this may also implicate the State of origin of the NGO where the organization is normally headquartered.[14]

The Commentary to the International Law Commission Articles on State Responsibility for Internationally Wrongful Acts (ARSIWA) stipulates that there occurs an "internationally wrongful act when conduct constitutes breach of an international obligation..." [Hence], "In that sense, international obligations may be regarded as the source of international responsibility".[15] The current author has previously mentioned some of the international law obligations (i.e., under the Geneva Conventions and the Additional Protocols I and II[16] thereto and under the United Nations Convention Against Torture and Other Cruel, Inhuman or Degrading Treatment or Punishment[17] owed also by non-State groups, including NGOs, when dealing with civilians and especially vulnerable groups such as children). Thus, NGO personnel, government officials, humanitarian education aid workers and workers associated with the UN operating in a conflict zones have a positive protection duty in respect of child civilians (i.e., schoolchildren) and other civilians such as teachers and humanitarian education aid workers who are specifically targeted for terrorist attack in an ongoing armed conflict situation. It has been suggested here that *intentionally* facilitating and encouraging school attendance *knowing that there is an absence of adequate security*, amounts to 'aiding and abetting': (a) the furtherance of terrorist objectives in perpetrating attacks on education (i.e., spreading terror and causing civilian casualties in that school attendance allows for a concentration of children and education-related persons at

---

[13]Lindblom (2010), p. 343.

[14]Lindblom (2010), p. 345.

[15]Lindblom (2010), p. 345.

[16]Provisions of International Humanitarian Law (specifically the Geneva Conventions and Additional Protocols 1 and 2) relevant to children http://www.essex.ac.uk/armedcon/story_id/000312.html (accessed 8 September, 2010).

[17]United Nations Convention Against Torture and Other Cruel, Inhuman or Degrading Treatment or Punishment entered into force 26 June 1987 http://www2.ohchr.org/english/law/cat.htm.

one locale and makes them easy targets at school or on the way to or from school along unsecured routes. Further, the attack will likely maim or kill several children and/ or civilian adults thus maximizing the terror impact by virtue of, for instance, who was killed or injured, the number of casualties and the undermining of an essential service as well as due to the damage or destruction of infrastructure namely school buildings associated with the essential service of education) and (b) increasing the likelihood of insurgent attacks on schoolchildren, education personnel as well as humanitarian education aid workers and on school buildings as well as other school sites. In this way, as explained previously, NGOs have unwittingly injected themselves into the conflict as a *de facto* if unofficial party to the armed conflict contributing unintentionally to the violence. Hence, though the term NGO (non-governmental organization) reflects the fact that normally the organization is subject only to domestic law; this is not the case, it is here argued, where there is international wrongdoing by the NGO or other of the aforementioned non-governmental parties such as UN human rights/humanitarian subsidiary organs (i.e., breach of international humanitarian law may be implicated in the conduct and, in addition, in respect of the subsidiary organs of the UN also violations of the UN Charter). In the latter instance, both the NGO, government or other policy leadership/decision-makers responsible for formulating the plan for the wrongdoing (those with 'superior responsibility'), and those on the frontline engaging in conduct that implements the plan which violates the fundamental human rights of civilians, can and should be held accountable under various relevant international law:

> ***The presence of international humanitarian organizations in situations of armed conflict [i.e., as in Afghanistan] has created a need for international law to adapt and encompass NGOs and other non-State actors in order to regulate their status, role, rights and obligations***. The special status of the International Committee of the Red Cross (ICRC) in the context of the Geneva Conventions and their Additional Protocols is the clearest example of this (emphasis added).[18]

Note that treaty law may be interpreted implicitly and often explicitly as conferring various obligations on NGOs under international humanitarian law (i.e., under Article 10 Geneva Convention I):

> *Perhaps the clearest example of obligations which may be placed on an NGO is [explicitly] expressed in article 10 of Geneva Convention I (with corresponding articles in other Geneva Conventions),* where it is stated that the High Contracting Parties [States] may at any time agree to entrust to an organization which offers all guarantees of impartiality and efficacy the duties incumbent on the Protecting Powers by virtue of the Convention (emphasis added).[19]

In Afghanistan, many NGOs are coordinating their efforts with the Afghan government and its allies. In some instances, the development initiatives of the NGOs are viewed as part of the overall military /security strategy for Afghanistan (i.e., the U.S./coalition 'hearts and minds' campaign). UNICEF also coordinates

---

[18] Lindblom (2010), p. 346.

[19] Lindblom (2010), p. 346.

with the Afghan government, as do not most if not all NGOs operating in Afghanistan, to provide various education supplies and other vital services to the children of Afghanistan who are in need. In providing any service to the children, NGOs and UN organs are obligated, on the view here, to do so in a way which ensures the children's safety in accessing the services such as community-based education. Further, NGOs operating in Afghanistan are arguably also bound by the principles of the UN Charter given that their home States are members of the UN General Assembly (as is also Afghanistan) and, as a consequence, responsible ultimately for their conduct when these NGOs violate IHL in a foreign State. In the situation described in this book, NGOs are often operating in hot conflict zones in Afghanistan to facilitate school attendance. It is argued here that the NGOs are not executing their duties under the Geneva Conventions to protect civilians when they send children to school knowing the children are high value targets for terrorists, and that such terror attacks are highly likely given the lack of security in the specific region at issue and for education in particular. It is here contended then that such a strategy which risks children's security represents, at least in part, the use of children as a tool for propaganda serving both NGO bureaucratic organizational and State interests. Hence: (a) the protection obligations of the State Parties to civilians under the Geneva Conventions and its Additional Protocols (transferred formally in some cases to certain NGOs under treaty law i.e., via Article 10 of Geneva Convention I) and (b) the direct responsibility of NGO personnel, in any case, to abide by customary humanitarian law (i.e., as articulated in the additional Protocols to the Geneva Conventions, Common Article 3 of the Geneva Conventions and the UN Treaty on Torture and Other Cruel, Inhuman or Degrading Treatment or Punishment) are not being, in all respects and at all times, adequately implemented. Note, in addition, that the 'UN Declaration on Human Rights Defenders' (a non-legally binding instrument in itself) clearly articulates the obligations of NGOs to protect humanitarian and human rights principles:

> ... non-governmental organizations have an important role to play and a responsibility in safeguarding democracy, promoting human rights and fundamental freedoms and contributing to the promotion and advancement of democratic societies, institutions and processes.[20]

Knowingly placing children at an increased risk of being victimized by a terror attack in Afghanistan and other conflict affected States, as do, it is here contended, certain NGOs, State bodies and UN agencies (by encouraging and facilitating school attendance at vulnerable sites in a conflict area) is inconsistent with promoting the children's basic human rights of security and survival. Further, indirectly contributing to an increased likelihood of terror attacks on education in this way does nothing to promote and advance democratic society or its institutions such as civilian schools dedicated to inclusiveness, and the promotion of equity, peace and tolerance. Rather, placing children, education personnel and humanitarian education aid workers at risk by operating schools without adequate security in a conflict-affected

[20] Lindblom (2010), p. 347.

State such as Afghanistan in areas within that country where terror activity is high greatly undermines democracy. This it does by furthering the objectives of terrorists (making schoolchildren easier terror targets) thus: (a) destabilizing the democratic government by contributing to an increase in terror attacks and (b) demoralizing the populace as a result of the increase in violence (i.e., terror attacks on schools, schoolchildren and education personnel as well as on humanitarian education aid workers in Afghanistan have, as discussed, increased dramatically in recent years according to independent UN and NGO reports).

Consider also the international obligations of the 'United Nations Assistance Mission in Afghanistan' (UNAMA). That body is mandated to implement a "Relief, Recovery and Reconstruction programme":

> One of the main functions of UNAMA's Relief, Recovery and Reconstruction programme is to coordinate the humanitarian development activities of UN agencies and to promote aid effectiveness and good development practice.[21]

To the extent that UN agencies promote school attendance even when security is still inadequate (i.e., UNICEF provides tents for open air schools as soon as possible after a school building is left nonoperational due to terror attack and without independent confirmation of an adequate security situation for the school with the intent that schooling will resume as soon as possible), they are arguably not performing a purely humanitarian function or carrying out the official mandate of the UNAMA as articulated nor abiding strictly by the principles of the UN Charter (since providing tents for an open air school where terror attacks on education are common facilitates children returning to school soon after a terror attack on a school building or an attack on an open air school children to potentially be put in harm's way once more). It can be argued that when exceeding the jurisdiction of the UN Charter by knowingly facilitating children being placed in harm's way, organs of the UN (and their individual personnel involved) have also violated their obligations under international humanitarian law (treaty and customary law) and can and should be held legally accountable. For instance, UNICEF clearly articulates its intention to carry on its work in the midst of the conflict in Afghanistan and to support school attendance despite security concerns as reflected in a 2007 report which reflects this perspective. The report does *not* set out any commitment by UNICEF to encourage and facilitate school attendance only where security for the children can be reasonably assured. Nor does the report articulate UNICEF's obligation under international law to reduce the risk of harm to children from terror attack *by suspending* the UNICEF school attendance initiatives in certain high conflict zones within Afghanistan until such time as security is adequate enough to allow for safe school attendance The burden for school security is clearly shifted by NGOs such as UNICEF entirely onto government and the local community leaders, elders and /or religious leaders. Yet, it would seem that UNICEF and other UN bodies and NGOs also bear a heavy legal and moral responsibility for any

[21]United Nations Assistance Mission in Afghanistan website, Frequently asked questions http://unama.unmissions.org/Default.aspx?tabid=1748 (accessed 12 September, 2010).

security risk to Afghan schoolchildren and education personnel due to terrorism to the extent that they are encouraging and facilitating school attendance in known high risk areas for targeted terror attacks on education. The issue of UNICEF's own international legal obligation *in the first instance* (applicable also to other NGOs working in the education aid sector in Afghanistan) to protect child civilians and others encouraged to access schools sponsored by UNICEF is hidden behind a barrage of rights rhetoric and a statement of UNICEF's promised support for local community initiatives to improve security for children attending school should such materialize:

> Afghanistan remains a volatile environment in which to work. But UNICEF is fully committed to supporting the Government and our other partners to continue upholding the rights of women and children [i.e., to education]. *Of course, there are times when it is difficult to work here, especially in areas where there is continued insecurity. But we are always looking for ways to continue our work* [i.e., providing access to education despite the lack of security]... UNICEF has a program of cooperation with the Government of Afghanistan and *there is significant donor interest in education*, in health, in the provision of water and sanitation... UNICEF is concerned that these incidents [attacks on schools] –and the intimidation in some communities aimed at stopping sending girls to school-could undo some of the excellent work undertaken so far in the education sector. **UNICEF believes that the solution to these challenges has to come from the communities themselves** ... [UNICEF] stand[s] ready to support any initiative that will keep children learning in safety.... . *Schools of course are a visible sign of reconstruction and progress, and there are those who perhaps fear such progress.* (emphasis added)[22]

Since the aforementioned 2007 UNICEF report, the situation in Afghanistan has deteriorated considerably generally and attacks on education increased significantly,[23] but still NGOs and UN organs have not critically examined their own unintended complicity in fostering attacks on education in the ways explained previously.

Let us return now briefly to the topic of the UNAMA. The UNAMA is mandated to promote and protect the human rights of Afghanis: "It [the UNAMA] has been mandated by the UN Security Council to assist Afghanistan's institutions in protecting and promoting international human rights standards, as well as to help the UN integrate human rights into its work".[24] It appears evident that the UNAMA has not intervened, however, to ensure that school attendance is encouraged and facilitated *only* when children's security can be reasonably assured. In failing to ensure that school attendance, in actual practice, is predicated on an adequate security situation at the school, and on the routes to and from school, the UNAMA has failed, it is here contended, in that important instance to protect the fundamental human rights of Afghan schoolchildren to security of the person and humane treatment (and failed to protect the parents' right to protection of family),

---

[22]United Nations Assistance Mission in Afghanistan website, Frequently asked questions http://unama.unmissions.org/Default.aspx?tabid=1748 (accessed 12 September, 2010).

[23]United Nations Assistance Mission in Afghanistan (UNAMA) (2010).

[24]UNICEF (2007).

thus falling far short of one of its key mandated objectives; namely to protect civilians. However, rather than the UNAMA and NGOs operating in the education sector in Afghanistan seriously scrutinizing: (a) their own potential role in facilitating terror attacks on education by not predicating school attendance on a secure safe environment, and (b) the violation of their obligations under international humanitarian law in this regard, these bodies instead simply call on the Taliban to comply with international humanitarian law and refrain from attacking civilians and civilian objects such as schools; to date a particularly futile effort.[25]

It has been contended by some scholars on the issue of NGO accountability under international law that:

> NGOs have some, but not many, legally binding obligations under international law. The binding force of most of these obligations have their source in an active decision of the NGOs to accept them, by entering into an agreement, seeking consultative status with an IGO (intergovernmental organization), *acting as a humanitarian organization in the meaning of the Geneva Conventions*, or by signing an instrument for self-regulation (code of conduct or standards of conduct for the organization and its members) (emphasis added)[26]

The focus in the analysis in the current inquiry, however, has been also on the obligations of NGOs as organizations and their individual personnel under international humanitarian customary law and the Geneva Conventions (i.e., Common Article 3) and/or its Additional Protocols (which have arguably attained the status of customary law). There is no possibility of 'opting out' of these international customary humanitarian law obligations unlike the situation perhaps where certain obligations of NGOs are set out by agreement for instance. Thus, States, NGO's as well as organs of the United Nations operating in conflict-affected States such as Afghanistan, it is argued here, have direct *humanitarian obligations* under international law (as do their individual personnel/delegates) and this is starkly apparent in the context of the war on terror.

7.2 Final Reflections

Following are a few final reflections on certain of the pressing human rights and humanitarian issues which arise in the context of widespread sustained terror attacks on basic education as are occurring in Afghanistan and several other conflict-affected States:

1. **Education cannot and should not be used as an alleged accurate key benchmark for level of security in conflict-affected States not yet firmly in the 'post-conflict' development phase** given that: (a) using education as an alleged indicia of security when the country is not yet genuinely in the 'post-conflict' stage is not consistent with the humanitarian agenda. Such an approach

[25] United Nations Assistance Mission in Afghanistan (UNAMA) (2010), p. v.

[26] Lindblom (2010), p. 352.

inevitably leads to operating schools even without adequate security and, hence, the increasing loss of life and injury for schoolchildren and teachers (and education aid workers) thus contributing to the people's suffering; and (b) targeted education attacks (i.e., burning or bombing school buildings and other sites where basic education classes are held, attacking schoolchildren on the way to and from school, assassinating teachers etc.) are a favoured propaganda tool used by organized terror groups still embroiled in the conflict.

2. **There is a need not only for monitoring of attacks on education internationally, but also for greater transparency and accuracy in the data gathered on such attacks, and on their implications for school enrollment and other educational measures.** At present, data on school enrolment in conflict-affected States still in the midst of the conflict is often inaccurate as it is collected at the beginning of the year and does not reflect the numbers of children who attend quite irregularly or who have dropped out due to fear of repeated terror attacks and for other reasons.
3. **There is a need to assemble accurate and comprehensive data regarding the potential role of the State, NGOs and/or certain UN bodies in inadvertently facilitating the number and deadly consequences of terror attacks on education.** Currently, there is virtually no discussion of whether i.e., NGOs may be complicit in facilitating terror group objectives by encouraging and facilitating school attendance despite the high risk of a terror attack on the school or on school routes in particular areas and regarding the inadequate protection afforded education at those locales within the CAFS.
4. **The model used by international humanitarian organizations to facilitate the education of schoolchildren in natural disaster areas and 'post-conflict' fragile States cannot and should not be generalized to high conflict locales within States with significant ongoing conflict that are experiencing systemic organized terror campaigns such as those targeting education.** This is the case as the notion of negotiating schools as 'safe havens' is not a reliable one in dealing with terror groups such as the Taliban which decline to renounce terror as the group's modus operandi.
5. **Development strengthens stability and security once there is a minimum acceptable level of security in the region already in place.** However, development cannot in itself create the baseline minimum level of adequate security needed at the outset in order that the beneficial effects of development (i.e., in the education domain) can emerge.
6. **Building and operating schools and encouraging school attendance in hot combat zones where targeted terror attacks on school buildings or sites, schoolchildren and school personnel are a foreseeable high probability risk: (a) does not serve the people's humanitarian nor development needs; and (b) is a violation of international human rights, humanitarian and criminal law.**
7. **Bureaucratic institutions, whether large international NGOs or organs of the UN or smaller national or international humanitarian organizations are potentially violating international humanitarian law (depending on the totality of the facts in each case) when they encourage and expect frontline**

aid workers to carry out their education aid work in known insecure areas where these workers are at high risk of terror attack as members of an NGO or UN organization.

8. **Government officials and humanitarian aid workers arranging for the building of new schools, the repairing and re-opening of schools previously damaged by terror attacks, or NGOs operating open air tent schools or community schools need to do so only in regions within the CAFS, if any, where security for educational activities can be assured (likely these will be areas that are in fact in a 'post-conflict' stage)**. There must be no pretence that community-based guarantees of security are sufficient to ensure the security of schoolchildren, teachers and other education personnel as well as education aid workers in for instance: (a) locales within Afghanistan that are not currently secured by allied troops, and/or (b) locales that have suffered terror activity with no significant added security being implemented subsequent to the attack and/or (c) locales where threats of terror attacks on education have been received and/or (d) locales that have been classed as inadequately secured by the UN Department of Safety and Security and/or the allied international State armed presence in Afghanistan. The international humanitarian community must refrain then from encouraging and facilitating schoolchildren attending education sites if schools are situated in areas where the conflict is ongoing and systematic terror attacks on schools and school routes are a real and high risk probability. Note in this regard, that the international, highly respected NGO 'Doctors Without Borders' withdraws from areas where security cannot be reasonably guaranteed.

   For the State and/or the national and international aid community operating in a conflict-affected country such as Afghanistan to facilitate the delivery of basic schooling services in locales where the risk of a targeted attack on education is high is to undermine prevention efforts in regards to terror attacks directed at education. 'After-the-fact' responses (i.e., the closing of schools for a time *following* a terror attack on a school or on school routes, or *after* some schoolchildren have been killed or injured attending the site) do not adequately fulfill organizational obligations under international humanitarian law regarding the protection of civilians (i.e., including schoolchildren who, as children, are entitled to a high standard of protection). Likewise, the re-opening of schools that have been subjected to terror attack before the school and the area in which the school is located is properly secured is (on the view here) a violation of international humanitarian and criminal law.

9. Children have a right under the UN Convention on the Rights of the Child (which countries such as Afghanistan and Iraq and many other conflict-States have ratified) to be educated for tolerance and peace and to learn to respect the fundamental human rights of *all* peoples (i.e., including those of various ethnic/cultural, religious and national backgrounds). **A curriculum dictated or requiring approval from an organized terror group is anathema to the notion of the right to education as set out in the UN Convention on the Rights of the Child.**

As discussed, UNESCO and certain other NGOs advocate negotiations with insurgents to end attacks on education. However, negotiations with terror groups to: (a) allow the reopening only of madrasas (religious schools) *to the exclusion of all others*, and/or (b) to have the terrorists refrain from attacks on schools on the condition that the curriculum conform to the terror group's dictates (such as that girls not be educated) is a violation of the children's right to education and to education equity and ultimately places the security of the children on an uncertain foundation.

10. **Humanitarian aid organizations cannot maintain the perceived political neutrality and independence that are critical to effective aid relief in the education domain when operating in conflict zones where they: (a) rely on coalition forces for security as they inevitably must (even though they may refuse to work closely with such forces) and/or (b) negotiate with insurgent groups regarding the establishment of school 'safe zones' when those organized terror groups have not renounced their violent and inhumane tactics.**
11. **Competition between aid agencies for donor money and the pressure to demonstrate progress in development to international donors has led to NGOs and other human rights/humanitarian organizations operating also in insecure areas in conflict-affected States**. Thus, schools are built and repaired, and school attendance encouraged in the midst of locales still undergoing terror attacks putting schoolchildren, their teachers and education aid workers (the latter often Afghan nationals hired by international NGOs to enter into these extremely insecure areas) at high risk of harm from terror attacks. The lack of accountability in these instances for the potential resultant violation of international humanitarian, human rights and criminal law must be addressed {i.e., via complaints filed to the international human rights courts and/or the permanent international criminal court in The Hague [if not by a special UN criminal tribunal set up to deal with violations of international humanitarian law (war crimes and crimes against humanity) perpetrated in Afghanistan by various parties]}.

7.2.1 The Six Grave Violations Against Children Affected by Armed Conflict

Finally, let us consider how attacks on education implicate all six of the grave violations against children caught up in armed conflict identified by the UN Under-Secretary General for Children and Armed Conflict and how *both sides* of 'the war on terror' contribute to these violations in different ways:

1. **Killing or maiming of children**: The Taliban perpetrate the attacks on education intended to kill or maim child and other civilians. The State and its national

and international NGO partners (as well as certain UN bodies) put children and education-related personnel at high risk of death and injury when they encourage and facilitate school attendance despite inadequate security to protect against terror attacks specifically targeting education.

2. **Recruitment or use of children as soldiers**: The children are put at high risk of such 'recruitment' when the State and its national and international NGO partners (as well as certain UN bodies) encourage and facilitate school attendance despite inadequate security at school or on the school route (i.e., the children are often abducted en route to school or at school by the Taliban to serve as suicide bombers and in other capacities within the terror group).
3. **Rape and other forms of grave sexual abuse of children**: The Taliban continue to perpetrate attacks on girls who are attempting to attend school in Afghanistan (as the Taliban generally oppose education for girls and girl's schools though attacks on boy schoolchildren are also prevalent). The attacks on girls especially not uncommonly involve sexual violence intended to shame the girl and her family. NGOs put children, especially girl children, at high risk of such sexual attacks when they encourage and facilitate school attendance despite inadequate security at school or on the route to and from school.
4. **Attacks against school buildings**: The Taliban and other insurgents are intent on destroying school buildings and school sites in an effort to undermine the Afghan government's attempts at reconstruction, normalization, stabilization and development. NGOs increase the risk of school buildings and other education sites being targeted for terror attack when they encourage and facilitate school attendance despite inadequate security for school or buildings and school sites (open air school sites).
5. **Denial of humanitarian access to children:** Humanitarians (i.e., NGOs and certain UN bodies dedicated to relief efforts) which are operating in the conflict-affected State of Afghanistan (and others) are too often *not* removing children from harm's way. Instead, they are placing child civilians in harm's way by encouraging and facilitating school attendance despite inadequate security for education in particular locales within the country. Depending on all the facts in any particular case, this may constitute a violation of international humanitarian and criminal law. Placing children in harm's way in the manner described means that the children are at high risk of being the victims of a terror attack at school or on a school route. It is contended thus that encouraging and facilitating school attendance despite inadequate security amounts to a form of denial to the children of access to genuine humanitarian assistance from NGOs and the State contrary to the obligation of these parties under the Geneva Conventions (Common Article 3 – children not being treated humanely) and their right to special protection under the laws of war.
6. **Abduction of children**: Children are abducted at school or on the route to or from school by the Taliban thus terrorizing the civilian community. These 'disappearances' arising from abductions by the terror group are significantly increased in likelihood as a result of the State, and the humanitarian community operating in Afghanistan encouraging and facilitating children going to school

despite the lack of security on routes to and from school and at the school site proper.

It is long overdue that the international humanitarian community be held accountable for violations of children's fundamental human rights and the infringements of international human rights, humanitarian and criminal law implicated. While there is no doubt that education over the long-term fosters stability and peace, we must be concerned with the realities of the war on terror and the security risks that children in Afghanistan and other conflict-affected States (not yet in a post-conflict phase) face in attending school (i.e., in the midst of conflict in locales within the country where security has not been adequately provided for education and the risk of terror attack is high).

Greg Mortenson, nominated for a Nobel for his selfless humanitarian work in establishing an NGO directed to education work, building community-based schools and facilitating girl's education in remote regions of northern Afghanistan and Pakistan, gives us insight into the NGO perspective more generally. (Mortenson attempts to provide a secure education environment but his NGO is not in any way affiliated with the U.S, military). Mortenson has pointedly commented as follows:

> Estimating the cost of one Tomahawk cruise missile tipped with a Raytheon guidance system at $840,000 ... [Mortenson,states]: "For that much money you could build dozens of schools that could provide tens of thousands of students with a balanced, nonextremist education over the course of a generation". Then he poses a provocative question: "Which do you think will make us more secure?"[27]

This book has, it should be noted, addressed a completely different issue than that of the value of education and development in the long-term for international peace and security; the latter issue being the one to which Mortenson refers in the previous quote. The issue addressed here rather has been children's fundamental human right to security of the person while pursuing their education; a right not to be infringed by encouraging and facilitating school attendance where the children are at high risk of being victimized by a terror attack at school or on the route to or from school (such that the right to education is treated as if it takes priority over the right to security when in fact security is a prerequisite for the implementation of the right to education in any meaningful sense). While the international community justifiably laments the launch of tomahawk cruise missiles and their wreaking havoc and causing civilian 'collateral damage', we must be no less concerned with children dying and being grievously injured by terrorists (i.e., being injured or killed in a bomb or arson attack on a school or blown up by an improvised explosive device on the roadside while being transported by school buses that were supposed to provide a modicum of security, or otherwise being violently attacked on routes to or from school). Humanitarian organizations, however, have in recent years and continue to encourage and facilitate school attendance also in specific locales where security is inadequate in conflict-affected States such as Afghanistan.

[27]Mortenson (2009), p. 251.

This has led to predictable outcomes in terms of child civilian and other civilian casualties. For this, it is suggested, there must be accountability in practice and not just in theory under international law both at the organizational level and at the individual level where all of the elements of an international crime have been met in the estimation of the international court (i.e., the ICC) (the latter in regards to the frontline workers that put such policies into practice and the higher level staff that create such polices and practices and those who ordered their implementation).

Sadly, failure to address the distressing topic of the use of schoolchildren as propaganda tools in the war on terror by the Afghan government and its allies as well as the national and international humanitarian aid community operating in Afghanistan (as reflected in encouraging and facilitating school attendance in virtually every locale with the conflict-affected State despite inadequate security) will only lead to a continued significant rise in the numbers of children, teachers, other school personnel as well as humanitarian education aid frontline workers in that conflict-affected State who are killed or maimed by terror attacks specifically targeting education. This issue must be made part of the narrative regarding education in conflict-affected States such as Afghanistan. However, currently the role of government and humanitarian organizations *themselves* in contributing to terror attacks by supporting school attendance even where security is lax or non-existent for the school and for the school children is not adequately addressed within government and humanitarian organizational circles if it is addressed at all (notwithstanding NGO calls for improved security). Furthermore, the national and international media in all forms plays into this code of silence on the topic; preferring instead a narrative focused on specific heroic humanitarians and school-children forging ahead with schooling despite the real and high risk of terror attack on education. This is reflected, for instance, in the highly respected paper the Christian Monitor reporting on the work of Mortenson in an article which only mentions ever so briefly that two of the schools built by the NGO he founded were in some undefined way besieged by the Taliban without reporting whether the schools in question were damaged, destroyed or merely threatened with a terror attack:

> Sarfraz [an ex commando serving as project director for the 'Central Asia Institute', Mortenson's non-governmental organization that oversees the schools built and run with the support of the CAI] and others have set a brave goal to build a string of girls' schools through the heart of Taliban country. They face a formidable opponent. *Out of hatred for girls' education, the Taliban have destroyed, damaged, or threatened many schools. Two of Mortenson's own schools have been affected.* Undaunted, he soldiers on (emphasis added).[28]

Education must occur in a safe environment and no legally or morally supportable humanitarian or human rights rationale can be proffered for placing the child's right to education as a priority over his or her right to security of the person (in any case the right to education, as discussed, presuppose a pre-existing at least minimum adequate security situation). Schoolchildren must not be made sacrificial

[28]Gardner (2009).

lambs by government or the international humanitarian community such that they are serving governmental or organizational (i.e., NGO) political, financial, and/or war propaganda agendas in the context of the war on terror. The latter is a tempting strategy given rich country donor interest in education and the fact that "Afghanistan has one of the highest proportion of school-age (7–12) children in the world: about I in 5 Afghans is a school-age child". The international humanitarian community; the States Parties to the war on terror in Afghanistan as well as all of the member States of the United Nations under international human rights/humanitarian law owe the children of Afghanistan much better; namely a safe learning environment. Disregard for the primacy of Afghan schoolchildren's right to survival and broader security of the person rights as compared to their right to education (where the latter is restrictively interpreted) inevitably then results, under international humanitarian/ human rights and criminal law, in potential culpability for grave violations. Nothing that was said in the foregoing pages, however, is to be interpreted as undermining the importance of education – *in a safe and secure environment immune from armed attack* – to the well-being of children and their communities in the short and long-term.

One very last but critical point must be made. It has been said that:

> ... the main rule for NGOs is that international obligations and responsibilities are accepted and taken on by NGOs themselves [they are consent-based obligations rather than automatic obligations]. *There are good reasons for not bestowing international legal obligations on NGOs as these organizations... do not use or promote violence* (emphasis added).[29]

In this inquiry into attacks on education, we have found, on the contrary, on the view here, that NGOs *are* facilitating violence ('promoting it' in that restricted sense), though unintentionally, when they encourage and facilitate (as they do) school attendance in conflict-affected locales where there is inadequate security. When children attend school under these insecure conditions, it provides an incentive for a terror attack given: (a) the importance of education to reconstruction; (b) the existence of operational schools acting as a symbol of progress in reconstruction; (c) the existence of highly viable and valued civilian terror targets namely: (i) an unprotected school and (ii) accessible large numbers of children and other civilians attending that unsecured school and travelling along unsecured routes to and from the school. Both the national and international humanitarian communities operating in Afghanistan in the midst of the conflict thus have compelling important international legal protection obligations. There must then be accountability under international law (perhaps in some instances incorporated into domestic law) for any and all wrongdoing attributable to those NGOs or organs of the United Nations (wrongdoing in regards to their violation of their obligation to protect the civilians with whom they work and those they serve to the extent they are in a position to do so; including schoolchildren whom they not uncommonly instead put in harm's way in the manner described instead of suspending educational activities until such time

---

[29]Lindblom (2010), p. 352.

as security for the children can be assured). It is time that international law adapted to the new reality of NGOs and organs of the UN working in the midst of conflict zones and held these non-State bodies to the international humanitarian obligations which in fact they *already* have (i.e., under the Geneva Conventions and customary law) as do State Parties.

References

Felbab-Brown V (2009) Negotiations and reconciliation with the Taliban: the key policy issues and dilemmas (Brookings Institution). Available for download at http://www.brookings.edu/articles/2010/0128_taliban_felbabbrown.aspx

Gardner M (2009) Review of Mortenson's "Stones into Schools"; Christian Monitor, (December 21, 2009). Available for download at https://www.ikat.org/2009/12/21/csm-dec-21-09/?fromFrame=. Accessed 9 Sep 2010

Lindblom A (2010) The responsibility of other entities: non-governmental organizations. In: Crawford J, Pellet A, Olleson S (eds), Parlett K (Assistant editor) The law of international responsibility: Oxford commentaries on international law. Oxford University Press, Oxford, pp 343–354

Mortenson G (2009) Stones into schools: promoting peace with books, not bombs, in Afghanistan and Pakistan. Viking, New York, p 251

O'Malley B (2010) Education under attack (a report commissioned by Mark Richmond, Director, Division for the Coordination of United Nations Priorities in Education, Education Sector, UNESCO), p 116. http://unesdoc.unesco.org/images/0018/001868/186809e.pdf. Accessed 9 Sep 2010

UNICEF report on Afghanistan (2007) General questions and answer sheet. http://www.unicef.org/infobycountry/files/updated_2007_QuandA_Afghanistan.pdf. Accessed 9 Sep 2010

United Nations Assistance Mission in Afghanistan (UNAMA) (2010). Afghanistan mid year report 2010: protection of civilians in armed conflict. Available for download at http:unama.unmissions.org. Accessed 12 Sep 2010

Index

S.C. Grover, *Schoolchildren as Propaganda Tools in the War on Terror*,
DOI 10.1007/978-3-642-17900-6, © Springer-Verlag Berlin Heidelberg 2011

Printed by Books on Demand, Germany